Bodies
and
Disciplines

MEDIEVAL CULTURES

SERIES EDITORS
Rita Copeland
Barbara A. Hanawalt
David Wallace

*Sponsored by the Center for Medieval Studies
at the University of Minnesota*

Volumes in the series study the diversity of medieval cultural histories and practices including such interrelated issues as gender, class, and social hierarchies; race and ethnicity; geographical relations; definitions of political space; discourses of authority and dissent; educational institutions; canonical and non-canonical literatures; and technologies of textual and visual literacies.

Bodies
and
Disciplines

INTERSECTIONS OF LITERATURE AND HISTORY
IN FIFTEENTH-CENTURY ENGLAND

Barbara A. Hanawalt and David Wallace, editors

Medieval Cultures
Volume 9

University of Minnesota Press
Minneapolis
London

Published by the University of Minnesota Press
111 Third Avenue South, Suite 290, Minneapolis, MN 55401-2520
Printed in the United States of America on acid-free paper

Library of Congress Cataloging-in-Publication Data
Bodies and disciplines: intersections of literature and history in fifteenth-century England / Barbara A. Hanawalt and David Wallace, editors.
    p.   cm. — (Medieval cultures ; v. 9)
    Contains revised versions of papers originally presented at a conference, Intersections — Fifteenth-Century Literature and History, held at the University of Minnesota in April 1993.
    Includes index.
    ISBN 0-8166-2714-2
    ISBN 0-8166-2715-0 (pbk.)
    1. Great Britain — History — Lancaster and York, 1399–1485 — Historiography — Congresses. 2. English literature — Middle English, 1100–1500 — History and criticism — Congresses. 3. Literature and history — England — History — Congresses. 4. England — Civilization — 1066–1485 — Congresses. 5. England — In literature — Congresses. 6. Fifteenth century — Congresses. I. Hanawalt, Barbara. II. Wallace, David, 1954–   III. Series.
DA245.R47   1996
942.04—dc20   95-32127

Contents

Contents

Acknowledgments

❖

In producing *Bodies and Disciplines: Intersections of Literature and History in Fifteenth-Century England,* the editors extend their thanks to a number of people and academic units that made both the initial conference possible and the subsequent volume a reality. Funding for the conference came from the College of Liberal Arts through the Center for Medieval Studies and from the Frenzel Chair through its holder, David Wallace. The Office of International Education, the Minnesota Student Association Educational and Diversity Grant, and a Cultural Activities Grant funded travel for our foreign visitors. The Carl D. Sheppard Fund provided some of the costs of publication.

The Center for Medieval Studies relies upon its research assistants for help in organizing its conferences and for editorial work on its volumes. The editorial assistants who worked on this volume included Mark Vesley, Gregory Prince, Patricia McGurk, Susan Burns, Morgan MacBain, and Jana Schulman. The graduate administrative assistants, Laura Staples and Donald Harreld, made travel arrangements and handled the finances and correspondence involved in the conference and the book.

Our relationship with the University of Minnesota Press in publishing the series Medieval Cultures has been a very fruitful one, and we are grateful for the collaboration with them.

Introduction

Barbara A. Hanawalt and David Wallace

The metaphor of "intersections" or crossroads as a model of inter-disciplinary work boldly offers itself to humorous critique (an offer generously accepted by the first and last essays in this volume): unfortunate things can happen at intersections. This metaphor does, how-ever, represent measurable progress over the introduction to the Center for Medieval Studies' predecessor volume, *Chaucer's England: Literature in Historical Context*, which spoke of territory raids and the carrying off of "facts" from archives or "qualitative evidence" from literary sources. Not only more civilized (in moving us from forest pathways to paved roads and a market economy), the intersections metaphor promises a more subtle modeling of the possibilities and perils of interdisciplinary exchange. Perhaps we have learned something from our predecessor vol-ume, from current advances in critical theory, and from our institutional experiences of cross-disciplinary teaching. The emphasis at Minnesota's Center for Medieval Studies has been for each teacher and graduate stu-dent to work *from* the strengths of a particular discipline (archaeology, classics, drama, history, literature, music, and philology) *toward* multidis-ciplinary understanding. Thus this initiating metaphor of "intersections" can be considered honest to our own current institutional practice; it promises, at least, to direct us away from the unmapped, boggy marsh-lands of a pandisciplinary "Medieval Studies."

But all such metaphors, of course, are of use only in *initiating* interdis-ciplinary discussion, rather than in defining its boundaries or possibilities. This volume traces its origins to a conference, "Intersections: Fifteenth-Century Literature and History," held at the University of Minnesota in April 1993, featuring papers from five historians and five literary scholars (with Paul Strohm as general respondent). The papers were relatively short, since a good deal of time was budgeted for cross-disciplinary discus-sion. The ten presenters were then invited to revise, refine, and some-times expand their papers in light of commentary from fellow contributors, from the editors, and from our audience. As editors, we have not sought to encourage or impose a particular theoretical model or set approach. Our Introduction here is short, since Ralph Hanna III's essay (it was gen-erally agreed) plays as something of an overture to the theoretical issues raised by this volume. Hanna's extended critique of the ways in which historians deploy literary texts offers something of a riposte to recent criticisms of the ways in which literati "borrow" from history. The fact that he chooses to concentrate upon a text first written in fourteenth-century England, *Piers Plowman,* forms part of his devious critical strategy: for as it was continually reread, glossed, and rewritten, Langland's poem became one of the most important of fifteenth-century texts.

Bodies and Disciplines, the somewhat austere main title finally chosen for this volume, represents our last, best assessment of the point to which contributors and commentators, through writing, discussion, and rewriting, have brought us. "Bodies" acknowledges "bodies of evidence," the time-honored term associated with the genesis of historical narrative; problematics of textual representation—from which the staging of civic, religious, or judicial "events" must be inferred—are exceptionally acute for those who would work on the English fifteenth century. "Bodies" also looks to the physical entities, the human beings, who found themselves caught up in such dramas; it hence provides a bridge to those acts of performance and ceremony, hospitality and celebration, coercion and restraint evoked by our second term, "disciplines". And "disciplines," of course, acknowledges not only things done to and by fifteenth-century bodies, but also our own efforts to reach them through organizations of knowledge known as "literature" and "history." Hence, then, *Bodies and Disciplines: Intersections of Literature and History in Fifteenth-Century England.*

The subject of fifteenth-century England is well suited to such adventures in interdisciplinary method: no anchoring canonical texts of the magnitude of Chaucer and Langland are authored, and there are prodigious obstacles to any Whiggish narration of social and political continuity. Fifteenth-century England is not, of course, terra incognita; it is, in fact, one of the most dynamic growth areas in both literary and historical scholarship. This may be, in part, because the fourteenth century has been overworked, but it may also be that medievalists, now somewhat more theory-literate, are better equipped to address the challenges of this difficult period. The extraordinary range of subject matters in this volume, some of them not previously considered fit or viable for sustained scholarly consideration, certainly attests to the emergence of a new fifteenth-century England. The Wars of the Roses, Caxton, and Malory—subjects that loom large in traditional accounts of this period—play a negligible role in this volume. Rather, the essayists direct our attention to the smaller, local dramas that occupied many and various segments of the population.

Such individual and community-based representations are drawn from a remarkable range of sources; readers will find the pairing of literary and record sources exceptionally rich and suggestive. Marjorie McIntosh, in evaluating communal disapprobation of social misbehavior, matches the leet court records of small market towns and rural villages with the language of fifteenth-century moral texts. Seth Lerer also goes to a market town record, that of Lydd, to consider how the theater scripted in these legal records might, or might not, compare with that of the *Croxton Play of the Sacrament*. Barbara Hanawalt uses London guild ordinances on apprenticeship and advice literature to explore the making of a concept of adolescence such as one finds in "The Childe of Bristowe." Ruth Mazzo Karras pairs church court records with *Dives and Pauper* in exploring sexual moralities. Felicity Heal moves from household books to *Sir Gawain and the Green Knight*; Rita Copeland takes a heresy inquisition as her chief source for understanding the hermeneutics of fifteenth-century dissent.

Several dominant themes emerge from the essays about fifteenth-century English life, literature, and popular culture; they emphasize the regulation and control of the human body, the need to establish community standards, the increasing concerns about identity of self and of community, and anxieties over religious orthodoxy. Such observations are hardly new, since they form subjects in Johan Huizinga's *Waning of the Middle Ages*. The shift of emphasis in these essays, however, moves from a sense of loss toward a sense of new definition and representation. The essays speak not of decay, but more of creating something new, perhaps in the name of the old, but with a full realization that all is not the same. Norbert Elias's great study, *The Civilizing Process*, also speaks to some of the issues in this volume, but he placed the developments in the sixteenth and seventeenth centuries and emphasized individual control more than a sense of communities also undergoing redefinition.

Many essays in this volume explore complex and porous relations between the physical body and the metaphorical body politic; freedoms and constraints endured and enjoyed by different bodies, or the same body at different moments, are considered as part of greater social strategies. In Miri Rubin's account, the medieval body emerges as an entity that can symbolize both harmony and unity as well as vulnerability, decay, and change. Seth Lerer focuses on bodily vulnerability in the public arena by considering legal scripts for public ceremonies, including the mutilation of thieves, in conjunction with simulated physical mutilation in the *Croxton Play*. The significant, meaning-making role played by spectators, as well as actors, in such drama is further explored by Sarah Beckwith. Her account of the Corpus Christi cycle considers commercial and political tensions that are played out through the ritual and commercial spaces of medieval York; she thereby troubles familiar notions of a society flawlessly integrated through the holistic image of Christ's body. Marjorie McIntosh ponders shifting relations of language to community conduct. Local court records show leading figures of villages and market towns across England becoming increasingly concerned with forms of activity and inactivity, such as gaming and idleness, considered offensive to communal sensibilities. In expressing their desire to discipline such malefactors, their language moves closer to that of "mirror for princes" literature and away from traditional moralism. Ruth Mazzo Karras, who also discusses the defining of behaviors considered offensive to the community, compares the teaching of sexual mores with the prosecution of sexual offenses in church courts (and finds a double standard). Gail McMurray Gibson considers the postchildbirth churching ceremony that transformed a mother's status from that of impure outsider to that of freshly purified and reintegrated communicant. Despite ambivalent feelings toward the female body expressed through church liturgy, women were able to make churching an occasion for the affirming of female friendship and the celebration of female fecundity.

The last three essays explore behaviors and strategies adopted by individuals in compliance with, or in resistance to, various kinds of prescriptive literature and disciplinary constraint. Barbara Hanawalt analyzes the moral and didactic poem, "The Childe of Bristowe," in the context of a rapidly expanding middle class that strove to define the parameters of acceptable behavior, including the creation of an ideal type of behavior for adolescents. Felicity Heal shows that in the complex workings of the medieval household reciprocity marked status. Exchanges of gifts, services, and hospitality helped establish immediate social standing (while playing a part in the governance of locality and kingdom). Rita Copeland reads the narrative of William Thorpe's interrogation as a textual site for the fashioning of a dissenter's historical identity and for the political framing of Lollardy; she further considers Thorpe's commitment to Lollard resistance through his own struggles as a professional intellectual.

The statute *De heretico comburendo* (1401), the *Constitutions* of Archbishop Arundel (1407–9), and the burning of Lollards such as Sawtry, Badby, and Oldcastle confirm that Lollardy inspired extreme anxiety in the secular and religious authorities of fifteenth-century England. Yet many of the essays in this book could be taken to resist the suggestion, one that the Lancastrians were anxious to encourage, that Lollardy be framed and isolated as the preeminent source and exemplar of all instability, religious and secular. Numerous local conflicts recounted in this volume — religious, judicial, domestic, and personal — suggest the inadequacy of confining accounts of instability and social disintegration in fifteenth-century England to analyses of Lollard trials, chapters from Malory's *Morte Darthur*, and battles from the Wars of the Roses. Yet other dramas considered here — through their discovery of movements of friendship, reciprocity, personal fantasy, and communal solidarity — resist subordination to any grand narrative that would pit an unruly English fifteenth century against the comforting, familiar (and hence, to us, stable) contours of Chaucer's England.

CHAPTER 1

❖

Brewing Trouble

On Literature and History — and Alewives

Ralph Hanna III

This essay places both its author and his subjects in a position of danger. For whatever the synergies "intersections" may provide, there are concomitant dangers — collisions and accidents, often of the mortal variety. Surveys always show, for example, that more pileups occur at the junctures of southern California freeways than occur in all the other miles they traverse. I put myself in such peril through my efforts to mediate between two disciplines. Similarly, my subject — alewives and taverns — defines an intersection both social and discursive, one potentially fraught with problems.

I began this chapter in what I thought was a throwaway footnote in an earlier article that discussed, in passing, representations of taverns in Middle English literature. On that occasion, I referred to "a common demonization of the tavern as feminized space."[1] In planning out this essay, I wanted to argue in full the point I had so blandly asserted. Alas, actual research intervened, and the only trouble I may brew in this essay will involve, not material alewives, but myself.

For rather early on in developing this study, I was directed to the fine historical work of Judith M. Bennett. Especially in her article "Misogyny, Popular Culture, and Women's Work," I discovered that Bennett assembles a vast amount of data, both about actual alewives (or brewsters) and about literary ones.[2] Yet I also found myself in a state of strange unease about Bennett's studies and about any possible intersection they might have with my own. Upon reflection, I realized that I was discomforted by what I took to be the differing evidentiary claims of two disciplines, literature and history, claims that presuppose incommensurate practitional self-definitions. Of course, the problem consumed me: what I present here, although I promise at least a peek at a literary text, will largely represent Low Theory, my take on the claims of the two professions. But I'm convinced, if only by my reading of past gatherings of the Center for Medieval Studies in Minneapolis, that such a generalized intervention should be of some value.[3]

The problem that bugs me is a very old one. I trace it back in some form to the implicit contention between Plato's banishment of the poets (*Republic* 10) and Aristotle's defense of poetry (*Poetics* 8 and 23). Plato, you will recall, objects to poetry as merely an imitation of reality and,

1

thus, a more distanced representation of his ultimate Real, the world of Ideas, than human reality itself. For him, the f/actual, the domain of history, is preferable. In contrast, Aristotle defends poetry against history. He argues that, in its reliance on the invented, the merely probable, rather than the actual, poetry is capable of attaining "a higher truth and higher seriousness" than history. Presumptively, he refers not simply to literature's formed presentation of allegedly universal values, but also to the presence of such values in those moral effects to be associated with *katharsis* in his affective dramatic theory.

It strikes me that the terms of this debate have not changed a great deal over the centuries. The self-styled interpreter of the two disciplines to one another, Hayden White, argues that traditional historians depend almost totally on literary tools: they, like the poets, must construct narratives to explain the past.[4] But for White, there is a fundamental seriousness to history that literature lacks: the reality of its referent; historical writing refers to and explains the f/actual. White's defense of history extends to what I can only call a peroration in hysteria: in a rearguard action against the postmodern, he threatens all humanist practitioners with irrelevance if they do not acknowledge the power that history gains because it has a real referent (pp. 44, 73–75). In comparison with this solid foundation in fact, as White sees it, literary study is merely frivolous, an indefensible lack of seriousness; history, and only history, can be the anchor discipline of the humanities.

However, White's Platonistic moralizing obscures two inelegant asymmetries to his argument. One can easily grant that both literary producers and literary critics rely on narratives, just as do historians,[5] but White first suppresses the fundamentally literary basis on which historical narratives are to be judged. He rather generally argues that historical narratives make sense and achieve either currency or the rubbish heap on the basis of "a correspondence to the real" (pp. 45–47, 76–78). By this White seems to mean some sense of the probable motivations of human action in the face of particular circumstances. Of course, at this point he has joined forces with Aristotelian notions of "plot" and thus with a purely literary form of analysis.

Moreover, White obscures the fact that the historian's Real is usually not (the medieval historian's, never) immediate. Just like literary critics, historians are, above all, readers: the evidence that—in White's terms, not mine—they must align with the Real is constituted of written documents. The historian's access to the real is, thus, always mediated by all those vicissitudes to which the act of reading is subject.

I certainly understand White's anxieties. Literary study does appear, even to many of its practitioners, unrestrained: in the absence of any possible claim to verification in the f/actual (as some would argue, even verbal verification), the discipline seems to proceed completely without rule. On the other hand, literary study, in its persistent concentration on a verbal document, has strengths from which history might well learn. The discipline has developed powerful tools for documentary interpretation—in recent years a bewildering plethora of them—for assessing, inter alia, the ideological bias of documents, broadly the way in which overt meanings are constantly undermined by silences, suppressions, and inadvertent admissions. Thus, especially as tools proliferate, literary study has disengaged and rendered contentious any claim to univocal meaning.[6] Of course, this tendency proves unsettling to White, as it does to many literary traditionalists, since such plurality vitiates any notion of an utterly common pursuit and of a determinate connection with anything outside the text itself.

The alternative reading strategy of "historians," a strategy thoroughly consonant with White's views, can be illustrated ubiquitously.[7] This kind of reading enacts what is in literary studies a retrograde swerve. It strives to see the text, not as a linguistic construction that represents the real, but as direct mimetic reflection of precise contemporary conditions. Let me give you an anecdotal example (lamentably true but here depersonalized). I once heard a discussion of the possible influence (which I would take as a given)[8] of Langland's character Piers the Plowman on Chaucer's description of the Plowman in *The General Prologue*; this study concluded in the negative. The only point of contact this investigator found was the Langlandian echo in Chaucer's "He wolde thresshe, and therto dyke and delve" (*General Prologue*, 536);[9] that line, the scholar averred, was insufficient to prove influence, for, this person asked with an air of thorough rhetoricality, "What else do people do in fields?"

This reading strategy is predicated upon pure mimesis. Its author assumes that language directly reflects human acts and ignores utterly that language mediates and selectively represents its referent. Within the space of literary history, this reading strategy also ignores Langland's revolutionary appreciation of manual labor, his motivated power to intervene in social usage and to redefine it, and the likelihood that there was nowhere in the years following 1386 for Chaucer to learn such an appreciation of field labor except in *Piers Plowman*.[10]

I want to suggest (and then test out on some of Bennett's readings) what I hope enacts a compromise reading strategy between these differing appropriations of texts to which literary scholars and historians want common access. While I believe in the materiality of the referents that literary[11] and historical texts represent, I equally believe that access to such referents occurs only in a medium, language. I'm acutely conscious, as well, that language has a history—not just of phonemes and lexicon, but of socially accepted modes of representing its various referents. These historically placeable language habits or codes, which I usually call "discourses," contextualize f/actual referents within one or another field of speech. Rather than there being a "plowman" with precise duties directly mirrored in Chaucer or Langland, we can reach only a polyvocalized medieval English plowman, a fragmented figure constructed out of a con-flicted range of social preoccupations and concerns, all expressed through often incommensurate value-laden descriptions in language. There is thus the plowman of husbandry manuals, of manorial court rolls, of labor leg-islation, of Cistercian rules and documents, of texts and deeds that protest rural exploitation. The totality of these descriptions, each the selective product of the diverse discourses I mention, all retrievable through doc-uments, construct the medieval English plowman we can "read." I would argue the power of such a reading strategy predicated on identifying ar-eas of social usage: whatever the vexed issue of its relation to the Real, such a reading in fact provides a more complete narrative, a fuller his-tory, than we can attain on the basis of purely mimetic readings. These, it seems to me, lift a single narrative device, the character "plowman," from a literary work and seek to analyze it, in isolation from other lin-guistic usages, as if it were thus the full medieval concept "plowman."

By this long "commodious vicus of recirculation" I return to Judith Bennett and our alewives. But before passing on to the specifics of Ben-nett's argument, I want to consider briefly her sources. I hope by this move to indicate the power of a discursive reading, that is, one that is ideological and simultaneously the utterly indispensible contribution of historical information in shaping it.

Analysis of Brigstock court records underlies most of Bennett's con-ceptions of alewives, their role and work.[12] The overwhelming majority of the relevant entries records "presentments under 'The Assize of Bread and Ale,'" fines levied against women brewers. However, this statute it-self cannot, in any reading, provide a logic for most fines imposed: the legal text, which I will discuss shortly, addresses quality of product and cost per unit and sets penalties for violation of only these regulations. Bennett's brewsters, in contrast, are fined simply for brewing—for prac-ticing a trade, itself legal and necessary, which provides the general occa-sion for the statute. Bennett notes this issue, but simply accepts it: she is happy with the demographic information the records provide, assum-ing a truthful record, a total survey of brewsters in Brigstock.

But to operate in this way, as a historian, Bennett must accept a fic-tion. Her documents record what is surely material fact, fines imposed for the act of brewing; and, as she notes, a statute intended to control malfeasance has been transformed into a simple licensing procedure. But this transformation relies upon a deliberated misreading of statute law, and the legal standing of Bennett's court rolls is surely qualified by their "punishment" of an act that is legal under the very document that li-censes the actions of the court. Of course, we deal here with a "legal fic-tion"—one rendered even more fictitious in locales other than Brigstock: in such places, wives apparently had no legal status and husbands were thus fined for brewing that they did not perform.[13] But the qualifying adjective "*legal* fiction"—which overfamiliarizes the records for us within a set phrase—seems to me less relevant than the following noun. For all their demographic substance, Bennett's documents report untruths: brewing is not a crime, and the statute requires no license to brew. The records, while they certainly record real events, material fines, do so within a context that significantly resembles literary narrative, a story wished for or feared, not the legalism on which the records ostensibly depend.

In coming to such a conclusion, I cannot function without Bennett's aid. As a historian, she has competence with a variety and range of documents I do not—their purposes, expected conventions, forms of record (even down to Latin abbreviations I've never seen before). From such reading skills Bennett can construct a material record of extreme value to me: it can create a horizon of expectation that may exclude from any reading strategy I would devise various naive assumptions. Her interpretation of the documents establishes a range of probability within which my readings can responsibly operate and provides some trace of material human experience to mediate the purely linguistic discursive features of the literary record.

Simultaneously, Bennett offers neither overt explanation nor apology for the fictive aspect of her documents. Yet part of the horizon she creates for me suggests a way of seeing the ideological work the untruth of "ale presentments" performs. From the documents Bennett reveals two important demographic facts about brewsters. First, brewing always functioned as an adjunct to an already packed domestic economy: it was a way in which women could utilize household space and implements to supplement family income. Second, women seldom brewed either frequently or for protracted periods; the work seems to have fitted around the edges of a normal routine, one would gather either to meet financial emergency or to fill slack time in the normal domestic economy.

Bennett's demographic data, dependent on reading the documents, organizing the information they present, and identifying biographical patterns in it, suggests that the fiction of "ale presentments" might be conceived as fulfilling a communal function (and thus a function analogous to the regulatory interests of "The Assize" itself). The community, through its legal institutions and those regulatory functions that strive to protect it, may here be involved in further self-protective gestures—taxing the excess profit of individual households. The fine imposed penalizes those in a position to accrue additional capital and returns some small measure of that profit to the now relatively impoverished community of nonbrewers. The special implementation of a statute that does not exist for this purpose strives to minimize, however marginally, potential social dissimilation, to restore the prior status of all village households. Certainly, the evidence of fines levied against nonbrewing husbands implies that, in locales other than Brigstock, "ale presentments" were perceived as a household—not a personal—"violation" of "The Assize," although such an ideology of equalizing households plainly cloaks the differential gendered effect of fining women's industry.[14]

This extension of Bennett's analysis may indicate what ultimately troubled me about her arguments concerning misogyny and women's work. For as the obverse of her strong material analyses, when Bennett turns to texts, she becomes unduly involved in the mimetic: she wishes to ask whether those negative attitudes toward alewives expressed in a variety of texts over two hundred years cannot be linked with a very real referent—the demise of women in the brewing industry, pretty much complete by the late sixteenth century. In this process, she singles out, among other instances, Langland's depiction of two alewives, Rose þe Regrater (5.217–25) and Beton þe Brewestere (5.296–306).[15] These, Bennett argues, represent part of a long line of popular depictions that show "female brewers and tipplers ... as unpleasant, unrespectable, and untrustworthy women," thus subject to public ridicule and ultimately, to be driven out of the profession in favor of male competitors.[16]

In this mimetic reading strategy, Bennett operates as if representations of alewives might be detached and treated discretely from complicated and intertwined medieval representations. These typically emphasize broader social institutions of which alewives form but a part—drinking and the tavern. (In fact, given both the paucity of overt references to alewives in the literature and women's prominence in the medieval brewing trade, the most misogynistic aspect of such depictions may be the general elision of the feminine.) Such representations occur widely in Middle English, across an array of genres—sermons and religious tracts (for example, the Dominican friar John Lacy of Newcastle's explanation of the decalogue), Chaucerian fabliaux and their imitations (for example, the Pardoner's performance and its reprise in the prologue to *The Tale of Beryn*), religious drama (for example, *Mankind*, the Winchester *Occupation and Idleness*, the Digby *Mary Magdalene*).[17]

Such depictions indicate the prevalence of discursive clusters that represent associations of women and alehouses and that frequently have little to do with gender in a misogynistic sense. As I hope one example will indicate, antifeminism is not a discursive universal, nor is it monovocally deployed in medieval texts. The author of the widely dispersed *Southern Passion* attacks taverngoing in an aside precisely because it demeans women. In this poet's rendition, men get drunk and voice their lascivious fantasies; they thereby defame both the sex and individual virtuous women alike:

Whanne men sitteþ in hare hayt vp hare ale-benche
And habbeþ þe pycher & þe coppe & þe botyler to schenche,
þanne is hare iangle & hare game to deme som sely wenche,
þat god ȝeue þat some of ham miȝte in þe ale-fat adrenche![18]

This author operates within a reconstructible and widely distributed sermon discourse: in it, taverns and drink produce, most immediately, a variety of evil speech-acts.[19] And in the most developed accounts of such behavior, tipplers pass beyond mere evil speech to violence, sometimes depicted as overtly misogynistic—adultery and wife-beating.[20] Not only does such a depiction attack misogyny, it is thoroughly indifferent to the gender of the tavern-keeper (here "þe botyler" is presumably male) and places primary blame upon the drunkard, not the institution that serves him.[21]

In her handling of *Piers Plowman,* Bennett detaches the character alewife from the supporting institution. From her, we learn about Rose and Betty, but nothing about Langland's extensive references to ale or taverns or drinking. Although I believe Langland, in certain contexts, an outstanding practitioner of misogyny, Bennett does not here acknowledge what she admits elsewhere—that forces other than misogyny may animate his depictions.[22] I want to suggest ways in which Langland may have shaped his accounts in response to a variety of circumambient social discourses, more diverse and more complicated in their interrelationships than the simple label "misogyny" would allow.

If I think of drinking, brewing, and the ale trade in *Piers Plowman,* four passages immediately come to mind, only three of them emphatically gendered, two of those male, a third more evenhanded. Within this range of uses, with which I can concord another forty or so loci in the poem, I think misogyny has much less play than do a variety of other available social discourses, primary among them an abiding distrust professionally demarcated, suspicion of victualing trades (a possibility Bennett acknowledges, p. 175). I want to run through these four passages very quickly to suggest how Bennett's mimetic eye, her claim that representation of alewives per se tells us about alewives, manages to ignore another history, characteristic of Langland's creation, one of social complexity and openness to different aspects of the fourteenth-century discursive universe.

The first passage about drink that leaps to my mind occurs in what literary critics always perceive as a seminal dialogue, that of the dreamer Wille and Holichirche in B passus 1 (lines 23–37).[23] The passage is particularly central to the poem in that, through its discussion of the three things necessary to mankind (23–26), it introduces Langland's persistent preoccupation with the world of dearth, a world in which harsh labor is necessary to provide for the entire commons.[24] In such a context, "reson" or "mesure" (restraint) is all, and overindulgence a fundamental social crime (25, 35–37; compare "mesurable manere," 19): it both deprives others of their due modicum and probably cloaks, on the part of the overindulgent, a criminous act, a theft in which one delights in what one has not earned by work. As I have indicated elsewhere, such lucubrations, one steady stream of medieval antitavern invective, are predicated upon an apparently "foreign" discourse—labor regulation and the presumption that one should earn one's keep (preferably, for a moderate price).[25]

Holichirche develops these points through the story of Lot. In certain respects this account echoes that of *The Southern Passion* and reflects the same pulpit background—appropriately, since the tale is spoken by a character representing The Institutional Church and takes a rhetorical form usual in sermons, the exemplum. Lot appears here as a figure of *dismesure*, the man who takes excessive delight in drink (27, 29–31, 33), then thinks of sex, and actuates his desire improperly. As a bad sexual "workman," his product turns out to be useless to anyone, merely "cherles" (33).[26]

But equally (and far from uniquely), Holichirche's explanatory anecdote is not entirely proportionate to the actual instruction at issue. For the Latin quotation and line 32 indicate that Lot is not simply an aggressor (as are the taverngoers of *The Southern Passion*), but also a victim. In fact, his daughters perform as biblical versions of the tapster-whore: they lead him on to his overindulgence and sexual sin.[27] Although the conclusion to the passage reasserts Lot's culpability, Langland plainly recognizes a misogynistic construction of tavern women like that Bennett discusses—as temptresses leading good men to their doom. This passage, especially insofar as Holichirche rambles away from her main point, strikes me as a gratuitously misogynistic joke. Not only is the exegesis of a piece with other medieval depictions of fallen patriarchs like Adam, David, Solomon, and Samson,[28] it allows Langland to express his distaste for feminine authority through characterizing it as competitively shrewish.

This passage immediately interfaces with a pair of early discussions, in this case thoroughly professionalized.[29] At the end of the poem's Prologue (226–30, note also 219), Langland's depiction of England degenerates into a cacophony of street cries; instructively, the most ubiquitous of these come from purveyors of food and wine. And early in passus 3, when Mede appears in London, she manages, through her engaging bribes, to get the mayor to suspend those restrictions that govern victualing trades (76–100). This action obviously piqued Langland, since in his final revision he thoroughly reworked it, ultimately doubling its length (see C 3.77–126).

At the end of the Prologue, the outcry of victuallers appeals to dietary sumptuousness. In contrast to what Langland will present as Piers Plowman's plain, yet perfectly adequate, peasant fare (6.179–96, 280–98), these figures encourage luxury consumption. Piers's diet, overtly short of protein, contrasts with the cooks' shilling for goose, pig, and roast; his water and ale, with the fancy imported wines available in the tavern.[30] These appeals, to paraphrase Holichirche, put "the gut" before "the ghost": they identify victualing with inherent appeals to *dismesure*.

8

Yet one should recognize that, socially, the representations of both Holichirche and the Prologue are directed toward only a single class. Fancy food, drinking with women, and "wasting" are not universal taboos in Middle English literary culture: indeed, the capacity, if not the responsibility, for indulging in such behavior defines one important cultural arena—hall society in the great house. One alliterative poet imagines the height of society as both "ladies full louely to lappen in my armes" and "With renkes in ryotte to reuelle in haulle." Sumptuous feasting and drinking, like the ornate verbal surface of courtly poetry, testify precisely to the aristocratic capacity to express power through wastage, conspicuous consumption. The work that most explicitly addresses such behaviors, *Winner and Waster*, apparently endorses Langland's very locales of indulgence—the wines of Cheap and the delicate meats available in Bread Street and the Poultry. The poet identifies these as a site "þer moste waste is of wele" (473), but accepts this sumptuousness as one appropriate focus of the noble life. Tellingly, he is open, as Langland here is not, about the class perquisites at issue: those for whom such indulgences may be licit can command others to work for them (see 286–90) and can take a laissez-faire attitude toward their social underlings: "Late lordes lyfe als þam liste, laddes as þam falles" (378, and see the following lines).[31]

Although Langland most typically concerns himself with lower-class overindulgence, the end of the Prologue contains the seeds of a more evenhanded and less class-marked discourse, for a flagrant and perverse expenditure of a sort uniquely Langlandian also occurs in this passage. The vernacular outbursts of victuallers (as well as Pro. 225's scrap of French, associated with lazy, self-indulgent workmanship) contrast with the notable Latinity of much of the Prologue. Simply consider the united voice of the commons, "Precepta regis sunt nobis vincula legis" (Pro. 145). Rich food violates basic rules of moderation, but, equally, it appeals to and encourages—as those dirty-talking bowlers of *The Southern Passion* would suggest—immoderate, in this case vernacular, speech. Langland's hope for the social power of the word presents speech as a spiritualized economic value in a way that overrides class distinctions: certainly, as a poet, and a vernacular one at that, he remains acutely conscious of social adulteration of language (and perpetually fretful over his inabilities to extract his poem from such wastage).[32]

The passage concerning Mede and the victuallers, equally professionalized and gendered male,[33] relies explicitly upon statute discourse—although not the labor legislation I have earlier mentioned. Passus 3, lines 77b-79 almost quote the "Iudicium pillorie" appended to "The Assize of Bread and Ale," and the entire passage examines the peculation potential in the retailing activies ("regratrie," 83), associated with victualing.[34] The statute itself, not just Langland's line 79a, links bakers and brewers, in part because it conceives their "just prices" as dependent on the same scale, the cost of their common raw materials, grains.

In its pricing, "The Assize" asserts one thing—and thereby implies another. Since it first sets specific per gallon prices on ale, tied to the cost of grain (*Statutes* 1:200), it simultaneously implies a quality standard, that some certain measure of grain produces each gallon of ale. As Langland's account proceeds, retailers' ability to enrich themselves depends on violating precisely these expectations. Selling "parcelmele" (82), in quantities smaller than the statutory gallon, obscures the actual costing involved and enables the retailer to take in more than the few pence a gallon the statute envisions.[35] And Langland gestures toward retail adulteration of the raw materials—rather than using whatever measure of grain the Assize imagines, one can attenuate the costlier stuff by mixing in draff or the dregs from the last batch—in his claim that victuallers "poisone þe peple pryueliche" (83).[36] The result is a perverse magic, that multiplier effect we would associate with capitalism per se: the poor victims' empty bellies become transformed into imposing architecture, the ostentatious mercantile home or the swarming tenement (which allows yet further profiteering through rent gouging). The passage implicitly harks back to Holichirche's three necessities—not only does victualing deny them to the poor, but the excess profit inherent in retailing violates the basic standards of "reson" and "truþe" (92, 85).

Finally, near the very end of the poem, after a last effort at reforming the Commonwealth according to Christian principles, Langland presents a (male) brewer as the unregenerate spokesman for the Commons' resistance to virtuous activity (19.396–402).[37] The brewer rejects that *spiritus iustitie* that should create an ideal state and demands the right to follow his inherent nature, his "kynde." That nature is, of course, fully professionalized: in rejecting just dealing, the brewer demands, implicitly, the nonenforcement of "The Assize of Bread and Ale." And, since they are framed within the same statutory language, he replicates the misbehaviors, the covert adulterations of product, also typical of Langland's Rose or the alewife of the Chester *Harrowing of Hell*: these are representations that speak less to gender than to abiding suspicions of victualing as a profession.[38]

I would suggest that these four passages (and a variety of other loci that I cite in the notes) place Langland rather precisely within discourses concerning brewing. These discourses are, for the most part, tied very closely to profession, "bakers and brewers," as Langland's repeated collocation (Pro. 219, 3.79; C 4.120) has it, and they concord with various permutations of Langland's broadly economic discourse. Brewing (and related trades) remain suspect in *Piers* because they render it impossible to ascertain what would constitute an appropriate return and they thereby cheat consumers, because they threaten the rule of laboring for what one eats (in retail, the brewer generates additional income without addi-

tional expenditure on materials or labor; the buyer is attracted to pleasure—not the sustenance that allows labor), and because they expend,
in a uniquely Langlandian twist, speech in trivial and nonproductive
ways.

How then should one assess Bennett's two "misogynistic" portraits?
I would make of them two rather different things, in neither case precisely Bennett's version of misogyny. Rose þe Regrater seems to me
largely a pendant to her husband Coveitise. As in several other instances,
here Langland utilizes marital metaphors to indicate one variety or another of allegorical linkage: in this case, he almost automatically assumes what Bennett demonstrates, that medieval women's economic en-
terprises merely supplemented a male-dominated household economy.
Rose's activities, like Coveitise's, are plural: she joins him in cloth making and depends on his investment to set up as an alewife. "I bou3te
hire barly; she brew it to selle," he says, and to his mind, his wife functions as a materially productive extension of his private capital.

Moreover, Rose's professional activities ape his (and those of male
brewers elsewhere in the poem). From the moment he is introduced—
"And lik a leþeren purs lolled hise chekes / Wel sidder þan his chyn"
(5.191–92)—we understand that Coveitise depends upon mercantile corruption of product, distortion of a preexisting raw material, all in the interest of the "leþeren purs." Thus, Coveitise describes his "donet," the
primer of his cloth trade, as "To drawe þe list along, þe lenger it semed"
(5.207–8). And we understand Rose's exercises in retailing, whether ale
or cloth, to be the same—the extenuation of raw materials. Rather than
uniquely gendered, she images her husband: in this typically misogynistic Langlandian gesture, the female member of a pair lacks any independent integrity, but such exemplary misogyny does not depend upon Rose's
professional affiliations.

Beton þe brewestere draws upon other aspects of contemporary social
usage, but ones well within Langland's general tavern discourse. Here, as
Owst pointed out long ago, Langland reproduces and develops dramatically
a pulpit stock, only explicitly voiced at C 9.98 ("beggares with bagges, þe
whiche brewhous ben here churches"), that the tavern is the devil's
church.[39] In fact, the most ubiquitous complaint against drink in medieval sources relies, not on statute labor discourse, but on the language
of spiritual instruction: the sinful antitype to the parish church dis-
suades and distracts people from carrying out basic redemptive Christian
duties.[40] Further, Beton is simply one part of the scene's elaborate and
constant parody of church services, another discursive bit well paral-
leled in pulpit literature; for example, playing forfeits in the tavern, the
game Langland calls New Fair, directly mirrors the penitential examination Glutton isn't engaging in as he refuses to give up his tavern life.[41]

But, although Beton is female, is an alewife, and does lead Glutton
away from proper religious duties, I think Bennett errs in linking her

with other alewives whom she may legitimately describe as harridan grotesques (for example, Skelton's Eleanor Rumming). In Langland's parody, Beton appears here as the antitype of the welcoming parish priest Glutton thinks he seeks. But she seems every bit as pleasant and forgiving as one might imagine that figure. Moreover, she is an accomplished professional, an accommodating and well-stocked hostess, even in her attention to fast-day diets. Quite in contrast to Langland's mordant presentation of Coveitise or to John Lacy's humorless satire of the demonic tavern (p. 22), Beton's establishment exemplifies—just as does the church—a place of fellowship and good cheer. Just as Langland might extend notions of victualing as waste to consider speech within the same discourse, so he is also capable of intervening in pulpit stocks to realize the tactile appeal of actions elsewhere marked, without hesitation, as virulent social ills.

This final example perhaps most trenchantly illustrates the possible power of the discursive analysis I am advocating. A century ago, during the period in which literary interest in *Piers* concentrated upon the poem's mimesis, its reflection of a living world, this scene always provided a central example of Langland's openness to a raw experience denied even to Chaucer. Certainly, for those with comparable modern experiences in juke joints and honky-tonks, Beton's tavern will convey a recognizable flavor of fellowship, joy, delight in low life, and plain disgust. Moreover, at points, this scene accords with those few surviving medieval snatches, mentioned in Felicity Heal's essay, that herald the joys of ale and fellowship.[42] Thus, even though this scene occurs within the most critical of evaluative frameworks—part of Langland's depiction of incontrovertible evil, the Seven Deadly Sins—it challenges, as much as confirms, the various social discourses on which Langland relies elsewhere. For this tavern scene, in some measure, reveals other representations as what they are—codes seeking the social restraint of pleasure, invoked for a variety of ideological motives.

Piers Plowman remains a source of perpetual fascination precisely because of such broad and often inconsistent openness to the polyvocality of fourteenth-century social discourses. The fascination of Langland's vast and imperfect efforts at mediation between the mundane and the celestial largely depends upon his ear for diverse social formulations, his ability to represent a confusing range of contemporary possibilities, in many cases ones unrecorded elsewhere. The poem thus resists closure and stasis; certainly, it never quite validates any single interpretation of its materials. (Simply consider, for example, that Langland's attack on retail victualing supports working-class needs for just pricing and healthy sustenance; in contrast, the discourses of the pulpit and of labor law display consummate indifference to the possible needs and interests of working people.) But such inconsistencies, resulting from the appropriation of social discourses diverse and noncommensurate, reveal in striking ways a history complicated and conflicted, the product of something more than Bennett's misogynistic apprehension of alewives.

Only by reading this diversely contoured record in its fullness do we gain whatever fitful hope exists of understanding What Was. But our attention must respect both the material record provided by historians and the imbrication of our access to the past in habits of contemporary language use. Just as we necessarily rely upon those skilled at handling the documentary record to direct our enthusiasms, we need also to comprehend medieval discursive habits, how materials of diverse origin interface and support or conflict with one another. Without both tools, our understanding is at best distorted, at worst functionally blocked off.

Notes

A number of Intersections conference participants offered comments, suggestions, and, in Barbara Hanawalt's case, unpublished materials that have made this a better essay. In addition to Hanawalt, I would single out contributions of Miri Rubin, Marjorie McIntosh, Ruth Karras, and Kathleen Biddick, all of which I have taken pains to incorporate. My colleague John M. Ganim has also made important suggestions that have improved the essay.

1. See Ralph Hanna III, "Pilate's Voice/Shirley's Case," *South Atlantic Quarterly* 91 (1992): 793–812, at 810 n. 14. Barbara Hanawalt, "Women Tavern Keepers, Servants, and Female Drunkenness in Medieval England," in *Was nützt die Schusterin dem Schmid? Frauenarbeit und Handwerk, 14.–19. Jahrhundert* (Vienna: Ludwig Boltzmann Institut für historische Sozialwissenschaften, forthcoming), argues that the tavern may have constituted a·unique site where the normally gendered division of labor and space broke down.

2. Judith M. Bennett, "Misogyny, Popular Culture, and Women's Work," *History Workshop* 31 (spring 1991): 166–88.

3. See Barbara Hanawalt, ed., *Chaucer's England: Literature in Historical Context* (Minneapolis: University of Minnesota Press, 1992), which records an extraordinary divide in the analytical methods utilized by historians and by literary scholars.

4. See Hayden White, *The Content of the Form: Narrative Discourse and Historical Representation* (Baltimore, Md.: Johns Hopkins University Press, 1987), esp. pp. 21–22, 24–25, 44.

5. Literary critics do this by providing some more or less covert (or, perhaps better, rhetorically transformed) narrative of their experience with the texts they analyze. See Northrop Frye's comment that criticism is simply a branch of allegory (*Anatomy of Criticism: Four Essays* [Princeton, N.J.: Princeton University Press, 1957], p. 89). I would note in passing that White's argument seems to me thoughtlessly self-canceling: if literary studies are so untrustworthy, what privileges the literary basis of White's historiography—what grants narrative, in literary circles taken as fiction, truth? Or, put another way, given that *De preliis Alexandri Magni* once passed current as a "true" account, is not "historical truth" subject to its own forms of mediation, its own fictiveness? At least one countermovement, quantitative history, of which Bennett is a practitioner, would evade this difficulty by laying claim to some scientist facticity.

6. However, it needs to be said that this openness replicates long-standing emphases in literary study. The now old New Criticism emphasizes rhetorical tropes, but its favorites—irony, paradox, ambiguity—all privilege devices of unsettled meaning. Precisely this long-held interest in uncertainty or polyvocality opens the way to the indeterminate text that allows, if not invites, readings resistant to overt thematics.

7. For example, in various essays in Hanawalt, *Chaucer's England,* or large tracts of F. R. H. DuBoulay, *The England of Piers Plowman: William Langland and His Vision of the Fourteenth Century* (Cambridge: Brewer, 1991).

8. Anne Middleton, in papers delivered to scholarly meetings (the 1991 Modern Language Association, the 1992 New Chaucer Society), has outlined with great sophistication a variety of ways in which Chaucer responds to Langland.

9. All references from Chaucer refer to Larry D. Benson et al., eds., *The Riverside Chaucer* (Boston: Houghton Mifflin, 1987). Compare the collocation "dike and delve" at *Piers*, Pro. 224, 5.545, 6.107 and 141; A 11.187. All citations from *Piers*, unless otherwise indicated, refer to George Kane and E. Talbot Donaldson, eds., *Piers Plowman: The B Version* (London: Athlone, 1975). I cite the other texts from George Kane, ed., *Piers Plowman: The A Version* (London: Athlone, 1960), and Derek Pearsall, ed., *Piers Plowman: An Edition of the C-Text* (London: Arnold, 1978).

10. See Elizabeth Kirk, "Langland's Plowman and the Recreation of Fourteenth-Century Religious Metaphor," *Yearbook of Langland Studies* 2 (1988): 1–21.

11. I assume that, for any literary text to have appealed to any audience, it must, in some measure, represent, not a Mimetic Real, but an actual concern of interest in the social context of its production.

12. Judith Bennett's primary studies include, in addition to the article cited in n. 2, "The Village Ale-Wife: Women and Brewing in Fourteenth-Century England," in *Women and Work in Preindustrial Europe*, ed. Barbara Hanawalt (Bloomington: Indiana University Press, 1986), pp. 20–36, and *Women in the Medieval English Countryside: Gender and Household in Brigstock before the Plague* (London: Oxford University Press, 1987), esp. pp. 115–26.

13. This seems the logical conclusion to draw about Bennett's control sample from Iver, where men accounted for seventy-three of all amercements for brewing, but see *Women*, pp. 121, 126–27. See also P. J. P. Goldberg, *Woman Is a Worthy Wight: Women in English Society c. 1200–1500* (Wolfeboro Falls, N.H.: Sutton, 1992).

14. Moreover, Bennett's analysis of brewsters' social status may suggest that the "community" protected by such actions is in fact the peasant aristocracy (not lower peasant orders). Fining brewers may reduce capital accumulation that would allow middling peasants to better themselves. In effect, the tax reaffirms that property ownership, possession of fields for agricultural production, remains the mark of peasant aristocracy, and extracting the tax marginally reduces the prospect of middling peasants intruding into this group through production unrelated to agriculture.

15. I think there are quite substantial gaps in Bennett's literary research; I cite in passing later a few examples of texts Bennett might have considered. However, Bennett offers important and fundamentally correct critiques of Rossell Hope Robbins, "John Crophill's Ale-Pots," *Review of English Studies* 20 (1969): 182–89, esp. 184 and notes; see esp. Bennett, "Misogyny," p. 184 n. 8. I have no desire to deny the propriety of Langland's two women to Bennett's argument, nor do I find much reason to disagree with her extraordinarily compelling summary conclusions about literary texts (see esp. p. 177).

16. Bennett, "Misogyny," p. 171 and, for the quote, p. 169.

17. For Lacy (fl. 1420s), see James Finch Royster, ed., "A Middle English Treatise on the Ten Commandments," *Studies in Philology* 6 (1910): 1–39, esp. 22; for "The Prologue to *The Tale of Beryn*" (s. xv med.?), see *The Tale of Beryn*, ed. F. J. Furnivall and W. G. Stone, Early English Text Society (EETS), e.s. 105 (1909), pp. 1–24; for *Mankind* (s. xv med.), see *The Macro Plays*, ed. Mark Eccles, EETS 262 (1969), pp. 153–84; for *Occupation and Idleness* (s. xv med.), see *Non-Cycle Plays and The Winchester Dialogues*, ed. Norman Davis (Leeds: University of Leeds School of English, 1979), pp. 192–208; for *Mary Magdalene*, see *Medieval Drama*, ed. David Bevington (Boston: Houghton Mifflin, 1975), pp. 689–753.

18. Beatrice Daw Brown, ed., *The Southern Passion* (s. xiii[2]?), EETS, o.s. 169 (1927), lines 1959–62: the passage occurs within a spirited defense of the propriety of the risen Jesus having first shown himself to a woman, the Magdalene. This text usually circulated within the very popular *South English Legendary*.

19. See Hanna, "Pilate's Voice," pp. 798–99 and notes.

20. See G. R. Owst, *Literature and Pulpit in Medieval England: A Neglected Chapter in the History of English Letters and of the English People,* 2nd ed. (New York: Barnes and Noble, 1961), p. 431.

21. See the way in which women, Glutton's wife and serving-girl, are left to pick up the pieces after his bender (*Piers* 5.357–63), or my discussion of Lot later.

22. See Bennett, "Misogyny," p. 175, for one acknowledgment of the variety of forces behind the depiction of brewsters. For Langland's antifeminism, see most notably the depiction of Meed, 2.7–5.33. But, more generally, given Langland's clerical pretentions, *Piers* is an extremely masculine poem.

23. R. E. Kaske's discussion probably overschematizes, but his interests would certainly be shared by many Langlandians and indicate the utter centrality of this passus to the poem; see Beryl Rowland, ed., "Holychurch's Speech and the Structure of *Piers Plowman,*" *Chaucer and Middle English Studies in Honour of Rossell Hope Robbins* (London: Allen and Unwin, 1974), pp. 320–27.

24. The issue first arises in the foundation of the Commonwealth at Pro. 112–22, and the dreamer figure Wille is still brooding over these problems (in a coda to the fourth passage I will discuss later) as late as the waking conversation with Need at the head of the poem's last passus (20.1–50).

25. See Hanna, "Pilate's Voice," pp. 795–96. Within *Piers,* see particularly 6.115, where bad laborers desert the field for the alehouse, and 6.305–20, where, once grain has been harvested, laborers become overindulgent in diet, a development immediately juxtaposed with their effort to violate the pay scales mandated by the Statute of Laborers. See more distantly, C 8.193 and 9.145; 13.250–52. Such a discourse underlies the typical morality play depiction of the tavern as alternative to holy labor and, consequently, holy living; see *Occupation and Idleness,* lines 171–94, 233–70, 421–24; *Mankind,* lines 273–76, 581–88, 609, 710–12, 729; *Mary Magdalene,* lines 305–571 (the tavern at 470ff.). And see Lacy's charge against taverngoers that "woon of ʒow distrith þat wolde susteyne mony mesurabul men in þe luste of glotene" (p. 22), a charge still alive in Elizabethan times (Hanna, "Pilate's Voice," p. 809 n. 11).

26. Langland returns to this discursive cluster—eating and drinking immoderately leads to crossing forbidden sexual lines—at 11.335–36 (compare the more extensive parallel, C 13.152–54, 182–90) and 14.71–84 (the example of Sodom). For alcohol and the misuse of Inwit, see 9.61–67; the C parallel cites Lot as an example (10.177). Both Chaucer's Pardoner (*Canterbury Tales* C 483–87) and the instructional handbook *Memoriale credencium* (s. xiv/xv), p. 131, lines 13–16, identify Lot as a prime example of that gluttonous excess that produces what the latter calls "vnskilful lecherie"; see J. H. L. Kengen, ed. (Nijmegen dis., n.d.).

27. For tapster-whores, see Chaucer's Pardoner, *Canterbury Tales* C 477–82, and the "Prologue" to *Beryn.* The association of taverns and prostitution recurs at 5.511–12, as well as in John Lydgate's "A Ballade on an Ale-seller" (s. xv2/4?), in *The Minor Poems of John Lydgate, Part 2,* ed. Henry Noble MacCracken, EETS 192 (1933), pp. 429–32 (although see n. 42 below); Thomas Hoccleve's "Male Regle," lines 137–59 (1405), in *Selections from Hoccleve,* ed. M. C. Seymour (Oxford: Clarendon, 1981), pp. 12–23; *Mankind,* line 609; *Occupation and Idleness,* line 400.

28. For women inveigling the patriarchs, see the originary bit of British misogyny, extant in over fifty manuscripts produced in England, Walter Map's "Dissuasio Valerii ad Ruffinum philosophum ne uxorem ducat," at p. 292 in *De Nugis Curialium,* ed. C. L. N. Brooke and R. A. B. Mynors (Oxford: Clarendon, 1983). Langland associates wine and whores at 14.250–53 and argues that indulgence in women and wine should debar one from the clergy at C 11.111. See more distantly 5.74 and 6.260–67.

29. I emphasize "early," because reading sequence certainly effects interpretation. Readers, as an initial gesture, try to assimilate passages later in their reading experience to the interpretative constructions that have helped explain to them earlier ones.

30. Following on his sense of dearth, Langland usually associates wine with overindul-

gence and depicts it as a luxury drink (weak ale should be good enough for everyone); see 5.177–79, 10.367, 14.230–33 (compare C 9.92) and 251; C 9.253. See Christopher Dyer, "English Diet in the Later Middle Ages," in *Social Relations and Ideas: Essays in Honour of R. H. Hilton,* ed. T. H. Aston et al. (Cambridge: Cambridge University Press, 1983), pp. 191–216.

31. The first two citations come from *The Parliament of the Three Ages,* lines 247 and 253; see Thorlac Turville-Petre, ed., *Alliterative Poetry of the Later Middle Ages: An Anthology* (London: Routledge, 1989), pp. 80–81. For the most flagrant example of the noble feast as expression of magnatial power, see Mary Hamel, ed., *Morte Arthure* (New York: Garland, 1984), lines 176–215. For the quotations from *Winner and Waster,* a poem that Langland knew and probably here rewrites, see Turville-Petre, ed., *Alliterative Poetry,* pp. 64–65, 55, and 60, respectively.

32. Hanna, "Pilate's Voice," pp. 809–10 n. 13, groups a large number of references to the tavern and debilitated speech; to these, one might add 6.266, 10.42, 13.399–403; C 6.435; and especially a raft of references in the B *Vita* to depraved speech (here amateur theologizing) at meals in great houses — "[þei] gnawen god in þe gorge whanne hir guttes fullen" (10.58). See also the discussion of lawyers' spending speech at 7.47–56. Directly relevant to Langland's poetic vocation are 9.99–106 and 10.168–71; compare C 5.9, 6.368 (where the poet surreptitiously places himself within Glutton's tavern). See further R. A. Shoaf, "'Speche þat spire is of grace': A Note on *Piers Plowman* B.9.104," *Yearbook of Langland Studies* 1 (1987): 128–33.

33. The archetypal scribe responsible for all B copies put line 79 into feminine forms, but both "men" (80) and A 3.68/C 3.80 indicate this reading is scribal (although certainly testimony to that scribe's misogyny). I'm not much of an alliterative poet, but I'm confident that Langland could have emphatically feminized the account, had he wished to, for example, "For þise are wommen in þis world þat wercheþ moost harm."

34. For the whole, see *Statutes of the Realm,* 11 vols. (1810; reprint, London: Dawsons, 1963), 1:199–204. Langland here cites "et si graviter deliquerit pluries, et castigari noluerit, paciatur judicium corporis, scilicet Pistor collistrigium, et Braciatrix trebuchetum vel castigatorium" (1:201). This is the penalty for habitual offenders, whom, Langland implies, are pandemic — for the first three violations one is allowed to make restitution (1:200).

35. Rose also sells "cuppemele" (5.23); on the basis of her claim that she sold a gallon for a groat (4d.), this probably represents a 200 to 300 percent markup. Compare Bennett, "Conviviality and Charity in Medieval and Early Modern England," *Past and Present* 134 (1992): 19–41, at 20 n. 2: "A bushel of malt yielded about ten gallons of ale, which would normally have sold for 1–2 d. a gallon."

36. The revision of C 3.88–89 adds a third statutory violation, the use of short measures; see *Statutes* 1:201, for methods of insuring standardization and 1:202 for the required inquiry into retailers' use of measures.

37. Myra Stokes deserves credit for recognizing the importance of this professional identification (and its reflection of earlier passages in the poem); indeed she returns to this brewer repeatedly in her account of early portions of B. See Stokes, *Justice and Mercy in Piers Plowman: A Reading of the B Text Visio* (London: Croom Helm, 1984), passim.

38. With the brewer, compare the similar comment of the "lewed vicory," "For *Spiritus prudencie* among þe peple is gyle" (19.455) and note Coveitise's reliance upon "þe grace of gyle" for mercantile profit (5.205). For the Chester *Harrowing of Hell* (s. xvi ex.), see David Mills, ed., *The Chester Mystery Cycle* (East Lansing: Colleagues, 1992), pp. 302–15, lines 277–336.

39. See Owst, *Literature and Pulpit.* pp. 434–41.

40. See further 5.450–54, 15.126, 20.221–23; C 9.190 and 194, and compare the discussion in chapter 5 by Marjorie McIntosh in this volume.

41. See Nick Gray, "The Clemency of Cobblers: A Reading of 'Glutton's Confession' in *Piers Plowman,*" *Leeds Studies in English* 17 (1986): 61–75.

42. See, for example, Rossell Hope Robbins, ed., *Secular Lyrics of the Fourteenth and Fifteenth Centuries*, 2nd ed. (Oxford: Clarendon, 1955), nos. 10–14, and probably Skelton's "Tunning of Eleanor Rumming," as well. However, the concept "fellowship" is far from unproblematized in the medieval discussions. Generally, such representations seem to me comic, attacks upon either "false friends" or professionally efficient tapsters used as a means of diminishing the self-indulgent drinker's responsibility. Hoccleve's lengthy account of his tavern life ("Male Regle," lines 105–208), beyond insisting on the intemperate excess of such pursuits (see n. 27), sees fellowship as inherently false, in fact a flattery encouraging one to expend one's purse, as well as one's person. Compare *Winner*, 277–90, or Woodburn O. Ross, ed., *Middle English Sermons Edited from British Museum MS. Royal 18 B.xxiii*, EETS 209 (1940), no. 85, pp. 26–37. Lydgate overtly genders the same topic. His poem to the Canterbury alewives parodies courtly complaints against the *donna*'s "doubleness": he charges that tapsters encourage male "affiaunce"—but not out of genuine passion, only to get patrons to spend their money.

CHAPTER 2

The Body, Whole and Vulnerable, in Fifteenth-Century England

Miri Rubin

As so many inherited grounding categories of historical explanation have been moved by the winds of plurality and difference, sweet winds whose effect has been welcome and fresh, historians and literary critics have returned to the body as a secure site of certainty and truth, as a grounding place for that which might connect people across their many differences.[1] We can no longer pretend that the world is anything but "messy,"[2] that motivation, self-understanding, aspirations, and desires are constructed in persons, whose consciousness is made of clusters of identifications, acting within and reacting to the salient narratives of their times. What has become an attractive notion, different from old humanistic essentialism and inspired by a most laudable commitment to human connectedness, to solidarity and compassion, is that there can be a shared, mutually if variably lived, communicable experience, in bodies, which can give ground and place for the postulation of a shared and similar humanity. We have in recent years read of a female religiosity grounded in the body, of social and political orders based on a shared metaphorical use of the body. These are imaginative approaches, yet we have a long way to go in applying them fully to historical cultures, in thinking of "a configuration of culture in which settled dichotomies become malleable or proliferate beyond the binary frame."[3]

Yet another type of thinking about the body is emerging, one that is less triumphant, more knowing: it is not based on the privileging or rejection of a single dichotomy; it tends to be more inclusive, less respectful of the distinction inner/outer; it sees the body as the vehicle of tentative will, the beginning of all social exchanges, the screen for fantasy, possessed by each and every one, yet only as a point of departure for the performances through which people live and interact. Foucault and his followers have stressed the body's subjection and making by institutions and the technologies that they imparted. Let us try to envisage some of the moments at which discourses intersect and conflict, creative moments where subjectivity and resistance can be experienced. Let us trace the trails of fantasy whenever our texts/traces allow us to touch medieval bodies, not only through the hegemonic pronouncements on the body, in Judith Butler's words, that rely upon "fixed sites of corporeal permeability and impermeability."[4]

While we try to retrace discourses of bodies, we shall engage with texts and try to learn from their affirmations and their evasions; about their usages, their silences, and their emphases; about some of the bodily hues that made medieval lives. I say "texts" bearing in mind recent warnings against the tempting elision of the body into texts, a practice that has satisfied some, but that can lose the social and political contexts of bodily performance. We historians can attempt to radicalize the Foucauldian legacy and to situate the specificity of experience, resistance, variety, and contradiction, as bodies were lived between and among the requirements of intersecting discourses—medical, religious, legal. Bodies, medieval and others, are subjected to such discourses, areas of understanding, fields of knowledge and power; these were lived by medieval people with and by the many messages and various teachings about their bodies, themselves. We can, thus, assume no prime grounding for the body, but an altogether primary place for the understanding of embodied existence. We would do well to redescribe such existence, even if it often seems as methodologically inaccessible as it is central to an engagement with the difference of the past.

I shall start with one of the ways, which differs from our ways, in which gender was made in a late medieval culture, fluid notions of sexual and bodily forms. The Galenic body was a complex humoral system, of a great variety of temperaments and inclinations, onto which law and religion attempted to impose a regulating dichotomy: feminine and masculine.[5] These attempts are the familiar part of the historical story; I shall try to present some images and notions of the body's sexual openness, its physical liquidity, its vulnerability and pliability. This is, after all, the context within which a particularly privileged body—Christ's own— emerged and dwelt, that of medieval corporeal anxieties and awareness of shapelessness and loss.

Embodied sexual identity was open to many possible understandings in late medieval culture. The humoral paradigm of the body meant that persons could be born in a wide range of shapes and with clusters of characteristics produced by the constellation of cosmic, climatic, spermatic, and humoral conditions at conception and generation.[6] Classifications of sexual types regularly claimed that there were men and women, but also hermaphrodites. This discussion is made without difficulty or moral condemnation, as a challenge that a good surgeon could confront with the help of Albucasis and Avicenna. Medieval medical discourse thus recognized different types of hermaphroditism: with full double genitals, with a concealed penis, or with a closed vagina. The recommended treatment was disposal of the redundant member (by cutting), by opening the closed vagina (in this case a true cul-de-sac), with suitable care to provide passages for urine. For doctors this was a surgical challenge, and Avicenna recommended treatment in the manner of surgical wounds. Albert the Great (circa 1200–1280) even acknowledged that he would be hard pressed to predict such a person's potential fertility. The body was full of secrets, it harbored many life forces.[7] The English translation of Guy de Chauliac's *Chirurgia* defines hermaphrodites as follows:

> Hermafrodicia is þe nature of double kynde. And it is in men (after Albucasis) after two maneres, for sometyme it is in þe place þat is apperynge under the stones [testicles]. In a womman forsothe þere is anoþer in the whiche a yerde [penis] and þrive stones apperen above þe prive chose [vulva]. And pai ben ofte tyme cured by kyttynge, as Avicen saith, but noght þat forsoþe þat maketh water, as Albucasis saith.[8]

A person had to choose a social persona from those on offer. The English legal tradition from Bracton required that this persona be the one "qui praevaleat," the more prominent identity among the two afforded to the hermaphrodite.[9] The hermaphrodite was neither monstrous nor threatening as long as a social and legal person was ultimately to be chosen and adhered to: for law, for marriage, for good.

Within bodies there were possibilities. The womb was temperamental, and in it future sexed bodies were cooked, and their characteristics defied dichotomy: these were bearded women, beardless men, combinations of heat, moisture, blood, semen. For social peace and order, for the sake of law and liturgy, a single person had to emerge, but the body retained its messy secrets.

The body also escaped the "governed wholeness" projected by political ritual and in Christian teaching by virtue of the fragmented nature of its apprehension. The "corps morcelé" of Jacques Lacan is a useful image of that experience, an acceptance of the discreteness of body parts and of the separate psychic relations between self and body parts through the very way in which a child comes to know them.[10] The use of saints' bodies reflects this apprehension: they were divisible in their economy and miraculously whole. The privileged signifier of this fragmented nature within medieval culture was Christ's own body, the body of the Passion. One image I have in mind is that of the *Charter of Christ*, a Middle English poem known in a number of versions of varying lengths from the fourteenth and fifteenth centuries.[11] The *Charter* was invented within the grand narrative of Incarnation and Redemption. It presents itself as the legal text of the document that bound by reciprocal agreement Christ and mankind, Incarnation for faith, Redemption for good Christian life. It is set out as a document made of parchment, in ink, sealed with wax, witnessed by the Evangelists. The dry legal language creates the dramatic opposition to the vibrant story of suffering in Christ's body and death on the cross. Pretending to be a metaphor, the *Charter is* the contract. It is made of Christ's skin, written in his blood, sealed in his blood, penned with the scourges that tore his flesh, in letters that are his wounds.

The long version of the *Charter* is told by Christ himself:

> Ne myght I fynd na parchemyne
> ffor to last with-outen fyne
> Bot als luf bad me do
> Myne awen skyn I toke þar-to.[12]

He recounts the making of the Last Supper and the giving of himself "With mete and drynk to saule fode / With haly word my flesch & blode" (lines 59–60). A little later Christ describes the making of the document on his body at the Passion: his skin was stretched like a hide and made into parchment, but this not on a tanner's frame but on the rood:

> Streyned to dry on þe rode tre
> Als parchemyne aw for to be
> Here now & yhe sall wyten
> How þis charter was wryten. [13]

And then another aspect of the charter/body is described:

> Opon my neese was made þe ynk
> With Iewes spyttyng on me to stynk
> þe pennes þat þe letter was with wryten
> was of skourges þat I was with smyten
> How many lettres þare-on bene
> Rede & þou may wyten and sene
> ffyue thowsand four hundreth fyfty & ten.[14]

Christ calls for his body to be read, and in savoring the document the reader is called to remember the pain in which it was made, to contemplate its colors, shape, smell, letters for the bodily liquids that had gone into its making. He leads the reader by reading the charter himself, addressing all men in the legal Latin of

> O vos omnes qui transitis per viam
> attendite & videte & cetera ...
> Sciant presentes et futuri & cetera.[15]

The story of the making is told by the bleeding wounded Christ, the English interspersed with phrases in mock-legal Latin idiom. The document/

body relives its past sufferings as it retells them, feeling pain, thirst, and the burning of wounds.

The image of writing and making the body is also used by Richard Rolle (circa 1290–1349) in his meditations on the Passion:

> More yit, swete Jhesu, þy body is like a boke written al with rede ynke; so is þy body al written with rede woundes. Now, swete Jhesu, graunt me to rede upon þy boke.[16]

Here the body, so pained, is a prerequisite for the "love-longing" of the author, and the reader as he or she engages with the body/poetic text.[17] The writing/making of Christ's charter is also the making of a female body, because of the deep correlation between the sense of Christ's vulnerability and submission in his Passion. The female body is likened to something to be made and written, receiving marks like those of pen on pliant wax, of ink on thirsty parchment.[18] The image of the female body as tablet for inscribing, for knowing, is current in other cultural contexts.[19] So many women are known to us by writings of men, who literally made them, bore them for us.[20] Writing is bound with the power of authority, authorship, mastery, and production, qualities linked with masculine principles within medieval culture, where women's bodies so often are adorned and made to carry marks offered by others. A very privileged type of marking was that sustained by mystical experience and through divine favor, the stigmata, and the first and most important recipient was Francis of Assisi. It is interesting to note, with Gillian Bennett, that women were never thus marked: medieval representations denied even famous female mystics this *particular* type of writing, which bespoke not submission but perfection. Even Catherine of Siena was deprived of the bodily marking in Christlike stigmata: hers was a strange mark on her left, not her right side.[21]

Bodies in parts were also dismembered and unmade in the context of burial, and the greater the person the more likely the fragmentation of his or her cadaver. The church repeatedly enjoined the preservation of bodily wholeness in burial—from Boniface VIII's first bull *Detestandae feritatis* of 1299, based on the current formulations of the psychosomatic understanding of the human person[22]—but dynastic aspirations demanded fragmentation of the body. Rituals of evisceration and ossification thus followed the death of the great, often far from their homes, and the piecemeal burial of the vital parts: heart, head, bones . . .[23] Fragments of the seigneurial body could mark family seats and, when distributed among religious houses for burial, could fulfill an elaborate program of intercession.

The body, like a legal charter or a book, unfolds only with the effort of engagement, but both have secrets to yield. Torture, love, surgery, translation, decoding, dizzying hermeneutic moves of empathy make the engagement with the body human as they make the encounter with God's body and the promise that had come with it.[24]

Such moves are always associated with pain, the pain of severing, the pain of loss. Yet an aestheticization and valorization of pain arises from multiple practices and uses. Pain, like the body, can yield goods and value: body relics produced cures, pain and suffering channeled grace. Even the abuse of children could be transmuted into virtue. A twelfth-century manuscript of Bury ("The Life of Christ and the Virgin") includes fifteenth-century additions — prayers and illuminations — related to Saint Robert of Bury, a boy allegedly martyred by the Jews in 1190:

> Ave dulcis puer beate Roberte qui infancie tempore floruisti martirii palma, ora pro nobis.
> [Hail, sweet boy, blessed Robert, you who flowered in the martyr's palm in your infancy; pray for us.]

The prayer then addresses God:

> Deus qui beato Roberto talem fortitudinem tribuisti ut in puerili corpusculo gloriosum pro nomine tuo subiret martirium, concede propicius, ut ipsius intercedentibus meritis ab omnibus nos absolvas peccatis.
> [God, you who gave blessed Robert such fortitude so that he could suffer martyrdom in his little boyish body, render favorably, that by his interceding merits, you will absolve all our sins].[25]

This alleged, cruel child-murder, child-martyrdom, at the hand of Jews has thus become assimilated into private prayer, but also into the aspirations of the monastery itself, the beneficiaries of his shrine and its merits. John Lydgate (circa 1370–1449), monk of Bury, wrote a prayer that in its last stanza invokes all the merits of the martyr:

> Have upon Bury þi gracious remembraunce
> That hast among hem a chapel and a shryne,
> With helpe of Edmund, preserve hem fro grevaunce,
> King of Estynglond, martir and virgyne,
> With whos briht sonne lat thy sterre shyne,
> Strecchyng your stremys thoruh al þis regioun,
> Pray for alle tho, and kepe hem fro ruyne,
> That do reverence to both your passioun.[26]

The martyrdom trope is thus alive as a younger martyr reinforces the merits bequeathed by an older one. Liturgically, literarily, in terms of its religious sentiment, little Robert's became a martyrdom par excellence, and yet it is the type of martyrdom that the church refused to recognize despite the abiding strength of its appeal and the quasi-formal location of its influence and cult. Church authorities discouraged new martyr cults and particularly those that sprang up around child martyrs.[27] Child martyrs just were—they had no history of saintliness, no life of growing merit, no biography of conscious religiosity; they were born and soon died, and were thus hard to evaluate, to grasp. Yet the precious suffering child-body was too dear in its promise for the people of East Anglia and the monks of Bury to pass by. His blood was too useful, so it was cherished.

Blood, the liquid of life, was a privileged signifier of the valences of life, material and spiritual. Blood could be offered as a sacrifice (of flagellants, at the altar) since it was the most vital expression of the gushing multitude of living capacities within the body. Blood conveyed nutriments and carried desire, together with all the ingredients that made up a person's character and that were passed on to the young through their mother's (or wet nurse's) milk, which was no more than a temporary form taken by the mother's menstrual blood.[28] This most potent liquid, life itself, was available at the altar under the appearance of wine for clerical consumption and for symbolic reception by communicants.[29] It colored the predominant representation of God, in Christ's suffering humanity on the cross, in images that invoked empathy and compassion.[30] It dramatized the sense of vulnerability, the ubiquity of pain, and the many other images of immolation, torture, and dismemberment that were practiced in late medieval towns. Blood flowed from tortured bodies as limbs were removed, "loosened," and disfigured in the course of judicial torture.[31]

Even the Virgin, immaculate, pure, came to be involved in the shedding of blood, as her son's crucifixion became a theater of blood in fifteenth-century devotional literature. She saw her son crucified, blood shed at the hands of those who became in medieval culture the "merchants" of blood, "collectors" of blood—the Jews.[32] Whether for magic, ritual, cosmetic improvement, or the pleasure of reenactment of the Passion, the desire for blood was imputed to Jews: desire for Christian blood, preferably that of a prepubescent child. Misunderstandings and fantastical elaborations of some of the Jewish hygienic and dietary practices provided the basis for the attribution of particular expertise and avidity in the extraction of blood by Jews. Christ's Passion came to be represented as a bloody crime par excellence. Devotional literature in late medieval England elaborated Christ's suffering at the hands of surgeons/magicians/executioners. *The Southern English Ministry and Passion of Christ* (circa 1275–80) is such a detailed account:

> Qwan þei þe rote of þi swete lyf [at þi herte ground] it souȝtte,
> Þat [i]s þe wil of euery mannys lyf—þei were loþ to leuyn owȝt.[33]

Here is a lurid discourse on the three types of human blood: flesh, veins, and heart—all three of which Christ was made to shed:

> þe ferste betwen fel & flesch [clene] ouȝtt was brouȝt
> þe þou were rent with scourgis; þer beleuyd in þe nouȝt.
> þe blood þat is ner þ[e] lyf, þat in þe veynys is,
> Wol clene þorwȝ þi fet & handys brouȝt was ouȝt iwis,
> & also þorw þe crounne of þornys þat in þe hed depe woode;
> þese þre stremys out of þi veynys wol clene souȝtte þi bloode,
> For þer is no veyne in mannys body but it tillyþ to þat on ende:
> To þe feet & þe handys & eke to þe hed þei don þeder wende.[34]

The death on the cross thus becomes a triple death, a thorough draining of Christ's body; Jews thus rendered Christ's sacrifice complete, his saving grace all-encompassing:

> With þe leste drope of þi blood þou myȝttyst us ha bouȝt,
> & þou ȝeve for vs euery drope þat þer belefte ryȝt nouȝt.[35]

In her eighth vision Julian of Norwich saw Christ in a gushing of blood:

> And aftyr this I sawe be haldande the bodye plenteuously bledande, hate and freschlye and lyfelye, ryȝt as I sawe before in the heede. And this was schewyd me in the senes of the scowrgynge, and this ranne so plenteuouslye to my syght that me thought, ȝyf itt hadde bene so in kynde, for þat tyme itt schulde hafe made the bedde alle on blode and hafe passede onn abowte.[36]

Blood is the essence of the body, of life, it is the ultimate and complete sacrifice, and it evades the boundaries of gender, age, corporeal containment. It is life and humanity experienced through pain—transcendent of shape, defiant of form.

Bodies—sites of fear, conduits of joy, objects of shame, victims of pain—were lived in the knowledge of their vulnerability, within an awareness of their *composed* nature, of their inherent disorder, which called for practical efforts at control in the pursuit of safety and respect. While ordering strategies were offered at confession, by laws and bylaws, by medical regimens—the unbounded nature of the body, in its seasonal changes and its porousness, was never obliterated. This meant that the many forms of persons that nature bore received explanation, and even when they were controlled for the purpose of social order, there was an ontological awareness that these were social conventions masking far more powerful, and threatening, states of being untouched by the ordering power of institutions, states of being that confronted medieval people, as they do us, with their breathtaking challenges—challenges that are also possibilities, to question the paths of determination, to reveal moments of imagination and agency, which do not easily upset established order, but which begin to subvert and undermine it.

Notes

I wish to thank the other contributors to this volume for helpful comments made about this essay at the Intersections conference.

1. George Sebastian Rousseau and Roy Porter, "Introduction: Towards a Natural History of Mind and Body," in *The Languages of Psyche: Mind and Body in Enlightenment Thought. The Clark Library Lectures, 1985–1986,* ed. George Sebastian Rousseau (Berkeley: University of California Press, 1990), pp. 3–44; Michael Featherstone, Michael Hepworth, and Bryan S. Turner, eds., *The Body: Social Process and Cultural Theory* (London: Sage, 1991).

2. David Wallace, "Chaucer's Body Politic: Social and Narrative Self-Regulation," *Exemplaria* 2 (1990): 221–40.

3. Caroline Walker Bynum, *Holy Feast and Holy Fast: The Religious Significance of Food for Medieval Women* (Berkeley: University of California Press, 1987); Mervyn James, "Ritual, Drama and Social Body in the Late Medieval Town," *Past and Present* 98 (1983): 3–29.

4. Judith Butler, *Gender Trouble: Feminism and the Politics of Identity* (London: Routledge, 1991), p. 132.

5. Alison M. Jaggar and Susan R. Bordo, eds., *Gender/Body/Knowledge: Feminist Reconstructions of Being and Knowledge* (New Brunswick, N.J.: Rutgers University Press, 1989).

6. On the development of the embryo, see C. S. F. Burnett, "The Planets and the Development of the Embryo," in *The Human Embryo: Aristotle and the Arabic and European Traditions,* ed. G. R. Dunstan (Exeter: Exeter University Press, 1990), pp. 95–112.

7. "Sed non puto quod impraegnet et impraegnetur" (Albert the Great, *Deanimalibus libri XXVI,* ed. H. Stadler [Münster: Beiträge zur Geschichte der Philosophie des Mittelalters, 1920], vol. 2, p. 1225).

8. *The Cyrurgie of Guy de Chauliac,* ed. M. S. Ogden, Early English Text Society (EETS), o. s. 265 (London: Oxford University Press, 1971), vol. 1, p. 529.

9. Bracton, *De legibus et consuetudinibus Angliae,* ed. G. E. Woodbine (New Haven, Conn.: Yale University Press, 1922), vol. 2, p. 31.

10. Jane Gallop, *Reading Lacan* (Ithaca, N.Y.: Cornell University Press, 1985), pp. 79–80, 86.

11. I am indebted to Jill Averil Keen of the Department of English at the University of Minnesota for kindly allowing me to read a chapter of her doctoral dissertation, "Documenting Salvation: Charters and Pardons in 'þou womman bouten were,' the Charters of Christ and Piers Plowman."

12. M. C. Spalding, *The Middle English Charters of Christ* (Bryn Mawr, Pa.: Bryn Mawr College Press, 1914), pp. 22–24, lines 51–54; the text here is Text A, Bodleian Rawlinson poet. 175.

13. Ibid., p. 26, lines 79–82.

14. Ibid., lines 83–89.

15. Ibid., following lines 94 and 98.

16. *The English Works of Richard Rolle,* ed. H. E. Allen (Oxford: Clarendon Press, 1931), p. 36; Kevin Marti, *Body, Heart and Text in the "Pearl" Poet,* Studies in Mediaeval Literature 12 (Lewiston, N.Y.: Mellen, 1992), pp. 28, 44–45.

17. On Rolle's English writings (such as "Swete Iesu") and their female audience, see Nicholas Watson, *Richard Rolle and the Invention of Authority* (Cambridge: Cambridge University Press, 1991), pp. 226–36, esp. pp. 232–36.

18. On this image, see Carolyn Dinshaw, *Chaucer's Sexual Poetics* (Madison: University of Wisconsin Press, 1989), pp. 13–14.

19. Page DuBois, *Sowing the Body: Psychoanalysis and Ancient Representations of Women* (Chicago: University of Chicago Press, 1988), pp. 130–66.

20. For an interesting recent consideration of the problems of mediation of the voices of female mystics, see Anne Clark, *Elisabeth of Schönau: A Visionary Life* (Philadelphia: University of Pennsylvania Press, 1992), pp. 50–67.

21. *Acta Sanctorum*, ed. Godefridus Henschenius and Daniel Papebrochius, Antwerp, 1675, April 3, 901. See Gillian Bennett, "Framing the Subject: Representation and the Body in Late Medieval Italy," (Ph.D. diss., University of London, 1993), pp. 100–126. On stigmatic women, see Bynum, *Holy Feast and Holy Fast*, pp. 212, 274.

22. Elizabeth Brown, "Death and the Human Body in the Later Middle Ages: The Legislation of Boniface VIII on the Division of the Corpse," *Viator* 12 (1981): 221–70; on intellectual background for the papal initiative, see Francesco Santi, "Il cadavere e Bonifacio VIII, tra Stefano Tempier e Avicenna intorno ad un saggio di Elizabeth Brown," *Studi Medievali*, 3rd ser. 28 (1987): 861–78.

23. Brown, "Death and the Human Body," passim, or see pp. 230–35.

24. Amos Funkenstein, *Theology and the Scientific Imagination from the Middle Ages to the Seventeenth Century* (Princeton, N.J.: Princeton University Press, 1986), pp. 23–115.

25. H. Copinger Hill, "S. Robert of Bury St. Edmunds," *Proceedings of the Suffolk Institute of Archaeology and Natural History* 21 (1931–33): 98–107, facing p. 104.

26. *The Minor Poems of John Lydgate*, ed. H. N. MacCracken, EETS, 107 (London: Kegan Paul, Trench, Trübner, 1911), p. 139, lines 33–40.

27. André Vauchez, *La Sainteté en Occident aux derniers siècles du moyen-âge d'après les procès de canonisation et les documents hagiographiques* (Rome: Bibliothèque de l'Ecole française de Rome, 1981), pp. 176–77; see also Miri Rubin, "Choosing Death? Experiences of Martyrdom in Late Medieval Europe," *Studies in Church History* 30 (1992): 153–83, esp. 164–70.

28. Shulamith Shahar, *Childhood in the Middle Ages* (London: Routledge, 1991), pp. 77–83; see also Istvan Begczy, "*Sacra infantia*," *Studies in Church History* 31 (1994).

29. On problems about reception of the wine/blood by the laity, see Miri Rubin, *Corpus Christi: The Eucharist in Late Medieval Culture* (Cambridge: Cambridge University Press, 1991), pp. 70–72.

30. Joanna Ziegler, *Sculpture of Compassion: The Pietà and the Beguines in the Southern Low Countries*, Etudes d'histoire de l'art 6 (Brussels: Institut historique belge de Rome, 1992).

31. For descriptions of torture perpetrated by the Visconti in 1362–63 in Milan, see David Wallace, "Writing the Tyrant's Death: Chaucer, Bernabò Visconti and Richard II," in *Poetics: Theory and Practice in Medieval English Literature*, ed. Piero Boitani and Anna Torti (Woodbridge, England: Boydell and Brewer, 1991), pp. 122–23; on the medieval literature of torture, see Edward Peters, *Torture* (Oxford: Blackwell, 1985), pp. 59–60.

32. Joshua Trachtenberg, *The Devil and The Jews: The Medieval Concept of the Jew and Its Relation to Modern Antisemitism* (New Haven, Conn.: Yale University Press, 1943), pp. 124–39, 140–55.

33. *The South English Ministry and Passion*, ed. O. S. Pickering (Heidelberg: Winter, 1984), p. 181, lines 2580–81.

34. Ibid., lines 2587–93.

35. Ibid., lines 2603–4.

36. *A Book of Showings to the Anchoress Julian of Norwich*, ed. Edmund Colledge and James Walsh, Studies and Texts 35 (Toronto: Pontifical Institute of Mediaeval Studies, 1978), p. 227.

CHAPTER 3

"Representyd now in yower syght"
The Culture of Spectatorship in Late-Fifteenth-Century England

Seth Lerer

Sometime during the mid-1470s, the corporation of the town of Lydd, in Kent, commissioned the transcription of their Customall, or custom book, the codified account of legal and community practices drawn from the inheritance of English customary law. In addition to the other records of the corporation—the chamberlain's books and the court books that were kept from the mid-fourteenth through the sixteenth century—this Customall offers a detailed picture of late medieval town life in both its public and its private ways.[1] Documents such as this one have long been the purview of social historians, from the great collections made for the *Reports of the Historical Manuscripts Commission* in the late nineteenth century through the more popular accounts of everyday life, ranging from Alice Green's *Town Life in the Fifteenth Century* of 1894 to H. S. Bennett's *The Pastons and Their England* (originally published in 1922 and frequently reprinted).[2] Among the many picturesque aspects of such life are the punishments deriving from traditional customary law, and one that had been singled out by local antiquarians and popular historians was the punishment for cutpurses from Lydd:

> Also, it is used, if ony be founde cuttyng purses or pikeyng purses or other smale thynges, lynyn, wollen, or other goodes, of lytille value, within the fraunchise, att the sute of the party, [he] be brought in to the high strete, and ther his ere naylyd to a post, or to a cart whele, and to him shalbe take a knyffe in hand. And he shall make fyne to the towne, and after forswere the towne, never to come ayene. And he be found after, doyng in lyke wise, he thanne to lose his other ere. And he be found the thirde tyme, beryng tokyne of his ii eris lost, or els other signe by which he is knowene a theffe, at sute of party be he jugged [judged] to deth.[3]

The editors of this report in the *Historical Manuscripts* volume from which I have quoted this text then explain: "The 'knife in hand' was delivered to him, that he might liberate himself by cutting off his own ear" (1:530).

This colorful account clearly spoke to the nineteenth-century imagination of a small-town Middle Ages, a world of penal curiosities in which the rigors of a centralized judicial system or the appeals to a written law had yet to take effect.[4] It was a world in which, as L. O. Pike had put it in the 1870s, "A petty thief in the pillory, a scold on the dunking-stool, a murderer drawn to the gallows on a hurdle, were spectacles familiar" to the eye, where "there was no town so little favored as not to receive ever and anon the ghastly present of an ear or a quarter, wherewithal to decorate its walls or its gates" (1:420–21).[5] Or, as Frederick Pollock and Frederick William Maitland put it, in their authoritative *History of English Law*, "many things were left to the rule of social custom, if not to private caprice or uncontrolled private force, which are now, as a matter of course, regulated by legislation, and controlled by courts of justice."[6]

But this account also addresses a more modern fascination with the theatrics of punishment and the cultural display of the marked and mutilated body. Its placement of the scene of legal action in the high street and its specificity of corporeal marking speak directly to Michel Foucault's construction of premodern punishment as public and spectacular, part of a ritual of marking that "is intended, either by the scar it leaves on the body, or by the spectacle that accompanies it, to brand the victim with infamy."[7] Its attentions, furthermore, to the tools of marking—its catenulate account of nail, post, cartwheel, and knife—articulate Elaine Scarry's contentions that the display of the weapons of torture and punishment "assists in the conversion of absolute pain into the fiction of absolute power," leading to a vision of torture and punishment as "a grotesque piece of compensatory drama."[8] And, in its ceremonialized aspects, this account fits into what a range of recent cultural and literary critics have seen as the workings of a "punitive aesthetics," a complex relationship between legal practice and social imagination that was designed to assure deterrence by creating memorable spectacle. As Stephen Wilf has put it, in a formulation synthesizing much recent historical and critical inquiry, what is at stake in the history of punishment may be not so much the ways in which societies define "what activities are criminalized or how seriously society will punish offenders" as "the way aesthetic conventions are used to fabricate punitive rituals."[9]

I have begun this essay by apposing late-nineteenth- and late-twentieth-century visions of medieval punishments not necessarily to chide the former and espouse the latter as to illustrate the shifting function of supposedly historical documents in the critical construction of late medieval cultural norms. It has become a commonplace to recognize that documents once valued for their purely historical content have come to be read as literary texts—a process characterized by Natalie Zemon Davis as the "fictionalization" of archival record, the construction of a crafted, culturally defining account out of the inherited forms of annal, chronicle, law book, and letter.[10] What Davis, along with a range of other recent cultural and literary theorists, sees as the potential readability of historical forms also reflects on the historical value of literary artifacts. Works of ostensible fiction, such as the contes and *nouvelles* of sixteenth-century France, are for Davis the literary vehicles for representing social realities, while at the same time they provided the writers of ostensibly "historical" pardon tales with the rhetorical principles of organization that make their stories, in effect, "literary" narratives.[11]

Davis's work provides one paradigm for my account of a particular example of the tensions between history and fiction in late medieval England: that of the relationships between late medieval legal practice and theatrical performance. Such documents of drama as the plays of the Wakefield Cycle and the *Croxton Play of the Sacrament* offer late fifteenth-century narrative and performative transformations of the legal and social practices of bodily torture and corporeal mutilation. But the difference between my texts and those of Davis's study is that mine are not offered as representations of social practices as "marks of their reality."[12] And even when such texts "claim ... to be retelling actual events" (as, say, in the *Croxton Play*), they do so not so much to mirror everyday norms as to affirm enduring ideologies: for example, the sacrality of the eucharist, the demonization of the Jews, the hierarchies of the church, the powers of liturgical symbolism.

The question, then, of what resemblance these plays bear to "fictions in the archives," in my case the records of the borough customs of late-fifteenth-century England, lies on the blurred lines between history and fiction, action and mimesis, or what I would label practice and performance. Can we productively draw the line between a community's response to the lived experience of bodily torture or punishment, on the one hand, and, on the other, their response to the mimetic representation of bodily mutilation as enacted in the medieval drama? The pervasive theatricality of legal practice in the Middle Ages finds its counterpart in the pervasive legalisms of theatrical performance. The plays that have come down to us as representative of medieval drama—the great Corpus Christi cycles of the northern towns, the saint's dramas keyed, perhaps, to particular feast days, and the moralities and miracle plays associated with local traditions of performance—are all, to some degree, imbued with a concern for bodies whole and broken, and with an awareness of the legal practices that judged offenses and worked punishments or tortures on the human form.[13] My argument will be that late medieval social and cultural habits facilitate the blurring of these lines between practice and performance and that we need to locate the theatrical aesthetic not just in the texts of medieval drama or the records of their playing but in what I hope to define as a spectatorial sensibility controlling audience reactions to both plays and punishments. Such a sensibility was the means by which individuals defined themselves as witnesses to power, viewers of drama, readers of documents, and participants in the public exercise of law. New ways of apprehending books and bodies in this period gave rise to what I consider the making of a seeing self, a sense of personal identity as viewer, spectator, or reader. Such a spectatorial sensibility, moreover, could be public or private, decorous or transgressive, participatory or voyeuristic, and part of my purpose here will be to outline some of the contexts, methods, and particular texts that may aid in the historical recovery of the public pleasure, horror, and interpretation of the marked and mutilated body.

Part of my purpose, too, will be to understand the literary representation of these cultural phenomena. The spectatorial impulse that may control new attitudes toward law or new approaches to the written page is thematized in the dramatic works themselves. The *Croxton Play of the Sacrament* — with its elaborate stage directions for the bleeding of the Host, the severing and restoration of the Jew's hand, the appearance of the *imago Christi* on the side of an oven, and the bursting of that oven to reveal Christ's body itself — is as much a play about the pleasures and the horrors of the vision of the mutilated *corpus* as it is a play that enacts or represents those phenomena. Similarly, the narratives of the Lydd customals (whatever social practices they may record historically) may be read as the illustrations of a communal fascination with display, whether it be the presentation of local theatricals, the trotting out of foreign exotica, the processions of royal or noble power, or the presentation of punitive pain.

Such concerns lead to a second set of potentially blurred distinctions I seek to investigate. What conditions the survival of the documents that chronicle legal action or record dramatic performance? My claim, developed at this chapter's close, is that certain texts may be preserved, copied, compiled, and relied upon not so much because they exemplify particular traditions as because they speak to certain preoccupations of their readership (for example, the pleasure of sensationalism). Such texts — and I take both the Lydd decrees and the *Croxton Play of the Sacrament* as my examples — may possess less a *historical* value for reconstructing the environments of original performance or enactment and offer more an *interpretive* value for helping us recover something of the climate of reception or the later personal or social function of these documents or traditions. The lines between the lived and the enacted, between practice and performance, then, may be redrawn not so much along medieval as along more modern lines, as Tudor fascinations with surveillance and dissent may have shaped the conditions of the manuscript survival of the *Croxton Play*, or as Victorian concerns with institutional policing and the history of English law may have guided the selection and publication of the documents from Lydd. What I hope to suggest in closing, therefore, is that these texts' preoccupations with wholeness and fragmentation reenact themselves in the processes of transmission and reception, as we are left in both the drama and the law with but the shards of old traditions and the bits and pieces of a literary history.

To understand some of the changing attitudes toward books and bodies in late-fifteenth-century England, it is necessary to review some of the cultural developments that distinguish the period's intellectual and literary history. Much recent work on English courtly and aristocratic culture has stressed the public and performative features of its discourse. The tournamentary and the chivalric impulses of the Anglo-Burgundian courts (from the time of Edward IV through that of Henry VII and the early years of Henry VIII's reign) found their expression in the range of allegorical romances and didactic dramas written by such figures as Stephen Hawes, John Skelton, Henry Medwall, and others. Moreover, the imported Italian humanist preoccupations with the monumentality of literary artifice, together with the new technology of print that reinforced that interest, led to changes in the spatialization of the ways of thinking. A fascination with the visual appeal of the book had developed, in part because of the lavishness of late medieval habits of illumination and in part because of the patterns of reorganization that shaped the pages of the early printed books.[14]

But part of these changing attitudes toward texts also developed from the changing habits of reading itself. The rise of silent reading as a social practice in the fifteenth century, together with the interest in the value of private study, had fostered what Paul Saenger considers to be a shift in northern European ideas of the book, and these shifts also affected the idioms of late-fifteenth-century theorizing on the act of reading. "References to the eyes and vision become more frequent in the rubrics of fifteenth-century prayers," Saenger notes, and there is a growing sense of visualization, rather than auralization, as the way of engaging with texts.[15] Perhaps nowhere is such a sense defined as clearly as in Guillaume Fillastre's *Toison d'or* of about 1470. Fillastre's work, the manual of Burgundian courtly ideals and the model for the English king Edward IV's ordinals of power, centered both royal display and private study in the field of vision, and his polemics on the cultivation of sign, on the power of the written word, and on the need for literate celebrants of aristocratic honor informed the fuller development of Anglo-Burgundian humanism under Henry VII.[16] For my purposes here, it is worth quoting some of Fillastre's text to illustrate the growing emphases on visualization in the period:

> Knowledge is not acquired by hearing alone, but also is acquired and increases by study, by reading and by subtly thinking and meditating on what one has read and studied.... The study of books is necessary in order to retain what one has learned by inquiry and

hearing.... For the sense of sight is much firmer than hearing and makes man much more certain, because the spoken word is transitory, but the written letter remains and impresses itself more on the understanding of the reader.[17]

These arguments articulate what I believe to be a cultural awareness of display, one that informs the practices of law, liturgy, and the drama in the late fifteenth and early sixteenth centuries. The poetry of Stephen Hawes, for example, often narrates the confrontations of its allegorical heroes as forms of reading. The heroic lover-traveler encounters engraved objects, signs and symbols, and pictorial displays, which instruct or guide him. Images are "grauen" in Hawe's poetry, and the lessons of the texts and preceptors are, variously, "impressed" or "enprynted" in the mind of the hero. So, too, in his religious verse, Hawes emphasizes the engraved, marked, or imprinted quality of spiritual experience. The *Conuercyon of Swerers* is described as a "lettre" offered to the reader to "prynte it in youre mynde" (lines 61–62), and in the version of this poem printed by Wynkyn de Worde in 1509 portions of the poem are shaped as a picture designed to arrest the reader's eye.[18] "See / me" one shaped section begins (lines 113–14), as it invites the reader both to meditate on Christ's signifying wounds and to marvel at the printer's craft. At the poem's end, Christ invites the audience to associate the body and the text, the incisions of his wounds with the impressions of both type and seal:

> With my blody woundes I dyde youre chartre seale
> Why do you tere it / why do ye breke it so
> Syth it to you is the eternall heale
> And the releace of euerlastynge wo
> Beholde this lettre with the prynte also
> Of myn owne seale by perfyte portrayture
> Prynte it in mynde and ye shall helthe recure. (lines 346–52)[19]

This textualization of Christ's relationship to Christian, and of author to audience, also informs what I believe to be the growing emphasis on visualization in late medieval legal practice and, furthermore, a growing self-consciousness about the theatricality of theater in the medieval drama itself. The marked and mutilated body constitutes a document to be interpreted or a text to be read, as the signs and symbols convey a specificity of legal meaning. The abscission of hands, ears, breasts, or other body parts, for example, defines the surviving criminal with all the directness and specificity of a badge. In some cases, transgressors were even branded with a letter for their crimes: unwilling workers were branded with an *F* in mid-fourteenth-century Yorkshire, while perjurers had the letter *P* burned into their forehead.[20] The criminal, on these occasions, becomes something of a readable text: a walking marker not just of the crime committed but of certain definite relationships of power between individual and community.[21]

Such relationships have long been considered to have focused not just on maintaining corporate or state power, but on figuring the exemplary or deterrent force of legal retribution. To terrify the criminal and frighten a potentially transgressive populace had largely been the purpose of the bodily mutilations of the wrongdoer; so, too, had been the purpose of the stocks and pillory, and their later descendant, the dunking stool. The punishment for scolds in Hereford defines the function of this particular engine of humiliation as bringing the offender within the purview of the populace. "The scold must stand with bare feet and let her hair down 'during such time as she may be seen by all passers-by upon the road.'"[22] Indeed, the need to see the victim—to make justice a thing beheld as well as simply done—informs much of the local records and chronicle histories of late medieval England and survives well into the juridical debates of the eighteenth century. From Bishop Alnwick's need to parade his Lollard heretics bareheaded and barefoot in the market place[23] to George Osborne's recognition, three centuries later, of the exemplary possibilities of spectacular execution, the masters of judicial pain recognized that "what was seen was less the suffering of the individual than the theater of justice."[24] "The more public the punishment," wrote George Osborne in 1733, "the greater influence it has commonly had," and to a large degree this tradition of theatricalized punishments and execution was what the later eighteenth-century reformers sought to bring out of the public's eye and locate privately and securely in prison walls.[25]

For late-fifteenth- and early-sixteenth-century England, however, such debates were far from the concerns of those who drew up and enacted the displays of mutilation in the English towns. The traditions of borough law were noted even to contemporaries for their specificities of pain. William Harrison's *History of England,* while praising the English for refusing the elaborate theatrics of the tortures of the Continent, nonetheless records in great detail the elaborate construction of a guillotine-like device for beheading witches in Halifax. With a curious blend of embarrassment and fascination, he describes the making of this "engine," its precise dimensions, its detailed workings, and its immense power, such that when the blade is released it "dooth fall downe with such a violence, that if the necke of the transgressor were so big as that of a bull, it should be cut in sunder at a stroke, and roll from the bodie by an huge distance." At the close of this remarkable account, Harrison avers: "This much of Halifax law, which I set downe onelie to shew the custome of that countrie in this behalfe."[26]

But of course, we must query if not Harrison's motives then at the very least his rhetoric. In setting down the "custome of the countrie," he offers us a script for the pageantry of horror, an account of local practice that, for all of his apology, resonates with his own pleas for "sharper law" against adultery and fornication: "For what great smart is it to be turned out of an hot sheet into a cold, or after a little washing in the water to be let lose againe vnto their former trades? Howbeit the dragging of some of them ouer the Thames betweene Lambeth and Westminster at the taile of a boat, is a punishment that most terrifieth them which are condemned therto."[27] Although writing in the later sixteenth century, Harrison gives voice both to specific surviving practices and to certain attitudes and images behind the English public sense of punishment. What he illustrates in discursive form is what the customals and borough records illustrate prescriptively or annalistically: that there is a theatrical mechanics to enacted law — that as important as the crime condemned or the judgment executed are the stagings, tools, machinery, and visible spectacle of the action. Late medieval law, much like late medieval courtiership or the Mass, is something that goes on before the field of vision.

But like its contemporary institutional practices, late medieval punishment also raises some questions as to the nature and function of the audience before it. Richard van Dülmen, writing of European habits, notes that for all of the displays of political power occasioned by punishments and executions, the citizens beholding such performances used them as occasions for "organized celebrations" and, at times, "quasi-religious festivals."[28] Spectators "became witnesses to a criminal's punishment as well as participants in a sacrificial rite that purged society."[29] Yet such emphasis on performance fostered a theatricalization of the law that may, at times, have overshadowed whatever participatory, ritualized, and purgative sense it might have had. In late-fifteenth-century Belgium, for example, "the people of Mons paid a large sum of money for a convicted brigand in order that they might enjoy watching him being quartered, while in 1488, the citizens of Bruges were so pleasurably excited by the sight of various tortures being inflicted on some magistrates suspected of treason that the performance was extended, long after it had achieved its desired ends, for the sole purpose of their gratification."[30]

The question remains where to draw the line between "purgative ritual" and "pleasurable excitement," a question that, as Eammon Duffy asks it, also motivates inquiry into the late medieval Mass.[31] The emphases on visualizing the Host, on the spectacular nature of sacramental observance, and on the "gruesome images of the Eucharistic miracle stories" (p. 106) all contribute to what Duffy identifies as the motivating visual imagination of lay piety. "Seeing the Host," Duffy writes, "became the high point of lay experience of the Mass" (p. 96), and to a great extent the devotional verse and public sermons of the later fifteenth century address the deep emotional response that every Christian celebrant would feel before the vision of the elevated bread and the artistically rendered or personally imagined wounds and blood of Christ. And yet, as

Duffy makes clear, such a spectacularism of the Mass did not necessarily foster the passive, nonparticipatory form of worship that some scholars have attributed to it. The uses of the veil and screen in parish churches to shield the altar and the Host were, by and large, things temporary in their function. As Duffy summarizes, "The veil was there precisely to function as a temporary ritual deprivation of the sight of the sacring. Its symbolic effectiveness derived from the fact that it obscured for a time something which was normally accessible; in the process it heightened the value of the spectacle it temporarily concealed" (p. 111). Such devices, redolent of the mechanics of stage prop, costume, and scenery, form what Duffy calls "a frame for the liturgical drama" of the Mass (p. 112), a drama in the course of which the congregation could be both spectators and participants.

"Spectators or Participants?" Duffy asks (p. 109). This is for me the central question in discerning the public response both to the social reality of legal punishment and the literary mimesis of cycle play or morality. It is a question, too, raised by the plays themselves, not simply in the ways that they work out the dramaturgy of the torturing of Christ or the mutilations of the Jews, but in the ways that they thematize the issue of theatricality itself, and in turn, the nature and social function of representation. As in the allegorical adventures of Hawes, the public acts of execution, or the showings of the Host, "behold and see" becomes the central trope of a self-consciousness of vision in the drama.[32] The characters within the play, together with the audience before it, bear witness to the sufferings and mutilations of the body. At times, the plays inscribe the idea of an audience within them, as for example in the Wakefield *Buffeting,* where Caiphas scripts out and stage manages Christ's torturing. His long speech toward the beginning of the play distills the approaching mutilation of Christ's body through specific references to tortured limbs and organs and through the controlling rhetoric of game.[33] He announces at the start, "I myself shall make examining" (line 128), and then goes on to detail each of Christ's body parts as the object of humiliation and pain. The ear and the mouth are the first parts of his threatened anatomy (129–35); his closed lips shall be forced open in pain (172); his eyes shall be put out (194), his head cut off (199), and even the feet that brought him to town are cursed in possible anticipation of their beating (255). Each of the *tortores* punishments imagined for the silent Christ is anticipated in Caiphas's speechmaking: he shall be put in the stocks (202–3), murdered "with knokys" (207), beaten (218), hanged (228), his neck wrung (237), struck even with Caiphas's own head (264), pelted (283), rapped on the pate (301), "knowked" on the head (314), hit so his head would throb (327), and finally knocked in a game among torturers (342).

This catalog—this "liturgy of punishment," in Foucault's words—delineates how Caiphas attacks Christ's body, and moreover, how his verbal taunts provide a kind of script for the play of torture we will witness at the close of the *Buffeting*. Caiphas has prepared for us, and for his *tortores*, the scene of torture we have yet to see, and he has done so by translating the brute force of bodily abuse into the spectacle of language. Before it happens, he presents the mutilation of the body as theatrical discourse, for by *talking* about torture Caiphas constructs a language of punishment, a way of representing the potential fear and horror of mutilation. In the process, though, he provides a model not just for his torturers but for the Wakefield playwright who created him. Caiphas is a figure for the dramatist here. Like him, he seeks a language for describing the indescribable. Like him, too, he performs that language through elaborate gestures and threats. His very questioning of Annas—why is Jesus so far from him? why cannot he lay a hand on him? (298–99)—are questions not just for the jurist but also for the stage director. Caiphas theatricalizes the torture of Christ by setting up the buffeting as theater: scripted, stage-managed, and directed by a governing authority. But if, as I am arguing, Caiphas is himself a figure for the playwright, then the questions that he raises go to the heart of dramatic authorship itself. For what the Wakefield Master does is both define and query the possibilities of scripting spectacle. Caiphas and his *tortores* give voice to the problematics of the cycle drama itself: to the relationship among individual author and civic performers. Both face the difficulty of describing mutilation and enacting it. Both, too, must devise a performative context for displaying pain. Caiphas, then, is not just a bully; he is an actor and an author. He writes the script for Christ's punishment long before the torturers perform it. It is he who makes Christ "King Copyn in oure game," he who mockingly invests him with the royal title, he who makes Christ into the "fatur," the impostor or actor in a drama of religious rule. When the *tortores* finally get their hands on him, they follow Caiphas's model, for before they touch him, they theatricalize their torture as a play:

> Go we now to oure noyte with this fond foyll
> We shall teche him, I wote, a new play of Yoyll. (343–44)

The point of these lines extends beyond the mere identification of the "new play of Yoyll" with the children's game of Hot Cockles, or for that matter, beyond V. A. Kolve's well-known arguments about the universality of playacting in medieval presentations of the Passion.[34] The purpose of these lines is to begin the enacting of Caiphas's own directions: to put into performance the script and staging he has already provided for his torturers.

The lines between action and mimesis, between practice and performance, are continuously and constructively blurred here, much as they are, as I have suggested, throughout the social practices of law and literature in late medieval England. In turning now to the archival records of the town of Lydd, and to the punishment for cutpurses that opened this essay, I will attend therefore not only to their documentary purpose but to their rhetorical effect. Lydd's records stand as evidence for a spectatorial sensibility in the late medieval town: one that informed not just a taste for theater or a punitive aesthetics but a rhetoric of customary law that makes this text into a set of stage directions for a public drama.

The documents assembled for the town of Lydd present a community accustomed to the regular performances of visiting professional drama, of aristocratic and royal minstrelsy and play, and of a strong local tradition (shared with the neighboring township of New Romney) of seasonal theatricals.[35] The records of the corporation note in detail the payments, both in coin and in "bred, wine and bere," to such performers, as well as the costs of stage props, costumes, and occasionally transportation. On certain Sundays, Lydd would stage its own plays, called *The May* and *The Interlude of Our Lord's Passion,* and these plays clearly had such regional influence that New Romney borrowed Lydd's Passion play and, at one point, even paid someone to return to Lydd "to see the original of our play there" in order to check on the traditions of local performance.[36]

The citizens of Lydd clearly loved a good show, and not just a scripted one. Such elaborate public gestures as the gift of a porpoise to the rebel Jack Cade in 1450—a gift designed to win his friendship just in case his rebellion succeeded—shows us a veritable dramaturgy of political protection.

> Paid for one purpoys, sent to the Captain [i.e., Cade] by the Jurats and commoners 6s. Paid for the hire of one horse, ledyng up the said purpoys from Herietssham to Londone to the Capitayn 12d. For the hire of a horse that John Menewode rode uppon to Londone the same tyme, for to helpe to present the porpys to the Capitayn 14d. Paid for an horse hire (sic) that Richard Alayn rode uppon from Lyde to Londone, with the purpoys 20d. For expenses the same time, in ledyng uppe of the purpoys 2s. 8d.... Paid to John Hays, for carrying a letter to the Captain, in excuse of this town 3s. 4d.[37]

To read this account within the context of the many records of largesse to visiting troupes and accompanying minstrels, or for the "exspense of our bane cryars of our play" (1:524) is to get a sense of how these records codify not just the act of payment for performance, but what might be thought of as the commodification of display. Against this story of the elaborate presentation of the porpoise and the prearranged remuneration of invited theatricals, we might compare the town's obvious delight at the serendipitous. Players show up on the "hyge strete" and are duly paid (five pence; 1:527); and to "the man who came through with the dromedary," the corporation offers eight pence (account in editorial remarks, 1:517). Within the record books of Lydd, these narratives of performance and display are interlarded with accounts of punishment, and both come to represent rhetorically the notarial construction of official, civic life. The reader of the record comes fresh from a record of payment "for making the buttys against the day for play, 9s 2d," to an account of "[t]he expenses made by the steryng [stirring] of Sir Andrew Ayllewyn agaynys the towne," and the note that "[t]he costes and expensis at that tyme made for counsell to be had for to have the feturs of yrone of his leggys and for [to] come out of prisone, comyth to 40s" (1:519).

In this environment of notarial record and social elaborations of theatrics, the story of the punishment for cutpurses takes on an interlocking set of possible interpretations. At one level, the account may be appreciated as but one of the most recent survivals of an old customary practice familiar from local laws and borough books. The Selden Society *Borough Customs* volume quotes and records nearly a dozen versions of this punishment in documents from the early thirteenth century through the early sixteenth century, in Latin, French, and English and ranging from the Scottish *Leges Burgorum* in the north to the records of Portsmouth to the south.[38] The mutilation of the body for larceny, too, had been a feature of Germanic law, stretching back to some of the earliest recorded documents of legal practice, and there is a certain obviousness to this kind of punishment.[39] First, it reenacts the crime of "cuttyng purses" on the criminal's body, severing if not the offending member of the hand, then at the very least a symbolic member, marking the criminal for his crime and thus distinguishing him to the populace. The wonderful symbolic value of this form of mutilation was recognized until well into the eighteenth century (there is a record of a thief in the German city of Freiburg in 1785 having his ear cut off),[40] and its survival may be as much a testimony to its theatricality as well as its convenience. For by publicly marking the criminal—by staging his mutilation as a kind of theater of punishment—the civic corporation provides a bit of local entertainment for a populace that had come to expect something of its judicial system.

At another level, this account—both in its narrative form and its civic function—might fit into the socioanthropological paradigms of Mervyn James, whose conception of the notion of the social body in late medieval culture has informed much work on the historical environments of medieval drama: "The concept of body provided urban societies with a mythology and a ritual in terms of which the opposites of social wholeness and social differentiation could be both affirmed, and also brought into a creative tension, one with the other."[41] Each element of the community was represented as a limb or organ of the body politic, and if the charge of civic government was to maintain the wholeness of that body, then at least part of that charge would have been to sever those diseased members that posed a threat to social health: "The persisting tension between whole and differentiation meant that the process of incorporation into the social body needed to be continually reaffirmed, and the body itself continually recreated. Ritual, in an effective and visual way, projected the tensions and aspirations, and the resolution of these, which this process involved" (pp. 8–9). For James, that ritual is the performance of the Corpus Christi drama and the growing civic pageantry around the feast of Corpus Christi that affirmed, in country towns like Wakefield and provincial capitals like York, the power of the urban magistracy and the later medieval ascendancy of the guilds.

From a Jamesian perspective, the dismemberment of the criminal's body enacts the severing of the offender from the body politic. At the heart of the Lydd decree is the spectacle of this dismemberment, as the criminal marks himself as a criminal and then severs himself from the body politic. He acts in contradiction, say, to the dictates of the Sarum Missal, which, as James points out, had counseled the citizen not to "sever himself from the fit joining together of all the members.... Let him be goodly, and useful, and healthy" (p. 9). Bound to a tree or a cart wheel, performing on the high street, this criminal cuts loose from the social body, and in so doing, renders himself an outcast damaged limb.

But in the narrative recorded in the Customall, there is a palpable gap in the description of the punishment. We are not told specifically just what the criminal does with the knife, nor are we told precisely what the relationship is between the "fyne to the towne" and the execution of this punishment. It is left to the nineteenth-century editors to explain these various relations, to fill in, in other words, the drama of self-mutilation carefully elided by the Customall. Now, where these editors derive their explanation is from the very tradition of punishment the Lydd decree reiterates. The other documents (here relying on the Selden Society volume) all make clear that the purpose of nailing the offender's ear to a tree, pillory, or cart wheel is that it be cut off:

> Portsmouth: "his ere to be nayled to the pelery, he to chese whether he woll kytt or tere it of."
> *Leges Burgorum*: "... et a quo captus est debet auricula amputari."
> Idem: "he shall be set on the pillory and then led to the end of the town and have his ear cut off by the man who caught him"
> Romney: "... et depuis a sa dite sute soit sa une oraile de soun chef trenché."
> Idem: "be set in the pillory, and then at the said suit one of his ears shall be cut from his head."[42]

Lydd's version of this punishment is unique, and I want to suggest that its uniqueness raises a problem not just of judicial practice but of dramatic theory. It is as if its text has taken out the very thing we want to read, as if it dares not to describe the actions that we (and everyone, for that matter) know must have been performed and that, both narratively and judicially, make sense out of this text. If the description from the Customall could be considered as a kind of script, then what it leaves out is the central stage direction for its actor. Drama begins at Lydd where the text leaves off; in the space between "take a knyffe in hand" and "he shall make a fyne" lies an action that may thrill but may not be described.

For what the Customall juxtaposes are the two concerns of civic sponsorship for theater, and the two concerns that fill the records of the corporation: object and money, stage prop and payment. Thus, it may come as no surprise to find, in the book of the corporation accounts for 1470, the entry "Payd for the naylyng of Thomas Norys [h]is ere 12d" (1:525). Here, what is recorded is not income from the "fyne" but the outlay for the performance. Just who is paid here we do not know, but the point, it seems to me, is that the nailing of Thomas Norys's ear constitutes as much a kind of theatrical expenditure as the performances of the minstrels of the Lord of Arundell or the king or the "plyars of Stone, crying the banes here" (all of whom, by the way, received 3s. 4d. in 1469). What I am suggesting, then, is that within the rhetoric of the notarial account, the line is blurred between the legal and the theatrical. The narrative of how to deal with cutpurses takes the inherited practices of a particular customary law and recasts them into a kind of theatricalized ritual. And it is the very familiarity of that ritual that, at one level, permits the writer to leave out the most obvious point of direction: the cutting of the criminal's ear.

It is this elision of what the modern scholar may most wish to read, and what the medieval spectator would no doubt see, that makes the Lydd decree so interesting—that shifts the focus of rhetorical attention away from the act of personal self-mutilation and the things that shape that act. This is a text, now, less about action than object, less about staging than stage props. It is a text (and I am arguing that, for the present, we must read it as a text) that, for all of its emphases on objects, placement, sequence, and performance, seems like the flip side of stage direction: a text that elides mention of the very act that all these actors and accoutrements have been assembled to perform. And it is this elision that distinguishes Lydd's version of the punishment from those similar accounts in other borough records. For what it does is transform this discourse from a record of social action into a shaped text of literary narrative. It makes the reader of this document pause and consider; it effects, in what it says as much as what it does not say, the shift from the archive to the fiction, from a record of unmediated social practice to a narrative shaped to the standards of rhetorical control. Its events transpire not so much in the lived time of public experience as in what Natalie Davis calls the "time of storytelling."[43]

If, as I am suggesting, Lydd's decree stands as something of a literary text, it also stands as something of a social gloss on those literary documents that had transformed the practices of law and liturgy, punishment and spectacle, into mimetic drama. It represents a social practice of what the *Croxton Play of the Sacrament* would transform into self-theatricalizing drama: a play so taken with the mutilations of its criminal Jews and the miraculous transformations of its Host that it comes off, much like the dramatic punishments of town and borough, as "overtly, explicitly and outrageously theatrical, drawing attention histrionically to its sense of show."[44] *Croxton* plays with the textuality of bodies, with the problems of mimesis, and with the uneasy relations between spectatorship and participation that had informed so much of legal, literary, and liturgical culture in late medieval England. Rather than reading *Croxton* as a drama of doctrinal argument or sacramental politics (although both, of course, inform its meaning), I see it as a drama about drama: a reflection on the raw materials of legal practice and religious imagery that restore a social harmony or, conversely, pander to individual attentions to the fragmentary, maimed, and bleeding.

Midway through the *Croxton Play of the Sacrament*, the Jews have gotten their hands on the Eucharist. Jonathas, Jason, Jasdon, Malchus, and Masphat proceed to mock the sacrament and its performance, and in the course of their blasphemy one of the Jews, Jasdon, suggests a clever way of testing the substantial quality of the host:

> Surely with owr daggars we shall ses on this bredde,
> And so with clowtys we shall know yf he have eny blood.
> (lines 451–52)[45]

To Jasdon, this idea is "masterly ment" (454), and the Jews mutilate the Host in an elaborate, and elaborately described, series of technical operations. They "smite" it, "stroke" it, "sese" it, "afeze" it, "punche" it, and "prike" it; they attack it with daggers and augers, announcing, "In þe middys of this prynt I thynke for to prene" (467). But their attacks are thwarted, for in their attempt to boil it, the Host sticks to Jonathas's hand. Trying to remove the Host, they nail it to a post, and when Jonathas attempts to pull his hand away, the play gives this direction: "Here shall thay pluke þe arme, and þe hond shall hang styll with þe Sacrament."

This horrific scene, which even by the standards of the medieval English drama seems bizarrely overdone, has long been appreciated for its challenges both to the presumed acting troupe who could perform it and to the modern critic who must reconcile its blend of sensationalism and risibility.[46] Together with the later episodes in which the image of the wounded Christ appears on the face of the cauldron boiling the Host and in which Jonathas's hand miraculously is restored, this moment in the *Croxton Play of the Sacrament* can serve as a touchstone for many modern scholarly presuppositions about the function of pain and game in medieval drama and, more generally, about the social function of dramatic representation itself. Surely, these scenes differ both in tone and effect from the playful jestings of the *tortores* in the Wakefield *Buffeting* and *Scourging* plays and from the cruel laughter of the soldiers in the York *Crucifixion*. Unlike the cycle plays, whose representation of the passion as a play and game grants, in V. A. Kolve's famous formulation, a kind of comically restorative technique "of making meaningful Christ's judgment on His tormentors ... and ... a dramatically exciting mode into which the humiliation and the death of Christ could be translated,"[47] the *Croxton Play of the Sacrament* has seemed to many scholars as little more than a bad joke irrevocably grounded in the limiting specifics of its time and place—an awkward blend of anti-Semitism and anti-Lollardism, didactically rephrasing the historical event that had inspired it and posing almost insurmountable problems for the nine players who, the manuscript announces, "may play it at ease."[48]

Within the contexts of theatricalized punishment and spectatorial sensibilities exemplified by Lydd's decrees, however, the sensationalism of this play may restage something of the public drama of the mutilations of the criminal. Both the play and the lawbook center their attentions on the nailing and dismemberment of body parts. Both, too, may be read as enacting Mervyn James's concern with the corporealization of the social entity, as the restitution of the Jew's hand, his ultimate conversion, and the concluding gestures of inclusion and celebration before the church all show the reincorporation of the severed member back into the body politic and illustrate how, through rituals of Christian rite and Christian drama (to take O. B. Hardison's old phrase, perhaps against itself),[49] the criminal or unbeliever may be reaccepted into Christian society. When the stage directions of the *Croxton Play* state, "Here shall Ser Jonathas put hys hand into þe cawdron, and yt shalbe hole agayn," they signal not just the directive to the players but the thematics of reincorporation for an audience. Jonathas returns to the body politic and symbolically mends the wound to that body by suffering the return of his own disjoined limb. Moreover, as if to signal the forgiveness granted him by admitting Jesus, the sign of Jonathas's torture is erased. No one can see the scar on his arm, much as none could see the scars inflicted in the Host after it has transformed itself from the *imago Christi* back into the bread.

One interpretation of these gestures, then, would be to claim that *Croxton* stages the possibilities of professional theater not just to entertain or shock an audience, but to effect a kind of social reintegration. At stake in the play is not so much the simple skill of the actors or producers in presenting the sensationalism of its stage directions, but rather how dramatic skill is thematized within the play and how the scenes of mutilation and dismemberment constitute a self-conscious reflection on the power of theatrical artifice to move an audience. The Jews appear here as professionals in crime, deployers of the tools of torture. Their display of the instruments of pain in the scene with the Host presents them as the figures who make drama, not just act in it. They are the agents of theatrical control and staged pain. Each of their words signals quite specifically the artifice of the metal shop, the wood cutter, the engraver, and the carpenter. Theirs is not so much an enactment of the *play* of pain — after the fashion of the playful, mocking, gaming *tortores* in the Corpus Christi cycles — as of the *job* of pain. Their mangling of the Host is less a game than a trial: a reenactment of the judicial procedure before Caiphas and Pilate and the courts of Roman law. Like the Caiphas of the Wakefield *Buffeting,* the Jews of the *Croxton Play* are directors of this legal show, agents of the theatrical control and staged infliction of pain on a bodily representation of Christ. But unlike Caiphas, who details the mutilations of Christ's body in terms solely of that body's parts and his own bodily contact with them, the Jews act through instruments. Their language both professionalizes and textualizes their mutilation of the Host, inscribing on the symbolized Corpus Christi the marks of a legal judgment coded in the misapprehensions of the Old Law and the suspicions of disbelief.

Malchus begins this process by recapitulating the beliefs of Christians who would try to convert the Jews. God, in the Christian sphere, is judge and ruler, and he notes:

> To turne vs from owr beleve ys ther entent —
> For that he sayd, "*judecare viuos et mortuos.*" (439–40)

Jonathas picks up this legal language to affirm the late medieval social practice of torture as an instrument of proof:

> Now, serys, ye haue rehersyd the substaunce of ther lawe,
> But thys bred I wold myght be put in a prefe
> Whether þis be he that in Bosra of vs had awe.
> Ther staynyd were hys clothys — þis may we belefe;
> Thys may we know, ther had he grefe,
> For owr old bookys verify thus.
> Theron he was jugett to be hangyd as a thefe —
> "*Tinctis [de] Bosra vestibus.*" (441–47)

The Jews as torturers now become the Jews as judges, reenacting in the trial of the Host's mutilation the search for truth that motivated the trial of Jesus. Judgment and control, torturing and texts all come together in this speech, as we see here the appeal to the "old bookys" that "verify" a fact of history, while the allusions to the stained garments of Christ himself affirm the marked or signed body as the locus of those force relations that both judged and branded him a "thefe." Now the assault on the Host becomes the symbolic, textualized reenactment of that hanging. As Jasdon affirms, "And with owr strokys we shal fray him as he was on þe rood" (455). But it is also a self-consciously staged performance: an enactment of a trial and torture by professionals of the theater of pain. Malchus announces:

> Yea, goowe to, than, and take owr space,
> And looke owr daggarys be sharpe and kene:
> And when eche man a stroke smytte hase,
> In þe mydyll part therof owr master shall bene. (461–64)

Malchus's plan defines the staging of a play. They are directives for performance, where each actor in the show should take his "space" and where each prop be carefully prepared for the display.

The line between action and stage direction—between the voicings of a character and the written stage directions of the manuscript—is blurred now. In the succeeding scenes with the bogus doctor, Master Brundiche, and his servant Colle, we witness the staging of attempted healing. Colle will announce, for example, what he has "told all þis audiense" (579), and Master Brundiche will aver:

> Here ys a grete congregacyon,
> And all not hole, without negacyon. (601–2)

Yet Master Brundiche cannot heal what only Christ can restore. After the terrifying visitation of the *imago Christi* on the oven that had received the mutilated Host, the Jews repent of their sins and enter Christian society. The apparitional Jesus advises Jonathas:

> No Jonathas, on thine hand thow art but lame,
> And ys thorow thyn own cruelnesse.
> For thyn hurt þou mayest þiselfe blame,...
> Thow wasshest thyn hart with grete contrycion.
> Go to the cawdron—þi care shalbe the lesse—
> And towche thyn hand to thy salvacion. (770–77)

It is at this point that the stage directions read, "Here shall Ser Jonathas put hys hand into þe cawdron, and yt shalbe hole agayn." Jonathas's restoration of his hand signals the reacceptance of the criminal or unbeliever into Christian society. The healing of his severed body part symbolically enacts the healing of the body politic. The Jew, the criminal, the mutilated outsider—all can, through *Croxton's* dramaturgy, reenter the community in wholeness and belief.

Croxton is, at one level, a drama of inclusion and restoration, and it is fitting that at the play's end its audience is invited to participate in the procession and the song that celebrate the miracles of Christ. The directions of the Episcopus suggest that the entire audience was to proceed, first to the Jews' house where they witness the restoration of the image of Christ into the bread, and then to the church itself where the Host shall be restored to its correct place in the service of communion.

> Now wyll I take this Holy Sacrament
>   With humble hart and gret devocion,
> And all we wyll gon with on consent
>   And beare yt to chyrche with solempne processyon. (834–37)

By enjoining the audience to proceed to the church, the Episcopus erases the boundary between staged performance and religious ritual. He holds up the newly restored Host in order to invite each member of the audience to share, now, in the celebration both of Christ's body and the social body, made whole by the performance of that ritual. The effect of this dramatic narrative is to affirm again the possibilities of finding social harmony in the performance of the holy rites, and furthermore, to confirm the possibilities of professional theater in the performance of a scripted play.

For where the force of this performance lies, and where it differs markedly from Wakefield or the other cycle plays, is in the way that *Croxton* defines its drama as that of the visiting professional troupe. The *Croxton Play* is not a play performed by members of a local guild or scripted by a civic author under the employ or patronage of merchant government. It is clearly a traveling play, one to be acted by outsiders who have been invited into a community.[50] What the *Croxton Play* enacts is the possibility of a visiting, professional theater to enter a community and restore the wholeness of the social body through its stagings of the rituals of torture, dismemberment, and reincorporation. The presentation of the Jew's hand nailed to the post becomes the fictive reenactment of the kind of mutilations witnessed by the populace at Lydd. The mutilations of the Host become the highly symbolized torturings of the body of the Christ reexperienced with each attendance of the Mass or each beholding of a play of Corpus Christi. *Croxton* is thus a kind of metadrama, a play about the possibilities of theater and its symbols. And if the *Croxton Play* is, in any sense, a miracle play, the miracle it stages may be not so much the transubstantiations of the Host or the forgivenesses of God or even the restoration of the hand of the offending outsider, but the miracle of the theater itself. What is miraculous about the play is how it uses the technologies of stagecraft or the skill of a performer to evoke the fear, the horror, or the pleasure of the spectacle of torture.

This professionalized, metadramatic quality of *Croxton* may explain one of the most distinctive features of its text: its stage directions. One of the points that I have tried to make is that, throughout the play, the actions of its characters are signaled through the rhetoric of dramatic direction. The Jews' announcements of just what they will do to the Host, Malchus's directive to "take oure space," Master Brundiche's announcements to his "audiense" and "congrecacyon," and the final directions of the Episcopus all give voice to the play's concern with controlling the actions of its characters and audience. But at its most sensationalist moments, the specificity and fullness of the stage directions takes precedence over scripted speech. Indeed, such moments in the play are met with only awe and wonder by the characters. When the Jews prick the stolen Eucharist, the stage direction reads, "Here þe Ost must blede," and Jonathas is left to exclaim "Ah! owt! owt! harrow! what deuyll ys thys?" (480). Similarly, when Jonathas's hand is torn away, having been nailed to the post, the stage direction reads, "Here shall thay plouke þe arme, and þe hond shall hang styll with þe Sacrament," and Malchus cries out: "Alas, alas, what deuyll ys thys?" (516). And, toward the play's end, when the staging directs, "Here the owyn must ryve asunder and blede owt at þe cranys, and an image appere owt with woundys bledyng," Masphat rejoins: "Owt! owt! here ys a grete wondere!" (713). At moments such as these, the exclamations of the Jews are voicings, not just of their own amazement at miraculous events, but of what must be the audience's wonderment at the miracles of stagecraft. They call attention to the skills of the prop master, and the object of their attention extends beyond the mimesis of theater to the education of the audience. It is as if these characters provide the spectator with a vocabulary of theatrical response, as if the viewer must exclaim, "Here ys a grete wondere!" and in the process further blur the line between spectatorship and participation.

These emphases on both the specificity of stage direction and the wonderment of character response realign the relations of the audience and the performers. They make the populace part of the directed actorship of theater, bringing them into the controlled space of dramatic performance. At the close of the play, when the audience becomes a congregation, the confines of theatrical disbelief may break down and liturgical reality may take over. But, as Sarah Beckwith has astutely argued, "alternatively, it is possible to see this ending of the play not so much as the movement out of theatrical space, but rather the absorption of procession into theater. The spectators, the 'congregation', become not so much processors, following the body of Christ (which is, after all, a stage prop), but actors, absorbed into the histrionic heart of the play."⁵¹ What I am suggesting is that the logic of this absorption has been controlling *Croxton* almost from its opening: a self-consciousness about the nature of theatrical performance and the powers of stagecraft to effect a reintegration of the severed limbs of the social body. Where I would differ somewhat, too, from Beckwith's emphases is in attending to the influences of the legal, as well as liturgical, theory and practice of the time.

For what the *Croxton Play* does is offer in mimetic, representational, staged form, a vision of bodily dismemberment strikingly akin to the forms of punishment still practiced on the high streets and the market-places of the towns in the late fifteenth century. What it also shares with the borough punishments is a rhetorical affinity with customary law. The language of stage direction and of borough law share a concern with direction and control. Both set themselves the task of placing action precisely in time and space: for customary laws, the constant rhetoric of "if" and "when" that introduces the announcement of a punishment and guides the sequencing of actions in the narratives, and moreover, the precise locations of those punishments in public places, complete with the props, machinery, and actors necessary to perform them. What the spectators have been absorbed into is not just the theatrics of the show but the legal system through which such theatrics may be pressed into the service of both punishment and salvation.

But if the close of *Croxton* offers up a vision of incorporation — a vision, much like that of Lydd's decrees, calibrated toward the maintenance of the social body and the exclusion or benign reincorporation of a community's *disjecta membra* — it also limns a view of fragments. The world conjured by the play's Jews, much like that evoked by Lydd's accounts, remains a world of things: of objects whose significance and social function have been radically transformed into the props of theater. The Host, the tools, the body parts, even, as in the case of Lydd, the knife and cartwheel, are the paid-for instruments of pain. For Croxton, the commodification of the Host rests with the merchant Aristorious. His bargaining over its price transforms its absolute and stable value as symbol into something that may be exchanged: a thing of fluid, and thus, ultimately, of debased worth.[52] For Lydd, the annalistic impulse to record places a value on everything. Indeed, one might say that the very principle of annalistic inclusion depends on whether a price can be set for object or for deed. That twelve pence was paid out for the punishment of Thomas Norys; that the man with the dromedary was paid eight pence; or that the minstrels, players, and performers of the local and the visiting troupes were reimbursed for expenses makes all these actions part of an economy of spectatorship.

The iterative feel of the account of Jack Cade's porpoise in the Lydd records, for example, takes this fish and centers it in an elaborate display of political fealty. By the time one reaches the end of this string of accounts, on cannot help but *see* this creature, and see it no longer as a simple gift or even as a piece of ritual exotica, but as an object of delectation. The very parade of the oddity (whether it be a porpoise or a dromedary or a self-mutilating cutpurse) becomes a source of entertainment and expense. The commodification of these objects of intrigue, then, goes beyond the simple civic act of payment and separates the thing paid for from its action. The objects of the Lydd records are foregrounded as objects: as props for the agency of pain or power that, in the end, come to replace the very actions of that power.

These fascinations with the props of legal and liturgical theatrics bespeak what may be a broader and more compelling affiliation between *Croxton* and the traditions of punitive spectacle. The banns that open *Croxton* deploy the polysemous linguistic resources of late Middle English to affiliate the drama of the play with the impulses of judicial visualization. The Second Vexillator announces at the close of the play's banns:

> And yt place yow, thys gaderyng þat here ys,
> At Croxston on Monday yt shall be sen;
> To see the conclusyon of þis lytell processe
> Hertely welcum shall yow bene. (73–76)

These lines have long been valued for their information on the provenance of the play: its "Croxston" has been identified as Croxton in East Anglia, and from this reference scholars have spun out a skein of associations on the play's affiliations with East Anglian dramatic and religious culture.[53] But as important as this reference to a place are these lines' definitions of a genre. For what the Second Vexillator does is define both the nature of the play and the expected situation of its viewership. The invitation is to "place yow," to take a present gathering of individuals and transform them into an audience for theater by directing them to both the time and locus of performance. What will be seen there and then is the conclusion of a process—not simply how the plot turns out but how the law works. Middle English *proces* meant not just story, tale, or action, but connoted also the proceedings of the law, an action, or a suit. The *Middle English Dictionary* cites a range of usages throughout the fourteenth and the fifteenth centuries that define the "proces" as a course of legal argument or judgment, and the sense of *Croxton*'s invitation to behold the "conclusyon" of this process evokes the ambiance of law court and of public judgment.[54] The emphasis on justice visualized here recalls the remarks of the Second Vexillator at the beginning of the banns:

> Souereyns, and yt lyke yow to here þe purpoos of þis play
> That ys representyd now in yower syght. (9–10)

The Middle English *representen*, too, has a set of late medieval legal connotations: to bring an offender or a prisoner into the custody of officers of the law.[55] To represent, conclude, or behold a process—all have about them the veneer of legal diction, and what I suggest is that this creates a context of allusion and connotation in which we may understand the function of the banns as (in addition to an invitation to behold a play) a summoning to bear witness before a legal action.

One function of these banns, then, is to associate theatrical and legal performance in a way that initiates those blurrings of the lines between drama and law, mimesis and action, spectatorship and participation that are the business of the play itself. The banns, together with the final notes on title, dramatis personae, and performance that end the text of the play in its manuscript, thus bracket the play text itself with two sets of remarks on generic, formal, and dramaturgical definition. The title of the play (*The Play of the Blyssyd Sacrament*), the historical event behind it (the miracle at Aragon in 1460), the list of dramatis personae, and the enigmatic remark that "IX may play yt at ease," all constitute the information that may help the reader understand the nature of this document. They situate the body of the play in the generic and dramatic norms of late medieval performance: in the familiarities of Eucharist miracle and of traveling theater. The purpose of these closing notes is to make the play playable and to redefine its subject as not one of action — "þe Conuersyon of Ser Jonathas þe Jewe," as the manuscript's title has it following the banns — but of thing. This is a play, now, of the blessed sacrament, of an event in the history of an object, a play that, for all its challenges to dramaturge or prop master, nine may play at ease.

Just what is, then, the *Croxton Play of the Sacrament*—a play, a representation, a process? A story of a miracle grounded in historical fact? A piece of itinerant theater, offered up, on this occasion, at a small town in East Anglia? These are the questions raised, not just by modern scholarship, but by the play itself. *Croxton*, as I have argued, thematizes the problems of drama, takes the details of liturgical and legal performance and self-consciously reflects on their effects on a viewing public, compelling them to play both spectators and participants. Its vivid presentations, as well as its specific directions for performance, draw on what I have sought to identify as the traditions of customary law—not just because both attend to the brutal mutilations of the body and the fascinations with the tools of punishment but, furthermore, because both blur constructively the line between viewer and actor, practice and performance, history and fiction. Such blurrings may help us to redefine the nature of late medieval theatricality by locating the spectatorial impulse not only at the stage but on the high street. The cultural connections between reading habits, religious devotion, and punitive spectacle made in the last decades of the fifteenth century (connections that I have only been able to sketch here) create the possibilities of interchange between what may have been traditionally separate forms of institutional expression. That law or liturgy appears theatrical, or that the drama draws on features of legal and liturgical practice, are cultural phenomena that share in a new emphasis on vision and display in late medieval English life and that associate the body and the book as inscribed documents of social understanding.

The fascinations with the fragment, therefore, are perhaps a natural result of seeing bodies whole and broken on the stage, the altar, or the high street. If *Croxton* is in any sense a "funny" play, or if the borough customs of bodily punishment have perhaps an unfortunate risibility about them, it may also be because of their emphases on fragmentation. Such texts are comic in a dark sense, one that, as Carolyn Walker Bynum has phrased it, "undergirds our sense of human limitation," and that, in its revelry in bodies shattered or disfigured, shows us a narrative of human history where "the pleasant [has been] snatched from the horrible by artifice and with acute self-consciousness and humility."[56] In effect, this is what the *Croxton Play* and Lydd's decrees have done. By offering a vision of incorporation and the miracle of Jewish conversion, *Croxton* snatches something, if not pleasant, than at least both amusing and redemptive from the horrible. And if the punishments at Lydd inflicted, to the modern eye, undue pain on the body of a pickpocket, they provided a drama of social control for a community accustomed to the theatrics of local play, visiting entertainers, and the occasional exotica of everyday life.[57]

Such fascinations with the fragment, too, remain the purview of the postmedieval reader, as well as the medieval spectator. The *Croxton Play* and Lydd's decrees survive as fragments in themselves: texts torn from the lost commonplace books of the Tudor scribe or disassembled from the collections of town clerks. The job of modern scholarship, as Theresa Coletti has observed in writing about the historiography of medieval drama, has been to take such fragments and restore them to a wholeness shaped by the trajectories of literary and legal history.[58] Just what the place of these texts might be in those histories remains a subject of debate, and the controlling self-historizing turn in recent medieval studies may provide one line of inquiry into the status, both historical and imaginative, of these documents. The contrasts I raised at this paper's opening — between the nineteenth-century preoccupations with the picturesque and the twentieth-century attentions to the violent, between an understanding of these texts as "history" and as "fiction" — I wish to return to now in closing to see how the problems of a culture of spectatorship inform not just the origins but the survival and transmission of these works.

Both the *Croxton Play of the Sacrament* and the records of the corporation of the town of Lydd come to modern scholars as the products of postmedieval cultural and critical environments. The *Croxton Play*, for all of its self-conscious grounding in a fifteenth-century event, is in many ways a Tudor text. The manuscript is datable by hand and watermark to sometime between the 1520s and the 1540s, and the occasion of its copying reflects the social concerns of that age.[59] The spectatorial sensibilities at the heart of the *Croxton Play* would certainly have spoken to the Tudor fascinations with display, surveillance, and spectacular judicial punishment that took medieval practices and transformed them into the unique apparatus of the Henrician state.[60] The play's preoccupations with the inscribed body as the locus of religious and legal power resonates with the "grauen" world of Stephen Hawes's allegorical poetry; and its presentation of the wounded, bloody Christ recalls, as Eammon Duffy has suggested, the beheld *imago pietatis* of Hawes's *Conuercyon of Swerers*.[61] In the manuscript of the play, too, the vivid stage directions are highlighted in yellow crayon, suggesting a particular attention to the details of bodily marking and mutilation they describe.[62] Such details fill the commonplace books of the early Tudor period—books that took texts of violent or erotic subject matter and apposed them against documents of political sedition or religious heresy.[63] The period from the 1520s to the 1540s was, indeed, an era prepossessed by rooting out the subversive and the heretical, and much of *Croxton* 's emphasis on doubt and heresy (whatever the immediate fifteenth-century contexts of Lollardy and anti-Semitism were to motivate them) would have addressed directly the preoccupations of those decades in which, as the Earl of Arundel had put it in a poem of the time, "blessings turned to blasphemies."[64] As a play about the power of the Host and the beliefs about its powers, *Croxton* must have seemed an eerie presaging of the iconoclastic debates of the late 1520s and 1530s. Eammon Duffy reports events of 1533 that curiously recapitulate the story told in *Croxton*: "By October 1533 it was even being reported in London that images were being taken from their places and cast out of the churches as 'stocks and stones' of no value, and that some 'will prick them with their bodkins to see whether they will bleed or no.' "[65] Such were the actions of the play's Jews, as the play's directions state, "Here shall þe iiij Jewys pryk þer daggerys in iiij quarters," as Masphat announces, "For with thys punche I shall hym pryke" (474), and as the stage direction commands, "Here þe Ost must blede."

The time of *Croxton* 's manuscript was one, too, in which issues of iconoclasm resonated with critiques of the theatricality of liturgical spectacle. The zeal to see the Host that so motivated fifteenth-century popular piety was seen, in the sixteenth century, as a form of idolatry. Thomas Cranmer had focused on the spectacular nature of the elevation of the sacrament in his critique of pre-Reformation practice: "What was the cause of all these [exclamations], and that as well the priest and the people so devoutly did knowck and kneel at every sight of the sacrament, but that they worshipped that visible thing which they saw with their eyes and took it for very God?"[66] Such arguments are part and parcel of a larger questioning about the nature of theatricality itself. Relationships between the power of dramatic spectacle and enforcement of state authority became the subject of much private and public debate.[67] *Croxton*'s self-consciousness of dramatic visualization—with its Jews' cries of wonderment at each of the play's more excessive mutilations or restorations—would certainly have spoken to the concerns of a polemicist like Richard Morison, who in writing to Thomas Cromwell noted, "Into the common people thynges sooner enter by the eies, then by the eares; remembryng more better that they see than that they here."[68] Greg Walker has detailed the uses to which popular dramatics were put in the Henrician court, and in turn, how the pressures of early Protestant reformers by turns suppressed or recast old theatrical traditions for new political ends.[69] Jörg Fichte, too, has chronicled the Protestant adaptations of the morality traditions, suggestively illustrating how texts originally anti-Lollard, anti-Semitic, or generally antiheretical could be pressed into the service of the antipapist polemics of the sixteenth century.[70] In sum, the occasion of writing down the *Croxton Play of the Sacrament* may have been conditioned by a constellation of events in early Tudor social life, and, in turn, the text of the play may thus have functioned not so much as a document of theatrical performance but as a response to current debates on iconoclasm and on the power of liturgical and theatrical representation. What we have in the *physical artifact* of the play, then, is testimony to issues in the sixteenth-century religious imagination, rather than a record of fifteenth-century theatrical practice.

In an analogous manner, the survival and compilation of the records of the town of Lydd may owe as much to the interests of nineteenth-century historians as to the habits of town clerkship in the fifteenth century. The whole project of the Historical Manuscripts Commission was designed to write out national histories through the investigation of privately held documents. "The most valuable records, even for general history," wrote John Bruce in a statement giving voice to the compelling antiquarian sentiments of the mid–nineteenth century, "are to be found among the records of private and personal experience."[71] What the antiquarians had found in opening these private documents for public display were, indeed, not only the historical accounts of great and small, but something of a romance of inspection itself: a compelling fascination with discovering the secrets of past families or townships. Such a romance had become, in the hands of mid-century novelists, a glamor of antiquarianism, as witnessed in Disraeli's *Sybil*,[72] and one that had been appropriated by the journalistic reportage of the Historical Manuscripts Commission itself. The *Standard* wrote, of the *First Report* published in 1870: "The whole story of our country as a state, the reputations of her famous men, the motives of her policy, the secret springs and wheels by which her power, from age to age, has been brought into action, are gradually being laid bare, as though we were digging open a Pompeii of literature."[73]

This archaeology of private life informed, specifically, the work of Henry Thomas Riley in his compilation of the Lydd acounts for the *Fifth*

Report. Reviewing the town records, Riley chose to edit and publish only "about one sixteenth" of the materials before him (1:516), and his principle of selection seems to have been one that stressed the theatricalities and spectacles of everyday town life. In his prefatory remarks to the excerpts published in the *Fifth Report,* Riley attends to the "troops of minstrels" and the "players from the surrounding country" who would regularly visit Lydd; to the Boy Bishop celebrations and the plays on Saint Nicholas Day; to the curious story of the porpoise for Jack Cade, the punishment for cutpurses, and the visitation of the man with the dromedary (1:516–17). His extracts seek to offer "characteristic passages" (1:517), and "passages among the more curious of these Ordinances" (1:530). Riley's selections may indeed overdetermine an analysis such as the one I have presented in this paper, for by offering an implied narrative of oddity and spectacle, they construct a vision of town life that, itself, explores the tensions between private and public. He lays bare, to appropriate the *Standard*'s words, things secret and hidden, not just in the archive but in human hearts, as well. His vision of the world of fifteenth-century Lydd is one of venal private motivations matched with great public exuberance. On the cover of the manuscript of the Customall of Lydd, Riley finds these words written twice, *"homo homini lupus"*—man to man is a wolf—and it would seem that Riley's following selections of the punishments for petty crimes are palpably designed to illustrate this adage.

The nineteenth-century cultivation of a spectatorial antiquarianism may, in some sense, cook the books on the recovery of a late medieval culture of spectatorship, much as the Tudor transcription of the *Croxton Play of the Sacrament* may tell us less about late-fifteenth-century performance history and more about early-sixteenth-century doctrinal and political foment. Yet I offer these closing reflections as a way of constructively problematizing my own project: calling attention to its own self-consciousness of method and approach and, at the same time, historicizing the conditions of transmission and reception that bequeath the medieval archive to the modern reader. A culture of spectatorship is one that, irrespective of its time, confronts the tensions between private vision and public performance: one that skirts the line between the beholding of things in the open and the delectation of things in the closet. The kinds of issues I have sought to raise here—about the nature of theatrical experience, about relations between legal practice and dramatic performance, about the status of surviving texts as historical documents or annalistic fictions—are those that may help us appreciate not just the texture of late medieval life, but the rewards and difficulties of recovering that texture, and in turn, of seeking to adjudicate between the literary, the legal, and the historical within the current climate of medieval studies.[74]

Seth Lerer

Notes

1. Selections from the records of the corporation of the town of Lydd have been edited by Henry Thomas Riley and published in the *Fifth Report of the Historical Manuscripts Commission* (London, 1876), vol. 1, pp. 516–33, and in Arthur Finn, ed., *Records of Lydd*, translated and transcribed by Arthur Hussey and M. M. Hardy (Kent, 1911). Records of dramatic activity at Lydd, culled from surviving volumes in the Lydd archives, have been collected and published by Giles E. Dawson in *Records of Plays and Players in Kent, 1450–1642, Collections Volume VII* (London: Malone Society, 1965), pp. 89–112. Only the Historical Manuscripts Commission volume has published excerpts from the Customall, and I quote from their text throughout. The editors of that volume believe the Customall to have been written down in 1476 by the town clerk, Thomas Caxton. Mrs. Beryl Coatts, honorary librarian to the Town Council of Lydd, informs me that the copy of the Customall used by nineteenth-century editors does not survive. What remains in the Lydd archives is a mid-sixteenth-century version of that volume (personal communication, July 26, 1993).

2. Alice Green, *Town Life in the Fifteenth Century* (New York: Macmillan, 1894); H. S. Bennett, *The Pastons and Their England* (Cambridge: Cambridge University Press, 1922; 2nd ed., 1932).

3. From the *Fifth Report of the Historical Manuscripts Commission*, 1:530. All future references to Lydd records in this volume will be cited in the text.

4. The current fascination with the origins of medieval studies in the nineteenth century has yet to come to terms with its construction of medieval legal history. Recent works that may chart future lines of inquiry into that construction, and that have informed my own perspective in this account, include the following: Lee Patterson, *Negotiating the Past: The Historical Understanding of Medieval Literature* (Madison: Univeristy of Wisconsin Press, 1987), pp. 9–18; Hans-Ulrich Gumbrecht, "'Un Souffle d'Allemagne ayant passé': Friedrich Diez, Gaston Paris, and the Genesis of National Philologies," *Romance Philology* 40 (1986): 1–37; and R. Howard Bloch, "New Philology and Old French," *Speculum* 65 (1990): 38–58. For a brief bibliographical review of nineteenth- and early-twentieth-century histories of crime and punishment in England, see John Bellamy, *Crime and Public Order in England in the Later Middle Ages* (London: Routledge and Kegan Paul, 1973), pp. 205–7.

5. Luke Owen Pike, *A History of Crime in England*, 2 vols, 1873–76 (reprint, Montclair: Patterson Smith, 1968), this quotation from 1:420–21.

6. Frederick Pollock and Frederick William Maitland, *The History of English Law before the Time of Edward I* (Cambridge: Cambridge University Press, 1895), 1:xxiv.

7. Michel Foucault, *Discipline and Punish: The Birth of the Prison*, trans. Alan Sheridan (Harmondsworth, England: Penguin, 1979), p. 34. The Foucauldian approach to the history of crime and punishment, both in detail and in the context of his larger project on the history of the body and of social force relations in Western societies, has been the subject of much critical debate since the translation of Foucault's work in the late 1970s. While this is not the occasion to review thoroughly the aspects of this debate and the legacy of Foucault's approach, some representative positions may be found in the following: Pieter Spierenburg, *The Spectacle of Suffering* (Cambridge: Cambridge University Press, 1984); Randall McGowen, "The Body and Punishment in Eighteenth-Century England," *Journal of Modern History* 59 (1987): 651–79; John B. Bender, *Imagining the Penitentiary* (Chicago: University of Chicago Press, 1987); Elizabeth Hanson, "Torture and Truth in Renaissance England," *Representations* 34 (1991): 53–84; Stephen Wilf, "Imagining Justice: Aesthetics and Public Executions in Late Eighteenth-Century England," *Yale Journal of Law and the Humanities* 5 (1993): 51–78.

8. Elaine Scarry, *The Body in Pain: The Making and Unmaking of a World* (New York: Oxford University Press, 1985), pp. 27, 28.

9. Wilf, "Imagining Justice," pp. 51, 54.

10. Natalie Zemon Davis, *Fiction in the Archives: Pardon Tales and Their Tellers in Sixteenth-Century France* (Stanford, Calif.: Stanford University Press, 1987).

11. For the critical inheritance in narrative theory, historiography, and reception history that informs Davis's work, see her bibliographical review, *Fiction in the Archives*, pp. 147–48.

12. I am appropriating Davis's phrasing from *Fiction in the Archives*, p. 5.

13. The place of the human body, marked and mutilated, tortured and controlled, in medieval drama has recently become the focus of a range of inquiries drawing on semiotics, feminist theory, and Marxist historiography. Some representative accounts that both inform and provoke my own analyses include the following: Peter Travis, "The Social Body of the Dramatic Christ in Medieval England," *Early Drama to 1600*, *Acta* 13 (1985): 17–36, and "The Semiotics of Christ's Body in the English Cycles," in Richard Emmerson, ed., *Approaches to Teaching Medieval Drama* (New York: Modern Language Association of America, 1990), pp. 67–78; Theresa Coletti, "Purity and Danger: The Paradox of Mary's Body and the En-gendering of the Infancy Narrative in the English Mystery Cycles," in *Feminist Approaches to the Body in Medieval Literature*, ed. Linda Lomperis and Sarah Stanbury (Philadelphia: University of Pennsylvania Press, 1993), pp. 65–95; Sarah Beckwith, "Ritual, Church and Theatre: Medieval Dramas of the Sacramental Body," in *Culture and History, 1350–1600*, ed. David Aers (Detroit, Mich.: Wayne State University Press, 1992), pp. 65–89; *Christ's Body: Identity, Culture, and Society in Late Medieval Writings* (London: Routledge, 1993).

14. Material in this and the next two paragraphs summarizes evidence and arguments from my *Chaucer and His Readers: Imagining the Author in Late-Medieval England* (Princeton, N.J.: Princeton University Press, 1993), pp. 182–91, with references and bibliography on pp. 275–79. A collection of specific studies that appeared too late for my account in that book, but which supports and qualifies some of its claims, is Sandra L. Hindman, ed., *Printing the Written Word: The Social History of Books, circa 1450–1520* (Ithaca, N.Y.: Cornell University Press, 1991), especially the essay of Michael Camille, "Reading the Printed Image: Illuminations and Woodcuts of the *Pèlerinage de la vie humaine* in the Fifteenth Century," pp. 259–91.

15. Paul Saenger, "Books of Hours and the Reading Habits of the Later Middle Ages," in *The Culture of Print*, ed. Roger Chartier (Princeton, N.J.: Princeton University Press, 1989), pp. 141–73, this quotation from p. 147. See also the remarks in Saenger, "Silent Reading: Its Impact on Late Medieval Script and Society," *Viator* 13 (1982): 367–414.

16. On Anglo-Burgundian cultural relations and the place of Guillaume Fillastre's *Toison d'or* as a manual of conduct and guide to political organization, see Gordon Kipling, *The Triumph of Honour: The Burgundian Origins of the Elizabethan Renaissance* (The Hague: University of Leiden Press, for the Sir Thomas Browne Institute, 1977), and "Henry VII and the Origins of Tudor Patronage," in *Patronage in the Renaissance*, ed. Guy Fitch Lytle and Stephen Orgel (Princeton, N.J.: Princeton University Press, 1981), pp. 117–64.

17. I quote from the translation in Saenger, "Books of Hours," pp. 167–68 n. 76.

18. On this section of the *Conuercyon* (lines 113–58), see the edition of Florence W. Gluck and Alice B. Morgan, eds., *Stephen Hawes: The Minor Poems*, Early English Text Society, extra ser. 271 (London: Oxford University Press, 1974), and their discussion on p. 147. The shaped portion of verse appears in de Worde's printing on sigs. Aiiiv-Aiiir; a reproduction of these pages may be found in my *Chaucer and His Readers*, p. 191.

19. For a brief discussion of this section of the poem in the context of the "imago pietatis" and the late-fifteenth-century fascinations with the wounded, bleeding Christ as man of sorrows, see Eammon Duffy, *The Stripping of the Altars: Traditional Religion in England, 1400–1580* (New Haven, Conn.: Yale University Press, 1992), p. 107.

20. These examples are from, respectively, Bellamy, *Crime and Public Order*, p. 182, and William Harrison, *An Historical Description of the Iland of Britaine*, printed as the introductory material to Raphael Holinshed, *Chronicles of England, Scotland, and Ireland* (London, 1807), 1:311.

21. On the "textualization" of the marked or mutilated criminal, see Foucault, *Discipline and Punish,* p. 34, and Michel de Certeau, *The Practice of Everyday Life,* trans. Steven Rendall (Berkeley and Los Angeles: University of California Press, 1984), pp. 139–41.

22. Bellamy, *Crime and Public Order,* p. 185.

23. See John A. F. Thomson, *The Later Lollards, 1414–1520* (Oxford: Oxford University Press, 1965), p. 231, and Beckwith, "Ritual, Church and Theater," p. 72.

24. McGowen, "The Body and Punishment," p. 666.

25. George Osborne, *The Civic Magistrates Right of Inflicting Punishment* (London, 1733), pp. 8–9, quoted in McGowen, "The Body and Punishment," p. 666. For a variety of perspectives on the eighteenth-century reformers' transformation of public punishment into private incarceration, see McGowen, passim; Bender, *Imagining the Penitentiary;* and Wilf, "Imagining Justice."

26. Harrison, *Historical Description,* 1:312. Harrison's attitudes toward customary law and the role of Holinshed's *Chronicle* in the transmission of medieval English legal traditions await further study. Some gestures in this direction have been made by Annabel Patterson, "'For Words Only': From Treason Trial to Liberal Legend in Early Modern England," *Yale Journal of Law and the Humanities* 5 (1993): 389–416, especially her remarks on pp. 389–91.

27. Harrison, *Historical Description,* 1:311–12.

28. Richard van Dülmen, *Theater of Horror: Crime and Punishment in Early Modern Germany,* trans. Elizabeth Neu (Oxford: Polity Press, 1990), p. 3.

29. Ibid.

30. Andrew McCall, *The Medieval Underworld* (London: Hamilton, 1979), p. 72.

31. Duffy, *Stripping of the Altars,* pp. 95–116, with specific references hereafter in the text. My brief review cannot do justice either to the remarkable depth of Duffy's research and analysis or to the potential controversy over his arguments in the historiography of late medieval religion. Suffice it to say that Duffy's arguments for the vigor and participatory nature of the lay experience of the Mass challenge some fundamental assumptions about the theatrics of the liturgy governing Gail M. Gibson, *The Theater of Devotion* (Chicago: University of Chicago Press, 1989) (see Duffy, pp. 110–11), and also Beckwith, "Ritual, Church and Theater," p. 76. For a sustained critique of Duffy's work—and a capsule account of an alternative approach to the study of late medieval religion—see David Aers, "Altars of Power," *Literature and History* 3, no. 2 (1994): 90–105.

32. For the thematics of vision in the Corpus Christi plays, see David Mills, "The 'Behold and See' Convention in Medieval Drama," *Medieval English Theatre* 7, no. 1 (1985): 4–12, and the discussion in Greg Walker, *Plays of Persuasion: Drama and Politics and the Court of Henry VIII* (Cambridge: Cambridge University Press, 1991), pp. 11–13, especially his remarks in n. 17 concerning the "stress upon the physical, observable, presentation of spiritual truths" in the cycle plays, in particular, that "the audience is asked to judge the veracity of the message expounded on the strength of their own observation. Hence characters repeatedly refer to what the audience has seen, does see or will see."

33. All references to the Wakefield *Buffeting* play are from the edition in David M. Bevington, *Medieval Drama* (Boston: Houghton Mifflin, 1975), cited by line number in the text.

34. V. A. Kolve, *The Play Called Corpus Christi* (Stanford, Calif.: Stanford University Press, 1966), pp. 175–205.

35. See the account in the Manuscripts of the Corporation of New Romney in the *Fifth Report of the Historical Manuscripts Commission,* 1:540, and the brief discussion in Green, *Town Life,* 1:148.

36. Green, *Town Life,* 1:148.

37. *Fifth Report,* 1:520. Further references are cited in the text.

38. M. Bateson, ed., *Borough Customs,* vol. 1, Selden Society Publications, vol. 18 (London: Selden Society, 1900), pp. 55–57. Let me note here that my central point about the

historicity of the punishment for cutpurses is that it was both a documented legal practice and a part of the rhetoric of punishment for late medieval and Renaissance writers. It is true that many of the borough laws were simply copied from the custom books of different times and places. Such documents, on their own, offer little in the way of evidence for the actual performance of particular punishments. Yet such records as the 12d. paid for the cutting off of Thomas Norys's ear do constitute such evidence, as do the records of contemporary chroniclers. One particularly vivid example is the Chronicle of the Monastery of Saint Albans, which describes the festivities around the coronation of the seven-year-old Henry VI in 1429 as follows:

> Quo die Londiniis, quia dies lucida et serena, millia millia populorum ad Coronationem confluebant. Ibi oppressus erat presbyter, una mulier, et plures alii; et scissores loculorum capti et incarcerati, et aures illorum a capitibus amputati.

> [On that day in London, because it had been clear and serene weather, thousands and thousands of people congregated at the Coronation. There, a priest, a woman, and many others had been crushed to death. And cutpurses were arrested and imprisoned, and their ears cut off from their heads.]

(*Chronicon Rerum Gestarum in Monasterio Sancti Albani*, in Henry Thomas Riley, ed., *Chronica Monasterii S. Albani*, Rolls Series no. 28, vol. 5, part 1 [London: Longmans, Green, 1870], p. 44, with the words *scissores loculorum* glossed as "cutpurses" by Riley. Translation mine.) The fact that the chronicle goes to no great lengths to explain the nature or purposes of the punishment for cutpurses implies that such a punishment was commonplace. See, too, the discussion in G. R. Elton, *Policy and Police* (Cambridge: Cambridge University Press, 1972), pp. 384–85.

39. Heinrich Brunner, *Deutsche Rechtsgeschichte* (Leipzig: Duncker und Humblot, 1887–92), 2:472. See, too, the discussion in van Dülmen, *Theater of Horror,* pp. 47–49.

40. See the account in van Dülmen, *Theater of Horror,* p. 48.

41. Mervyn James, "Ritual, Drama and the Social Body in the Late Medieval English Town," *Past and Present* 98 (1983): 3–29 (further references are cited by page number in the text). A valuable critique of James's methods and presuppositions can be found in Chapter 4 by Sarah Beckwith in this volume.

42. Bateson, ed., *Borough Customs,* pp. 55–57.

43. Davis, *Fiction in the Archives,* pp. 1–35.

44. Beckwith, "Ritual, Church and Theatre," p. 68.

45. All quotations from the *Croxton Play of the Sacrament* will be from the edition of Norman Davis, *Non-Cycle Plays and Fragments,* Early English Text Society, suppl. ser. 1 (London: Oxford University Press, 1970), pp. 58–89. I have also occasionally preferred the emendations in the edition of David Bevington, *Medieval Drama,* pp. 754–88, and have checked, too, the facsimile of the unique manuscript (Dublin, Trinity College MS F.4.20, fols. 338r-356r) as reproduced and analyzed in Norman Davis, *Non-Cycle Plays and the Winchester Dialogues* (Leeds: School of English, 1979), pp. 93–131.

46. See, for example, the remarks in Bevington, *Medieval Drama,* p. 755: "The theatrical devices seem obvious and even comic.... Surely a medieval audience would have recognized these stage contrivances as entertaining theatrical illusions." See also the comments of Richard L. Homan, "Devotional Themes in the Violence and Humor of the *Play of the Sacrament,*" *Comparative Drama* 20 (1986–87): 327–40, especially pp. 328–29: "Any performance which hazards the use of horrific special effects risks appearing ludicrous.... The success of this pattern of action and of the stage effect must depend, therefore, on the skill with which the scene is written and on the effect executed." For an account of some possible historical contexts for recovering the medieval staging of the *Croxton Play,* together with some reflections on modern attempts to recreate their effects, see Darryll Grantley, "Producing Miracles," in *Aspects of Early English Drama,* ed. Paula Neuss (Cambridge: Brewer, 1983), pp. 78–91.

47. Kolve, *Play Called Corpus Christi,* p. 180.

48. In addition to the studies cited above, see the arguments of Ann Eljenholm Nichols, "The Croxton *Play of the Sacrament*: A Re-Reading," *Comparative Drama* 22 (1988): 117–37 (who considers the play less a piece of anti-Lollard propaganda than a "reflection of fifteenth-century Eucharistic piety," p. 117). More detailed attempts to ground the play in the various cultural traditions of late-fifteenth-century England include those of Eammon Duffy, *Stripping of the Altars*, pp. 105–9 (who sees the function of its Jews as concerned less with the virulence of living anti-Semitism than with the stock symbolism of the "unbelieving Jews [who] regularly feature in Eucharistic miracle stories," p. 105), and Beckwith, "Ritual, Church and Theatre" (who deploys a range of historical and methodological approaches to understand the play as problematizing the nature of sacramental symbolism and the theatricality of the liturgy). The final words of the manuscript, "IX may play yt at ease," have long been understood as evidence for *Croxton* as a "touring" play, appropriate for itinerant players of limited company. For an attempt to use this scribal remark as evidence for the recovering of the historical environment of the play's performance, see Gibson, *Theater of Devotion*, pp. 34–35.

49. O. B. Hardison Jr, *Christian Rite and Christian Drama in the Middle Ages* (Baltimore, Md.: Johns Hopkins University Press, 1965).

50. See the materials assembled in Gibson, *Theater of Devotion*, pp. 34–35.

51. Beckwith, "Ritual, Church and Theatre," p. 78.

52. Ibid., p. 79.

53. Bevington remarks, "Although a number of places named 'Croxton' have been found in the Midland area, local allusions to 'colkote a lytyll besyde Babwell Mill' make it clear that the play was performed near Bury St. Edmunds in Suffolk" (*Medieval Drama*, p. 756). This information is pressed into the service of Gibson's argument that the *Croxton Play*, in spite of its exotic location in Aragon, Spain, "is pointedly East Anglian in its topography of mind and purpose" (*Theater of Devotion*, p. 34). Beckwith develops Gibson's claims to aver that "it is evident that the play has definite connections with Bury St Edmunds, and was possibly written for performance there in the first instance" ("Ritual, Church and Theatre," p. 70), and her note to this passage affirms, "Arguments about the authorship and production of the play are inevitably speculative; the Bury St Edmunds connection seems, however, irrefutable" (p. 85 n. 25). Except for the mentions of Croxton and "colkote a lytyll besyde Babwell Mill" (which Gibson believes is "the 'Tolcote' or tollhouse just opposite the friary near the North Gate of Bury," p. 34), there is no other evidence to link the play irrefutably with Bury St Edmunds. As I will argue at the close of this chapter, what counts as evidence in understanding the *Croxton Play* as a *document* are the details of its manuscript—details that locate it in environments specific to the second quarter of the sixteenth century, not the last half of the fifteenth.

54. *Middle English Dictionary*, ed. Hans Kurath et al. (Ann Arbor: University of Michigan Press, 1954–), s.v. *proces*, def. 4. The *MED* offers a definition (3.f.) of the word as "a play, pageant, or performance," but cites only this passage from the *Croxton Play* as evidence.

55. *MED*, s.v. *representen*, def. 1.b.

56. Carolyn Walker Bynum, *Fragmentation and Redemption* (New York: Zone Books, 1990), pp. 24–25.

57. Let me affirm here that, for all my interest in the rhetoric of punishment and the cultural construction of a punitive aesthetics and theatrical sensibilities, I am not insensitive to the fact that in these punishments real people suffered real pain. As Bynum reminds us, "It is important not to forget that tales of mutilation and fragmentation are about human pain" (*Fragmentation and Redemption*, p. 305 n. 28). Scarry's *Body in Pain* is a valuable corrective to the Foucauldian-inspired New Historicist dispassion and suspicious playfulness concerning rituals of pain and power. The larger problem, it seems to me, and one not within the scope of my brief essay here, is the relationship between what Scarry calls pain and imagining (see pp. 161–80): that is, the relationship between pain as a somatic condition and as an imaginative construction. A useful analogy to my discussion, and one that I hope to develop in another context, is provided by Carol Clover, "Her

Body, Himself: Gender in the Slasher Film," *Representations* 20 (1987): 187–228, and the development of these arguments in *Men, Women, and Chainsaws* (Princeton, N.J.: Princeton University Press, 1992). In addition to her focus on the weapons of the slasher and the viewer's need to "see with our own eyes the 'opened' body" ("Her Body, Himself," p. 198), Clover deftly adjudicates between the critic's need to explain horror in an interpretive framework and the viewer's need to respond to horror in a visceral one. She quotes James B. Twitchell, in a formulation that may stand as something of a guidepost for my own work: "The critic's first job in explaining the fascination of horror is not to fix the images at their every appearance but, instead, to trace their migrations to the audience and, only then, try to understand why they have been crucial enough to pass along" ("Her Body, Himself," p. 191). My goal, in part, has been to appreciate the horror of the medieval stage *as horror*: not as typology or symbol, or as risible theatrics, but as an event that resonated with the public experience of watching officially inflicted pain. From this perspective, my concern has been with those "migrations" between the stage and an audience that was inured to, or at least educated in, the rituals of punishment and thus to try to understand why certain aspects of those rituals were crucial enough to pass along.

58. Theresa Coletti, "'Fragmentation and Redemption': Dramatic Records, History, and the Dream of Wholeness," *Envoi* 3 (1991): 1–13, and her more fully developed critique of the ideologies and critical presuppositions of the Records of Early English Drama project in "Reading REED: History and the Records of Early English Drama," in *Literary Practice and Social Change in Britain, 1380–1530*, ed. Lee Patterson (Berkeley and Los Angeles: University of California Press, 1990), pp. 248–84.

59. See Norman Davis's analysis of the manuscript in the facsimile edition, pp. 93–94.

60. The rise of surveillance culture and the official preoccupations with heresy, sedition, and political propriety during the reign of Henry VIII have been the subject of a variety of recent reassessments of Henrician rule and early Tudor life. While this is not the place to review the entire bibliography on the subject, those studies that have sought to locate Tudor literary writing in these environments, and that have shaped my own thinking about the period, include the following: Elton, *Policy and Police*; Stephen Greenblatt, *Renaissance Self-Fashioning* (Chicago: University of Chicago Press, 1980); Suzanne Westfall, *Patrons and Performance: Early Tudor Household Revels* (Oxford: Clarendon Press, 1990); and Walker, *Plays of Persuasion*. A. C. Spearing writes of the voyeuristic world of the *Squyr of Lowe Degre*, a poem of the early Tudor period, as one full of "enclosed and private spaces, but equally of *huote*, surveillance, of spies and opportunities for spying. It is a world, like the early Tudor court as evoked in the poetry of Skelton, Hawes, or Wyatt, where 'treason walketh wonder wyde.'" From *The Medieval Poet as Voyeur* (Cambridge: Cambridge University Press, 1992), p. 178. Spearing's general discussion of this poem (pp. 177–93) and his general assessments of the cultural thematics of looking in medieval European literature (pp. 1–50) are relevant to the concerns of my study. Studies of later sixteenth-century literary culture that remark in passing on the Henrician origins of these phenomena include the following: Katherine Eisaman Maus, "Proof and Consequences: Inwardness and Its Exposure in the English Renaissance," *Representations* 34 (1991): 29–52; Hanson, "Torture and Truth in Renaissance England"; and John M. Archer, *Sovereignty and Intelligence: Spying and Court Culture in the English Renaissance* (Stanford, Calif.: Stanford University Press, 1993).

61. Duffy, *Stripping of the Altars*, p. 107.

62. See Norman Davis's remarks in the facsimile edition, p. 93. The highlightings appear in the black-and-white facsimile as smeared shadings over the handwriting.

63. I have discussed an example of this phenomenon in *Chaucer and His Readers*, pp. 213–18, with references and bibliography to the practice in general on pp. 281–83.

64. From a poem in Bodleian Library MS Rawlinson poet. 291, fol. 16, attributed to the earl of Arundel, and printed by Duffy, *Stripping of the Altars*, pp. 377–78.

65. Duffy, *Stripping of the Altars*, p. 381; see, too, his entire account of this period on pp. 379–423.

66. Quoted in Duffy, *Stripping of the Altars*, p. 98.

67. See, for example, Sydney Anglo, *Spectacle, Pageantry, and Early Tudor Policy* (Oxford: Clarendon Press, 1969), and Walker, *Plays of Persuasion*, especially pp. 6–36.

68. Quoted in Walker, *Plays of Persuasion*, p. 11.

69. Ibid., passim.

70. Jörg O. Fichte, "New Wine in Old Bottles: The Protestant Adaptation of the Morality Play," *Anglia* 110 (1992): 65–84.

71. John Bruce, preface to the *Verney Papers* (Camden Society, 1853), quoted in Roger H. Ellis, "The Royal Commission on Historical Manuscripts: A Short History and Explanation," in *Manuscripts and Men: An Exhibition of Manuscripts, Portraits, and Pictures ... to Mark the Centenary of the Royal Commission on Historical Manuscripts, 1869–1969* (London: Her Majesty's Stationery Office, 1969), pp. 1–39, this quotation on p. 1.

72. Ellis, "Royal Commission," pp. 4–5.

73. *Standard*, 4 April 1870, quoted in Ellis, "Royal Commission," p. 13.

74. This chapter represents the initiatory gestures of a larger study in progress funded by a 1993 Guggenheim Fellowship. Earlier treatments of some of its material have been presented to audiences at the Medieval Association of the Pacific, Stanford University, and the University of Michigan, and I am especially grateful to R. Howard Bloch, Hans-Ulrich Gumbrecht, and Karla Taylor for comments and encouragement. In the course of preparing it for presentation at the Intersections conference, I profited from the responses of my students and colleagues, especially Mary F. Godfrey, Michael Jones, and Mary F. Wack. That it appears at all in its present form in this volume is due to the professional generosity of David Wallace and the perceptive criticisms of Paul Strohm.

CHAPTER 4

Ritual, Theater, and Social Space in the York Corpus Christi Cycle

Sarah Beckwith

God is only a figurative expression of the society.
—Emile Durkheim

Christianity provides in the condensed symbolic economy of the passion an image of the body that converts the suffering of one individual into the redemption of the world.[1] In the passion and resurrection sequences of the York Corpus Christi cycle, that symbol that clerical culture had sought to establish as hegemonic (universal, yet exclusive to them through their rights of mediation and officiation)—Christ's body in the host—is subject to an inventive, brutal, and alarming series of reworkings.[2] The passion sequence gradually comes to subsume the theatrical and ritual energies of the city of York, as over the course of its production, it comes to account for half of the cycle. It is the silent object of the competing juridical claims of the secular and ecclesiastical establishment, represented in the plays by Pilate, Herod, and Annas and Caiphas. The object of Judas's betrayal and subsequent remorse, Christ's body is ritually tortured in an agonizingly extended sequence culminating in the reconstruction on stage of the central icon of the culture—Christ on the cross, dramatically played as both reenactment of the crucifixion and a construction of its central representation. Mourned for longingly and with anguish and only eventually relinquished by his mother and Mary Magdalene, its absence in the tomb signifying its miraculous escape from confinement, the impossibility of its constraint, the wounded body reappears in the resurrection sequences as the very proof of the sacramental system it underwrites, to become the vehicle of a drama of doubt, disbelief, and evidential testing. Groped by Thomas, whose fingering of Christ's side is extensively investigated,[3] Christ comes back in his wounded shirt in the Last Judgment pageant, the final pageant, so that the Christian cosmology can complete the sequence it has followed in the pageants, accounting for the very beginning of the world in its creation, as it looks forward and gives a rendition of its end. That symbol of which every little piece was a *pars pro toto*, a synecdoche for the whole, is subjected then, both literally and symbolically, to extensive, protracted, and vicious fracturing.

The York Corpus Christi pageants are an unprecedented encounter with the central imaginary significations of late medieval culture. Through their rearticulation of the body of Christ on the streets of York the representations that organize social existence in York are examined: "Who are we as a collectivity? [they ask.] What are we for one another? Where and in what are we? What do we want; what do we desire; what are we lacking?"[4] This chapter looks at some of the ways in which the articulation of the body of Christ in the pageant plays of the Corpus Christi cycle points at and presses those questions and at some of the ways in which criticism has conventionally addressed and thought about the ritualized social space of York itself. In looking at some of the implications of such examinations I want to show how and at what cost certain understandings of ritual have severed culture from social and political relations, structure from history, and ritual itself from theatrical practices in their analysis of these plays. I will argue that the analysis of these pageants in terms of a theory of ritualization will help us to see the way in which cultural reproduction is connected to temporal change, spatial configuration, social relations, and political form in the productions of York and in our critical reproductions of this theater.

Social Wholeness or the Part for the Whole

"Among all human communities," Aquinas, following Aristotle, reminds us, "the city is most perfect." And "because the things which come into the use of humans are ordered to humans as to their end, it is therefore necessary that the whole which constitutes the city is the principle of all other wholes which can be known and constituted by human reason."[5] The city is assured its composite status, its integrity, by that other "principle of all other wholes," Corpus Christi itself, according to the pioneering analyst of the celebrations of this theme in late medieval English town life. In his article published in *Past and Present* in 1983, Mervyn James writes:

> The theme of Corpus Christi is society seen in terms of body. The concept of the body provided urban societies with a mythology and ritual in terms of which opposites of social wholeness and differentiation could be affirmed and brought into creative tension, one with the other. The final intention of the cult was, then, to express the social bond and to contribute to social integration.[6]

This viewpoint is based on a particular interpretation of Durkheim by way of Mary Douglas; the body is the site for the close interrelation of symbolic classification, ritual process, and the formation of social solidarity.[7] This approach, brilliant and deservedly influential, as was its elucidation in this particular article, has tended to reduplicate at the level of functionalist anthropology the very hegemony that the medieval theologies and politics of Corpus Christi sought to accomplish: social integration and unity in the name of a single administering body. Functionalist anthropology will thus merely reiterate the very clerical project it seeks to articulate. In both cases, and they share a twin idealism, the hegemonic project that allows a part to speak for a whole can be simply edited out, for that part will already have been mistaken for the whole. One can therefore hardly be used as a historical account of the other.[8] James's appropriation of Durkheim has problems explaining and exploring the processes by which the town is reproduced as a whole. His inability to do this is linked to the way in which his model of ritual derives from a holistic version of culture that cannot separate out or identify sociopolitical structures.[9] Neither is his model capable of engaging in any explicit way with the theatrical practices of the plays themselves.[10] This is perhaps not surprising, for the model of ritual wielded in these analyses is a better tool for examining and constructing a sense of overall structure than it is, say, at dealing with the manipulation of bodies in space in the individual pageants, or their sophisticated attention to the phenomenological dichotomy of the actor's body (simultaneously sign and signified).[11] Yet any understanding of the complex festivity of Corpus Christi cannot afford to avoid a more detailed confrontation with these pageants if it is to be able to account for the ritual of Corpus Christi festivities and the manipulation of Christ's body at the center of their practices.[12]

In James's model of ritual, ritual is a discrete, identifiable object characterized in particular by its splitting of action from thought and by the function of its action: the resolution of contradiction and the closure of social conflict.[13] The endemic fissures and tensions in late medieval urban life, between the mercantile oligarchy and an artisanate that it increasingly sought to delimit by repressive labor legislation, could all be assuaged by the sense of wholeness and participation represented by, but more crucially generated by, the composite, sacral, and unified body of Christ.[14] The body of Christ can unify in this view because it is itself invested with the intense levels of social interaction that surround it in the festivity, which is then invested in the object taken to represent collective ideals.[15]

The ministry of Christ pageants of the York Corpus Christi cycle depict Christ's break with the Old Law via a demonstration of his superior scriptural knowledge (miracuously mediated) and his powers of salvific healing, and the drama is consistently self-conscious about its enactment and articulation of a prior text.[16] Thus Christ will tell Peter to fetch the ass on which he will ride into Jerusalem so that he can fulfill the prophecy, and yet this consciousness of scriptural precedent, particularly marked in the pageants most concerned with the move from the Old to the New Testament, disappears in the skinners' pageant of the

Entry into Jerusalem. Here we are swept up in a process of ritual participation in which York becomes Jerusalem and in which the lyrical and repetitive hailing of Christ as king is both a construction and a recognition of him as such. Structures of belief and doctrinal considerations are here utterly unimportant. The theatrical and ritual effect is one of being swept into an inevitable, visceral, and committed response to his passage. Exploiting the processional nature of the staging, the burghers in the play await the entrance of Christ; the blind man, the lame man, and Zacchaeus come out of the crowd to halt the procession, in such a way that Jerusalem and York are superimposed one on the other. Through the medium of Christ's passage, one has been converted into the other.[17] It is just such moments that James's model seems good at reading, but he is less successful at others. Indeed we might say that his article deals entirely at the structural level of ritual organization in the abstract rather than reading the substance of the pageants in terms of their performative practice. Part of the problem lies in the way he locates ritual as a discrete, autonomous object of study. For as Durkheim says in "Value Judgments and Judgments of Reality":

> Collective ideals can only be manifested and become aware of themselves by being concretely realized in material objects that can be seen by all, understood by all, and represented to all minds.... All sorts of contingent circumstances determine the manner of its embodiment, and the object once chosen, however commonplace, becomes unique.[18]

But what precisely here is the object of representation? What, indeed, is the nominal object of festivity, of celebration? Who and what is Christ's body in the performance of the Corpus Christi pageants in York? At this point we will need to go beyond the notion of an integrated and wholesome body being traced onto the city as if it had no resisting shape, no already delineated contours, no marked and contested spaces to make a rougher surface, a more difficult screen on which to draw the shape and outline of Christ's body and the ideology that supposedly comes along with it.

Signifying God: Symbolic Practice

How is God signified? On the one hand God as a supernatural concept is what underwrites the entire belief system and cosmology of late medieval culture. But on the other hand it is the very impossibility of his representation that determines the way in which God as an imaginary signification might generate the creative mythologies through which that society looks at itself:

Whatever points of support his representation may take in perceived reality, whatever his rational effectiveness may be as an organizing principle of the environing world for certain cultures, God is neither a signification of something real, nor a signification of something rational. . . . God is neither the name of God nor the images a people may give him, nor anything of the sort. Carried by, pointed at by all these symbols, he is, in every religion, that which makes these symbols religious symbols—a central *signification,* the organization of signifieds and signifiers into a system. . . . And this signification which is neither something perceived (real) nor something thought (rational) is an imaginary signification.[19]

God, or God as Christ, does not actually denote anything as such, but in the very vagueness and indeterminacy of that denotation, he may connote everything.[20] The symbol may be overdetermined, then, through its very indetermination.[21] These hints from Cornelius Castoriadis and Pierre Bourdieu may help us to extend the notion of ritual practice from Mervyn James to incorporate the more precise ways in which cultural form is not so much imposed on the city of York as actually articulated by and through that city. In extending James's Durkheimian-Douglasian version of ritual into a reading of bodily practice, it will be possible, too, to overcome the dichotomy of ritual and theater that has bedeviled criticism of medieval Corpus Christi theater. Historians who have used the concept of ritual have by and large shied away from reading the pageants themselves, and critics of the theater have been constrained by the inadequate (for performative readings) tenets of formalist literary criticism. In the process we may be able to reconnect the political and aesthetic effects of the drama.

My argument is that ritual does not so much assert a set of monolithic beliefs as construct a series of tensions. As Catharine Bell has put it: "This orchestration is not a perfect and holistic order imposed on minds and bodies but a delicate and continual renegotiation of provisional distinctions and integrations so as to avoid encountering in practice the discrepancies and conflicts that would become so apparent if the whole was obvious."[22] This view further implies that ritual does not so much designate an object as a process of relation. As Bourdieu says: "Ritual practice, which aims to facilitate passages and/or to authorize encounters between opposed orders, never defines beings or things otherwise than in and through the relationship it establishes practically between them, and makes the fullest possible use of the polysemy of the fundamental actions."[23] In such an understanding of ritual practice no objective meanings can be assigned independently of material processes, and such meaning restores the practical moments of human agency that James's model of ritual has found it hard to locate. Space, which is perhaps too simplistically conceived by James as the tabula rasa of the procession, comes to have meaning through practice itself.[24]

Integration through Division

The theoretical inflections of Bell and Bourdieu are not necessarily in complete opposition to the Durkheimian approach pioneered by James. Durkheim, for example, tends to use "sacred" as an adjective, not as a noun.[25] For him the sacred is arguably a situational rather than a substantive category: "Sacred and profane are transitive categories; they serve as maps and labels, not substances; they are distinctions of office, indices of difference."[26] Such an understanding is not just one that is offered by contemporary theorists of ritual; it is also built into articulations of ritual practice in the late Middle Ages itself. Take, for example, an anonymous sermon on Corpus Christi that constructs itself quite conventionally around a scriptural text, gloss, and a series of exempla.[27] The text, "Whosoever eats my flesh and drinks my blood, will dwell in me and I in him. And therefore I will go to the place from which I came," is first translated from the Latin and then linked with the text from 1 Corinthians 11:29: "For he that eateth and drinketh unworthily, eateth and drinketh damnation to himself, not discerning the Lord's body." Then follow a series of exempla designed to make the point that the mass is not an empty rite, and the host not an object whose magic is preexistent. Its capacities for transformation depend upon the way it is approached, and such an approach requires preparation. The parable concerns a woman who goes to mass out of charity in hatred of a poor neighbor. At the mass, her priest says he will withold her "ryghtes" unless she forgives her neighbor and reconciles herself with her. She does this, but out of "shame of the world" rather than "awe of God." When after the service her hated neighbor comes to her house and she admits that she forgave only with her mouth and not with her heart, "the devil strangles her even there." The host will not magically resolve discord or disharmony. Its properties, of course, lie in the structures of relation that are established between the ritual participant and the ritual object. Although transformative powers might be ascribed to the little host itself, they operate according to a mutual, and mutually structuring, relation. It was such a relation that was subject, as here, to clerical definition and attempts at control. The ritual object is then not magically or ontologically efficacious. Bell, developing a theory of ritual practice informed by both Bourdieu and Foucault, argues for an understanding of ritual different from that developed by James, one that will see it as a practice whose self-differentiation is an intrinsic part of its efficacy. Ritualization will, according to her reading, involve the establishment of a privileged contrast, loosely homologized to suggest but never define solutions. In this way, sacred and profane (never in any case ontological referents for Durkheim) are produced through the very performance of their differentiation. So, in the York Corpus Christi plays, the body of Christ, the sacrament that is the ritual object par excellence, does not simply operate according to a static binary opposition: divinity versus humanity. Rather it catches in its network of association a range of oppositions that, because they are mutually constructed through the way the body of Christ conflates them, nuance, add to, and so defer any final signification. Christ's body alludes to numerous oppositions: inner and outer, transcendent and immanent, spirit and flesh, male and female, left and right, up and down, noisy and silent, just and unjust, passive and active, noumenal and phenomenal, public and private, hierarchical and collective, unified and multiplicitous, transcendent and immanent, and so on.[28] Each set of terms invokes the others; they imply a loose coherence, but this is actually constituted by a "redundant, circular and rhetorical universe of values and terms whose significance keeps flowing into other values and terms."[29] Each set of categories transcodes and refers to the others, and meaning is constructed and deferred through those interrelationships. There is no definitive statement, then, nothing that may be subject to assent and denial. Integration is established paradoxically through division, and ambiguity is essential to ritual's efficacy. When the centurion comes rushing in to explain to his overlords the miracle of Longinus's regained sight, for example, he declares that it is a "misty thing to mene."[30] His words refer us back to that pageant where the unequivocal truths of the revelation of God in Christ have been asserted:

> O wondirfull werkar iwis,
> þis weedir is waxen full wan
> Trewe token I trowe þat it is
> þat mercy is mente unto man.[31]

Yet when we hear him again in the Resurrection pageant, the full complexity of the word "mene" becomes marked. For it carries the double significance of meaning, intention, and intermediary, and the very mistiness of the communication here is not an isolated incident in the resurrection sequences but a central part of their ritual efficacy. It is as if the centurion's role is reflexively marked here to acknowledge not merely that he is an intermediary, but that to mean something, to intend a meaning, is necessarily to have to go through the vagaries of representation, of mediation. What is meant needs to be meant by someone and understood by someone, and the complexities, difficulties, and frustrations of this "meaning" complicate greatly any simple act of witnessing that had seemed so simple in the "trew token of truth" asserted in the "Death of Christ" pageant. The other latent meaning of "mene" is doubt (surely contextually agitated here), and it is through the exploration of doubt and disbelief, of the difficulty of understanding, that a complex relation with the ritual object is established, and this, rather than the simple communication of the doctrine of the resurrection, is precisely the point of the extended sequence that contemplates the repetitive return of the wounded yet ascended body. We understand the body of Christ through the relation developed with it by Mary, Mary Magdalene, Thomas, the pilgrims at Emmaus, and the other disciples. It is through the changed relation that the new identities are reformed. The continuous and agonizing return of Christ's bleeding body in these sequences, then, is not just the return of the incontrovertible proof of the central doctrine that underscores the medieval sacramental system,[32] but the insistence on its central cultural contradiction.[33] In the Death of Christ pageant we are shown the central miracle that is the very axis of the play cycle: the regained sight that shows that we, too, can see that Christ is the sign of God. But it is neither the cognitive statement of belief that we are meant to understand by the time the play is over, nor the mindlessly ritualized incantation that through its sheer repetition and formalization will eventually manage to succeed in incorporating all in its ecstatic embrace.[34] The plays as a whole consciously encode an argument about the relation of cognition to incorporation, and we need a model of ritual able to read the complexity of such interactions.[35]

City as Theater: Actor and Space

In these sequences the body as the bearer of social and cultural meaning is absolutely central, not just because the pageants intimately concern a theology of incarnation and embodiment, but also because in theater, it is the very body of the actor that becomes the chief vehicle of semiosis. If, as Robert Weimann has stated, "to explore [the] connections between the technical arrangements and the unformulated intellectual assumptions of the medieval theater is to find that there is no such thing as a unified or homogeneous concept of a stage,"[36] then that stage was in fact articulated into being at the very moment when an actor assumed a role in the streets of York. Given that the acting area had no inherent symbolic significance, the "tension between fictive locality and public space"[37] is called into being through the very body of the actor. Although the pageants are concerned with mapping the body in many overdetermined ways, surprisingly there has been almost no attempt to develop a systematic understanding of the kinds of bodily inscription involved in the Corpus Christi pageants, or of the implications of such an account for an investigation of the interrelations of ideology, religion, and corporeal identity. What is learned by the body is not (as Bourdieu has reminded us) what one has, but what one is.[38] Incorporating practices such as theater and ritual are powerful means of articulating the reproduction of the social order in habit-memory, in the innocent injunctions of the body's choreography. It is because the body somaticizes culture,[39] because the

70

world is affectively as well as semantically structured[40] in powerful—because mute—ways, that "every group trusts to bodily automatisms the values and categories which they are most anxious to conserve."[41]

In addition, this is a processional theater whose very stage (or series of stages) is the city of York itself.[42] The topography of the city is spatially reorganized through the mutual restructuring of body and environment involved in this performative inscription. The route, for example, and so the shape of the city and the body that is mutually implicated was subject to argument, which had a direct bearing on who was able to control and profit from the ritual forum intended to encompass all its citizens. In 1399, the commons presented a petition to determine where the stations of performance were to be located. It requested that the stations be positioned at the doors of the important civic officials as well as at other more obviously public places.[43] In 1417, at a meeting described as the most representative meeting of the community that the Memorandum book has registered, the populace complained about the profit being made by those before whose houses the plays were performed:

> Seeing that everyone according to his condition bears his burden in the maintenance of the said play, it was unanimously ordained that for the benefit of the community the places for playing of the aforesaid play shall be altered, unless those, before whose houses it was formerly played, shall pay to the community some fixed sum in return for their own individual advantage, which they thus receive each year. And that in all subsequent years as long as that play shall happen to be played, it shall be played before the doors and houses of those who are willing to pay most richly and well to the chamber, and to do most for the benefit of the whole community for the sake of having the play in the same place—not showing any favour to any person for any individual advantage, but only what is held to be the public welfare of the whole commons of York.[44]

The very shape and timing and positioning of the performance of the Corpus Christi pageants, then, were subject to local bargaining in which the interests of private property and profit competed with the interests (of) "tocius communitatis." The rhetorical conversion of individual profit to public-spirited generosity is a fascinating sleight-of-hand here and merits further consideration. For Charles Phythian Adams, this is the demonstration of his dictum that "ceremony completed the transformation of wealth ownership into class standing for the upper levels of society."[45] But there may be more ramifications to such arguments than the principle of increasing ceremonial presence. The subtext of the 1417 meeting is the appropriation and definition of civic space as private property against a competing definition of common use. It seems that the scaffolds erected before the houses of the eminent, in front of which some

71

of the stations were to be located, functioned virtually as private theaters in the public city space for which those who could afford it might
pay:

> Nevertheless, the mayor, the honourable men, and the whole said
> commons, by their unanimous consent and assent, order [that] all
> those who receive money for scaffolds which they may build in the
> foresaid places before their doors on public property at the afore-
> said sites from those sitting on them shall pay the third penny of
> the money so received to the chamberlains of the city to be applied
> to the use of the said commons.[46]

The scaffolding that the householders erected rested, it was pointed out,
on city property, and so the city should profit. It is a veiled protest against
the conversion of communal drama into private entertainment and is
emblematic of wider contests in which the body of Christ was challenged
to assume its universalizing, common, and generous invitation. In his
analysis of the York Corpus Christi cycle as ritual, Richard Homans
uses this incident as an indication of the "common interest prevailing
over the interest of the few," a representation that ignores the rhetorical
conversion of "individual advantage" into "public welfare," through the
power of property and payment. Wealthy householders, through paying
money to the city, could literally inscribe their own property into the
very inscription of the route of the Corpus Christi pageants, because their
houses were part of the processional staging of the cycle. The twenty-
five surviving station lists between 1399 and 1569 indicate how this inscription was regularly invoked and exploited by incumbent mayors and
the aldermanic elite of the city.[47] For Homans, following James, this is
an instance of "the Corpus Christi cycle's function as an arena in which
actual conflicts could be ritually resolved."[48]

Such arguments require a more supple and flexible way of being able
to conceive of the ritual and theatrical carving up of space in York than
is currently on offer. They require of us the difficult task of thinking of
the boundaries they delineate, in Georg Simmel's terms, as less a "spatial
fact with sociological consequences" than a "sociological fact that is
conceived spatially."[49]

The 1417 memorandum, for example, invokes the public utility of
the whole commons, and yet through converting their wealth into their
generosity, the rhetoric of the passage allows the maintenance of what
are effectively private theaters within the public space of the city.[50] They
function as private theaters in that what they display is the illustrious
houses that then become the backdrop of the theater. These are the
points that at least for the day define the shape of Corpus Christi, but
because the space itself is rented from the city council by the private

owners, who are making money by renting out seats on scaffolds erected on "community ground,"[51] it is riven with contradictory meanings. The space itself carries no essential meaning; it comes into being through the complex relation and actions of the ritual and theatrical practices through which it is enacted. The metaphor of the city as stage has been invoked before,[52] but here I wish to say that we need to see in more concrete terms how the densely significant social space of the city and its topography can figure as part of the polysemousness of the theater.

By 1394, the route of the Corpus Christi play seems already to have been established.[53] The contest over space and who was to control it can already perhaps be seen in the wording of the decree requesting that the pageants be played in their assigned stations and not at any others, and that there be a fine if that decree were infringed.[54] Over the years the stations changed in number and position, and it would certainly be interesting to establish a more concrete sense of the meanings of those changes. Here I wish merely to establish how the city as stage might help us to conceptualize the kind of theater this is, how it might contribute to that sense of the sheer overdetermination that we have established as being central to the ideological mechanisms of this play's workings. Anna Mill and Meg Twycross have mapped out the location of the stations in some detail. From their work we can establish — if we take, for example, some of the earliest records, those of 1398–99, as exemplary — that the Corpus Christi pageants first collected on Toft Green outside of the city gates, and then passed through the following stations: Holy Trinity Gates at Micklegate, the house of Robert Harpham, the house of John Gysburn, the end of Skeldergate and the end of Northstreet, the Castlegate end of Coney Street, the end of Jubbergate, the house of Henry Wyman, Coney Street, near the Common Hall at the end of Coney Street, the house of Adam del Brigg in Stonegate, the Minster gates, the end of Girdlergate at Petergate, and finally the Pavement. What is the (necessarily changing) significance of some of these sites? First of all we might say that the territory of the city itself (before any pageant, actor, or procession transforms it) was already hardly a single area of franchise. As E. Miller has said, "It was honeycombed with other franchises, some of them older than the liberty of the city."[55] One of the stations outside the Minster gates represents the edges of one of these liberties, at which, for example, the dean could hold a court for all transgressions "in the land of the court both within and without the city."[56] The Minster gates then represent an area where the city's authority could not extend. The territorial marking of one of the stations at the gates of a minster that was itself not involved in the Corpus Christi procession[57] represented at once an enclosure of mayoral jurisdiction and a breach into the jurisdiction of the minster. It could thereby be a physical reminder that this interlacing of privilege and exemption, which as Miller says, "early manifested itself in disputes over the claim of the privileged churches that their property was exempt from the common burdens," was an irritant, sometimes erupting into a violent conflict.[58]

Obviously there is some sense, then, in which the Corpus Christi pageants may be seen to be marking territory in the same way in which boundaries were "ridden." The ridings of the citizens and the mayor, for example, were requested by the citizens in 1465 "for that we may know our liberties and lose no part of our right that is due to the city."[59] These ridings did take place frequently (although not with annual regularity)[60] and were only stopped in 1830, because at this point enclosure, outright extinction of common rights, as well as replacement by strays whose "boundaries were precisely known" and mapped, made the perambulations "unnecessary." The Corpus Christi procession and pageants may then have a similar understanding of the marking of space as the beating the bounds ceremonies performed during "rogation days" about three weeks before Corpus Christi in the liturgical calendar. The task of the rogation days was to ratify boundaries, but they too display the ambivalence of festival in that they also offered the community license to transgress those boundaries.[61] The rogation processions designate the common rights of the city; through priestly blessing they are sanctified; through the beating of the bounds they are inscribed in the physical memory of the processioners. E. P. Thompson describes a late rogation procession in which "small boys were sometimes ducked in the ditch or given a clout to imprint the spot upon their memories."[62] The rogations designated the city as a political corporation with rights and responsibilities before the common law.[63] Thompson describes rogation processions as examples of the contested nature of custom at the interface between law and agrarian practice. Custom, as Thompson in his pathbreaking examination shows, is at one extreme "sharply defined and enforceable at law, and (as at enclosure) . . . a property."[64] But it also depended on the "continual renewal of oral tradition, as in the regular perambulation of the bounds of the parish," and as such it passes into more blurred areas: "unwritten beliefs, sociological norms, and usages asserted in practice but never enrolled in any by-law."[65] Rogation ceremonies plotted out space, then, in such a way as to "imprint its topography on the popular memory."[66] It becomes indeed, historically, the very site of competing definitions of space as property as against use, away from a broadly feudal notion of custom as reciprocal obligation to a reification of usages into properties.[67] For "beating the bounds" conventionally signified at once a ritualization of space and a consecration of property.[68] When the 1547 Royal Injunctions curtailed many of the religious processions associated with "popery," the rogation perambulation was retained. In 1559, Bishop Grindal refined the procession still further: it was to be carried out by the curate and "substantial men of the parish boundaries."[69] Grindal thus redefined the procession as a "perambulation" and restricted it to property holders.[70] In this reading, ceremony is not simply the confirmation or revelation of a preconceived holism, but rather a place of "unqualified class conflict."[71] In York, the ceremonial ridings of the sheriffs are, after 1537, associated with the Corpus Christi productions.[72] Persistent attention is paid in the records of the city to the way in which disputes over the "commons" become an important theme of civic politics.[73] Miller documents the incidents of arguments between the citizens and Lord Lovell in 1479, between the citizens and Saint Mary's Abbey in 1480, and between Saint Nicholas Hospital and the commons in 1484, which erupted into riot in October of that year.[74] The city authorities tried to avoid disputes by seeking recognition of the citizens' common rights. Such "recognition" often took the form of an annual rent to substitute for the use of common rights, as for example when the vicars choral agreed to pay rent to the city to "extinguish the common rights" over commonage in the Vicars Leas.[75] The weavers protested again in the form of riot and took down the hedges surrounding the disputed land.[76]

The debate about the stations of the city may be seen then as part of an endemic and long-standing argument over physical space, in which it was the literal ground of competing definitions, at once of possession and usage.[77] We need to develop a way of reading these plays and festivities, then, not as the reflection of a homogeneous collective understanding that will reveal the very principles of a social structure,[78] but in ways that make their spatial configurations, as they extend in time as well as space, a dynamic and component part of their articulation. If, as David Harvey says, space is a "source of social power,"[79] then its homogeneity can only be achieved through its total "pulverization and fragmentation into freely alienable parcels of private property, to be bought and traded at will on the market."[80] Festival, which insists on visibility, on publicity, makes claims on space in altogether different ways.[81]

The York Corpus Christi festivities reconfigure space, then; they argue over it in many ways. But we also need to be able to see how such reconfigurations will interact with a city that organizes its division of labor, its social polarities, in visible because spatial ways.

Generally speaking we can talk about a concentration of the larger and bigger households with the greater retinues of servants in the central prosperous districts of York, while many poor districts contained houses with only one member (frequently female), to be found in the poorer suburban districts.[82] In addition, as P. J. P. Goldberg points out elsewhere, by about 1450–1500 the commercial sector, comprising the mercers and drapers who clustered in Fossgate and the parishes of Saint Crux and All Saints, shrinks and appears to become more closely defined.[83] This may well be a topographical enactment of an increasingly wide gap between the artisanate and the mercantile oligarchy, which (I have argued elsewhere) it may have been part of the very purpose of the

Corpus Christi celebrations to enact.[84] Here it may be significant that as the commercial sector appears to shrink in the actual physical space it takes up in the city, it extends its command over ceremonial space. Anna Mill's figures indicate that as the stations take in spectacularly less rent in the sixteenth century, there appear to be more and more "freeplaces" commandeered for the use of officials and dignitaries.[85]

In any case, trades may well have been associated with certain specific sites that they filled with their wares, the physical tools of their trade, and the symbolic values that attached to them: the metal trades were to be found, for example, in Petergate and Coney Street, the drapers in Ousegate and Jubbergate, and the butchers were in the Shambles near the Pavement and had their own hall.[86]

But there were other ways in which the material space of York must have set up interesting interactions as the pageants rolled by the different temporary stages of their procession. As they passed the Castlegate end of Coney Street they may have passed the prisons;[87] as they came onto the Pavement that space would have signifed the central marketplace of York, where not merely goods but people were traded since servants had to collect to sell themselves there to new masters;[88] it was the place, too, where proclamations were made and punishments enacted. What significance would the Last Judgment have if it were performed in such a place? Would it be different from the performance, say, of the Crucifixion or of the various jurisdictions, especially of the secular ones, that tried Christ in the plays? Would the differing versions of justice indict or underwrite (more likely both) the mayoral administration? What about when they were performed before the house of that mayor himself, John Gysburn? Gysburn was chased out of the city in 1381 by rioters who subsequently broke into the guildhall and swore in Simon Quixley as mayor.[89] Quixley and Gysburn were both rich merchants, but it seemed that Quixley had the support of the nonmercantile crafts.[90] The dispute was described as one between Gysburn and the "communitas."[91] When Gysburn had the pageants performing outside his door he was claiming space in the city, although the way that space would be interpreted, as his house became part of the theater, would never be subject to his interpretive control.

If we see and continue to devise ways of seeing the sheer ambiguous density of the interaction between city and theater as each transformed the other in the production of the York Corpus Christi cycle, then we will also see that the ritualization of the city is not about the imposition of a homogeneous kind of unity onto the city but rather an implication of its webs of signification. The politics we need to talk about, then, will not be those of dominance and subversion or resistance and containment, but rather the politics of mobility and access.[92]

The stage provided by the city of York was not the bounded, contained place that we have been used to thinking about; indeed, it would be hard to think of a theatrical space that is as polysemous as York's. But as I suggested earlier, it is not the essential meaning of the spaces themselves so much as the uses to which they are put, their construction through agency, that enhances still further our understanding of the multiple dimensions of meaning that they can inhabit. In the Corpus Christi pageants, overdetermination is the principle of the acting, as well. There may be as many as thirty different actors playing, for example, Christ, as many as thirty playing Mary, and several different Gods. In each instance the identity of the performer, the actor, the persona, and the way it might be crafted in the individual pageant may all play against each other. And there is no determining the relation of the pageants to one another. It is hard to imagine that the order of the pageants would in any sense be the order in which any spectator might want to observe them. The possibilities of perspective, of interrelationship, are at once bewildering and exhilarating.

One of the ways that the pageants work, then, is not so much through an assertion of doctrine or belief, but through the central manipulation of the symbol of Christ's body in ritualized performances. Such a structure helps to avoid those problematic areas that occur where awkwardnesses of doctrine are particularly foregrounded—such as the Purification pageant, where Mary, purest of the pure, untainted by the normal carnal sin attendant upon giving birth, must still be ritually purified, or the Baptism pageant, where Jesus (to the evident surprise of John the Baptist) must be baptized.[93] The paradox here is that the very foundation and legitimation of Christ's Church on earth, Jesus himself, has to participate in the ritual structures that he supposedly actually instituted. The text registers this awkwardness, and it is not of course a problem that can be logically resolved at the level of belief, a problem that the cycle itself implicitly acknowledges in the Harrowing of Hell pageant. In response to Satan's subtle poking at the contradictions of the dispensation of mercy and the existence of hell, Christ reponds quite unequivocally that it is not simply virtue, but allegiance and love, belief in his law, that is important to the attempt to stay out of hell: "Who will noght trowe, þei are noght trewe."[94] The plays themselves cannot altogether avoid the problem of belief, for they are after all partially concerned with commanding assent to those beliefs. However, theological readings of the plays that perceive them as sermons in drama have no account of their symbolic working, for in such a view they merely encode simple messages whose "truths" will be passively absorbed by their audiences.

One can, after all, speak only symbolically about Christ. If the symbolizing process involves a movement across a classificatory system, thus problematizing a region where language intersects with the world, a symbol may call both the describing language and the world into question. That is why the symbolic utterances that circulate around the symbol of Christ's body are the very densest sites of signification. It is because that symbol violates the classificatory lines of the system (and therefore the order upheld through those divisions and definitions) that contests for new configurations of meaning obsessively locate themselves here. But it is for this reason, too, that violent hierarchies may be reinscribed, just as symbolic utterances paradoxically, through the very act of boundary crossing, reveal the lines of the system in the very act of rudely violating them.[95]

An interpretative practice, I have tried to suggest, based on a concept of ritualization rather than either ritual or doctrine and belief might begin to understand and plumb the symbolic resources of the bodily symbol at the center of this drama and so help to articulate both its affective reach and its relation to structures of domination (for the real power of a dominant model is "its ability to produce and reproduce itself, continually to impose the principles of the construction of reality.")[96] But it would not be sufficient to understand such a symbol through a set of cognitively understood binary oppositions; rather, these oppositions need to be seen as being articulated in and through the space that is actually only produced through social, that is bodily, practice.[97] Such bodily practices are at once subject to diachrony and to intense theatricalization—to the simultaneity of production and communication rendered possible by performance.[98]

Such a reading might finally be able to begin to understand the defining religiosity of the Corpus Christi cycles. For we cannot, as in the discourse of rationalism, await some anticipation of an unambiguous set of symbols; rather, that ambiguity is central to the social mechanisms of Corpus Christi. And if, like Merleau-Ponty, we are able to see that "religion is not a veil for some other more true meaning which is hidden beneath it, even if it helps sustain a culture that is closed and narrow compared with a possible social existence," then we will see that religion is neither reducible to the orthodox doctrine "expressed" in these plays nor simply false consciousness.[99] It does not finally constitute a doctrine to be transmitted, but a world of significance to be explored.

Notes

This chapter is part of a larger study in progress on the cultural history of the York Corpus Christi cycle; the current working title is "Signifying God: Symbolic Act and Social Relation in York and the York Corpus Christi Plays." I would like to thank my interlocutors at the History, Body, Identity Conference held in March 1993 at the University of Pittsburgh and the participants of the Intersections: Fifteenth-Century Literature and History Conference at the University of Minnesota in April 1993, who heard versions of this essay that they helped to improve. I also benefited from stimulating discussions with audiences at Harvard University, the Literature Program at Duke, the University of North Carolina at Greensboro, and the University of Virginia. Finally I would like to thank David Wallace, for his meticulousness and his encouragement as editor.

1. Dorinda Outram, *The Body and the French Revolution* (New Haven, Conn.: Yale University Press, 1989), p. 1.

2. Alexandra Johnston, in "The Continental Connection: A Reconsideration," a paper presented at a conference entitled The Stage as Mirror: Civic Theater in Late Medieval Europe held at Penn State in March 1993, reminds us that we need to think in terms of discrete passion and resurrection sequences rather than the full cycle, for the recent records indicate that this was in fact the most common mode of production in England as a whole.

3. Richard Beadle, ed. *The York Plays* (London: Edward Arnold, 1982), p. 371.

4. These questions are the ones used by Cornelius Castoriadis to describe the necessary "social imaginary" through which any society is instituted. See *The Imaginary Institution of Society*, trans. Kathleen Blamey (Cambridge, Mass.: MIT Press, 1987), pp. 146–47.

5. Thomas Aquinas, "Commentary on Aristotle's Politics," in *Medieval Political Theory — A Reader: The Quest for the Body Politic, 1100–1400*, ed. Cary Nederman and Kate Langdon Forhan (London: Routledge, 1993), p. 137.

6. Mervyn James, "Ritual, Drama and Social Body in the Late Medieval Town," *Past and Present* 98 (1983): 3–29.

7. James specifically cites Mary Douglas, *Natural Symbols: Explorations in Cosmology* (Harmondsworth, England: Penguin, 1973), on p. 6 of his article.

8. Sometimes it must be said that the subtle and dynamic complexity of James's article is reduced in its reproduction. See, for example, Eamon Duffy's recent invocation of James to underwrite his location of "traditional religion" in the late Middle Ages: "Mervyn James has written eloquently of the way in which the Corpus Christi procession in late medieval communities 'became the point of reference to which the structure of precedence and authority in the town is made visually present.' This was the 'social miracle,' the sacramental embodiment of social reality," (*The Stripping of the Altars: Traditional Religion in England c.1400–c.1580* [New Haven, Conn.: Yale University Press, 1992], p. 11). It is possible to see in this sentence the swift move from "late medieval communities" to, in James's words, "the structure of precedence and authority in the town," to Duffy's "social reality" itself. In the process there is a quite characteristic erasure of any understanding of the mechanisms of representation by which the part has come to stand for the whole.

9. See also Charles Phythian Adams's pioneering discussion of ceremony in the "life-cycle" of the Coventry citizen, "Ceremony and the Citizen: The Communal Year at Coventry, 1450–1550," in *Crisis and Order in English Towns, 1500–1700*, ed. Peter Clark and Paul Slack (London: Routledge, 1972), p. 106, where the "fit" that functionalism describes between social structure and expressive form is elucidated: "This exploratory analysis will seek first to demonstrate some simple congruities between Coventry's late medieval social structure (that relatively enduring but adaptable framework of institutionalized positions and connective relationships) and its ceremonial or ritualized expression in action, in time — with respect to the local calendar — and on the ground." In the process Phythian Adams explains that in his examination of the "perennial" customs of Coventry from 1450 to 1550, "known structural modifications ... have to be sacrificed at the altar of brevity." But given Phythian Adams's dense and pioneering analysis and the development in book-length form of the role of ceremony in Coventry, it is, I would say, the altar of synchrony, rather than brevity, that underlies the principle of omission. Phythian Adams has recently reconceptualized some of the problems of the very versions of community and locality of which he was such an eloquent exponent in his *Rethinking English Local History* (Leicester: Leicester University Press, 1987). See especially p. 25, where he discusses the difficulty of the relation between function and structure in the local historian's designation of the object of study: "Having defined a territory and then having discovered a community within it, the danger is that he will relate the community once again to the territory."

10. For a recent wide-ranging and interesting discussion of one possible way of conceiving the interrelation between ritual and theater, see Anthony Gash, "Carnival and the Poetics of Reversal," in *New Directions in Theatre*, ed. Julian Hilton (New York: St. Martin's Press, 1993), p. 93: "The doubleness which is only embryonic in ritual becomes the

basis of theatre, where every coronation, marriage or trial is, by definition, a mock-coronation, mock-marriage or mock-trial." Gash criticizes both Barber's understanding of "festive comedy" and Donaldson's understanding of "the world upside down," as well as more recent New Historicist understandings of "staging carnival," for an insufficient observation of the distinctions between ritual and theater. Gash develops a poetics of reversal from a nuanced reading of Mikhail Bakhtin, William Empson, and Arthur Rossiter.

11. The reference to the "phenomenological dichotomy" of the actor's body is from John Harrop, *Acting* (London: Routledge, 1992), p. 80.

12. Neither Mervyn James nor Richard Homans look at the possibilities of staging or at the version of the pageants that we have in the Register (the civic document, property of the corporation, British Library, Add. MS 35290). This is a constitutive, structural omission, rather than an accident or oversight. Their models of ritual simply cannot read theatrical practices, because those practices complicate functionalism's understanding of social orders as social systems. For James, "this structure projected the nature of the society whose world view it expressed" ("Ritual, Drama," p. 16). Where James talks about the play cycle, he uses it to distinguish that part of the festivity from the more rigid and hierarchical principles at work in the procession. The argument is that the "temporal mutation" within the urban body could work itself out through the more fluid medium of the play cycle as a "necessary complement to the Corpus Christi procession, which defined the static order prevailing in the urban world" (p. 18). James is quite clear, then, that the play cycle, as the means of registering change, "provided a mechanism by means of which status, and the honour which went with status, could be distributed and redistributed with a minimum of conflict resulting." The play cycle is the vehicle of diachrony precisely so that the procession itself can reveal "the static order prevailing in the urban world" (p. 18). But it is only by conceptually separating the synchronic from the diachronic that such an "order" can be analytically understood. It is temporal change itself that is the price James's model pays for its location of order.

13. See Catharine Bell, "Discourse and Dichotomies: The Structure of Ritual Theory," *Religion* 17 (1987): 97–98. For the famous and founding Durkheimian distinction between belief and rite, see Emile Durkheim, *The Elementary Forms of the Religious Life*, trans. Joseph Ward Swain (New York: Free Press, 1965), p. 51.

14. I have analyzed the social and political divisions not so much resolved as actually effected by the production of the Corpus Christi plays in "Making the World in York and the York Corpus Christi Cycle," in *Framing Medieval Bodies*, ed. Sarah Kay and Miri Rubin (Manchester: Manchester University Press, 1994).

15. See Lynn Hunt, "The Sacred and the French Revolution," in *Durkheimian Sociology: Cultural Studies*, ed. Jeffrey C. Alexander (Cambridge: Cambridge University Press, 1988), p. 27. Douglas's inability to conceptualize the nature of the interactions between the body and society is, however, more notorious among anthropologists than it has appeared to be among literary critics. See, for example, Jean and John Comaroff, "Bodily Reform as Historical Practice," in *Ethnography and the Historical Imagination* (Boulder, Colo.: Westview Press, 1992), p. 79. For an inspired reexamination of Douglas's central paradigm, see Peter Stallybrass and Allon White, *The Politics and Poetics of Transgression* (London: Methuen, 1986).

16. It is possible that there is some degree of reflexivity here about the pursuit of a preordained script. Such self-consciousness may be particularly acute at those moments of transition from "old" to "new"; see especially *The Annunciation and the Visitation, The Purification*, and *Christ and the Doctors*, in *York Plays*, ed. Beadle, pp. 110–17, 149–60, 174–81. The commitment of the play texts to the Register and the "keeping" of the Register are very much in the interests of oligarchic control against extempore performance and traditions of improvisation.

17. See Alexandra Johnston, "The York Corpus Christi Play: A Dramatic Structure Based on Performance Practice," in *Theatre in the Middle Ages*, ed. Herman Braet, Johan Nove, Gilbert Tournoy (Leuven, Belgium: Leuven University Press, 1985), p. 372, where

she describes the way the Entry into Jerusalem pageant is modeled along the lines of a royal entry.

18. Durkheim, *Elementary Forms*, p. 94.

19. Castoriadis, *Imaginary Institution*, p. 140. For Castoriadis's refutation of the adequacy of functionalism, see pp. 119, 124, 130, 136. See especially p. 122: "A functionalist may consider it self-evident that, when a society provides itself with an institution, it gives itself at the same time, as something it can grasp, all the symbolical and rational relations that this institution carries or produces—or at any rate, that there can be no contradiction, no incoherence between the functional 'ends' of the institution and the effects of its actual functioning, that whenever a rule is set down, the coherence of each of its innumerable consequences with the set of all the other previously existing rules and with the ends that are consciously or 'objectively' sought is guaranteed." Castoriadis's words quoted in the text may be read as an extended gloss on Durkheim's statement, "God is only a figurative expression of the society" (*Elementary Forms of Religious Life* [London: Allen and Unwin, 1915], p. 226), taking that statement in an uncharacteristically (for the Durkheiminan tradition) nonfunctionalist direction.

20. Castoriadis, *Imaginary Institution*, p. 138. See also Kenneth Burke, *The Rhetoric of Religion* (Boston: Beacon Press, 1961), p. 15, for the necessary link between indeterminacy, polysemousness, and the simultaneous foundation and antifoundation established through "God" in the symbolic system: "Since 'God' by definition transcends all symbol systems, we must begin, like theology, by noting that language is intrinsically unfitted to discuss the 'supernatural' literally. For language is empirically confined to terms referring to physical nature, terms referring to socio-political relationships and terms describing language itself. Hence all words for 'God' must be used analogically—as were we to speak of God's 'powerful arm' (a physical analogy), or of God as 'lord.' "

21. Pierre Bourdieu, *Outline of a Theory of Practice*, trans. Richard Nice (Cambridge: Cambridge University Press, 1977), p. 110.

22. Catharine Bell, *Ritual Theory, Ritual Practice* (Oxford: Oxford University Press, 1992), p. 125. The influence of this work on the formulations I am making here is pervasive.

23. Bourdieu, *Outline of a Theory of Practice*, p. 120.

24. See Henrietta Moore's use of Bourdieu in *Space, Text and Gender: An Anthropological Study of the Marakwet of Kenya* (Cambridge: Cambridge University Press: 1986), p. 77.

25. See William Paden, "Before the 'Sacred' Became Theological: Rereading the Durkheimian Legacy," *Method and Theory in the Study of Religion* 3, no. 1 (1991): 11, 14, 17. See also Durkheim's analysis of the "churinga" in *Elementary Forms* (p. 141) and Jonathan Z. Smith's comments on these passages in his book, *To Take Place: Toward Theory in Ritual* (Chicago: University of Chicago Press, 1987), pp. 106–7.

26. Smith, *To Take Place*, p. 105.

27. The sermon is from MS Royal 18 B. 23 and is printed in *Middle English Sermons*, ed. Woodburn O. Ross, Early English Text Society (EETS), o.s. 209 (London: Humphrey Milford, 1940), pp. 61–69.

28. These binary oppositions are not cognitively understood schemata but are learned through the bodily practice through which that space comes to have meaning in the first place.

29. Bell, *Ritual Theory, Ritual Practice*. See also Bourdieu, *Outline of a Theory of Practice*, p. 120.

30. Beadle, *York Plays*, p. 345.

31. Ibid., p. 330. The rest of the passage is worth quoting in full: "Full clerly consayue þus I can / No cause in þis corse couthe þei knowe, / Yitt doulfull þei demyd hym þan / To lose þus his liffe be þer lawe, / No rigte. / Trewly I saie / Goddis sone verraye / Was he þis daye, / þat doulfully to dede þus is digt."

32. What possible kind of proof does this constitute in theater's simulation of miracle, in any case?

81

33. See Burke, *Rhetoric of Religion*, p. 2: "For regardless of whether the entity named 'God' exists outside his nature sheerly as key term in a system of terms, words 'about him' must reveal their nature as words."

34. By far the most sophisticated, imaginative, and compelling version of ritual as formalized repetition is articulated in Maurice Bloch, *Ritual, History and Power: Selected Papers in Anthropology* (London: Athlone, 1989). His version of ritual restricts its usage as a "special strategy" of "traditional authority" (p. 45). The literature on ritual is now vast. For a preliminary survey that usefully reviews "the turn to history" and the questions it has raised for anthropology, see John Kelly and Martha Kaplan, "History, Structure and Ritual," *Annual Review of Anthropology* 19 (1990): 119–50.

35. One would have to think at length about the significance of the commitment of the "originals" to text in the Register, and of the tensions around extempore performance frequently expressed in the records of performance, to explore this more fully. I wish to stress here, though, that the Durkheimian model of ritual as expounded in James has not much room for such examinations.

36. Robert Weimann, *Shakespeare and the Popular Tradition in the Theatre* (Baltimore, Md.: Johns Hopkins University Press, 1978), p. 77.

37. Ibid., p. 80.

38. Bourdieu, *Outline of a Theory of Practice*, p. 73.

39. Peter McLaren, "On Ideology and Education: Critical Pedagogy and the Politics of Empowerment," *Social Text* 9, no. 20 (Fall 1988): 175 ff.

40. Lawrence Grossberg, "Teaching the Popular," in *Theory in the Classroom*, ed. Cary Nelson (Urbana: University of Illinois Press, 1986), cited in McLaren, "On Ideology and Education," p. 175.

41. Paul Connerton, *How Societies Remember* (Cambridge: Cambridge University Press, 1989), p. 102. He goes on to say, "They will know how well the past can be kept in mind by habitual memory sedimented in the body."

42. The most concerted and developed attempt to work through an analysis of the city as stage to date is the chapter on the York cycle in Martin Stevens's book, *Four Middle English Mystery Cycles: Textual, Contextual and Critical Interpretations* (Princeton, N.J.: Princeton University Press, 1987), pp. 17–87.

43. *Records of Early English Drama: York*, 2 vols., ed. Alexandra Johnston and Margaret Rogerson (Toronto: Toronto University Press, 1979), pp. 11–12, and translation, pp. 697–98 (hereafter cited as *REED: York*). For a detailed examination of the stations of the York Corpus Christi play over the course of its performance, see Anna J. Mill, "The Stations of the York Corpus Christi Play," *Yorkshire Archaeological Journal* 37 (1948–51): 492–502; Meg Twycross, " 'Places to Hear the Play': Pageant Stations at York, 1398–1572," *REED Newsletter* 2 (1978): 10–33; Eileen White, "Places for Hearing the Corpus Christi Play in York," *Medieval Theatre* 8, no. 2 (1986): 23–63; and White's doctoral dissertation, "People and Places: The Social and Topographical Context of Drama in York, 1554–1609" (University of Leeds, 1984). See also David Crouch's essay, "Paying to See the Play: The Stationholders on the Route of the York Corpus Christi Play in the Fifteenth Century," *Medieval English Theatre* 13 (1991): 64–111.

44. *REED: York*, p. 714; *York Memorandum Book*, vol. 125 (1388–1419), Surtees Society, (London, 1914) (hereafter cited as *YMB*), p. xlv, and in Latin, p. 64: "Cum unus quisque juxta statum suum onus sum portet pro ipso ludo sustinendo, unanimiter, igitur, ordinaverunt pro utilitate communitatis quod loca ad ludendum ludum predictum mutentur, nisi ipsi, ante quorum loca antea ludebatur, aliquod certum quid solverint communitati pro ipso comodo suo singulari sic annuatim habendo, et quod in omnibus annis sequentibus, dum ludus ille ludi contingerit, ludatur ante ostia et tenementa illorum, qui uberius et melius camere solvere et plus pro commodo tocius communitatis facere voluerint pro ludo ipso ibidem habendo, non impendendo favorem alicui persone pro aliquo commodo singulari, sed tantum quod consideretur utilitas publica tocius communitatis Ebor."

45. Charles Phythian Adams, "Ceremony and the Citizen: The Communal Year at Coventry, 1450–1550," reprinted in *The Early Modern Town*, ed. and intro. Peter Clark (London: Longman, Open University Press, 1976), p. 114.

46. *YMB*, 125:63: "Nichilominus maior, probi homines et tota communitas predicta eorum unanimi consensu et assensu ordinarunt quod omnes illi qui pro skafaldis, quas ante eorum ostia super solum communitatis edificant in locis predictis, de supersedentibus monetam recipiunt, solvant tercium denarium monete sic recepte camerariis civitas, ad usum communitatis ejusdem applicandum." I briefly discuss these issues in "Making the World," p. 267 n. 10.

47. Most of the station lists are derived from entries in the Chamberlains' Books, which give the amounts paid by householders for having the play performed before their houses (see White, "Places for Hearing," p. 48).

48. Richard Homans, "Ritual Aspects of the York Cycle" *Theatre Journal* 33 (1981): 313. See also his adjacent comments, stating that the festival of Corpus Christi must be looked at "as a microcosm of the political and economic structure of the town in which economic inequalities, unresolvable in fact, could be resolved, and most importantly, in which the central anomaly of the city government could be ritualistically put right." Homans's formulation here is surely a very precise instance of the way in which functionalist ritual theory conceives of cultural facts as working in support of a structure that preexists their articulation. As Robert Ulin puts it, "The intersubjective constitution of meaning of cultural facts is reified as logically reconstructed rules for the technical maintenance of a total social system" (*Understanding Culture: Perspectives in Anthropology and Social Theory* [Austin: University of Texas Press, 1984], p. 19). The effect of such constitution is to render totality "coincident with nature" (p. 20). For a detailed refutation at the level of the evidence, see my "Making the World."

49. Cited in David Frisby, *Simmel and Since: Essays on Georg Simmel's Social Theory* (London: Routledge, 1992), p. 105, from Simmel, "The Sociology of Space," originally published as "Sociologie des Raumes," *Jahrbuch für Gesetzgebung, Verwaltung und Volkswirtschaft* 27 (1903): 27–71.

50. Thus it accentuates the already contradictory space of the street. For an analysis of the street facade's function, see James Holston, *The Modernist City: An Anthropological Critique of Brasilia* (Chicago: University of Chicago Press, 1989), p. 118: "It defines by containment and separation, interior and exterior, private and public, house and street (and all that is associated with these contrasting domains of social life) and yet provides for numerous kinds of passages between them. As a selectively porous divider, therefore, the street facade constitutes a liminal zone of exchange between the domains it holds apart."

51. See Mill, "Stations," p. 493. Also see White, "Places for Hearing," Twycross, "Places to Hear," and Crouch, "Paying to See the Play." The uniformity and stasis of the stations from year to year has been exaggerated.

52. Most extensively by Martin Stevens, *Four Middle English Mystery Plays* (Princeton, N.J.: Princeton University Press, 1987).

53. Mill, "Stations," p. 492.

54. *YMB*, 120:47. The pageants should be played " 'in locis antiquitus assignatis et non alibi sed ut sicut premunientur per maiorem ballivos et ministros suos."

55. E. Miller, "Medieval York," in *A History of Yorkshire, the City of York*, ed. R. B. Pugh, *Victoria History of the Counties of England* (London: Institute of Historical Research, University of London, Oxford University Press, 1961), p. 38.

56. Ibid. In addition, as Miller tells us, the king's justices (1250) were forbidden to try pleas concerning the Minster or its tenants anywhere but at the Minster door.

57. For details of the competing Corpus Christi processions in York, see Douglas Cowling, "The Liturgical Celebration of Corpus Christi in Medieval York," *REED Newsletter* 1, no. 2 (1976): 5–9. As well as the procession regulated by the corporation of the city,

there were two other processions, one associated with the Minster and one associated with the Abbey of Saint Mary (pp. 6–7).

58. Miller, "Medieval York," p. 38.

59. Ibid., p. 315.

60. Ibid. They had to be requested again in 1485.

61. See François Laroque, *Shakespeare's Festive World: Elizabethan Seasonal Entertainment and the Professional Stage*, trans. Janet Lloyd (Cambridge: Cambridge University Press, 1991), p. 14.

62. E. P. Thompson, *Customs in Common: Studies in Traditional Popular Culture* (New York: New Press, 1991), p. 98.

63. For a fascinating analysis of the relation between Corpus Christi and rogation processions, see Steven Justice, "The Idiom of Rural Politics," in *Writing and Rebellion: England in 1381* (Berkeley: University of California Press, 1994), pp. 165 ff.

64. Thompson, *Customs in Common*, p. 98.

65. Ibid., p. 100.

66. Laroque, *Shakespeare's Festive World*, p. 13.

67. Thompson, *Customs in Common*, pp. 127, 135. Enclosure is thus, as Thompson classically describes it, the "climax" of this reification of usages as properties (p. 136). Roger Manning reminds us that there is no "clear and unqualified" definition of property in any legal dictionary or works of any legal writer before the eighteenth century (*Village Revolts: Social Protest and Popular Disturbances in England, 1509–1640* [Oxford: Clarendon Press, 1988], p. 5).

68. Laroque, *Shakespeare's Festive World*, p. 13.

69. Keith Thomas, *Religion and the Decline of Magic* (London: Weidenfield and Nicholson, 1970; Peregrine, 1980), p. 72.

70. David Underdown, *Revel, Riot and Rebellion: Popular Politics and Culture in England, 1603–1660* (Oxford: Oxford University Press, 1987), p. 47.

71. Thompson, *Customs in Common*, p. 175. At least, Thompson so defines ceremony "at the point when commons were enclosed."

72. *REED: York*, p. xvi; see also p. 263: "Item it is agreyd that Master Shyrryffes of this Citie shall Ryde uppon Corpuscristy day with men in hernesse accordyng to the ancyent Custome of this said Citie."

73. See Miller, "Medieval York," pp. 82–84.

74. Ibid., p. 83. It was Richard III who seemed to spark off the incident of 1484 when he asked the council to give up common rights in a close belonging to Saint Nicholas Hospital. The council agreed "if the commons will agree to the same." The commons disagreement took the unequivocal form of a riot. See *York Civic Records*, vols. 1–8, ed. A. Raine, York Archaelogical Society Record Series, 1938–52, vol. 1, pp. 89, 102–5.

75. Miller, "Medieval York," p. 83.

76. Ibid.; *York Civic Records*, 1:107–23. The leading rioters were imprisoned by the mayor, and under pressure from the king, who threatened to replace the civic authorities unless they could keep the peace, the council and the commonalty relinquished their common rights in Vicars Leas.

77. The classic account of the redefinition of property in the seventeenth century is C. B. Macpherson, *The Political Theory of Possessive Individualism*. See also his "Capitalism and the Changing Concept of Property," in *Feudalism, Capitalism and Beyond*, ed. Eugene Kàmenka and R. S. Neale (London: Edward Arnold, 1975), p. 105, where the conceptualization of property under precapitalist conditions is discussed: "a) Whereas in precapitalist society property was understood to comprise common as well as private property, with the rise of capitalism the idea of common property drops virtually out of sight and property is equated with private property — the right of a natural or artificial person to exclude others from some use or benefit of something. b) Whereas in pre-capitalist society a man's property had generally been seen as a right to a revenue, with capitalism property comes to be seen as a right in or to material things, or even as the things themselves.

c) There is a change in the rationale or justification of private property; before capitalism, various ethical and theological grounds had been offered; with the rise of capitalism, the rationale came to be that property was a necessary incentive to the labour required by the society."

78. See Don Handelman, *Models and Mirrors: Towards an Anthropology of Public Events* (Cambridge: Cambridge University Press, 1990), pp. 9, 12.

79. David Harvey, *The Condition of Postmodernity* (Oxford: Blackwell, 1989), p. 239. Harvey develops four dimensions of spatial practice: accessibility and distantiation, appropriation of space, domination of space, and production of space; see p. 222 for details.

80. Ibid., p. 385. The classic text here is Henri Lefebvre, *The Production of Space*, trans. Donald Nicholson-Smith (Oxford: Blackwell, 1991).

81. The literature on festivity is increasing at a rapid space. Here I confine myself to mentioning three recent works that examine the interrelationship between ritual and space in densely socially located ways. Roberto DaMatta effects a comparative analysis of carnival in Rio and New Orleans in his *Carnivals, Rogues and Heroes: An Interpretation of the Brazilian Dilemma*, trans. John Drury (Notre Dame and London: University of Notre Dame Press, 1991). Mono Ozouf provides a nuanced Durkheimian reading of the reconfiguration of festivity in the French Revolution in the brilliant *Festivals and the French Revolution*, trans. Alan Sheridan (Cambridge, Mass.: Harvard University Press, 1988). Finally, Don Handelman examines the Palio of Siena in his *Mirrors and Models* (pp. 116–35) as part of the development of an anthropology of public events. The power of these analyses is that, although they are interested in examining the material relations of power in festive space, they refuse to do so in terms of blanket or ahistorical descriptions of the essential activity of festival. To me, they are therefore exemplary models for the possibilities of reimagining the York Corpus Christi festivities.

82. See P. J. P. Goldberg, "Urban Identity and the Poll Taxes of 1377, 1379 and 1381," *Economic History Review*, 2nd ser., 43, no. 2 (1990): 197.

83. P. J. P. Goldberg, *Women, Work and Life-Cycle in a Medieval Economy: Women in York and Yorkshire, 1300–1520* (Oxford: Clarendon Press, 1992), pp. 64 ff.

84. I have argued this at length in "Making the World."

85. Mill, "Stations," p. 499. By 1486, she points out, it seems to be established that the Pavement, the last station, will be rent free. The station at the common hall, she says, is by the early years of the sixteenth century reserved for the mayor and aldermen. This, of course, precisely ties in with the decisive reorganization of the systems of representation in 1517 whereby a new common council was appointed in which the role of the merchant body increased at the expense of the manufacturing guilds. See Heather Swanson, *Medieval Artisans: An Urban Class in Late Medieval England* (Oxford: Blackwell, 1989), p. 123, and Jennifer Kermode, "Merchants, Overseas Trade, and Urban Decline: York, Beverley and Hull c. 1380–1500," *Northern History* 23 (1988): 51–73.

86. Goldberg, *Women, Work.*

87. The Ousegate "kidcotes," the set of cells that are recorded at least in 1435 as standing beside the doorway of a chapel (*Victoria County History* (City of York, 1961) (hereafter cited as *VCH*).

88. Goldberg, *Women, Work*, pp. 176–77. Also see Jean-Christophe Agnew's illuminating comments on the situatedness of markets in *Worlds Apart: The Market and the Theater in Anglo-American Thought, 1550–1750* (Cambridge: Cambridge University Press, 1986), p. 18: "These markets were, in every possible sense of the term, *situated* phenomena; that is to say, they were assigned to precise sites—in space and time—in societies where the particularities of place and season were intricately linked to the dominant patterns of meaning and feeling, and where the configuration of the landscape was itself used as a mnemonic repository of collective myth, memory, and practical wisdom."

89. *VCH*, p. 81.

90. Ibid.

91. Ibid.

92. Doreen Massey, "A Global Sense of Place," in *Studying Culture: An Introductory Reader*, ed. Ann Gray and Jim McGuigan (London: Edward Arnold, 1993), p. 235. Place, as she puts it, will not then be "bounded, homogenized ... having a special history based on a long internalized history but constructed out of a particular contestation of social relations." She articulates the critical consequences: "If places can be conceptualized in terms of the social interactions which they tie together, then it is also the case that these actions are not motionless things, frozen in time. They are processes" (p. 239). It is less likely, in this way of thinking, that place will be misidentified as community.

93. In the Purification pageant, the needlessness of the ritual for the purposes of purification is pointed out by Joseph (Beadle, *York Plays*, p. 154). Mary insists on participating in the ritual to fulfill the law and as a "sample of mekenesse." In the Baptism pageant when John points out that Christ is clean and does not need to be baptized, Christ says that "Mankynde may no3t unbaptymde go / Te endles blys." Since he is an example to mankind, he has to be baptized, too (pp. 183–84). See also the Harrowing of Hell pageant, ibid., pp. 341–42.

94. Ibid., p. 341.

95. I am borrowing lines here from the conclusion to my book *Christ's Body: Identity, Culture and Society in Late Medieval Writings* (London: Routledge, 1993).

96. Moore, *Space, Text and Gender*, p. 170.

97. For Bourdieu's decisive rejection of the location of incorporation at the level of representations such as body image, see *The Logic of Practice*, trans. Richard Nice (Stanford, Calif.: Stanford University Press, 1990), pp. 72–73.

98. Tadeusz Kowzan defines the art of performance in ways that resonate with this discussion of ritualization: "This is what the circumscribed definition of performance implies: a work of art which must, by necessity, be communicated in time and space" (*Litterature et Spectacle* [The Hague: Mouton, 1975] p. 24).

99. See Maurice Merleau-Ponty, *The Visible and the Invisible*, ed. Claude Lefort (Evanston, Ill.: Northwestern University Press, 1968). See also Roberto DaMatta, *Carnivals, Rogues and Heroes*, p. 62, for a discussion of ritual in relation to Marx's camera obscura image of ideology in *The German Ideology*: "In all ideology men and their relations appear upside down as in a camera obscura" (Marx, "The German Ideology," in *Collected Works*, 3rd rev. ed., vol. 5 [Moscow: Progress, 1976], p. 36). See also Tony Gash's discussion of this same image in relation to the characteristic role of reversal as it is ascribed to ritual, in "Carnival and the Poetics of Reversal," p. 94. Stuart Hall discusses ritual as a "metaphor of transformation" in his memorial essay for Allon White in *Carnival, Hysteria and Writing: Collected Essays and Autobiography* (Oxford: Clarendon Press, 1993), pp. 1–25, in relation to the theme of "the festival of revolution," especially pp. 1–2.

CHAPTER 5

Finding Language for Misconduct
Jurors in Fifteenth-Century Local Courts

Marjorie K. McIntosh

During the fifteenth century, the heads of established families in many English market towns and villages expressed growing concern with certain forms of social misconduct. Some actions appeared to local leaders to threaten the social peace and concord of their communities; issues like malicious gossip and eavesdropping were particularly troublesome during the first half of the century. By around 1460 attention was shifting to actions that violated good governance and control, such as sexual misdeeds or operating a rowdy alehouse. Problems associated with poverty and a refusal to labor likewise mounted in the later fifteenth century. Local leaders expressed their uneasiness in their role as "presentment jurors" within the courts of their own communities. Using the records of these courts, we can examine how social attitudes and the language jurors used to describe misconduct—the terms that simultaneously expressed and helped to shape their perceptions—changed over the course of the fifteenth century. We can also see how local language was related to a broader textual environment: to didactic moral tracts, dramatic and poetic works, parliamentary legislation, and instructions for rulers as produced by more educated and influential men.[1] This examination of texts suggests some parallels but also some contrasts between the language and ideas put forward in local courts and those of the wider cultural context. Furthermore, the comparison does not explain the chronological changes seen in the types of offenses reported locally. To elucidate those variations, we will turn to developments within the material or nondiscursive context—to demographic, economic, and social factors that may have created new challenges to the social stability and effective control that local leaders were at all times trying to maintain.

This study suggests that as local leaders attempted to articulate their concerns and to justify why offenders should be punished, they faced a lack of congruity between traditional ideas and language on the one hand and the new circumstances they confronted on the other. The customary habits of thought and expression with which they had grown up and which surrounded them as adults proved inadequate to identify, describe, and attack what they perceived as new threats to their village or town.[2] While traditional concepts provided a broad justification for local actions, the particular reasons for opposing socially disruptive behavior offered by moral, literary, and legal texts were not identical with the issues mentioned by local jurors. In the earlier fifteenth century, their concerns focused instead upon preserving peace and goodwill within their neighborhoods. The gap becomes more apparent when we examine violations of governance and control in the middle and later part of the century. Although some of these offenses were deemed sins in the moral literature (such as fornication and adultery) or were proscribed by law (such as the playing of specified games), jurors expressed their disapproval in terms of disruption of the good order and regulation of their communities. Local people employed language and ideas that resembled the instruction manuals addressed to rulers or the "mirror of princes" literature. Problems of poverty and labor received little serious attention in contemporary writing (a thoughtful analysis was not to emerge until the sixteenth century); jurors, too, expressed their views about these matters in a narrow range of labels and images. Yet at the same time local court leaders were experimenting vigorously with new procedures and new punishments to increase their actual power over the poor and idle, hence creating a lag between practice and a revised cultural statement.[3] The imperfect fit between community responses and the largely traditional language about social misconduct and poverty evokes David Aers's discussion of the possible incompatibility between "received cultural categories and the demands posed by present practical realities."[4]

Local Practice, Local Language, and the Textual Environment

Male heads of stable families of middling rank dominated the local courts responsible for maintaining order within late medieval market towns and rural villages. While the policies of the Crown and Parliament did, of course, have some impact on local patterns, and while noble and gentry families shaped events at the county level, many of the decisions that affected daily life for the bulk of the population were made within their own courts. These local bodies and their officials likewise implemented any orders made at higher levels of government or the law. Within such courts agricultural yeomen and husbandmen, people holding perhaps thirty to two hundred acres in the fifteenth century, were joined as presentment jurors and officers by substantial craftsmen-traders and local merchants. A public court, one authorized to exercise leet jurisdiction, was the vehicle through which these men attended to the well-being of the community.[5] Manors, boroughs, hundreds, and honors could have leet courts.[6]

At public court sessions a body of jurors was sworn in and asked to "present" or report people whose actions had broken the law of the land or local bylaws. The list of offenses normally included violations in the preparation and sale of food and drink, assaults, and poor maintenance of drainage ditches, roads, and bridges. In addition, jurors might report people for forms of misconduct that may not have been officially illegal but that seemed to them to impair community order. Although the court was presided over by a steward appointed by the lord, by the sheriff, or by a borough official, he was dependent upon the information provided by the jurors. It was they who also determined the punishments for guilty parties, which were carried out by locally elected constables or bailiffs.[7] Local court records therefore reflect middling people's attitudes about social values and conduct.

In tracing the reactions of such jurors, we draw upon the records of 178 courts that enjoyed public jurisdiction, spanning nearly every county and chosen because good rolls survive within the period from 1370 to 1599.[8] The residents of England's smaller communities have tradition-ally received scant historical attention, although they constituted the majority of the population. To help remedy that neglect, this study deals only with courts held in agricultural villages and market centers with fewer than four thousand people.[9] For each court studied, presentments were analyzed from between two and five years within each of a series of thirty-year periods (hence covering about one generation each) begin-ning in 1370, 1400, 1430, 1460, and 1490. Although use of sampling means that the numbers reported here are probably somewhat low, they should provide a generally accurate reflection of concerns: once a community began to express worry about a given type of misbehavior, it normally reported offenses of that kind every year or two, a pattern continuing usually for at least a generation. The lords of the courts were of many sorts (private families, religious bodies, colleges and hospitals, and the Crown), but no correlation has been found between the type of lordship and the type of offenses presented.

Our analysis of misbehavior utilizes two approaches. We will first sur-vey the problems reported in local courts by period and examine the lan-guage in which presentments were recorded, to see how the jurors laid out their concerns and what attitudes appear to have underlain their re-sponse.[10] We can then turn to the broader textual environment, assess-ing the relationship between these local statements and those produced by clerics writing on moral topics, by the authors of dramatic or poetic works, and by the framers of parliamentary legislation or advice manu-als for monarchs. Direct transmission through these written texts is not assumed, since many of the village and town leaders would have been entirely illiterate or only partially educated. Our approach emphasizes rather the extent to which such media as sermons, plays, poetry, and dis-cussion of contemporary social and political issues provided a context sufficient to the needs of local leaders in their attempts to describe and regulate conduct and the problems of poverty.

We must acknowledge that the language recorded by local court clerks provides only an indirect, filtered reflection of the jurors' actual terms for misconduct. The surviving accounts were translated from spoken English into written Latin, and in some cases the clerks may have tried to make the actual charges conform more closely to conventional legal terminology. Clerks familiar with parliamentary legislation and the language of the upper law courts may have drawn upon that phraseology. Yet the range and individuality of the specific terms used to describe offenses suggests that the clerks, who must have been taking notes as the jurors spoke, often translated the original English vernacular presentments into comparable Latin words, rather than using set formulas. We do not gain from these texts rich and detailed personal statements in the speaker's own language such as one finds in the best court testimony or depositions, but the local presentments certainly offer better evidence of individual concerns than do the almost entirely formulaic charges made before the central common law courts.

Disruptions of Social Peace and Concord within the Community

The four types of offenses reported most often during the first half of the century (scolding, nightwalking, eavesdropping, and gaming) were generally described by local people as threatening amicable interactions and the social tranquility of the community. The attention of jurors focused normally upon the actions themselves, not upon the kinds of people who performed them or the settings in which they occurred. Although each of these offenses was embedded within a long tradition of moral analysis and social condemnation, and although the church's teachings may well have influenced local jurors' personal reactions to these misdeeds, matters of sin lay within the purview of ecclesiastical courts rather than secular courts. Defining misconduct as morally wrong was thus not an option in the jurors' presentments. Nor could they argue in most cases that the action was against the law of the realm, for only gaming was clearly a statutory violation. Forced to develop their own, secular justifications for their decision to report and punish offenders, they did so in terms of disruption of community harmony. While their moral concerns are thus obscured, their choice of language makes clear their emphasis upon peace and concord.

Scolding was the most common presentment within this cluster during the first half of the century. As Figure 1 shows, nearly a quarter of all courts under observation between 1400 and 1459 reported at least occasional instances — more than twice the level of the later fourteenth century. Scolding fell into two main categories: quarrelsome or argumentative speech with another person, and the spreading of malicious gossip or false tales about other people behind their backs. Scolding could occur either between a named offender and another individual, or it could

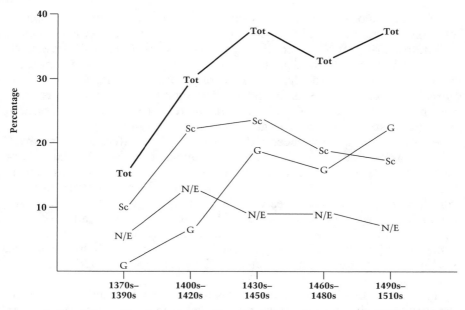

Figure 1. Percentage of local courts reporting disruptions of social peace, 1370–1519. This figure displays the percentage of all courts under observation within each thirty-year period that expressed concern with one of the offenses listed here, either by presenting individuals for misconduct or by enacting bylaws proscribing such behavior. The number of courts analyzed for each period is as follows: 1370s–1390s, 96; 1400s–1420s, 96; 1430s–1450s, 111; 1460s–1480s, 138; 1490s–1510s, 153. The precise nature of each offense is described in the text. For sources, see note 8. Sc, scolding; N/E, nightwalking/eavesdropping; G, gaming (because of the change around 1450 in how gaming was described, the values for gaming in the final two periods actually fall better into the category of violations of good governance, as in Figure 2; see text). Tot, total (percentage of courts that reported one or more of the preceding offenses. Because some courts dealt with several of these problems in a given period, the total does not represent simple addition of the three component offenses. If gaming were excluded, the total would show a slight decline in that final period as compared with the previous one).

be done "commonly," with unspecified people. The great majority of those presented for scolding were women, although men formed a tenth to a fifth of the total number in most places and periods. The most common form of punishment was a small money fine, but women who were reported more than once were sometimes ordered to face the public ridicule that accompanied sitting in a tumbrel or cuckingstool for a stated period of time.[11]

Because parliamentary legislation never declared scolding illegal, local jurors maintained that it disturbed, disrupted, or broke the peace, harming the neighbors or tenants—that it was "to the grave and common harm of the king's liege people." The frequent association of local peace with "the peace of the lord king" served a double purpose: it stressed that peace was a virtue supported by the weight of the Crown while also suggesting (incorrectly) that scolding should indeed be punished since it violated the generic legal requirement of maintaining the king's peace.

The precise nature of scolding was not always described. Several of the most common Latin descriptors, including *objurgator/-trix* and *garrulator/-trix* do not specify the kind of spoken offense. Many of the phrases, however, carried meanings that enable us to distinguish between the two varieties of scolding.[12] In the first usage, a scold was quarrelsome, casting insults or engaging in heated arguments with others. The Latin term may have been a translation of the English word "shrew," which was applied to evil-disposed or malignant men from the later thirteenth century and to railing or turbulent women by the late fourteenth. This sense is suggested by common terms like *litigator/-trix* and *rixator/-trix* (both originally meaning "a contentious person") or less frequent descriptors like *conviciator/-trix* (from "abusive") and *contrabator/-trix* (from "beating against"). Other accounts include such verbs as *maledicant* ("revile") and *redarguit* ("reprove" or "rebuke"). In this sense, scolding was sometimes associated in the presentments with participation in physical fights.

The second meaning of scolding was termed "backbiting" in fifteenth-century English, an apt phrase for the deliberate spreading of false or malicious gossip. It was often described quite fully, in phrases like being "a creator of false tales" or "a sower of discord between his neighbors, who caused controversy, rumors, and dissension"; a woman called "a scold with her tongue" was said "to provoke controversy in poisonous fashion [*venemose*] between her neighbors." Because it disrupted local harmony indirectly, in hidden ways, backbiting was seen as particularly damaging. One man was said to be a "perturbator mendax et factor fabul' mal' de vicin' suis ac scandalizator dictis vicinorum et populorum domini Regis et est causator diversis insultis cum verbis maliciosis" (a lying disturber and maker of evil tales about his neighbors and a slanderer of his said neighbors and the people of the lord King and a causer of divers insults with malicious words).[13] Scolding might thus destroy another person's reputation or credit, concepts that were to be of such importance by the sixteenth century. In its second meaning scolding was associated in the presentments with eavesdropping.

The next two types of misconduct, nightwalking and eavesdropping, were closely related and have been grouped together in Figure 1. The right of local courts to deal with nightwalking was not well defined, and reports of this offense were relatively uncommon.[14] Those accused as being wrongly out at night (nearly all men) were usually described as a *noctivagator*, a wanderer at night; occasionally they were called night watchers. The verb *vagor/vagari* (deponent) stressed that the offender lacked a good reason for being out, as contrasted with someone walking purposefully and legitimately from one place to another. Nightwandering was commonly said to be against the peace (or the king's peace) or to the harm of the neighbors, and it was sometimes connected with other forms of wrongdoing: listening to the secrets of others, or, less often, carrying arms, committing a rape, or watching other people's houses or animals, apparently with an eye to theft.

Eavesdroppers—both men and women—normally listened to people's private conversations from outside their houses but might also observe their private actions. They were said, for example, "to stand under the eaves [*projectiones*] of the tenants, listening to their secrets," "to hide under the windows of the tenants of the manor to listen to what they were doing in their houses," or "to lie under the walls of his neighbors, snooping into [*explorans*] what is said in the house." Eavesdropping, never the topic of legislation, was usually described in socially harmful terms, such as being a disturbance of the peace. While eavesdropping was clearly connected in some cases with nightwalking, it was also related to scolding: one person was "a listener at windows and sower of discord between the neighbors," while another was "a common listener at night who followed the said listening by increasing disputes."[15]

Playing certain proscribed games was the only offense within this early group that was clearly against English law. The language of the courts reflects local awareness of this fact, citing the illegality of gaming as well as the familiar ascriptions of social faults. Many kinds of gaming had been illegal since 1388, but, as Figure 1 displays, local courts rarely enforced the statute prior to the second third of the fifteenth century.[16] Since it is unlikely that the prohibited games were never played, jurors were apparently prepared to ignore the legislation unless the actions seemed to undermine community stability. Prior to around 1450 nearly all those presented were people who had been playing themselves, not the owner of the establishment in which the actions occurred. The kinds of games mentioned included both indoor and outdoor activities—dice, cards, hazard, checkers, tables, pennyprick, closhing, "kowteryng," (hand)ball, tennis, "buttering," "quekkyng," and bowling.

In the first half of the century jurors' language indicated that gaming caused harm if it occurred at improper times or places or disrupted the peace by causing "other neighbors to congregate." Some courts were worried about its financial impact. People who played for money were presented, as were a chaplain and several servants from Sherburn-in-Elmet, in Yorkshire's West Riding, who played dice at night, "not having the ability to continue such illegal games."[17] By the mid-century, however, the reasons for discomfort with gaming were changing, placing the later presentments more appropriately into the category of offenses against governance and control.

In attempting to situate these local concerns and uses of language within a broader environment, we may consider first the didactic moral writings produced by educated clerics. Here we confront at once the conservative, even static quality of much fifteenth-century moral discussion.[18]

Although this may well have been a period when the clergy were making a more strenuous effort to educate the laity in Christian ethics through active translation of continental texts, new versions of earlier didactic works, and expanded use of such forms as the exemplum, ideas about moral behavior show little sign of change.[19] *Jacob's Well*, for example, prepared probably in the 1440s, was the newest addition to the series of redactions of the thirteenth-century French work *Somme le Roi* and resembled its predecessors fairly closely in terms of content.[20] While local people may thus have been more fully aware of the details of Christian morality, the traditional ethical environment was unlikely to respond quickly to the new concerns emerging at the village and town level.

Whereas scolding or quarrelsome uses of the tongue were routinely proscribed throughout the fourteenth and fifteenth centuries, backbiting formed an exception to the general pattern of stable attitudes. Malicious words received more attention and a somewhat more complex analysis during the first half of the fifteenth century than before or after. *Jacob's Well*, for example, presents a detailed discussion of ten "sins of the tongue," under the heading of gluttony. Backbiting is described as "whan þou spekyst euyll be-hynde a man, & turnyst all þat þou mayst þe gode dedys of an-oþer man to þe werste."[21] Backbiters are compared to adders: such offenders "byte & sle iij. at oo strook, þat is, þe bacbytere, þe herere, & him þat he bacbyteth." The sowing of discord, which the author classifies as a deadly sin, was "whanne þou makyst hem enemyes þat were freendys, & makyst stryif & debate wyth talys & lesynges [falsehoods] berynge aboute."[22] Other moralists attempted to explain the circumstances that led to backbiting. At the turn of the fifteenth century, the author of a Worcester Chapter sermon launched a long attack on backbiting, which he argued stemmed from envy and was associated with circumstances in which some people were getting richer while others lagged behind.[23]

The relationship between backbiting and envy was developed in dramatic and poetic texts as well. In the early fifteenth-century play *The Castle of Perseverance*, Backbiting (or Detraction) acts at various times as a servant or messenger to Envy, Worldliness, Covetousness, the Bad Angel, and the Devil.[24] Backbiting, who calls on his fellows to "make debate abowtyn to sprynge / Betwene systyr and broþyr," is ordered by Envy to attack any of Mankind's neighbors who are thriving, killing them "wythowtyn knyve"; he is told to "Speke þi neybour mekyl schame, / Pot on hem sum fals fame, / Loke þou vndo hys nobyl name / Wyth me, þat am Envye." Mankind replies that more envy is now reigning than at any time "syth Cryst was kynge." In keeping with the teachings of didactic authors, the only character always capable of destroying Envy is Charity.[25]

Backbiting had potential political ramifications, too. The extended poem *The Assembly of Gods* shows malicious murmurers, feigners of tales, seekers of debate, and maintainers of quarrels among the host of commons led by the character Idleness.[26] By including in this group "makers of clamours" and "traytours," the author implies that there were dangers to the state as well as dangers to society from misuse of the tongue. An undated advice poem called "Think Before You Speak" lists war and disease among the consequences of evil tongues.[27] Certainly we have here the background to the intense Tudor concern with the spreading of political rumors.

It is interesting that one finds no suggestion in any of these works that offenses of the tongue were especially associated with women. The author of the Worcester sermon from the turn of the century was clear that backbiting was common to both men and women: he speaks always of "þis man or þis womman," and his most vivid example refers to a man.[28] While the mother in the fourteenth-century poem "How the Good Wijf Tauȝte Hir Douȝtir" does indeed advise her daughter to be of good tongue, "How the Wise Man Tauȝt His Son" (from circa 1430) puts even more weight on this point.[29] The father warns, "þin owne tunge may be þi foo," especially in carrying tales; a word you say today may return to make trouble in the future. The most colorful abuser of the tongue in fifteenth-century drama, Noah's wife in the mystery cycles, who is cross, argumentative, and disobedient to her husband (going as far as to strike him in several of the versions), is counterbalanced by the portrayal of Cain in the Towneley plays, who complains, argues, speaks crudely, and curses his horse, his boy servant, and Abel before finally killing his brother.[30] Even when the image of bridling the tongue was used, it was not applied particularly to women.[31] This gender neutrality contrasts with the predominance of women among those actually reported for the offense in local courts and with the exclusively female images of scolding produced in the later sixteenth and seventeenth centuries.[32]

Fifteenth-century discussion of scolding was but one component within a powerful and widely shared feeling about the importance of peace and harmony within the community. This goal, often described as "living in charity with one's neighbors," was defended in spiritual, social, and political terms. The old-fashioned moralist John Audelay said that people should not cause debate or discord with their neighbors, because if a person is "euer out of charyte; / To al payne ent domysday he schal go."[33] In a more secular vein, "The Good Wijf" stresses to her daughter the importance of being on friendly terms with one's neighbors. If she is financially able, the younger woman should welcome them "with mete, drinke, & honest chere," for the utterly pragmatic reason that in the future she may need help from "þi neiȝboris þat dwelle þee biside."[34] At the furthest end of the spectrum, an undated political poem, "Advice to the Several Estates," exhorts the English people to "set all yovr myndes to norysshe amyte; / for vnto a royalme the syngvler defence / restyth en love, concorde, and vnete"; it warns the commoners against rebellion, "for certaynely dyscorde / es rote and mother of carefvll poverte."[35] The importance of avoiding discord was heightened by the spiritual requirement that the laity be "in ful charyte with frynd and with foo" when going to confession before receiving the communion.[36] This idea was defended in such popular works as *The Lay-Folks Mass Book* and John Mirk's collection of homilies known as the *Festial*.[37]

Neither nightwandering nor eavesdropping received much attention from the clerical authors of didactic works, but they did appear occasionally in other kinds of texts. As in the court records, they were usually portrayed as types of behavior suspect largely through association. Roaming around at night was connected sometimes with staying too late at a tavern, sometimes with eavesdropping. "The Wise Man" tells his son not to stay out in the evening or to sit drinking, because "of late walking comeþ debate."[38] A moral poem laid out as the inverse of all true virtue advises its reader to "Rechelesly þe gouerne, / Day and ny3t; walke late / At cokes hostry and tauerne," while in *The Assembly of Gods*, "stalkers by nyght" are paired with eavesdroppers in the company that follows Idleness.[39]

The limited worry about gaming seen in local courts during the first half of the century lay within a context of firm moral and practical objection. *Jacob's Well*, with its customary thoroughness, identifies nine distinct kinds of sin connected with playing games.[40] Here, as in many other sources, game playing was linked with betting—the lure of money that led men to risk whatever resources they might have. The poem "Money, Money!" from the late fourteenth or early fifteenth century includes both indoor and outdoor games among the settings in which "money hathe euer the floure."[41] When a virtuous Bristol apprentice asks his master for more money after having spent his inheritance to rescue his father's soul, his master accuses him of having "played atte dice, / or at som other games nyce, / and lost vp sone þt thu had."[42] Other authors emphasized the association between game playing and idleness. Lydgate, for example, in *Reson and Sensuallyte*, portrays Venus's son Deduit (or Pleasure) as the god of games, who himself specializes in dice, tables, and chess; *The Assembly of Gods* lists players of cards and such games as hazard and closhing as among the followers of Idleness.[43] The location of dicing and the other indoor games—frequently in alehouses—was likewise to their discredit. Thus, "The Wise Man" warns his son to beware of dice, which in his mind were connected with taverns.[44] The negative associations of dicing may have been increased by the scene in the mystery plays that shows dice being used to divide up Jesus' clothing after the crucifixion.[45] More vivid still for the laity of at least a few parishes were visual reminders of the spiritual damage of gaming. Wall paintings in their churches showed Christ surrounded by a group of implements, thought to represent the concept that sins committed in our daily lives wound him. Among the objects that cause him to suffer are dice and cards.[46]

Violations of Good Governance and Control

Some new forms of social misconduct began to appear in local courts during the second quarter of the century, developing rapidly after around 1460. Jurors apparently saw these as a loss of governance and control, both the self-regulation expected of individuals and the control exercised by authority figures over the behavior of those subject to them. Sexual misconduct, problems in alehouses and inns, the playing of illegal games (according to the terms in which this action was presented in the later fifteenth century), and a group of offenses loosely described as "bad rule or governance" all challenged good order. Also new in the jurors' discussion of these matters was a shift of focus away from the nature of the action itself to the nature of the person who committed the misdeed. Three groups of people were starting to receive special attention: the poor, young people, and outsiders or newcomers to the community.[47] Moreover, jurors now extended blame to those who permitted or promoted misbehavior — operators of brothels, panderers, and keepers of disorderly alehouses, inns, and gaming establishments — because they failed to provide the supervision demanded of those in positions of power within households. It is presumably no coincidence that this strong emphasis on governance and control emerged among local leaders at the very time when more literate men were addressing a small flood of instructive works to the nation's rulers on how to govern effectively. Both groups were probably influenced by the weakening of power associated with the Wars of the Roses, affecting the monarchy, Parliament, and, to some extent, the upper level courts of the common law system between the 1430s and the 1480s.

In reporting fornication and adultery, jurors were on questionable legal ground since the church courts, not secular ones, had jurisdiction over sexual matters.[48] Yet, as Figure 2 displays, in the second half of the century more than 10 percent of all courts under observation were presenting sexual misconduct. Jurors bypassed the morality issue by claiming that sexual misdeeds formed a practical threat to good order within their communities. Although some women were charged simply with being a common whore (*meretrix*), many of the presentments ʾ ʾ460 attempted to define more carefully why sexual misconduct c a secular offense. Women and occasionally men were now d "badly governed in their bodies," suggesting that their own inadequate; as well as being a whore, a woman might "live s

97

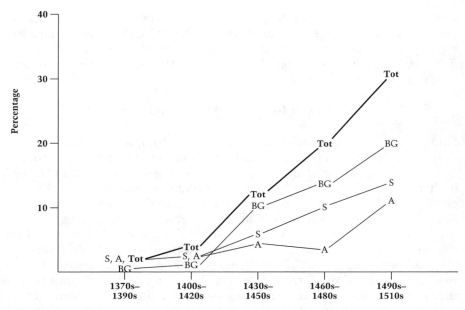

Figure 2. Percentage of local courts reporting violations of good governance, 1370–1519. This figure displays the percentage of all courts under observation within each thirty-year period that expressed concern with one of the offenses listed here, either by presenting individuals for misconduct or by enacting bylaws proscribing such behavior. The number of courts analyzed for each period is as follows: 1370s–1390s, 96; 1400s–1420s, 96; 1430s–1450s, 111; 1460s–1480s, 138; 1490s–1510s, 153. The precise nature of each offense is described in the text. For sources, see note 8. S, sexual; A, alehouse; BG, badly governed; Tot, total (percentage of courts that reported one or more of the preceding offenses. If gaming were included here [see Figure 1], the rise in the total for the 1490s–1510s would be even more pronounced.

implying unnamed other offenses. The accounts often indicate that the men who utilized the services of such women were themselves of bad condition (one woman was termed "a common whore ... who receives suspect men"). Presentments also named the people who made bawdry possible, the keepers of brothels and any procurers or panderers. Brothel keeping could be associated with other problems, too: several female bawds were presented as scolds, another "gives hospitality to divers suspect persons, causing controversy and discord between her neighbors," and a male brothel keeper "receives and supports men and women of bad living through whom the goods of the neighbors are stolen."[49]

In describing sexual misbehavior, jurors used several interesting kinds of language. Frequently the terms employed indicated an inversion or distortion of customary social virtues and relationships. Heads of households, for example, together with the keepers of any kind of public establishment, were expected to receive and care for visitors but also to maintain discipline among their families and guests. Two of the verbs most commonly used for taking in people of bad governance or for keeping a whorehouse, alehouse, or gaminghouse were *hospituere* ("to harbor" or "to give hospitality") and the less readily translatable term *fovere* (meaning originally "to keep warm," thence "to tend" or "to nourish").[50] Thus, a couple was said to keep a brothel, giving hospitality to divers badly governed persons at nighttime, to the bad example and grave harm of others; a woman "nourished" (*fovet*) a common brothel with a chaplain, while another man was a regular procurer for them.[51] The indignation that permeates this language suggests that the jurors felt that such misdeeds not only represented a breakdown in governance but also made a mockery of behaviors intended to be socially nurturing. Likewise, men who abandoned their normal roles as husbands by acting as procurers for their wives received comment. The unspecific nature of many of these terms is striking, culminating in the most general accusation of all: to be "a suspect person" or "to live suspiciously."

Reports of problems associated with alehouses, taverns, and inns similarly increased in frequency.[52] Between the 1430s and the 1480s only one in twenty courts mentioned such offenses, but by the end of the century the figure had risen to one in eight. Rarely was a person reported for *frequenting* such establishments: those named were almost always the keepers of the houses. As with sexual misconduct, local concern focused upon the quality of order maintained in the houses, the kinds of people received there, and the other offenses with which it was associated. A man might be charged with "receiving in his tavern divers suspect men who are not well governed" or "keeping divers men and women who are suspect and of bad condition."[53] Poorly run alehouses were associated with the playing of illegal games, with prostitution, and with receiving vagabonds.

Although I have suggested that reports of gaming during the first half of the fifteenth century were based primarily upon concepts of local tranquility, a change in the language used to describe gaming after around 1460 implies that it, too, was now seen primarily as a matter of control and order. Most of those presented were the operators of establishments where gaming took place, who were accused of allowing people to play at night or other illegal times or with receiving strangers or "divers suspect persons." Further, the jurors displayed a new and marked concern with the problem of disrupted labor, especially among young people. The heads of establishments were charged with permitting gaming, which kept servants and/or apprentices from their work: with "soliciting divers servants and aiding and abetting them [in playing games]," and with permitting people to play tennis, "causing divers servants of the tenants to quit their service to their masters." The constables of North Curry, Somerset, were ordered "to report all players at tennis and dice in feast days and work days, to the hindrance of the service of the tenants."[54]

The last category within this group of offenses is a composite of various presentments that refer to "bad governance or rule" but with no indication of a specific offense. In these cases, the most loosely described of any considered here, we cannot be sure of the precise nature of the behavior that the jurors found objectionable. When applied to women, it may sometimes have referred to sexual misconduct, but often one suspects that the jurors did not have evidence of any more specific misdeed or they would have reported that as more certain to lead to punishment. This was nevertheless a common presentment, with the numbers rising from one in ten courts in the period 1430–59 to one in five by the end of the century. Because they were on particularly shaky legal ground, in that they had no definable misconduct to report, the jurors frequently described their concerns in fuller language. A man might have kept "bad governance and riot in his house" or "received, given hospitality to, and maintained in his house ... badly governed people and of suspicious life," while another "nourished [*fovet*] suspect persons within her house." The concern with servants is again apparent: one man kept "bad governance in his house at night, especially in giving hospitality to servants of the tenants," through which he made "the said servants withdraw their service from their masters, to the grave damage of the tenants."[55]

In trying to implement their concern with these types of misbehavior, few of which fell within the statutory headings of local court jurisdiction, jurors experimented with new procedures and punishments. Through the technique of the bylaw or local ordinance, the jurors could at a given court proscribe a certain action from that time onward, under penalty of a stated punishment in case of infraction. Whereas bylaws were rarely employed prior to the middle of the fifteenth century, they came into increasing use thereafter when dealing with offenses that were not against national law — regulation of the local economy in many places, and sometimes social misconduct, as well. Further, many courts had obviously become aware by the later fifteenth century of the inefficacy of the traditional reprimand of a small cash fine. In addition to more frequent use of the stocks and tumbrel, a new form of punishment — expulsion — was now being employed for the most severe cases.[56] In the 1460s through the 1480s, 4 percent of the courts under observation threatened or carried out permanent eviction from the community, a penalty used almost entirely for the offenses in this second category, especially sexual misconduct; by the 1490s through the 1510s, the figure had reached 11 percent.

The wider textual setting of these concerns resembles in some respects that described for our first category of offenses. Sexual wrongs, misconduct in alehouses, and gaming were all proscribed in moral and literary texts and/or in legislation, providing a potential basis for local court attitudes. But the fairly traditional approach of those works did not offer a statement of the specific reasons that led local officials to want the offenses punished, nor could jurors allege whatever moral considerations may have affected their thinking. In developing their own formulations of the dangers of such misbehavior, they instead used terms and ideas similar to those employed by more educated people when describing the nature and duties of the monarch. Local figures may therefore have appropriated for their own purposes language found within the debate over government at the national level.[57]

Moral discussion of these kinds of misbehavior appears to have changed relatively little across the fifteenth century. While spiritual condemnation of fornication and adultery, of course, continued, there is no indication of intensified disapprobation around the middle of the century or of a new concern with those responsible for such behavior.[58] Alehouses and taverns had likewise been regarded with suspicion by moralists of many hues. By the later fourteenth century such places were associated with overindulgence in food and drink as well as with linguistic abuses.[59] Although there may have been a new emphasis upon alehouses as centers of waste and loss of economic substance in the earlier fifteenth century, criticisms from later in the century do not castigate them especially as centers of bad governance.[60]

Revisions of the gaming statutes passed in the later decades of the century show a delayed reflection of the concerns we have seen locally, reminding us that Parliament responded to new circumstances more slowly than did village and town bodies.[61] The first of the enactments, from 1477–78, imposed fines upon keepers of gaming houses, as well as upon players, and expressed a concern with the economic impact of gaming: it notes that people play "to their own Impoverishment, and by their ungracious Procurement and encouraging, do bring other[s] to such games, till they be utterly undone and impoverished of their Goods."[62] This position is similar to the attitudes observed in local courts prior to 1460. The revision of 1495 focused upon when and where games might be played and whether the masters of servants were present at the time, thus paralleling the concern with labor, especially among young people, seen in the local context from around 1460.

As they tried to articulate their own sense of anxiety about issues of control, village and town leaders used language that resembles the ideas of contemporary political commentary at the highest level—the analyses of royal governance that flourished during the reigns of Henry VI and Edward IV. How the country should be ruled had obviously been debated long before this time, with attention traditionally concentrated upon the king's role as a bestower of mercy, forgiveness, and reward.[63] Early in Henry VI's reign, however, a change in focus becomes apparent, with a new emphasis upon the need for control by the king as maintained through punishment. During the 1420s and 1430s, works in the tradition of such continental forms as the *Speculum Regis* or *Miroir au Prince* together with more original pieces all called for forceful governance. This was expressed within discussions that defined the nature of government, identified the characteristics of a powerful ruler, and formulated guidelines for practical matters of administration. Such works as Hoccleve's *Regement of Princes* and James Yonge's mirror for the Earl of Ormond emphasize that rulers must maintain order and control through the use of the royal right to punish offenders.[64] By the third quarter of the century, a variety of works were insisting upon the obligation of the king and his representatives to implement their authority by subduing miscreants: by enforcing the law, they will inspire appropriate fear in their subjects.[65]

The similarity between local court language and analyses of rule at the level of the monarchy or state is intriguing. While it is unlikely that many local leaders were familiar with the advice manuals to the king through their own reading, such works may well have expressed ideas that were being discussed more generally in the country. Jurors could thus take from the broader debate concepts and language that served to express and justify their own concerns. Whereas it is not surprising that sermons, plays, poems, and laws formed part of the cultural experience of local figures of middling status, it is interesting that such men may have been at least indirectly familiar with the nature of the educated debate over royal or national governance.[66] Further, the reason that so many writers were providing advice to the ruler was precisely because, as we have seen, the actual authority of the central government and courts was declining during the middle decades of the century. In many areas of the country, nobles and gentlemen were distracted by factional disputes. The leaders of local courts may have been consciously aware that if they wanted to see good governance and control maintained in their own communities, they had to act themselves, through the vehicle of their own courts, because there was no assurance that anyone above them would do so.

Problems of Poverty and Labor

The final group of offenses revolved around issues of poverty and labor. This cluster, which emerged in the second half of the century, was to become more acute in the sixteenth century; we are witnessing only its early stages here. A quarter of all courts under observation reported hedge-breakers, vagabonds, or people who refused to work by the decades around 1500, but the language of the jurors in making these presentments was restricted. The paucity of ideas and terms among more educated writers in their meager discussions of the problems associated with poverty, geographic mobility, and their relationship to labor limited the ability of local people to define and express complex reactions. Rather than developing their own critique, jurors took practical action against miscreants but did not try to describe the reasons for their concern in anything beyond the brief and simplistic language provided by their social and cultural superiors.

Taking wood from common hedges for use as fuel, known commonly as hedgebreaking, was an offense primarily of the poor. Some people lacked rights to the common woodlands of the manor, because they held no arable land or perhaps no land or all, while others were physically unable to cut wood from trees (especially elderly women and children).[67] This problem was negligible before the 1430s but by the end of the fifteenth century had appeared in 17 percent of all courts examined (see Figure 3). In nearly all cases the language used to describe hedgebreaking was minimal, suggesting either that the offense did not carry a great moral or social burden in the eyes of the jurors or that they lacked a richer vocabulary in which to characterize and discuss it. A hedgebreaker was normally said to be "a common breaker of hedges" or "of the hedges of his or her neighbors." Only rarely was a longer wording employed (that someone was "a common trespasser in breaking hedges of the tenants" or "a breaker of hedges and taker of firewood").[68] Nor was much comment given to why the action was wrong—just an occasional statement that it was "to the harm of her/his neighbors." The size of the small money fines used against hedgebreakers reinforces our sense of the poverty of the perpetrators.

Receiving vagabonds or beggars or living idly, offenses grouped in Figure 3, were likewise described in a narrow range of terms. These problems began to emerge around the middle of the century and were reported in 16 percent of the courts by the decades after 1490. The first element within this group includes vagabonds and, less often, beggars; the presentments seldom speak of *being* such a person but focus instead on those who received such wrongdoers into their houses.[69] In the generally short and matter-of-fact language used in these presentments, by far the most common term stems from our friend *vagor/vagari*, the inherently suspicious form of aimless movement that appeared in descriptions of nightwalking. Traveling directly from one community to another to take up employment or visit a relative was fine, but wandering from place to place was not. Fear of the wandering poor could overcome traditional attitudes toward charity and hospitality: in an order rare in its fullness, the jurors of the manor of Ombersley, Worcestershire, stated in 1502 that no one "shall give any hospitality to any poor people unless they are weak or enfeebled [*debil'*], and then for only one night per month." (Six years before they had ordered the constables "to see that outside and suspicious wandering beggars are not permitted to remain here.")[70] The goal here, as in many of the presentments, was doubtless to prevent poor and idle strangers from settling in the community, but the court records seldom state this concern directly or attempt to justify it. Gender issues are hinted at, too, as in an order that "no tenant shall receive any masterless or female vagabonds to live within their

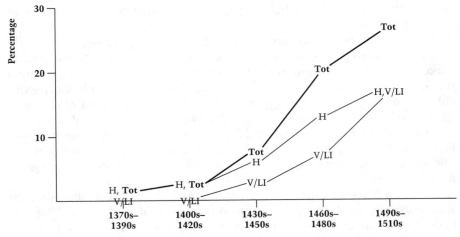

Figure 3. Percentage of local courts reporting problems of poverty and labor, 1370–1519. This figure displays the percentage of all courts under observation within each thirty-year period that expressed concern with one of the offenses listed here, either by presenting individuals for misconduct or by enacting bylaws proscribing such behavior. The number of courts analyzed for each period is as follows: 1370s–1390s, 96; 1400s–1420s, 96; 1430s–1450s, 111; 1460s–1480s, 138; 1490s–1510s, 153. The precise nature of each offense is described in the text. For sources, see note 8. H, hedgebreaking; V/LI, vagabond/living idly; Tot, total (percentage of courts that reported one or more of the preceding offenses).

holdings." Vagabonds were likely to be associated with other types of misconduct, either explicitly or implicitly, as in the charge that a man "keeps his house open at night and is suspected of taking in vagabonds, wanderers, and frequenters of taverns" or that they "keep beggars and [other] people playing illegal games at night in their houses."

Closely related were accusations that a person was unwilling to labor: charges of living idly, of having no income but living suspiciously, or of refusing to work. Local people were usually presented only if they were mistrusted for other reasons. A resident woman and her daughter, for example, were said to "live suspiciously with large expenses but earning nothing through which [they can support themselves]," while a man who was living with a woman other than his wife compounded his offense by having "no honest means of livelihood." Outsiders were named more frequently. (New arrivals who immediately sought work might be welcomed into the community, but not the idlers.) Thus, one local person "received in his house a man who is a vagabond and suspect in not working," while a rector in Devon maintained "suspect houses for divers women and vagabonds walking the country having no honest work."[71]

Whereas the evidence we have examined thus far derives from court records that paint the local response to poverty in negative colors, this stance was partially balanced in many communities by a variety of efforts to assist those poor people regarded as worthy of help.[72] The defining criteria for aid were that the poor had to be unable to labor to support themselves, that their poverty must not stem from their own negligence, and—in most cases—that they be established local people, not newcomers. The positive response may be illustrated through a characteristic fifteenth-century charity, the founding of an almshouse to provide free housing (and usually some kind of a stipend, food, and/or fuel) for elderly poor people. Among the residential institutions founded between 1400 and 1500, almshouses largely replaced the hospitals so popular during previous centuries, which had provided a staff as well as housing for ill or bedridden poor.[73] Almshouses were often set up by people of less wealth than the founders of the great medieval hospitals. Many of them were intermediate landholders, local merchants, or craftsmen-traders within the community in which their house was endowed—the same sorts of people who served as jurors in the courts. Foundation documents from fifteenth-century almshouses therefore provide another view of local attitudes about behavior, in this case within a setting in which the poor had been gathered into a residential unit. Although the respectable old folks admitted into an almshouse were unlikely to be violent disrupters of the good order of their village or town, a concern with their behavior is nonetheless apparent. Almshouse dwellers, whose actions could be observed, regulated, and disciplined, were to be models of appropriate conduct, as well as of devout religious observance.[74]

The founding documents reveal a familiar set of attitudes about proper behavior.[75] Maintaining the peace of the house, as in our first category of court offenses, was high on the list. The occupants of Saffron Walden's almshouses were to be "of good and honorable intercourse, not ... quarrelsome nor chiding one another."[76] At God's House in Ewelme, "charytye, peas, & rest" were to be preserved among the thirteen poor men: they were to keep themselves "from iangling and chiding" and from "euill sclaunder."[77] John Isbury, founder of an almshouse in Lambourne, Berkshire, said that "yf anye of my saide pore be ... a brawller amongst his fellowes or any the inhabitants of Lamborne, a quarifer or maker of debate," he was to be punished by subtraction of his salary or expulsion from the house. Among the grounds for removal from Westende's Almshouses in Wokingham, Berkshire, were being a scold, "a night stroller," or "other notorious offender." Concern with self-governance and control, with the ability to regulate one's own actions, was also visible in the foundation charters. At Ewelme, the thirteen poor men were not to be "incontynent, com[m]only dronk, or a glutton, ... a taverne haunter or of any other suspect or unlawfull place." If any of the poor at John Isbury's almshouses in Lambourne "be a dronckerd, a haunter & frequenter of alehouses, inns, or taverns," he would be punished. Wandering was forbidden. The poor men of Ewelme were not to leave the precincts of their almshouse and the church for more than an hour, nor were they to "walke much about in the sayd paryssh, nether without the sayd parysh wythout a reasonable cause to be alowyd." At John Isbury's almshouses, the poor were not to go "wandering or traveling" unless they had obtained leave.[78]

Obedience to the ordinances or the master of the house was required in virtually all the charters. At Ewelme, for example, if any of the poor men "be rebell in ded or in word agaynst the correction of the foresayd master, that then he correct such a rebellious man by subtractio[n] and taking away of such wages after his discretion"; should the inmate remain "incorrigible, obstinat & froward," he was to be put out of the house forever. These statements echo language we have heard before: we observe no distinction between what was tolerated among unruly or idle vagrants and residents as presented to local courts and what was accepted among the elderly and godly poor living within charitable almshouses.

The broader textual environment offers a confined range of analysis and some significant absences. Hedgebreaking does not appear at all in either moral or legal works. This lack of a verbal context is consistent with the singularly brief statements in the court records. With respect to vagabonds, the fifteenth century had at hand a small stock of pejorative vocabulary drawn largely from parliamentary legislation of the middle and later fourteenth century. The Ordinance and then Statute of Labourers passed within a few years of the plague of 1348–49 and the subsequent Commons' petitions express considerable hostility toward people who refuse to work and able-bodied beggars; this repressive language arose within the context of Parliament's rather desperate attempt to force people to remain in employment within their own communities and to accept traditional wages.[79] The first use of the term *vagabond* in official legislation came in the comparably charged atmosphere that followed the Peasants' Revolt, when all justices and sheriffs were given power to try and punish such wanderers; in 1388 a provision labeled "Punishment of wandering beggars" ordered that "every person that goeth begging and is able to serve or labour" is likewise to be punished.[80] Vagabonds were commonly associated in legal texts of the later fourteenth century with other offenses we have encountered. After the Peasants' Revolt, for example, a man was hanged who had been "a vagabond in various counties" during the disturbance, carrying "lies as well as silly and worthless talk from district to district"; while passing on his news at a tavern in Cambridge, he criticized John Ball's execution.[81]

A simple and fairly mechanical dichotomy underlay the thinking of these statements. The idle poor who were capable of working but chose not to do so were to be ignored or punished, whereas the worthy or deserving poor who were unable to labor for their own support qualified for charitable assistance within their own communities. When the able-bodied poor left home to wander, they were viewed with suspicion and fear.[82]

This distinction between the lazy and the worthy poor and between mobile outsiders and "our poor" formed part of the fifteenth century's collection of inherited ideas, available to be invoked if needed.

Idleness was an active topic of discussion right through the fifteenth century, but the reasons for concern changed.[83] In keeping with the traditional moral stance, poetic or dramatic representations from the earlier decades of the century focus upon the spiritual harm caused by sloth or suggest that it is harmful in both spiritual and practical terms. Lydgate, for example, characterizes Idleness as having a shield that displays a barren tree: by encouraging many vices and voluptuous desires as well as lack of thrift, Idleness "in vertu maketh a man ful bare." *The Castle of Perseverance* likewise figures Idleness's ability simultaneously to pull a man into hellfire and to put him into poverty on this earth.[84] Yet through the mid-century, the character Idleness was occasionally allowed to express the traditional social virtues of good fellowship with which he was associated.[85] After around 1460 most works talk only about pragmatic issues. Whereas idleness had been seen earlier as conducive to nearly all the other forms of misconduct we have examined (scolding, nightwalking, eavesdropping, gaming, sexual immorality, lingering in alehouses, and vagabondage), it was now associated especially with poverty. The poetic "Advice to the Several Estates" notes that "where slovth hath place, there welth es faynt and small." George Ashby, writing his political commentary in the 1460s, advocated reviving the cloth industry in order to keep the common people out of idleness and to put the poor into work.[86]

In general, however, it is striking how little serious attention was devoted to the poor in fifteenth-century texts. In contrast to the second half of the fourteenth century, poverty was not a central issue.[87] Traditional and more positive definitions of poverty had not, to be sure, disappeared. Images of the poor as filling a special spiritual and social role (God's poor) were still being used in didactic moral works and occasionally in other contexts, especially during the earlier decades of the century and among more conservative authors and regions of the country.[88] Similarly we find restatements of customary ideas about the importance of charity to relieve the poor and needy, principally the seven works of mercy.[89] In the 1420s both the old priest, John Audelay, and a poem, "Loue That God Loueth," repeat the familiar emphasis on the acts of mercy, a theme forcibly represented in the scenes of the Last Judgment in some of the cycle plays.[90] In Lollard writings, too, the Christian obligation to help the poor was a powerful theme.[91] But even in favorable depictions, no attempt was made to analyze or even to describe carefully the nature and causes of lay poverty. Fifteenth-century authors did not pursue or develop Langland's painfully honest (if not fully successful) efforts to wrestle with the actual manifestations of poverty and the reasons for these problems;[92] they did not investigate the forms of poverty among the laity in their own world or explore the relationship between them and opportunities for employment. While *Piers Plowman* remained part of fifteenth-century culture, the work seems to have evoked no particular interest among its scribes and readers in Langland's often passionate descriptions of the nonclerical poor.[93] Nor did the debate over mendicant poverty develop into a more sophisticated examination of lay poverty.[94] Parliament itself did not attempt even a slightly more thoughtful discussion of the various sorts of poor people, their needs, and the response appropriate to each until 1495.[95]

What limited interest we can discern focused upon the rich and their relation to the poor. A few texts mention the forms of exploitation whereby the wealthy take advantage of the poor, criticizing manipulation of their legal knowledge and lending money at excessive interest, but these were generally brief poems or popular moral tales, such as "The Childe of Bristowe," not detailed critiques.[96] A more emotionally charged issue in fifteenth-century texts was whether wealthy people, especially those who had risen through their own efforts, could indeed find salvation. This question is analyzed in *Dives and Pauper* through a debate between Dives, presented as a rich layman, and Pauper, a well-educated mendicant preacher. When Pauper persuades Dives that he has risked his chance of gaining "the entree of heuene blisse" by pursuing worldly gain, Dives asks, "How schulde I losyn myn rychesse fro me?"[97] Pauper responds reassuringly that God does not hate the rich, only the covetous and selfish rich; it is enough to dispense alms wisely without having to give away all one's wealth. Reginald Pecock carried the idea of limited assistance even further, saying that after his service to God, man should attend first to himself and only then do good works for his neighbors, an emphasis that modified customary teachings about Christian charity.[98]

In similar vein, most of the arguments used in the fifteenth century to encourage almsgiving among people of means emphasized not the needs of the poor but rather the value of charitable acts to the donors in terms of their own salvation.[99] Frequently mentioned was Saint Bernard's suggestion that the poor will be doomsmen upon the rich at the Day of Last Judgment, that they will report to God which wealthy people assisted them during their lives. John Audelay, writing as an old (and poor) man in the 1420s, portrayed this image with some compassion: "þe pore schul be made domysmen / Apon þe ryche at domysday; / Let se houe þai cun onswere þen / For al here ryal, reuerent aray; / In hunger, in cold, in þurst, weleaway, / Afftyr here almes ay waytyng, / þay wold not vysete vs nyȝt ne day; / þus wyl þai playn ham to heuen Kyng, / þat is aboue."[100] Most later texts, however, implied that not a great deal of sacrifice was expected from the wealthy. *Jacob's Well*, for example, exhorts its readers to give away their excess money and unused goods, rather than storing them until they moldered: "Pore men schul aske vengeaunce on þe a-fore þe ry3tfull iuge, þat my3te haue be releuyd wyth þi rust-fretyn monye, wyth þi vytayles perysched, wyth þi mothe-etyn clothis, & were no3t holpyn þerwyth."[101] A serious attempt to fit the poor, including outsiders, into a wider social and economic construct would have to await the attention of moral, social, and political thinkers of the sixteenth century.

The Changing Material Context

Since the textual environment does not provide a clear explanation of the changes seen over time in the offenses reported by jurors, we may ask what other factors may have influenced the response of these middling-level leaders. Such a question directs our attention to the material context within which the courts functioned, in particular to possible alterations in the demographic, economic, and social conditions of local communities across the fifteenth century. What practical changes were occurring that might have heightened local concern with maintaining social harmony in the first half of the century and with ensuring good governance and controlling the problems of poverty and idleness in the second? Were certain types of misconduct and certain groups of people indeed becoming a more serious problem?

Our interest in the material context is reinforced if we break down the figures on court presentments by type of community. After eliminating the twenty-seven courts that covered several different kinds of places (the hundred and honor courts), so that we are looking only at those held within either market centers or rural villages, we find that the commercial communities showed earlier and more intense concern with all the issues under consideration. As Table 1 displays, disruptions of social peace were reported much more heavily in market centers than in villages. The cluster of offenses against good governance and order began to appear sooner in the market centers, blossomed in the period 1430–59, and remained higher there during the later decades as well. The problems associated with poverty and labor likewise emerged in market communities before they appeared in villages and stayed at a higher level for the rest of the century. The contrast is seen, too, in the number of different types of offenses reported by courts in the two kinds of places. Table 2 shows that market centers mentioned more types of offenses in each of the periods. Especially interesting are the percentages under the heading of four or more different offenses, indicating a variety of problems and/or a heightened level of anxiety among the leading families.[102] The market communities that demonstrated most acute concern were of four sorts: trading centers on main roads outside the London area; lesser outlying ports; manufacturing areas (woolen cloth or mining); and smaller towns within twenty miles of London through which consumer goods were sent into the capital. Among the agricul-

**Table 1. Percentage of local courts reporting social misconduct,
by type of community, 1370–1519[a]**

	Market Centers (Number of courts under observation = 54)[b]	Villages (Number of courts under observation = 97)[b]
Disruptions of social peace[c]		
1370s–1390s	20%	13%
1400s–1420s	45	18
1430s–1450s	69	28
1460s–1480s	44	20
1490s–1510s	60	21
Violations of good governance[c]		
1370s–1390s	7%	0
1400s–1420s	10	0
1430s–1450s	31	2%
1460s–1480s	31	10
1490s–1510s	49	18
Problems of poverty and labor[c]		
1370s–1390s	0	2%
1400s–1420s	3%	2
1430s–1450s	22	3
1460s–1480s	27	10
1490s–1510s	45	14

[a]For the types of reports included, see note to Figure 1. For sources, see note 8.
[b]This is the total number of courts under observation at some time between 1370 and 1519; the number of courts for which records survive within each thirty-year period varies but is generally slightly lower.
[c]The particular offenses included within each category are shown on Figures 1, 2, and 3. The values used here are the totals as shown on those figures, which equal the percentage of all courts under observation within each period that reported one or more of the specific offenses within that category.

tural villages, by contrast, nearly two-thirds were reporting no offenses of any kind even at the end of the fifteenth century. The clear variation in response between market towns and villages, and the nature of those places that showed the strongest response to change, together emphasize the importance of practical circumstances.

The fifteenth century experienced the cumulative impact of the massive demographic, economic, and social changes initiated in the fourteenth century. Among these were the dramatic drop in population from the 1348–49 plague and resulting demographic conditions that held the population at a low level until at least the end of the fifteenth century, higher rates of geographic mobility, changes in landholding patterns caused by leasing of the demesnes of most great estates and consolidation of many

Table 2. Number of different types of social misconduct reported by local courts, by type of community, 1370–1519[a]

	Market Centers (Number of courts under observation = 54)[b]			
	0 types	1 type	2–3 types	4+ types
1370s–1390s	77%	13%	7%	3%
1400s–1420s	52	26	19	3
1430s–1450s	25	25	28	22
1460s–1480s	44	20	20	16
1490s–1510s	23	13	47	17
	Villages (Number of courts under observation = 97)[b]			
	0 types	1 type	2–3 types	4+ types
1370s–1390s	87%	11%	2%	0
1400s–1420s	80	17	4	0
1430s–1450s	68	23	8	0
1460s–1480s	72	14	12	3%
1490s–1510s	63	19	13	5

[a]This table analyzes the eight specific offenses (or pairs of offenses) shown on Figures 1, 2, and 3. It counts the number of these types of offenses reported by each court within a given period. For the kinds of reports included, see the note to Figure 1; for sources, see note 8; for the distinction between market centers and villages, see note 9.
[b]See the second note to Table 1.

smallholdings, weakening of the constraints imposed by villeinage, and the consequences of increased woolen cloth production. The well-defined socioeconomic groupings of the preplague generations, in which the landholding of most peasants within a given community fell within a fairly limited range of acres, were now breaking down into a more complex stratification. Some local people were becoming conspicuously wealthier while others remained at the customary levels. Many market centers were prospering as foci of local trade, welcoming new workers — often young and sometimes female — from outside to sustain their activities. The economic and social disparities caused by these developments, accompanied in the case of the market centers by the arrival of unmarried newcomers, may well have shaken the social harmony of many communities. Reports to local courts concerning disruptions to the community's tranquility beginning in the first half of the century may thus have been an attempt by jurors to maintain in a changing environment the peace and goodwill necessary to a stable social and economic life.

The period between 1400 and about 1460 seems to have witnessed relatively few problems with poverty outside the larger towns.[103] The substantially lowered population meant a greater amount of land per capita, many peasants had gained greater freedom and mobility, vacant housing abounded, and agricultural wages were high. Opportunities for secondary employment in cloth manufacturing were available in some regions, and access to urban life and jobs was open to many, especially the young. For most regular workers, the good wages and low prices of the fifteenth century brought newfound economic security.[104] The less diligent poor who did not like steady employment presumably found it possible to get by with occasional or part-time labor. The absence of poverty as a serious issue within local court records and other texts during the first half of the fifteenth century accords with these observations.

The decades from 1460 to 1500 saw considerable regional variation in England.[105] Whereas the northeast and probably the northwest suffered demographic and economic decline, southeast England, parts of the southwest, many market centers, most industrial towns, and some ports thrived. This contrast was intensified by the transition from arable to pastoral forms of land use in areas of mediocre soil and low population, especially the Midlands — a process accompanied in some cases by enclosure.[106] The successful regions saw an increase in the scale of agricultural production, greater specialization of crops for urban markets (often based upon labor-intensive forms of land use), and a rise in cloth manufacturing. Since all these changes meant heavier reliance upon wage labor, they led also to immigration from surrounding rural communities into market towns and from less successful areas into the southeast. They must therefore have enlarged the number of poor people and newcomers in the successful communities. Additional labor — both male and female — was probably provided during the later fifteenth century by an expansion of adolescent service. This institution had previously been concentrated in the large cities but now appears to have become more common in lesser communities as well.[107] The kinds of market centers most acutely concerned with social misconduct and poverty in the second half of the century were precisely the sorts of places that were becoming more reliant upon wage-dependent workers and were experiencing an unfamiliar rise in the numbers of poor people, outsiders, and the young.

For local court jurors, the need to maintain control in the face of these changes was paramount: they sought both to regulate the life of their communities and to retain their own power. They were faced with the presence of new kinds of people and styles of behavior that undermined traditional patterns of good order, yet they lacked specific legal authority with which to address many of the issues that seemed most threatening. They therefore utilized whatever language they could appropriate that permitted them to formulate and express their worries; even when none was available, they developed practical responses within their community courts. Their sense of urgency in responding to the problems can only have been intensified by the political uncertainties of the higher levels of government.

This study has suggested that responses to problems of misconduct and poverty within local communities during the fifteenth century were affected by several different factors. Village and town leaders operated within a perceptual framework shaped by the traditional concepts and language of correct moral behavior; their reactions and forms of expression appear also to have been influenced by Parliamentary legislation. This inherited ideology was not, however, entirely sufficient to describe and justify their specific emphasis upon social peace. Customary ideas were even less able to express the worries about control and order that emerged in the second half of the century; for such concerns jurors employed a language of governance and regulation similar to that used in manuals of advice addressed to the king. When tackling the problems of poverty and idleness, local leaders were restricted in their ability to describe the offenses and issues by lack of careful analysis of the nature, causes, and consequences of poverty within the broader climate. A strong practical emphasis on order and discipline is nonetheless visible both in the court records and in the foundation charters of almshouses. In attempting to explain the changes observed over time in their specific concerns, I have pointed to developments within the material environment. The problems created by the demographic, economic, and social changes of the fifteenth century demanded new responses from the leaders of many market centers and some villages. The records of their courts enable us to observe the interplay between the jurors' attitudes, words, and actions and those of the surrounding culture. In particular we can watch them working energetically to overcome the gaps between their "received cultural categories" and current practical problems.

Notes

I am grateful to David Aers, David Wallace, and Margaret Ferguson for their helpful reading of a draft of this paper and to Paul Strohm, Ralph Hanna, and Larry Scanlon for their generous advice.

1. As Paul Strohm has suggested, delineating the environment or "field of shared knowledge" "within which both texts and actions are produced and received" can help to "overcome the incommensurability of texts and actions, and hence to narrow the gap between them" (Strohm, *Hochon's Arrow: The Social Imagination of Fourteenth-Century Texts* [Princeton, N.J.: Princeton University Press, 1992], pp. 6, 66).

2. Many theoretical discussions of "practice" are hampered by their inability to explain how changes are introduced into an inherited set of values and terms: see, for instance, the critique of Bourdieu's concept of habitus in Richard Harker, C. Mahar, and C.

Wilkes, *An Introduction to the Work of Pierre Bourdieu* (New York: St. Martin's Press, 1990), esp. chap. 9, and Michel de Certeau's comments on Bourdieu and Foucault in *The Practice of Everyday Life,* trans. S. F. Rendall (Berkeley: University of California Press, 1984), esp. ch. 4.

3. For the possibility of such lags, defined often in terms of Louis Althusser's concept of the relative autonomy of various domains, see, for example, Raymond Williams, *Marxism and Literature* (Oxford: Oxford University Press, 1977).

4. David Aers, "Introduction," in *Community, Gender, and Individual Identity* (London: Routledge, 1988), p. 4, commenting on Bakhtin. Aers notes that "the 'praxis' of medieval people ... involves practical reference which put their cultural systems at risk in changing historical circumstances" (ibid., p. 6).

5. These public courts might be styled a View of Frankpledge, a Curia Legalis, a Tourn, or a Leet (*Leta*). There is no modern study of leet jurisdiction; see F. J. C. Hearnshaw, *Leet Jurisdiction in England* (Southampton: Cox and Sharland, 1908), and W. A. Morris, *The Frankpledge System* (New York: Longman, 1910).

6. A hundred was an administrative and legal subdivision within a county; an honor (or liberty or fee) was a group of manors held by a given noble family or branch of the royal family.

7. Although a person reported for an offense was legally entitled to bring in witnesses or oathhelpers to establish his or her innocence, almost none of those reported ever challenged the presentment.

8. The full chronological range will be considered in my forthcoming book on the maintenance of social order in England, 1350–1600; only those prior to 1520 are included in the present chapter. The records used here stretch wherever possible from the later fourteenth century through the end of the fifteenth. Courts from every county except Rutland and Westmorland are included. I would be happy to provide a detailed list of the courts studied and the document references.

9. Forty-seven communities have been excluded from this study: those with populations of more than about four thousand and/or tax yields of above about #850 in 1524, plus all county towns. In the cities and larger towns, higher levels of immigration, more densely packed housing, a larger percentage of employed women, and a greater contrast between the richest and the poorest exaggerated the difficulty of maintaining social order and good governance and accentuated the problems of poverty. Although patterns similar to those observed in the lesser places considered in this study appeared in the major centers, they often emerged somewhat earlier and in more intense form. Market centers have been distinguished from villages (see Tables 1 and 2) on the basis of the lists provided in Alan Everitt, "The Marketing of Agricultural Produce," in *The Agrarian History of England and Wales,* vol. 4, ed. Joan Thirsk (Cambridge: Cambridge University Press, 1967), pp. 466–592.

10. In examining changes in the offenses reported, it is important to recognize that we cannot distinguish between variations in the actual amount of misbehavior within a given community and variations in the sensitivity of local officials to the problem and hence the thoroughness with which they reported whatever violations did occur.

11. A tumbrel was originally a chair or stationary cart situated in a public place in which female offenders against the rules for baking and brewing were confined as a punishment; it was equivalent to the stocks or pillory for men. By the fifteenth century such a chair, now described in English as a cuckingstool, was used solely for female scolds. The very few references prior to 1600 to any "dunking" or "washing" of women while confined in a movable cuckingstool come from England's larger cities. Men were never punished in this fashion, for any kind of offense.

12. I am grateful to Ruth Karras for discussing the types of scolding with me and for letting me see the proofs of her fine paper on gendered sin in Bromyard's "Summa Predicantium."

13. Norfolk Record Office N.R.S. 6024, 20 E 2 (Manor of Cawston, 1474) and N.R.S. 6025, 20 E 3 (Manor of Cawston, 1492); Lincolnshire Archives Office ANC 3/14/55 (Manor of Spilsby cum Eresby, 1481); Dorset Record Office D/BKL CF 1/1/49 (Badbury Hundred, 1467).

14. The Statute of Winton of 1285 had called only for the arrest of strangers walking around at night in towns (13 Edward I, c. 4); this was extended in legislation of 1331 that authorized the arrest of suspicious strangers passing in the night, to be delivered to the sheriff, as well as the arrest by local constables at any time of people suspected of manslaughter, robbery, or other felonies (5 Edward III, c. 14). No specific legislation empowered local courts to punish residents of the community who were out at night.

15. Cambridge University Library E.D.R. C/11/2 (Manor of [Little] Downham, 1421–22); British Library, Add. Ch. 18,478 (Manor of Castle Combe, Wiltshire, 1437); D. L. Powell, ed., *Court Rolls of the Manor of Carshalton, from the Reign of Edward III to That of Henry VII*, Surrey Record Society, vol. 2 (London: Roworth, 1916), p. 74 (1450); Cornwall Record Office ME 1747 (Manor of East Stonehouse, Devon, 1509); Cambridge University Library E.D.R. C/6/6 (Manor of Ely Barton, 1442–43).

16. 12 Richard II, c. 6. This measure prohibited such games ostensibly because they kept men away from archery, seen as necessary to the country's military strength. Parliament's fear of gatherings of the poor, especially in alehouses, during the repressive atmosphere after the Peasants' Revolt may also have been a factor.

17. Cambridge University Library E.D.R. C/6/6 (Manor of Ely Barton, 1447–48); West Yorkshire Archive Service, Leeds, GC/M3/42 (1444).

18. For a general discussion of this literature, see Morton W. Bloomfield, *The Seven Deadly Sins* (East Lansing: Michigan State University Press, 1952).

19. I am grateful to Larry Scanlon for discussing with me the efforts to improve moral awareness and for letting me see, prior to publication, several chapters from his *Narrative, Authority and Power: The Medieval Exemplum and the Chaucerian Tradition* (Cambridge: Cambridge University Press, 1994). Ralph Hanna supports my own impression of the lack of change in the substantive content of didactic literature in this period (personal communication).

20. See Richard Morris, ed., *Dan Michel's Ayenbite of Inwyt; or, Remorse of Conscience in the Kentish Dialect, 1340 A.D.*, Early English Text Society (EETS), o.s. 23 (London: Trübner, 1866); W. Nelson Francis, ed., *The Book of Vices and Virtues: A Fourteenth Century English Translation of the "Somme Le Roi" of Lorens d'Orléans*, EETS, o.s. 217 (London: Oxford University Press, 1942); and Arthur Brandeis, ed., *Jacob's Well: An English Treatise on the Cleansing of Man's Conscience*, EETS, o.s. 115 (London: Kegan Paul, Trench, Trübner, 1900). The latter offers more complex categorization and a few new images through which to analyze human sinfulness.

21. Brandeis, ed., *Jacob's Well*, pp. 147–58; ibid., p. 83.

22. Ibid., pp. 150 (from Proverbs 23:32); ibid., pp. 99, 83. Backbiters were represented in somewhat more complex fashion as witnesses in Stephen Spector, ed., "The Trial of Mary and Joseph," in the N-Town cycle: *The N-Town Play*, vol. 1, EETS supp. ser. 11 (Oxford: Oxford University Press, 1991), pp. 139–52. I am grateful to Gail Gibson for this reference.

23. D. M. Grisdale, ed., *Three Middle English Sermons from the Worcester Chapter Manuscript F.10*, Leeds School of English Language Texts and Monographs, no. 5 (Leeds: University of Leeds, 1939), pp. 35–40. This sermon was written circa 1389–1404. The possibility of regional variations in the production and dissemination of texts is not considered here, but see the "Changing Material Context" section in this chapter for parallel issues within the material context.

24. Mark Eccles, ed., *The Macro Plays*, EETS, o.s. 262 (London: Oxford University Press, 1969), pp. 1–111. Probably written circa 1405–25, this is the earliest and most comprehensive English morality play extant.

25. Ibid., pp. 55, 36, 50.

26. *The Assembly of Gods,* previously attributed to Lydgate, as by Oscar L. Triggs, ed., EETS, extra ser. 69 (London: Kegan Paul, Trench, Trübner, 1896), pp. 20–22. The work was probably written around 1420.

27. Carleton Brown, ed., *Religious Lyrics of the Fifteenth Century* (Oxford: Clarendon Press, 1939), pp. 280–82. Lydgate's and Burgh's *Secrees of Old Philisoffres,* ed. Robert Steele, EETS, extra ser. 66 (London: Kegan Paul, Trench, Trübner, 1894), written in the 1440s, develops another angle by talking of the dangers to the prince of flattery and duplistic speech (p. 28).

28. Grisdale, ed., *Three Middle English Sermons,* p. 35. He tells of a monk who went one night into the choir of his church to pray, where he found seated "a man as blake as ani pich in al þe world." He watched the stranger "stretch owt his tunge, þat brente as brith as ani veir'. euen vrom his mowþ down to þe erþe, & with a scher' þat a hadde in his hond, a began ate neþer ende'. & clippid a-wey euche meel euen til a com to þe mouth & whan a was ter'. þis tunge sodeynliche wax as long' as it was'. & a clippid rith as a dide before. & tus a was o-cupied a long' tyme with alle, þat it was doel & ruthe to be-holde hym." When asked who he was, the dark man replied that he was "a misspekir', a bakbiter & sueþ ofte-tymes þe sed of detractiun." So "ich am punschid e þe same membir' þat I trespasid with, þat is mi tunge, & schal be þre hundred wynter her'-afterward" (pp. 39–40).

29. F. J. Furnivall, ed., *Early English Meals and Manners: The Babees Book, etc.,* EETS, o.s. 32 (London: Trübner, 1868), pp. 36–47, esp. p. 37 (for the revised dating of this work, see the introduction to Tauno F. Mustanoja, ed., *The Good Wife Taught Her Daughter, The Good Wyfe Wold a Pylgremage, The Thewis of Gud Women* [Helsinki: Suomalaisen Kirjallisuuden Seuran, 1948]); for "How the Wise Man," see *Early English Meals and Manners,* pp. 48–53, esp. p. 49.

30. R. M. Lumiansky and David Mills, eds., *The Chester Mystery Cycle,* vol. 1, EEETS, suppl. ser. 3 (London: Oxford University Press, 1974), play 3, *Noah,* esp. pp. 46–53; George England and A. W. Pollard, eds., *The Towneley Plays,* EETS, extra ser. 71 (London: Oxford University Press, 1897), play 2, *The Killing of Abel,* pp. 9–19.

31. In an attack on evil tongues ("fals detraccioun, lesyng & Dysclaunder / Hath slay mor peple than dud kyng Alys[under]"), an undated poem commented, "Oft yll reportis engenderyth sorw[e and c]are; / Were-for in spekyng at no tyme [is] he ydill / That can hys tong at all tyme wysly bridill" ("See Much, Say Little, and Learn to Suffer in Time," in *Religious Lyrics of the Fifteenth Century,* ed. Brown, pp. 279–80).

32. See, for example, Susan D. Amussen, *An Ordered Society: Gender and Class in Early Modern England* (New York: Blackwell, 1988), esp. p. 123; and David Underdown, "The Taming of the Scold: The Enforcement of Patriarchal Authority in Early Modern England," in *Order and Disorder in Early Modern England,* ed. Anthony Fletcher and John Stevenson (Cambridge: Cambridge University Press, 1985), pp. 116–36.

33. Ella K. Whiting, ed., *The Poems of John Audelay,* EETS, o.s. 184 (London: Oxford University Press, 1931), pp. 46–47, 117, written around the 1420s. A poem called "Love God, and Drede," probably from just after the turn of the century, likewise emphasized the importance of maintaining unity and reconciling quarrels (in *Twenty-Six Political and Other Poems,* ed. J. Kail, part 1, EETS, o.s. 124 [London: Kegan Paul, Trench, Trübner, 1904], pp. 1–6).

34. Furnivall, ed., *Early English Meals and Manners,* pp. 44–45. For the sake of goodwill, the mother advises that if any discord should arise between her neighbors, the daughter should "make it no worse, meende it if þou may" (p. 44).

35. "Advice to the Several Estates, II," in *Historical Poems of the Fourteenth and Fifteenth Centuries,* ed. R. H. Robbins (New York: Columbia University Press, 1959), pp. 233–35.

36. Whiting, ed., *The Poems of John Audelay,* p. 38. The author of a Worcester sermon instructed lay people coming to confession that "þe schalt ben e charite with þyn

emcristen," and a religious poem from around the 1420s said that people should not receive the communion while "in synne and stryf" (Grisdale, ed., *Three Middle English Sermons*, p. 60; "Of the Sacrament of the Altar," in *Twenty-Six Political and Other Poems*, ed. Kail, part 1, p. 105.)

37. Thomas F. Simmons, ed., *The Lay-Folks Mass Book: or, The Manner of Hearing the Mass*, EETS, o.s. 71, (London: Trübner, 1879), pp. 46–49; Theodor Erbe, ed., *Mirk's Festial: A Collection of Homilies*, part 1, EETS, extra ser. 96 (London: Kegan Paul, Trench, Trübner, 1905), p. 168. *The Lay-Folks Mass Book* said that the requirement of being at peace with others when receiving the communion is symbolized by the kissing of the Pax (pp. 48–49). The kiss of peace was part of lay interactions, too: the poem "Love God, and Drede" says that "if a man do a-nother mys, / Neighbores shuld hem auyse, / The trespasour amende and kys, / Do bothe parties euene assise" (*Twenty-Six Political and Other Poems*, ed. Kail, part 1, p. 6).

38. Furnivall, ed., *Early English Meals and Manners*, p. 50.

39. "To Lyf Bodyly, Is Perylous," in *Twenty-Six Political and Other Poems*, ed. Kail, part 1, pp. 25–27 (written perhaps around the start of the century); *The Assembly of Gods*, p. 21.

40. Brandeis, ed., *Jacob's Well*, pp. 134–35, including playing for gain and keeping the profits of gambling.

41. Robbins, ed., *Historical Poems of the Fourteenth and Fifteenth Centuries*, pp. 134–37.

42. "The Childe of Bristow, " ed. Clarence Hopper, Camden Society Miscellany, vol. 4 (London, 1859), p. 22; and see Chapter 8 by Barbara Hanawalt in this volume.

43. Ernst Sieper, ed., *Lydgate's Reson and Sensuallyte*, vol. 1, EETS, extra ser. 84 (London: Kegan Paul, Trench, Trübner, 1901), pp. 63–64, written at the beginning of the century; *The Assembly of Gods*, p. 21.

44. Furnivall, ed., *Early English Meals and Manners*, p. 50.

45. See, for example, *The Chester Mystery Cycle*, vol. 1, pp. 306–9.

46. A. Caiger-Smith, *English Medieval Mural Paintings* (Oxford: Clarendon Press, 1963), pp. 55–58 and Plate 20.

47. By the sixteenth century, these groups seemed to constitute a particular threat to three meanings of the concept of order: a stable *social order*, in the sense of hierarchy and location; eagerness to prevent *disorder* or violations of local security; and concern with *good order*, meaning harmonious or amicable interactions within the community.

48. The ecclesiastical courts were dealing actively with sexual issues in the second half of the fifteenth century, as they had done before and would continue to do thereafter: see, for example, Richard M. Wunderli, *London Church Courts and Society on the Eve of the Reformation* (Cambridge, Mass.: Medieval Academy of America, 1981), chap. 4; and Christopher Dyer, *Lords and Peasants in a Changing Society: The Estates of the Bishopric of Worcester, 680–1540* (Cambridge: Cambridge University Press, 1980), pp. 362–65.

49. Public Record Office SC 2/172/38 (Manor of Havering, Essex, 1497); Hampshire Record Office Eccles I 81/9 (Manor of Alverstoke, 1462); Cambridge University Library E.D.R. C/6/11 (Manor of Ely Barton, 1475–76); Norfolk Record Office N.R.S. 6025, 20 E 3 (Manor of Cawston, 1494); Somerset Record Office DD/L P28/13 (Manor of Minehead, 1468).

50. For a discussion of the language and symbolism of hospitality, see Felicity Heal, *Hospitality in Early Modern England* (Oxford: Clarendon Press, 1990), esp. chap. 1.

51. Norfolk Record Office N.R.S. 20743, Box 41 D 4 (Manor of Fakenham [Lancaster], 1503), and Wiltshire Record Office 490/1169 (Manor of Downton, 1465).

52. This was not the result of any new parliamentary legislation: no statutes concerning alehouses were passed between 1400 and 1489. Only in 1495 was it ordered that alehouses be licensed by the justice of the peace after appropriate sureties for good behavior had been provided (11 Henry VII, c. 2, heading 5). Simple violations of the licensing laws are not counted as offenses in this study.

53. Devon Record Office CR 341 (Hundred of Tiverton, 1454), and Greater London Record Office M95/BEC/9 (Manor of Tooting Bec, Middlesex, 1483).

54. Wiltshire Record Office 490/1169 (Manor of Downton, 1465); Norfolk Record Office N.R.S. 6025, 20 E 3 (Manor of Cawston, 1494); Somerset Record Office DD/CC 131903/5 (1467).

55. Norfolk Record Office Y/C 4/153 (Borough of Great Yarmouth, 1446), Lincolnshire Archives Office 6.Ancaster 1/85 (Manor of Langtoft and Baston, 1467), and Somerset Record Office DD/L P28/15 (Manor of Minehead, 1496); Cambridge University Library E.D.R. C/11/3 (Manor of [Little] Downham, 1491–92). Allegations of bad governance were not merely a warning, as a number of such offenders were expelled from their communities.

56. Physical violence (as opposed to restraint *cum* ridicule) was not used in the kinds of courts described in this paper at any time during the fifteenth century. Even whipping of vagrants was not recorded (nor was it authorized by statute until 1531: 22 Henry VIII, c. 12). For the suggestion that the later fifteenth century saw a heightened concern with violent punishments in some urban settings as a tool of governance, see Chapter 3 by Seth Lerer in this volume.

57. For the appropriation of elements of ideology by specific social groups, see Strohm, *Hochon's Arrow*, esp. the introduction.

58. Even Lollard authors concentrated less upon the moral conduct of the laity than upon other issues. Whereas Wycliffite writers were deeply concerned about the righteousness of the clergy, and while they may have attempted more vigorously to implement appropriate social behavior, they appear to have offered no innovative ideas about or even special emphasis upon lay social actions in their writings. See, for example, Anne Hudson, ed., *Selections from English Wycliffite Writings* (Cambridge: Cambridge University Press, 1978); Anne Hudson, ed., *English Wycliffite Sermons*, vol. 1 (Oxford: Clarendon Press, 1983); and Gloria Cigman, ed., *Lollard Sermons*, EETS, o.s. 294 (London: Oxford University Press, 1989).

59. For heightened opposition to alehouses in this period, part of a class-based set of worries centered on peasant misconduct, see Ralph Hanna III, "Pilate's Voice/Shirley's Case," *South Atlantic Quarterly* 91 (1992): 793–812, and chapter 1 by Hanna in this collection.

60. For the former, see, for example, "La Male Regle de T. Hoccleue," in *Selections from Hoccleve*, ed. M. C. Seymour (Oxford: Clarendon Press, 1981), pp. 12–23. Ralph Hanna, who kindly suggested the previous reference, agrees with my sense that attitudes toward alehouses remained relatively static across the fifteenth century (personal communication).

61. For a fuller discussion of this point, see Marjorie K. McIntosh, "Local Change and Community Control in England, 1465–1500," *Huntington Library Quarterly* 49 (1986): 219–42.

62. 17 Edward IV, c. 3; for the revision of 1495, see 11 Henry VII, c. 2, heading 5.

63. Much of my discussion here derives from Pat McCune, "Late Medieval Strategies of Retribution and Reconciliation," paper read to the American Historical Association, December 1991. I am grateful to Dr. McCune for permitting me to use and cite her work.

64. F. J. Furnivall, ed., *Hoccleve's Works*, EETS, extra ser. 72 (London: Kegan Paul, 1897), pp. 97–113, and Robert Steele, ed., *Three Prose Versions of the Secreta Secretorum*, EETS, extra ser. 74 (London: Kegan Paul, 1898), pp. 127–45, both as cited by McCune, "Late Medieval Strategies." See also "Tractatus de Regimine Principum," written circa 1435–50 for Henry VI, in *Four English Political Tracts of the Later Middle Ages*, ed. Jean-Philippe Genet, Camden Society, 4th ser. 18 (London: Royal Historical Society, 1977) pp. 48–168, esp. pp. 49 and 72–78.

65. Even the most innovative thinker of the century, Fortescue, employs in his works of the 1460s and 1470s the now familiar rubric of governance within which to offer a more sophisticated analysis of the actual nature of control within different types of political structures. See, for example, Sir John Fortescue, *De Laudibus Legum Angliae*, ed. A. Amos (Cambridge: Cambridge University Press, 1825); Charles Plummer, ed., *Gover-*

nance of England (Oxford: Clarendon Press, 1885); and Arthur B. Ferguson, *The Articulate Citizen and the English Renaissance* (Durham, N.C.: Duke University Press, 1965), esp. chap. 5.

66. Scanlon notes the parallels between use of exempla in moral sermons and in political works of the later medieval years (*Narrative, Authority and Power*, chap. 4), but this speaks to the shared experience of the authors of such works, not necessarily establishing that they had similar audiences.

67. While removing a certain amount of deadwood was good for a hedge, taking too much old wood or any live wood might harm it. Hedgebreaking was never proscribed by statute except through a general application of theft, but the latter was difficult to apply to common property. By the sixteenth century, reports of hedgebreaking serve as an a priori indicator of a rising level of poverty within a given community. The offense considered here has sometimes been confused by historians with the deliberate knocking down of newly erected hedges as a protest against enclosure.

68. Somerset Record Office DD/L P28/13 (Manor of Minehead, 1468); Berkshire Record Office D/ESk M13 (Manor of Cookham, 1484).

69. In the Assize of Clarendon of 1166, the king had prohibited people from receiving a vagabond ("that is, a wandering or an unknown man") anywhere except in a borough, and then only for one night. The next legislative mention came only in the 1380s.

70. Worcestershire Record Office (St. Helens) 705:56/BA 3910/22/10, and ibid., 1496. For the next three quotations, see University of Durham MSS Dept., Prior's Kitchen, DCD Halmote Court, autumn 1460 (first entry, place name damaged); Devon Record Office CR 81 (Hundred of West Budleigh, 1494); Lincolnshire Archives Office ANC 3/14/66 (Manor of Spilsby cum Eresby, 1505).

71. Cornwall Record Office ARB 75/84 (Manor of Fowey, 1456); Devon Record Office CR 124 (Hundred of Hayridge, 1502); Wiltshire Record Office 490/1169 (Manor of Downton, 1465); Devon Record Office CR 81 (Hundred of West Budleigh, 1494).

72. For a fuller discussion, see Marjorie K. McIntosh, "Local Responses to the Poor in Late Medieval and Tudor England," *Continuity and Change* 3 (1988): 209–45.

73. Whereas 88 percent of 112 residential institutions for the poor and sick founded between 1300 and 1399 that gave themselves a title called themselves hospitals, only 45 percent of 103 houses founded in the period 1400 to 1459 were named hospitals, the rest being almshouses; between 1460 and 1499, just 21 percent of 61 new foundations were hospitals and the rest almshouses. For fuller information and discussion of the sources and methods of this study, see Marjorie K. McIntosh, "The Foundation of Hospitals and Almshouses in Medieval and Tudor England," paper read at the Wellcome Unit for the History of Medicine, Oxford, October 1990.

74. All houses stipulated daily attendance at church and prayers for the souls of the donor(s) and other Christian dead. Residential institutions for the poor marked by careful regulation bear obvious resemblance to the ideas of Michel Foucault but in a rather different time frame: see, for example, *Discipline and Punish: The Birth of the Prison*, trans. Alan Sheridan (New York: Pantheon, 1977).

75. In addition to those cited in the text, we have statements from Sherborne Almshouse in Dorset, founded 1438 (Dorset Record Office D/SHA D24); Roger Reede's almshouse in Romford, Essex, founded 1483 (Essex Record Office D/Q 26); Heytesbury Almshouse, Wiltshire, founded circa 1442 with statutes of 1472–74 ("Ancient Statutes of Heytesbury Almshouse," *Wiltshire Archaeological and Natural History Magazine* 11 (1869): 289–308); Hosier's Almshouses in Ludlow, Shropshire, founded 1486 (Shropshire Record Office 356/Box 315); and Pykenham's almshouses in Hadleigh, Suffolk, founded 1497 (Hadleigh Town Records MS 25/29).

76. Francis W. Steer, "The Statutes of Saffron Walden Almshouses," *Transactions of the Essex Archaeological Society*, n.s. 25 (1955–60): 160–221 (quotation here translated from the Latin text). This Essex house was founded by a group of local merchants, with ordinances from the very beginning of the fifteenth century.

77. University of Nottingham Library MSS Dept. MS Mi 6/179/18 (a copy made circa 1500). Alice, duchess of Suffolk, and her husband William de la Pole created this house in Oxfordshire around 1437; it is the only institution discussed here whose founders were members of the nobility.

78. Berkshire Record Office D/Q1 Q7/15, and D/QWo 35/1/1 (calendar entry). The house in Lambourne was founded by Isbury, a local gentleman, in 1501; Westende, a clerk, set up his institution in 1451.

79. 23 Edward III, Ordinance Concerning Labourers and Servants; 25 Edward III, stat. 2. As Aers has noted, classifying mobile workers as idle mendicants and beggars was an important rhetorical weapon within the social and political struggle waged by England's leadership at the time ("*Piers Plowman*: Poverty, Work, and Community," in *Community, Gender, and Individual Identity*, pp. 20–72, esp. p. 30).

80. 7 Richard II, c. 5; 12 Richard II, c. 7.

81. Hanna, "Pilate's Voice/Shirley's Case."

82. For the emergence in the later fourteenth century of the stereotype of the mobile, able-bodied beggar, see Aers, "*Piers Plowman*," p. 37.

83. For a general discussion of this topic, see Siegfried Wenzel, *The Sin of Sloth: Acedia in Medieval Thought and Literature* (Chapel Hill, N.C.: University of North Carolina Press, 1960).

84. *Lydgate's Reson and Sensuallyte*, vol. 1, pp. 181–82 (idleness was also an important character in *The Assembly of Gods*, see, for example, pp. 20–22); Eccles, ed. *The Macro Plays*, p. 51.

85. As in *Occupation and Idleness*, from around the mid-century: in *Non-Cycle Plays and The Winchester Dialogues*, ed. Norman Davis, Leeds Studies in English (Leeds: University of Leeds, 1979), pp. 192–208.

86. Robbins, ed., *Historical Poems of the Fourteenth and Fifteenth Centuries*, p. 233; "Active Policy of a Prince," in *George Ashby's Poems*, ed. Mary Bateson, EETS, extra ser. 76 (London: Kegan Paul, 1899), p. 29.

87. This observation disagrees with historical studies that describe severe practical problems with poor people and intense concern with and antagonism to them throughout the later fourteenth and fifteenth centuries (for example, Michel Mollat, *The Poor in the Middle Ages: An Essay in Social History*, trans. Arthur Goldhammer [New Haven, Conn.: Yale University Press, 1986]; *Etudes sur l'Histoire de la Pauvreté*, ed. Michel Mollat, 2 vols., [Paris: Publications de la Sorbonne, 1974]; and Miri Rubin, *Charity and Community in Medieval Cambridge* [Cambridge: Cambridge University Press, 1987]). Such portrayals err, I think, by failing to discriminate with sufficient care between rhetoric and reality, between attitudes of the second half of the fourteenth century and the rather different concerns of the fifteenth century, and between continental and English texts. For the suggestion that poverty was not a serious problem in practical terms in England between about 1400 and 1460, see the final section of this chapter.

88. *Mum and the Sothsegger*, for example, says when talking about support for the church and clergy that God's part of the church's wealth should be given to God's men, namely the poor (ed. Mabel Day and R. Steele, EETS, o.s. 199 [London: Oxford University Press, 1936], pp. 46–47, written at the turn of the fifteenth century).

89. Interest in the works of mercy may have lingered with particular power in the north (see P. H. Cullum, "Hospitals and Charitable Provision in Medieval Yorkshire, 936–1547" (D.Phil. thesis, University of York, 1989). They were also represented visually in a number of fifteenth-century wall paintings in parish churches (Caiger-Smith, *English Medieval Mural Paintings*, pp. 53–55).

90. Whiting, ed., *The Poems of John Audelay*, p. 7; Kali, ed. *Twenty-Six Political and Other Poems*, part 1, pp. 73–75.

91. See, for example, the references in note 58. This provides additional interest to John M. Bowers's suggestion of a link between the *Piers Plowman* tradition and Lollardy

in the fifteenth century: "Piers Plowman and the Police: Notes toward a History of the Wycliffite Langland," *Yearbook of Langland Studies* 6 (1992): 1–50.

92. Useful editions of the texts are *Piers Plowman: The A Version*, ed. George Kane, rev. ed. (London: Athlone, 1988); *Piers Plowman: The B Version*, ed. George Kane and E. T. Donaldson, rev. ed. (London: Athlone, 1988); and *Piers Plowman by William Langland: An Edition of the C-Text*, ed. Derek Pearsall, York Medieval Texts, 2nd ser. (Berkeley: University of California Press, 1979). Among recent discussions of Langland's analysis of poverty are David Aers, "*Piers Plowman* and Problems in the Perception of Poverty: A Culture in Transition," Leeds Studies in English, new ser. 14 (Leeds: University of Leeds, 1983), pp. 5–25; Geoffrey Shepherd, "Poverty in *Piers Plowman*," *Social Relations and Ideas*, ed. T. H. Aston et al. (Cambridge: Cambridge University Press, 1983), pp. 169–90; R. E. Kaske, "The Character Hunger in *Piers Plowman*," and Derek Pearsall, "Poverty and Poor People in *Piers Plowman*," both in *Medieval English Studies Presented to George Kane*, ed. Edward D. Kennedy et al. (Bury St. Edmunds: St. Edmundsbury Press, 1988), pp. 187–97, 167–86; Aers, "*Piers Plowman*: Poverty, Work, and Community"; Wendy Scase, "*Piers Plowman*" *and the New Anti-Clericalism* (Cambridge: Cambridge University Press, 1989); and Lawrence M. Clopper, "Need Men and Women Labor? Langland's Wanderer and the Labor Ordinances," in *Chaucer's England: Literature in Historical Context*, ed. Barbara A. Hanawalt (Minneapolis: University of Minnesota Press, 1992), pp. 110–29.

93. For fifteenth-century copies of *Piers Plowman* and the topics that seem to have drawn attention, see Marie-Claire Uhart, "The Early Reception of Piers Plowman (Ph.D. diss., University of Leicester, 1988), and Scase, "*Piers Plowman*" *and the New Anti-Clericalism*, both of which document interest in *clerical* poverty. I am grateful to Dr. Uhart for permission to consult her thesis and to John M. Bowers for loaning his copy of it to me.

94. For the suggestion that the debate could be transferred to an attack on lay beggars, see Aers, "*Piers Plowman*: Poverty, Work, and Community," pp. 29–30; for the equation between clerical beggars and illegitimate lay beggars, including discussion of the "gyrovague," a false religious within a type of antireligious satire who went from house to house in search of hospitality, see Scase, "*Piers Plowman*" *and the New Anti-Clericalism*, esp. chap. 3 and pp. 125–37. Anticlericalism could also be tied to grand plans to eliminate poverty: see Margaret Aston, " 'Caim's Castles': Poverty, Politics, and Disendowment," in *The Church, Politics and Patronage in the Fifteenth Century*, ed. Barrie Dobson (New York: St. Martin's Press, 1984), pp. 45–81.

95. 11 Henry VII, c. 2.

96. For example, the undated poem "Advice to the Several Estates, II," in *Historical Poems of the Fourteenth and Fifteenth Centuries*, ed. Robbins, pp. 233–35; "The Childe of Bristow," pp. 10, 12.

97. Priscilla H. Barnum, ed., *Dives and Pauper*, vol. 1, parts 1 and 2, EETS, o.s. 275 and 280 (London: Oxford University Press, 1976 and 1980), part 1, pp. 55–56. Dives sounds like just the sort of person who might have founded an almshouse in his town. Pauper also expressly disavowed any necessary connection between poverty and misbehavior, saying that wealth is occasion of more sin than is poverty. That idea, expressed here in the first decade of the 1400s, was coming under question by the end of the century.

98. Reginald Pecock, *The Reule of Crysten Religioun*, ed. William C. Greet, EETS, o.s. 171 (London: Oxford University Press, 1927), pp. 377–78. Pecock later found himself in trouble with the church for some of his beliefs, but there is no indication that this one was deemed erroneous.

99. For example, the poem "Man, Know Thy Self, and Lerne to Dye" talks about which kinds of poor people should receive alms but goes no further than separating the "nedeles gredy" from two kinds of legitimately "pore and nedy" (in *Twenty-Six Political and Other Poems*, ed. Kail, part 1, pp. 27–29).

100. Whiting, ed., *The Poems of John Audelay*, pp. 9–10.

101. Brandeis, ed., *Jacob's Well*, p. 121, citing Saint Bernard and with a curious use of James 5:2–3.

102. See note 10.

103. For a fuller discussion, with references, see McIntosh, "Local Responses to the Poor."

104. Their excess income permitted at least a few to indulge in that clothing whose richness so offended their superiors. For the emphasis on dress among workers in the sumptuary legislation of this period, see 3 Edward IV, c. 5, and 22 Edward IV, c. 1.

105. A more detailed discussion of this period, with references, is given in McIntosh, "Local Change and Community Control."

106. Enclosure is thought by most recent historians to have been the *result* of depopulation rather than a major *cause* of eviction and vagrancy, as was assumed by many previous writers. See, for example, Ian Blanchard, "Population Change, Enclosure, and the Early Tudor Economy," *Economic History Review*, 2nd ser., 23 (1970): 427–45; and Christopher Dyer, "Deserted Medieval Villages in the West Midlands," *Economic History Review*, 2nd ser., 35 (1982): 19–34.

107. Local court records from the 1460s onward begin to list many more servants among those entered into the Frankpledge and named for minor local offenses. Even a relatively limited expansion of service in the market centers could have attracted enough additional young people to heighten local sensitivity to them.

❖

CHAPTER 6

Two Models, Two Standards
Moral Teaching and Sexual Mores
Ruth Mazo Karras

During the Middle Ages, although a clearly articulated set of official teachings stipulated what sexual behavior was permitted and what was forbidden, not everyone followed it. In addition, even if standards of sexual morality were the same for both sexes, men could much more easily flout them without risking punishment or opprobrium. These truisms tell us little that is specific about late medieval England. Yet the intersection of these two propositions does reveal a good deal about the degree to which believers internalized the teachings of the church. Both didactic literature and court records from the fifteenth century indicate that they did so to a much greater extent with regard to women's behavior than to men's.

The concept "teachings of the church" deserves some elaboration, because the church was, of course, composed of many groups and individuals teaching many different things. I use the term here to mean the body of writings by canonists and theologians that was generally accepted as doctrine. Obviously there was not universal agreement, and some issues remained contested. By the late Middle Ages, though, the church's basic positions on the various sorts of sexual behavior were fairly well established.[1] This does not mean that what every parish priest preached was in line with official doctrine. There were a host of texts directed at the parish clergy that attempted to set out for them the orthodox point of view on each of the *praedicabilia,* the matters that were to be preached to the laity at least four times a year.[2] Despite these educational efforts, I would not suggest that the views of any given parish priest were necessarily closer to those of the theologians or canonists than were those of the laity. The laity are here contrasted with scholars and prelates, not with the parish clergy.

Two Models of Sexual Behavior?

Some people in any society violate approved norms of sexual behavior. If they do so while accepting those norms as fundamentally valid, then there is a disparity between theory and practice. If, however, they substitute another set of norms, then the disparity is not between theory and practice, but between two competing models of acceptable sexuality. One group not only breaks the other group's rules, it also has some belief or rationale, if not a fully elaborated theory, that justifies that behavior. Competing models like this often arise where two cultures meet: for example, in the age of European expansion, Europeans labeled polygamous practices as promiscuous and deviant.[3] They also arise when one social class imposes its norms on another, for example labeling as prostitution relationships that those involved in them consider practical living arrangements or normal social interactions.[4] In high medieval Europe, Georges Duby has suggested, two models clashed as the church sought to control marriage as a sacrament while lay magnates considered it an issue of property and dynastic alliance.[5]

The problem of the extent to which the laity in the Late Middle Ages absorbed the church's teaching extends beyond the area of sexuality and marriage. Recent work on medieval religion has emphasized that the laity had their own understandings and interpretations of text and doctrine. Some medievalists argue that popular belief was "folkloric" and had little relation to the great debates over doctrine—indeed, that much of medieval culture can hardly be termed "Christian."[6] Others argue that by the Late Middle Ages, lay people commonly knew and accepted the basics of the faith as taught by the church, but developed their own ways of understanding them.[7] The issue of lay and ecclesiastical models of sexual behavior is part of the wider question of the thoroughness of European Christianization.

Since marriage was considered the appropriate locus for sex, we can look briefly at marriage to see whether the laity either ignored the church's teaching or developed (or retained) their own model in competition with it.[8] In the realm of behavior, as opposed to doctrine, late medieval English people seem to have accepted the church's definition of what constitutes a valid marriage. Richard Helmholz has argued that many people regarded the exchange of vows, which under canon law constituted an indissoluble marriage, as a betrothal or contract to marry.[9] This would imply not just disregard of the church's definition but an alternative model. Yet there is evidence that already by the thirteenth century secular law courts had accepted the church's position on the exchange of vows.[10] Less educated people may have entered into unions more informally than canon law dictated, but by the fourteenth century, as Michael Sheehan has shown, the church was regularizing marriage among the poor by recognizing informal relationships as clandestine marriages. Clandestine marriage, which the church deemed illicit although indissoluble, did continue during the fourteenth and fifteenth centuries, but such unions are overrepresented in the court records, since they were much more likely to be in dispute than those celebrated publicly in church. L. R. Poos found in his study of late medieval Essex that the popular culture of marriage generally regarded vows, clandestine or otherwise, as permanent.[11]

Even if there had been a lay model of marriage that differed from that put forward by the church, then, the church's model was winning out by the fifteenth century. The mid-fifteenth-century gentleman and civil servant Peter Idley advised his son, in his explication of the Sixth Commandment, not to marry clandestinely and not to anticipate marriage:

> I sey oonlye for spousaille and wedloke,
> In the face of the churche it oweth to be hadde,
> And not in derke corners behynde thy bakke.
> . . . .
> And if thow be ensured and purpose the to wedde
> And fleisshelie thow knowest the woman to fore,
> Deedly thow synnest.[12]

Idley was an educated man; his *Instructions* drew heavily on the thirteenth-century pastoral manual *Handlyng Synne,* of which they are basically an abridgment. Robert Mannyng had written:

> No trouþ oghte to be ȝeue wyþ ryght
> But yn holy cherchys syȝt

and

> Ȝyf þou ly by here seþen
> Aftyr þou hast þy troupë ȝyven
> Y sey þe weyl certeynly
> þat þou synnedyst þere dedly.[13]

Yet even though he drew on the earlier treatise, it is significant that the same teaching emerged in a text written not for a parish priest to teach from but for a layman to read, and written by another layman. The extent to which such ideas would have been absorbed by the uneducated is still questionable, but records of marriage litigation do not show much difference among social classes (to the extent this can be determined), and the church's efforts to make the marriages of the poor conform to official teaching seem to have been gradually successful.[14]

The laity accepted the church's model of nonmarital sexual behavior (at least for men) less than they did the ecclesiastical view of marriage. Again, this is not simply a question of practice that did not conform to norms; rather it is a question of competing models. One place to look for a lay model of appropriate sexual behavior is in pastoral literature, written either for the laity directly or for the parish clergy. This literature does not, of course, directly represent lay views, but it shows what the church thought they thought, what views needed to be reinforced and what needed to be eradicated (or perhaps preempted). There are, of course, a number of caveats to be observed here. The teachings that the church directed at the laity at any particular time depended not only on current moral conditions, but also on the sources for the particular text, as fifteenth-century writers were as prone as any to repeat traditional topoi. In addition, because of the international circulation of devotional literature, any given text may not reflect specifically English conditions. On the other hand, Peter Biller has demonstrated, regional differences in devotional literature can be identified, which can be linked to differences in demographic and behavioral patterns.[15] We may fairly take a popular English text as indicative of what issues were important in England.

Such a text is *Dives and Pauper,* a treatise on the Ten Commandments written in English between 1405 and about 1410. The work exists in eight manuscripts and several fragments, all from the first two-thirds of the fifteenth century; it was also printed in 1493 by Pynson and again by Wynkyn de Worde in 1496. It thus appears to have had a reasonably wide circulation. Priscilla Heath Barnum, the text's editor, suggests that the audience was "the growing number of newly literate, worldly, some-what credulous yet pious laymen."[16] The three wills that mention the text are all of laymen, as is the heresy trial in which it is mentioned.[17]

As its mention in a heresy trial indicates, *Dives and Pauper,* although orthodox in its theology and ecclesiology, was in some ways a suspect work. A group of sermons written some years later by the same (proba-bly Franciscan) author, possibly for a lay patron, was assumed by a mod-ern cataloguer to be Lollard, although in fact some of the sermons seem to be directly anti-Lollard.[18] The author noted in the prologue to the ser-mons that the earlier work had caused some problems: "I haue wretin þe gospel to ȝou in wol gret drede and persecucion ... now prechinge and techinge of þe gospel and of Goddys lawe is artid and lettid more þan it was wone to ben."[19] The suspect aspects of *Dives and Pauper* stemmed from its reformist attitude toward the church hierarchy and the clergy for their wealth, corruption, and dereliction of duty, and for its implied criticism of Archbishop Arundel's 1407 *Constitutions* restricting access to scripture in the vernacular, rather than from any doctrinal error.[20] At the same time that it was used as evidence in a heresy case, the Abbot of Saint Albans was ordering a copy for his library.[21]

Dives and Pauper is somewhat unusual for texts of this sort in its rel-atively sympathetic attitude toward women. This is apparent through-out the work, as the author refers to "men and women," instead of as-suming women are subsumed under "men." This general attitude is also reflected in its discussion of the double standard.[22] Throughout the discussion of the Sixth Commandment, dealing with sexual morality, Pauper (a friar) defends not only church doctrine but also women against the arguments of Dives (a worldly layman), and, not surprisingly given the genre, Pauper wins the argument.

In the discussion of sexual morality, Dives says to Pauper, "Y may wel assentyn þat avouterie be a wol greuous synne boþin man & in woman, but þat simple fornicacion atwoxsyn sengle man and sengle woman schulde ben dedly synne Y may nout assentyn þerto, and comoun opynyon it is þat it is non dedly synne."[23] Pauper responds by quoting Saint Paul to the effect that fornicators may not enter the kingdom of heaven. Dives continues by claiming that "when a sengle man medelyth with a sengle woman he doth no man ne woman ony wrong, for eyþir of hem is in his own power."[24] The author's putting these words into the mouth of his lay protagonist would certainly seem to indicate that he thought the laity took premarital or nonmarital sex too lightly, as would the fact that he goes to great lengths to prove with biblical texts that it is in fact a mortal sin.[25] This was not a contested issue among theologians, although some writers went into detail as to the reasons it was a mortal sin.[26]

This theme, that many people — "summe foolis," in the words of another fifteenth-century text on the Ten Commandments — believe simple fornication between two single people is not a mortal sin, is also found in other late medieval treatises, although none of them develop it to the same extent as *Dives and Pauper*.[27] By contrast a number of earlier texts stress the sinfulness of fornication but do not note that people have called it into question. *Handlyng Synne* says of fornication, "þe lest hyt ys of allë seuene [branches of lechery], ȝyt hyt forbarreþþe blys of heuene."[28] The fourteenth-century *Lay Folks' Catechism* lists fornication as "a fleshly syn / Betwix ane aynlepi man, and ane aynlepi woman, / That forthi that it is ogaynes the lawe/And the leue, and the lare that hali kirk haldes, / It is dedly syn to tham that dos it," yet adultery is a "greuouser and gretter" sin.[29] *Jacob's Well* calls fornication "þe firste fote depthe" of the sin of lechery, "& þis is dedly synne."[30] It is easy to see why the stress on fornication as the least of the varieties of lechery might have led some to think it was not mortal. The *Fasciculus Morum*, compiled in the first half of the fourteenth century, implies the same thing when it refers to those "who claim that simple fornication is not a mortal sin because it is a natural act."[31] The disagreement is thus not new in the fifteenth century, but these earlier texts do not imply that it was widespread or that there was an articulated lay point of view over against the church's teaching.[32]

Neither *Dives and Pauper* nor these other texts mention widespread lay disagreement with the church's teaching on any other aspect of sexuality, although Dives's arguments against Pauper may represent such disagreement. Obviously, if writers of tracts on the Ten Commandments, the Seven Deadly Sins, or other elements of the faith did not think people were breaking the church's precepts (whether through unfamiliarity or through disobedience), they would not have found it necessary to catalog those precepts. But only in the case of simple fornication is it suggested that people generally recognize the church's teaching on the subject but do not agree with it. In this respect at least we may suggest that there was a different model of sexual morality than that the church promulgated.

The extent to which the objections put forward by Dives really represent a disagreement with the church's model of sexual behavior may be judged by looking at how the text treats other topics. For example, usury and other financial dealings, like sex, constitute an area where lay practice often disagreed with the church's teaching. Yet in the discussion of usury and other sins related to money, Pauper's teaching is not contested. The author uses Dives merely to ask questions to prompt Pauper's teaching—"How many spycys ben þer of vsure?"—or to break up long passages of Pauper's exposition with expressions of agreement—"I assente wel to þin wordis"—or to paraphrase.[33] Only once does Dives argue with Pauper or express an alternative view: "Contra, God ʒaf leue to þe Iewys to takyn vsure of oþir nacionys."[34] This does not directly contradict Pauper's argument, and he easily explains it away. This contrasts with the discussion of the Sixth Commandment, where Dives constantly raises objections or counterarguments from scripture or practice, or indeed raises new topics by taking positions that Pauper then defeats (for example, "Womanys aray steryt mychil folc to lecherye"[35]). The difference is striking and indicates that the existence of actual argument—both over whether fornication is a mortal sin and over the double standard—is not a rhetorical strategy common to the entire text but a reflection of issues that were actually contested in the culture out of which the text came.

The alternative model or point of view about fornication that I am suggesting is not necessarily a pre-Christian or non-Christian view. It may have developed as a consequence of preaching about adultery that gave people the impression that the unmarried did not incur the same degree of sin. Indeed, it may have developed to some degree in resistance to the church's model, in full awareness and rejection of it, as a way of spurning clerical dominance. Yet that dominance was not spurned in respect of feminine behavior. With regard to women, the church's teaching seems to have been far more accepted by the laity—at least by those members of the laity whose views are reflected or inscribed in the sources that have come down to us.

The Double Standard

Dives and Pauper indicates that the laity held a different view of sexual behavior from the official teaching of the church. But that teaching, as expressed in this text and in others, was distinctly gendered. Although these didactic texts mostly preach a common standard of sexual morality for men and women, they seem to be addressed only to men: descriptions of sexual behavior are phrased from the man's point of view only. A poem by the chantry priest John Audelay, for example, in a discussion of adultery, refers only to adulterous husbands: "When he as chosen hyr to his make / And plyȝt here trowþto here y-take / Hy schuld neuer here foresake / Euen ne morne."[36] This is not simply a case of the masculine standing for the general, the "default," as Leo Carruthers has suggested, for religious literature generally.[37] The specifics of the precepts in many texts simply do not apply to women. For example, *Dives and Pauper* includes in the list of types of lechery "lecherie with comoun women ... defylyng of maydynhod," offenses phrased as though only committed by the male partner. The Latin terms are given; "meretricium" could as easily be translated as "prostitution" or being a common woman, but it is not.[38] Even "libidinosus coitus coniugalis," "synful medlyng togedere atwoxsyn housebounde & wife," which seems a gender-neutral phrasing, is elaborated in accordance with the question, "In hou many wisys may þe housebond synnyn medlyng with his wif?"[39] The answers are all given in terms of occasions in which it is a sin for him to "medle with his wyf."

The notion of a woman being presented as the passive partner in sexual intercourse, grammatically as well as physically — as the *Memoriale Credencium* puts it, "þe man þat doþ and þe womman þat suffreþ"[40] — is not a surprising one. It functions here, if not to absolve her of the responsibility, at least to make her insignificant as a player, or to make her sin or lack thereof not the subject of focus. Similarly, the text on the Ten Commandments in Harleian MS 1197 refers to a man who "hadde lyved neuer so weel and plesingly to god alle his lyf before, and after fill doun in lecherie bi a sengle womman." This is the behavior that "summe foolis" think is only a little sin, but there is no comment on the sinfulness of the woman's behavior.[41] Other discussions of sexual sin, including those organized around the Seven Deadly Sins rather than around the Ten Commandments (for example, the *Fasciculus Morum*), also take the masculine point of view exclusively, phrasing the sin as lying with a certain kind of woman.[42] Mirk's *Instructions for Parish Priests*, also from the early fifteenth century, gives instructions for questioning about each sin: on lechery, the one confessing is to be asked whether he sinned with "wyf or may ... sybbe or fremde ... ankeras or nonne, wydowe ... or any that haþ a-vowet to chastyte, or comyn womman." Mirk also adds a series of questions to be asked of women, but the focus once again is on the men. There is much more detail in the questions to be asked of men, and even when questioning women the text still regards the man as the active party: "Byd hyre telle, ȝef heo con, / Of what degre þe mon was / That synned wyþ hyre in þe cas."[43]

The stress on the masculine audience is consistent with the view expressed in *Dives and Pauper* that adultery is a greater sin for a man than for a woman, because "þe heyere degre þe harder is þe fal & þe synne mor greuous," and because he is supposed to govern his wife and there-fore should be a model of behavior to her. When Dives suggests that wives who have sex with their servants are brought into court and shamed, whereas husbands who do the same with their maids are hardly ever brought before the court, Pauper responds that it is not God's law but "þe schrewidnesse of man þat makyth man lesse gylty þan woman in þe same synne." The author here recognizes both the existence of the dou-ble standard and its enforcement in the courts. Men are punished less for adultery than women because they testify on each other's behalf and cover up for each other, not because they are less guilty. "In woman is seldam seyn auouterie & therfor it is wol slaundrous whan it fallyt & hard punchyd."[44] The text here argues that women's sexual misdeeds are commonly treated as more serious, and that is why men need to be reminded that theirs are in fact more serious as well as more common. Women have to be chaste because they are guarded by their husbands; men must guard themselves.[45]

This attitude that adultery is worse when committed by men than when committed by women is not typical for medieval English (or other) writers: Bromyard in the fourteenth century, for example, argued that it was worse when committed by women: "adultery is worse and more cruel in a woman than in a man, and she is more criticized, because an adulterous man does not disinherit his own sons, but the sons of him with whose wife he sins, and it is more against nature to exercise cru-elty upon one's own than upon others."[46] Indeed, John of Freiburg, one of the main sources used by the author of *Dives and Pauper,* similarly noted in his *Summa Confessorum* that woman's adultery is worse than men's because she sins against two of the goods of marriage (faith and legitimate children), whereas he sins against only one.[47] *Dives and Pau-per* is a pro-woman text in this way and many others—it recognizes that women tempt men to sin, a common theme in medieval preaching, but also "many mo women han ben deceyuyd be þe malyce of men þan euere wer men deceyuyd be malyce of woman."[48] But it also recognizes in its discussion a prevailing societal attitude: that men had a different idea of what was appropriate sexual behavior for them and what was ap-propriate for women.

This critique of the double standard was obviously not new, although the observation that men favor each other in legal proceedings may have been. The author of "Dives and Pauper" cites and draws heavily on Au-gustine's *"De decem chordis"* in this section. It is unusual among me-dieval English texts in doing so, and the author may have known Au-gustine's sermon itself rather than using it via a florilegium.[49] This work may have picked up the critique of the double standard where others did not because of the author's relatively pro-woman tendency (it can hardly be called feminist when he suggests that men should be held to a higher standard because of their superiority) and perhaps, we may speculate, because it addressed the contemporary situation.

The sexual double standard was part of what I have been calling the lay model of sexual behavior.[50] The church was not arguing that men needed to behave differently from women; the texts discussed men's behavior more than women's because it was a more contested area. The laity accepted the church's standards of behavior for women far more readily than it did for men. Virginity was valued for women much more than it was for men outside the monastery. Sexual sinfulness was an important part of the complex of misogynistic commonplaces that appear in a wide variety of literary genres throughout the medieval period.[51] Women's supposedly innate lustful nature did not mean that their transgressions were more excusable than men's; on the contrary, it made them more dangerous.

Not only were men's sexual transgressions generally treated (by the church courts and by society) as less significant than women's, but there was also, as argued in the first section of this chapter, a competing model of behavior that held that they were not even transgressions. This is why treatises focused on the masculine. People had to be convinced that these things were wrong for men to do; they did not have to be convinced that they were wrong for women. This does not mean that there was not an alternative model held by at least some women for women, but it never became textualized; it was not widely enough held to compete with the church's model, because many women had accepted that model. The church's model was a masculine model (although not the only masculine one), but there is little evidence of what the feminine alternative might have been.

The acceptance of the church's standards for women can be seen in the records of the ecclesiastical courts. People often ended up in church court for sexual offenses because they were gossiped about or informed on by their neighbors, suggesting that standards of morality were being imposed from within the community as well as from without.[52] Chaucer's *Friar's Tale* describes just such informing: "For subtilly he hadde his espiaille, / That taughte him wel wher that him myghte availle. / He koude spare of lecchours oon or two, / To techen hym to foure and twenty mo."[53] By the end of the fifteenth century, as Marjorie McIntosh argues in her essay in this volume, people also ended up in manorial courts for sexual offenses, again because of local concerns.[54]

We can also determine something about attitudes toward men's and women's sexual behavior from defamation cases, which are intimately related to the gossip networks that brought sexual behavior to the courts' attention. One of the reasons defamation of one's character was so damaging was that it could lead to prosecution in ecclesiastical court.[55] Defamation cases show very distinctive gender patterns. For example, in London church court records from the late fifteenth century, women were defamed of sexual offenses far more often than men. Women also defamed others, both men and women, of sexual offenses far more often than did men.[56] Data from other jurisdictions, including some from earlier in the century, confirm the much greater number of sexual defamations against women.[57] The London pattern suggests not only an identification of women with the sexual (whereas men had a much wider range of insults that could be hurled at them), but perhaps also a restricted range of ammunition available to women who wanted to attack their enemies.

The acts referred and alluded to in the records of ex officio cases in the ecclesiastical courts commonly involved one party of each sex, but the parties were often viewed and treated differently. In accusations of fornication or adultery, correspondents were generally named, even if not accused, and men and women were charged and purged at an approximately equal rate.[58] When women were accused of being whores (*meretrix*, which did not necessarily mean "prostitute," although it often did), however, their partners were not accused.[59] A woman risked being labeled for her promiscuous behavior far more than did a man. The differing rates of defamation also indicate that sexual reputation was far more important for women than for men: either sexual insults were not used as much against men, or they were not considered defamatory. Other accusations — dishonesty in business, for example — might affect them much more.

The use of sexual defamation against women is an indication not only of a double standard of sexual behavior, but also of a lack of an alternative to the church's model of appropriate sexual behavior for women, as there was for men. The ecclesiastical view — chastity outside of marriage, without exception — fitted with popular notions of what women should be like (although not necessarily notions of what women *were* like). When they did not adhere to that model it was not only the church but also the community at large that called them to task for it. Men's behavior, however, was measured against two competing standards: if they did not measure up to the church's standard, the community minded a good deal less.[60] As McIntosh discusses, by the second half of the fifteenth century, sexual offenses were becoming a concern to local communities who treated them as disturbances of the peace, but even then only women were whores, women more often than men were "ill governed of their bodies" or "lived suspiciously," and the sorts of sexual offenses for which men were presented most often involved their control of women's sexuality: brothelkeeping or pandering.[61]

Because the court records used here do not run over a long period and therefore do not lend themselves to the analysis of change over time, and because the literary works cited do not differ markedly in emphasis from those of the thirteenth and fourteenth centuries, it is difficult to locate either of the phenomena discussed here—an alternative model of male sexual behavior and a sexual double standard—very specifically in the fifteenth century. Demographic patterns, in particular the presence of unmarried women, may suggest some reasons why the double standard may have been a major concern in the later Middle Ages.

The existence of unmarried women, who were not under the control of a particular man, could be seen as a threat to the social order. This may have been the case when, because of population pressure, women could not accumulate a sufficient dowry to make a suitable marriage.[62] In the late fourteenth and the fifteenth centuries, however, as the labor shortage following the Black Death improved women's economic situation, unmarried women did not become less of a threat; on the contrary, economic independence may have made them less eager to marry and more choosy about their marriage partners.[63]

Economic independence allowed a certain degree of personal independence that was perceived as threatening; fear of this independence could lead to attempts to control women's sexuality.[64] In the later part of the century, when recession forced more women to rely on marriage for their support, independent women might also have been seen as endangering social stability: skewed sex ratios in the towns meant that there were women who would not be able to find marriage partners, and the lack of good alternatives to marriage meant that even if a larger proportion were marrying than before, those who did not posed more of a problem for the society.[65] The presence of a large number of single women, perceived as more of a problem than a large number of single men, could have contributed to the need for a means of control of their sexuality. Where men were concerned, on the other hand, demographic factors such as rates of nuptiality did not occasion a secular push for conformity with church doctrine. The demographic situation does not explain the emergence of the double standard at a particular time, as indeed it should not, because it was an ongoing feature of European society. It may, however, help explain why it was important at this time.

In arguing for two models of masculine sexual behavior I do not wish to draw a sharp dichotomy between them. The human mind has a great capacity for believing two mutually contradictory things simultaneously—or, to put it another way, for participating at once in two discourses. Obviously we cannot separate low and high culture, or the teaching of the church and the views of the laity, because individuals both of the clergy and the laity participated in both. But we can see that the discourses about masculine sexual behavior were more conflicted and contradictory than those about feminine behavior, where the hegemonic model of appropriate sexual conduct found much more acceptance. Individual women did resist the standards of behavior placed upon them, but late medieval society was ready to suppress—or ignore—such resistance.

Notes

I thank Ralph Hanna, Marjorie McIntosh, Miri Rubin, Larry Scanlon, and Paul Strohm for helpful comments on the version of this essay presented at the Intersections conference; David Boyd, Baber Johansen, Christopher Karras, Larry Poos, Paul Szarmach, and John Van Engen for advice on the longer written version; and Barbara Hanawalt and David Wallace for their extensive and constructive editorial suggestions. Larry Poos was kind enough to share with me in advance of publication work that has influenced this paper, and Priscilla Barnum was most generous with her time and her knowledge of *Dives and Pauper*.

1. James A. Brundage, *Law, Sex, and Christian Society in Medieval Europe* (Chicago: University of Chicago Press, 1987), is the indispensable reference on the canonists. Pierre J. Payer, *The Bridling of Desire* (Toronto: University of Toronto Press, 1993), while not as comprehensive, gives an account of the theologians' view.

2. The matters to be preached were set out by Archbishop Pecham in 1281 at the Council of Lambeth, and repeated in other episcopal constitutions. See F. M. Powicke and C. R. Cheney, eds., *Councils and Synods, with Other Documents Relating to the English Church*, vol. 2 (Oxford: Clarendon Press, 1964), p. 886. For accounts of the literature this generated, see W. A. Pantin, *The English Church in the Fourteenth Century* (Toronto: Medieval Academy of America, 1986), pp. 220–43; D. W. Robertson Jr., "Frequency of Preaching in Thirteenth-Century England," *Speculum* 24 (1949): 376–88.

3. For example, John D'Emilio and Estelle B. Freedman, *Intimate Matters: A History of Sexuality in America* (New York: Harper and Row, 1988), pp. 6–9.

4. See, for example, Linda Mahood, *The Magdalenes: Prostitution in the Nineteenth Century* (London: Routledge, 1990), pp. 3–13; also, discussion by Judith R. Walkowitz, *Prostitution and Victorian Society: Women, Class, and the State* (Cambridge: Cambridge University Press, 1980), pp. 192–213.

5. Georges Duby, *Medieval Marriage: Two Models from Twelfth-Century France*, trans. Elborg Forster (Baltimore, Md.: Johns Hopkins University Press 1978), and *The Knight, the Lady, and the Priest: The Making of Modern Marriage in Medieval France*, trans. Barbara Bray (New York: Pantheon, 1983).

6. John van Engen, "The Christian Middle Ages as an Historiographical Problem," *American Historical Review* 91 (1986): 519–52, reviews and critiques a number of works taking this approach.

7. Much of this work has grown out of studies of women's spirituality: for example, Caroline Bynum, *Holy Feast and Holy Fast: The Religious Significance of Food to Medieval Women* (Berkeley: University of California Press, 1987); and Clarissa Atkinson, *Mystic and Pilgrim: The Book and the World of Margery Kempe* (Ithaca, N.Y.: Cornell University Press, 1983).

8. The discussion in this chapter of lay attitudes toward sexual morality focuses on the groups who would have been the audience for preaching by the parish clergy, who would have read devotional manuals, or who would have appeared in ecclesiastical court. It thus largely ignores the behavior of the upper aristocracy. Court culture no doubt exhibited the same features — disregard for the church's norms and stricter standards for women than for men — as the rest of lay society, but their alternative model may have been different, more influenced, for example, by genealogical considerations or by different literary traditions. See, for example, the tracts on love found in a manuscript made in 1500 for Prince Arthur: Leslie C. Brook, ed., *Two Late Medieval Love Treatises: Heloise's Art d'Amour and a Collection of Demandes d'Amour*, Medium Ævum Monographs 16 (Oxford: Society for the Study of Mediaeval Languages and Literatures, 1993).

9. R. H. Helmholz, *Marriage Litigation in Medieval England* (London: Cambridge University Press, 1974), pp. 72, 168, 189, and passim; see also Michael M. Sheehan, "The Formation and Stability of Marriage in Fourteenth-Century England: Evidence of an Ely Register," *Mediaeval Studies* 33 (1971): 228–63. For background, see Sheehan, "Marriage Theory and Practice in the Conciliar Legislation and Diocesan Statutes of Medieval

England," *Mediaeval Studies* 40 (1978): 408–60. For subsequent developments see Ralph Houlbrooke, *Church Courts and the People during the English Reformation, 1520–1570* (Oxford: Oxford University Press, 1979), p. 66; Martin Ingram, *Church Courts, Sex, and Marriage in England, 1570–1640* (Cambridge: Cambridge University Press, 1987), esp. pp. 217–18. The church continued to regard private exchange of vows as a valid marriage, although punishable because clandestine. It was not until 1753 that marriage in church was required by law, although in Catholic countries this came in the sixteenth century with the Council of Trent. See Christopher Brooke, *The Medieval Idea of Marriage* (New York: Oxford University Press, 1992), p. 139, and Lawrence Stone, *Uncertain Unions: Marriage in England, 1660–1753* (New York: Oxford University Press, 1992), pp. 17–22.

10. Richard Smith, "Marriage Processes in the English Past: Some Continuities," in *The World We Have Gained: Histories of Population and Social Structure*, ed. Lloyd Bonfield, Richard M. Smith, and Keith Wrightson (Oxford: Blackwell, 1986), p. 57. Henry Ansgar Kelly argues that Chaucer knew and accepted the church's view of clandestine marriage, indeed based his *Troilus and Criseyde* on it ("Clandestine Marriage and Chaucer's 'Troilus,'" *Viator* 4 [1973]: 435–57).

11. Michael M. Sheehan, "Theory and Practice: Marriage of the Unfree and Poor in Medieval Society," *Mediaeval Studies* 50 (1988): 457–87, esp. pp. 484–87; L. R. Poos, *A Rural Society after the Black Death: Essex, 1350–1525* (New York: Cambridge University Press, 1991), pp. 135–40.

12. *Peter Idley's Instructions to His Son*, ed. Charlotte d'Evelyn (Boston: Modern Language Association, 1935), p. 135, lines 1672–79, 1686–88. He goes on to discuss how nevertheless a clandestine contract is binding even without witnesses — a completely orthodox position.

13. *Robert of Brunne's "Handlyng Synne,"* ed. Frederick J. Furnivall, Early English Text Society (EETS) 119 (London: Kegan Paul, Trench, Trübner, 1901), p. 59, lines 1633–34, 1637–40.

14. Sheehan, "Marriage Theory and Practice."

15. P. P. A. Biller, "Marriage Patterns and Women's Lives: A Sketch of a Pastoral Geography," in *Woman Is a Worthy Wight: Women in English Society c. 1200–1500*, ed. P. J. P. Goldberg (Wolfeboro Falls, N.H.: Boydell and Brewer, 1992), pp. 60–107.

16. *Dives and Pauper*, ed. Priscilla Heath Barnum, vol. 1, part 1, EETS 275 (Oxford: Oxford University Press, 1976), p. x. Barnum's third volume, containing an introduction (including sources, analogues, genre, audience, and so on), has not yet appeared, but she was kind enough to share with me some of her notes as well as to discuss the text.

17. Norman P. Tanner, ed., *Heresy Trials in the Diocese of Norwich, 1428–31*, Camden Society, 4th ser. 20 (London: Royal Historical Society, 1977), pp. 98–102; the book was alleged to contain "plures errores et hereses quampluros."

18. Anne Hudson and H. L. Spencer, "Old Author, New Work: The Sermons of MS Longleat 4," *Medium Aevum* 53 (1984): 229–30.

19. Quoted in Anne Hudson, *The Premature Reformation: Wycliffite Texts and Lollard History* (Oxford: Oxford University Press, 1988), p. 420 n. 131.

20. On the reform movement and *Dives and Pauper*'s place in it, see R. N. Swanson, *Church and Society in Late Medieval England* (Oxford: Blackwell, 1989), pp. 312–29.

21. Hudson, *Premature Reformation*, pp. 417–20.

22. The suggestion has been made that the author was the chaplain of a women's monastic house and that this led him to place more importance upon women in his writing than did many clerics. The work, however, is clearly not intended for a monastic audience (Priscilla Heath Barnum, personal communication, January 5, 1994). The suggestion about the author's possible affiliation was made orally to Barnum by John Fines.

23. *Dives and Pauper*, vol., part 2, EETS 280 (1980), bk. 6, chap. 8, p. 76.

24. Ibid., p. 77.

25. It is not only extramarital sex that *Dives and Pauper* comments on; it is also concerned with the appropriate use of sex within marriage, another area of potential disagree-

ment between church and laity, although it is not the focus of the current discussion. It should be noted, though, that there is no mention here of lay disagreement with the official position.

26. The use of Ephesians 5:5 here may be drawn from Thomas of Chobham, *Summa Confessorum* pt. 7, bk. 2, chap. 5a, sec. 2, ed. F. Bloomfield, Analecta Mediaevalia Namurcensia 25 (Louvain: Nauwelaerts, 1968), p. 342. The sermon of Augustine from which the author of *Dives and Pauper* draws other parts of his discussion of the sixth commandment also goes to some length to demonstrate that fornication is against that commandment, but his argument is entirely different (Augustine, "De Decem Chordis," Sermon 9, in *Sermones de Vetere Testamento*, ed. Cyril Lambert, Corpus Christianorum Series Latina 41 [Turnhout: Brepols, 1961], pp. 135–38).

27. For example, British Library (BL), Harleian MS 1197, fol. 1r; Harleian MS 665, fol. 68v (late fifteenth century).

28. *Handlyng Synne*, p. 235, lines 7355–56. The text also refers, some fifteen lines earlier, to lechery as the last of the seven deadly sins, but the greatest but not the least, since it damns two people rather than one (p. 234, lines 7339–40). When referring to fornication as the least of seven, the author clearly is referring to the "seuene maners" of lechery (p. 235, line 7349).

29. *The Lay Folks' Catechism, or the English and Latin Versions of Archbishop Thoresby's Instruction for the People*, ed. Thomas Frederick Simmons and Henry Edward Nolloth, EETS 118 (London: Kegan Paul, Trench, Trübner, 1901), pp. 94–96, lines 546–53.

30. *Jacob's Well*, ed. Arthur Brandeis, EETS 115 (London: Kegan Paul, Trench, Trübner, 1900), p. 160.

31. Siegfried Wenzel, ed. and trans., *Fasciculus Morum: A Fourteenth-Century Preacher's Handbook* (University Park: Pennsylvania State University Press, 1989), bk. 7 chap. 7, p. 669.

32. On "nature" and attitudes toward sexuality in France in the same period, see Jacques Rossiaud, *Medieval Prostitution*, trans. Lydia G. Cochrane (Oxford: Blackwell, 1988), pp. 72–85.

33. *Dives and Pauper*, 7:1–28, pp. 132–210.

34. Ibid., 7:14, p. 197.

35. Ibid., 6:13, p. 90.

36. *The Poems of John Audelay*, ed. Ella Keats Whiting, EETS o.s. 184 (London: Oxford University Press, 1931), p. 5, lines 113–16. Audelay also writes about the value of chastity for women, but with regard to adultery discusses only men.

37. Leo Carruthers, "'No womman of no clerk is preysed': Attitudes to Women in Medieval English Religious Literature," in *A Wyf Ther Was: Essays in Honour of Paule Mertens-Fonck*, ed. Juliette Dor (Liège: Département d'anglais, Université de Liège, 1992), p. 53.

38. *Dives and Pauper*, 1:2, 6:1, p. 58.

39. Ibid.

40. *Memoriale Credencium: A Late Middle English Manual of Theology for Lay People, Edited from Bodley MS Tanner 201*, ed. J. H. L. Kengen (Nijmegen: n.p., 1979), p. 141.

41. BL, Harleian MS 1197, fol. 1r. The discussion of the Sixth Commandment here is apparently taken from *Jacob's Well*, except that it has added the phrase "þe which summe foolis holdin litel synne," which is omitted in Salisbury Cathedral MS (fol. 196r), the only extant manuscript of the full text of *Jacob's Well*. I am once again most grateful to Priscilla Heath Barnum for making available to me her transcription of the unedited second half of *Jacob's Well*.

42. *Fasciculus Morum*, 7:7, p. 669.

43. John Mirk, *Instructions for Parish Priests*, ed. Gillis Kristensson, Lund Studies in English 49 (Lund: Gleerup, 1974), pp. 138–39, 141, lines 1239–46, 1288–90.

44. *Dives and Pauper*, 2:2, 6:5, pp. 67–69.

45. Ibid., 6:6, p. 71.

46. John of Bromyard, *Summa Praedicantium* (Venice: Domenico Nicolino, 1568), s.v. *adulterium* a.17.3, fol. 44r: "et in hoc casu peius et crudelius est adulterium in muliere, quam in viro, et ipsa plus vituperatur, quia vir adulter non exhaeredat filios proprios, sed filios illius cum cuius peccat uxore, et plus est contra naturam crudelitatem exercere in proprios, quam in alienos." The "hoc casu" refers to the circumstance where a previous marriage contract made a subsequent marriage adulterous, but the dictum was probably meant to apply to adultery in general, because it is hard to see how the adulterous non-marriage of a precontracted woman disinherited anyone.

47. John of Freiburg, *Summa Confessorum* (Augsburg: Günther Zainer, 1476), bk. 4, chap. 24, sec. 11 (no foliation): "Plus tamen peccat mulier contra iura matrimonii uno modo quod vir, altero modo equaliter. Nam mulier plus peccat contra bonum prolis, sed contra bonum fidei equaliter peccat uterque." On John of Freiburg's reliance on Aquinas, see Leonard E. Boyle, "The *Summa Confessorum* of John of Freiburg and the Popularization of the Moral Teaching of St. Thomas and of Some of His Contemporaries," in *St. Thomas Aquinas, 1274–1974: Commemorative Studies*, vol. 2 (Toronto: Pontifical Institute of Medieval Studies, 1974), pp. 245–68.

48. *Dives and Pauper,* 1:2, 6:10, p. 80. All of chapters 10 to 12 hammer on this theme, so much so that Dives accuses Pauper of excusing women's sin and accusing only men's.

49. Augustine, "De Decem Chordis," pp. 111–13, 128. Many manuscripts of Augustine's sermons were in circulation; the most recent editor of *Dives and Pauper* believes the author may have read them at the Franciscan library in Oxford (Priscilla Heath Barnum, personal communication, January 5, 1994).

50. See Keith Thomas, "The Double Standard," *Journal of the History of Ideas* 20 (1959): 195–216, for some suggestions about the history and development of the double standard, relating it to property in women.

51. On misogyny in general, see R. Howard Bloch, *Medieval Misogyny and the Invention of Western Romantic Love* (Chicago: University of Chicago Press, 1991). For the sexualization of misogyny in various genres, see, for example, Ruth Mazo Karras, "Gendered Sin and Misogyny in John of Bromyard's 'Summa Predicantium,'" *Traditio* 47 (1992): 244–50, 256–57, and Theresa Coletti, "Purity and Danger: The Paradox of Mary's Body and the En-Gendering of the Infancy Narrative in the English Mystery Cycles," in *Feminist Approaches to the Body in Medieval Literature,* ed. Linda Lomperis and Sarah Stanbury (Philadelphia: University of Pennsylvania Press, 1993), pp. 71–72.

52. The distinction between "without" and "within" the community is not that between clergy and laity, but rather between central doctrinal authority and local understanding.

53. *Riverside Chaucer,* ed. Larry Benson, 3rd ed. (Boston: Houghton Mifflin, 1987), p. 123, lines 1323–26.

54. Marjorie K. McIntosh, "Finding Language for Misconduct: Jurors in Fifteenth-Century Local Courts," chap. 5 in this volume.

55. L. R. Poos, "Sex, Lies, and the Church Courts of Pre-Reformation England," *Journal of Interdisciplinary History* 25 (1995): 585–607.

56. For the sample year November 1489 to December 1490 (Guildhall Library MS 9064/4, fols. 1–191), in cases where women are accused of defaming men, 32 of the insults are sexual, 41 nonsexual, 4 both; in cases of women accused of defaming women, 95 are sexual, 12 nonsexual, 8 both; in cases of men accused of defaming men, 21 are sexual, 22 nonsexual, 2 both; in cases of men accused of defaming women, 52 are sexual, 2 nonsexual, 7 both. See also charts in Richard Wunderli, *London Church Courts and Society on the Eve of the Reformation* (Cambridge, Mass.: Medieval Academy of America, 1981), pp. 76, 78.

57. Poos, "Sex, Lies, and the Church Courts." Poos's article initially stimulated my interest in this topic and led me to analyze the data for London on the question. Poos also discusses the way sexual insults were used for women even when the real issue was something else. He states some important caveats about the use of this evidence, notably its

fragmentary nature, which prevents the observation of change over time, and the extreme brevity of the cases, which makes it impossible to determine any details about the social position of either defamers or defamed.

58. Wunderli, *London Church Courts*, p. 86.

59. Ruth Mazo Karras, "The Latin Vocabulary of Illicit Sex in English Ecclesiastical Court Records," *Journal of Medieval Latin* 2 (1992): 6–9.

60. Kristine L. Rabberman, in her dissertation research currently in progress on fifteenth-century church courts in the diocese of Hereford, finds that in ex officio accusations of adultery, the male defendant is as a rule named first, except when there are specific witnesses who brought the adultery to the court's attention. This would tend to support the point that the laity objected primarily to women's transgressions.

61. McIntosh, "Finding Language for Misconduct."

62. Margaret Spufford suggests that this was the case in the late thirteenth and early fourteenth centuries, when population was rising (Margaret Spufford, "Puritanism and Social Control?" in *Order and Disorder in Early Modern England*, ed. Anthony Fletcher and John Stevenson [Cambridge: Cambridge University Press, 1985], pp. 41–57). She discusses the late thirteenth and early fourteenth centuries by way of analogy to the sixteenth and early seventeenth centuries, in order to argue that the imposition of a strict moral code of behavior was due more to demographic than to religious factors.

63. P. J. P. Goldberg, *Women, Work, and Life Cycle in a Medieval Economy: Women in York and Yorkshire c. 1300–1520* (Oxford: Oxford University Press, 1992), esp. pp. 324–61, discusses the relationship between employment opportunities and age at marriage for towns in the north of England. See also Poos, *A Rural Society*, pp. 133–58, on late age at marriage in the later fourteenth century.

64. See Paul Strohm, *Hochon's Arrow: The Social Imagination of Fourteenth-Century Texts* (Princeton, N.J.: Princeton University Press, 1992), pp. 121–44.

65. Caroline Barron, "The 'Golden Age' of Women in Medieval London," *Reading Medieval Studies* 15 (1989): 48, suggests that the erosion of opportunities came later in London than elsewhere. These changes must be seen in the context of an overall tendency for women's work to be lower paid and less prestigious than men's. The situation was not unchanging; it was better for women at some times than at others, but, like the double standard, the lack of opportunity for working women is characterized more by continuity than by change (Judith Bennett, "Medieval Women, Modern Women: Across the Great Divide," in *Culture and History, 1350–1600: Essays on English Communities, Identities, and Writing*, ed. David Aers [New York: Harvester Wheatsheaf, 1992], pp. 147–75).

CHAPTER 7

Blessing from Sun and Moon
Churching as Women's Theater
Gail McMurray Gibson

After her miraculous and inviolate childbirth, the Virgin Mary remained at the Bethlehem manger for forty days: thus did the *Meditationes vitae Christi* instruct the unnamed nun (a Poor Clare) for whom the famously influential devotional text was first penned in the latter part of the thirteenth century. Mary waited humbly "as though she were like any other woman of her people and the boy Jesus an impure human who must observe the law," and so, too, must the pious, attending female reader wait those forty days of Mary's confinement, for as the author of the *Meditationes* urged, "Every faithful soul and especially a religious should visit the Lady at the manger at least once daily in the period between the Nativity of the Lord and the Purification, to adore the infant Jesus and His mother, thinking affectionately of their poverty, humility, and benignity."[1] After the forty days prescribed by Jewish law have passed, both Mary and the meditating reader leave the stable of Matthew's gospel and proceed, as the second chapter of Luke described, to the Temple for the Hebrew rituals that Luke's gospel conflated there—the purification of the mother's womb after childbirth and the offering up of the firstborn son.

About 1410, Nicholas Love, prior of Mount Grace Charterhouse in Yorkshire, translated the pseudo-Bonaventure's *Meditationes* as *The Mirror of the Blessed Life of Jesus Christ,* an adaptation for lay readers that became the single most influential devotional guide for lay men and women in fifteenth-century England.[2] In Love's version, "þat riȝtwisman Simon, lad in spirite by þe holi gost," joyfully embraces the Christ child and speaks the words of Luke 2:29–32, the exultant Nunc Dimittis hymn of the medieval liturgy, in homely English: "Lord I þonk þe, for nowe þou letest þi seruant aftur þi word in pece. Forwhi I haue seene with myn eyen þi blessed son oure sauyoure ... "[3] The old prophetess Anna also adores and celebrates the infant; then the baby stretches out his arms to his mother, who bears him in her arms, says the *Mirror,*

> in maner of procession toward þe autere, with þe childe, þe which procession is represented þis day in alle holi chirch, with liȝt born to goddus wirchipe. And þan þei wenten in þis manere. First þo tweyn wirchipful olde men Joseph & Symeon goon before, ioyfully

eyþer haldyng oþer by þe handes, & with gret mirþe singyng & sey-
ing, "Lord god we haue receyuet þis day þi gret mercy in middes of
þi temple, & perfore after þi gret name so be þi louyng and þi
wirchippe in to þe ferþest ende of alle þe world." Aftur hem foloweþ
þe blessed modere & maiden Marie berynge þe kynge of heuen Jesus, & with hir on þat one side goþe þat wirchipful widowe Anne
with gret reuerence & vnspekable ioy louvyng and presyng god.[4]

This joyful procession hand in hand to the altar was, explains Nicholas
Love, a "solempne & wirchipful procession of so fewe persones, bot gret
þinges bytokenyng & representyng. For þer bene of alle states of mankynde sume, þat is to sey of men & women, olde & 3onge, maidenes &
widowes."[5]

In its explication of the symbolic inclusiveness of the Temple procession, the *Mirror of the Blessed Life of Jesus Christ* shared with other
popular late medieval texts an eager interest in that communal procession reenacted "in alle holi chirch" at the feast of Candelaria, in England called Candlemas — the feast forty days after Christmas that com-
memorated the Purification of the Virgin Mary in the Temple. The
Legenda Aurea of Jacobus de Voragine had offered an antiquarian gloss
on the origin of the candlelit procession on the second day of February,
explaining that the candles were derived from Roman torchlight processions in honor of Proserpine and those in the first days of February in
honor of the goddess Februa, mother of Mars. "As it is always difficult
to wipe out such a custom," Jacobus de Voragine wrote, "Pope Sergius
decreed that in order to give to this one a Christian meaning, the Blessed
Virgin should be honored each year on this day, a blessed candle being
carried in the hand to this end. Thus the ancient usage was preserved,
but at the same time transformed by a new intention."[6]

Mindful of Proserpine and Februa or not, men and women of the late
medieval parish joined in procession on the feast of Candlemas. On the
second of February, all — men and women, young and old, maidens and
widows — ritually enacted the words of the second chapter of Luke's
Gospel by a blessing of candles in parish churches and by a joyful public
candlelit procession that celebrated the coming of the infant whom
Simeon had proclaimed the Light of the World "before the face of all
peoples." In the hands of the whole parish the candles burned to represent the light of Christ but also, the *Legenda Aurea* explained, to represent the chaste body of the Blessed Virgin Mary. "To impress her purity
upon the minds of all, the Church ordered that we should carry lighted
candles, as if to say: 'Most blessed Virgin, thou hast no need of purification; on the contrary, thou art all light and all purity!'"[7]

These familiar late medieval parish Candlemas processions are mirrored in the processional staging of the fifteenth-century plays of Mary's
Purification in the Temple that appear in the York and N-Town drama

cycles—and even more elaborately in the minstrelsy and festive dancing of the early-sixteenth-century Digby Candlemas play, which instructs that Anna Prophetissa be accompanied as she processes to the altar by "virgynes, as many as a man wylle [who] shalle holde tapers in ther handes," virgins who at the end of play are called on by the Poeta to dance "with alle your cumpany."[8] So, too, in the festive parish processions on the second of February, the virgins, wives, and widows of the parish—as well as men old and young—carried lighted candles in their hands as they walked the sacred precincts of church aisles or parish streets to converge at the altar. This procession made visible in joyful mimesis the figures of Simeon and Anna, who had recognized the child who would "lighten the Gentiles"; it ritually celebrated both the Messiah and the virgin mother whose purity shone forth like a lighted candle; and that shining candle, as the *Legenda Aurea* glossed, also imaged the believers of the parish themselves, for it "signifies faith with good works."[9] In the devotional theater of the parish streets, Candlemas was transformed from sacred history into symbol of the corporate body of parish believers.

Both David Mills and Eamon Duffy have focused upon this parish Candlemas ritual as a particularly resonant example of the corporate symbolism of late medieval liturgical and paraliturgical theater. Parish Candlemas procession, writes David Mills, was both "a symbolic interpretation of the historical event and an act of communal celebration in which each member of the congregation, by processing, affirms faith in the underlying myth and, re-enacting the event, becomes the bearer of divine truth into the darkness of ignorance."[10] Eamon Duffy concurs, adding that the talismanic power of the candles so blessed and processed added to the significance of the ceremony in ways that included communal practical utility as well as corporate symbolism, since "the people took blessed candles away from the ceremony, to be lit during thunderstorms or in times of sickness, and to be placed in the hands of the dying."[11] Late medieval Candlemas processions thus functioned as a kind of census—an ocular proof and numbering of the ranks of the parish—as well as a drama of consensus, an affecting visible display of shared conviction and creed.

Both Mills and Duffy have analyzed in detail the most useful archival source for reconstructing the spectacle of the English Candlemas processions, a fourteenth-century record of a Candlemas processional pageant that survives from the English town of Beverley. The Beverley text tells us that the procession there included "all the brethren and sisteren" of the Guild of Saint Mary and that it was led by "one of the gild ... clad in comely fashion as a queen, like to the glorious Virgin Mary, having what may seem a son in her arms." The Virgin and Child were followed by others costumed as Joseph and Simeon and by angels who processed with twenty-four thick wax candles; all with "music and gladness" walked through the streets to the parish church.[12]

The surviving fifteenth- and early-sixteenth-century archival records of the Candlemas pageants of Aberdeen suggest, however, that there may have been even more elaborate spectacle in the streets there; those records, if more laconic, at least seem to argue against Alan Nelson's conclusion that at Aberdeen, "the entire spectacle consisted of marching figures from random subjects."[13] In fact, the pageant list of 1442 begins with Caesar Augustus ("the emprioure and twa doctourez") and "the three kings of Cologne," followed by "Our Lady and Joseph," and "Simeon and his disciples,"[14] all expected characters in a Bethlehem and Candlemas drama. Mary, who is both virgin and mother, was flanked by figures representing "Sanctea bride" and Saint Helena, hardly the "random subjects" Nelson has called them. "Sancte bride," as Anna Jean Mill long ago pointed out,[15] was Brigid of Kildare, the Celtic virgin saint whose feast day was Candlemas Eve, and Helena was the famous mother saint of European Christendom, mother of the Roman emperor Constantine the Great and herself the legendary finder of the True Cross. As for the messenger and Moses and "two or four woodmen" of the Aberdeen pageant list, they were surely the enactors of a tableau of Moses and the burning bush, since the eleventh century a familiar Old Testament type of Mary's virginal conception of Christ[16] and an especially relevant prefiguration of the burning candle of Mary's purity. As the records of fifteenth-century Aberdeen pageantry likewise reveal, then, the Candlemas processional drama was both in and out of time; it linked the streets or aisles through which the candlelit procession moved and the altar that was the culmination of the journey; it telescoped Old Testament types of Mary's miraculous purity with New Testament story and conjoined the saints of the ancient past with the present body of believers. The Candlemas processional ritual annihilated the differences and fissures in the body of believers to make a statement — as emphatic as the symmetry of old Anna and old Simeon in Luke's gospel — of a corporate, double-gendered community of believers.

Despite the visibility of Candlemas in recent discussions of civic drama and ceremonial, however, no commenter on Candlemas ritual and drama, as far as I have been able to determine, has acknowledged the very strangeness of Candlemas as a public drama of the corporate Christian body. No one has conceded the incongruity at the heart of those late medieval Candlemas processions and pageants encompassing as they did all believers, male and female. For the feast of Candlemas conflated, we must recall, the epiphanal recognition of the light of the Christ child "to all the Gentiles" with commemoration of the Virgin Mary's submission to the Hebrew ritual requirement of women's purification after childbirth, a Levitical ritual that was the Old Testament type and exemplar of the continuing, prescribed, and noninclusionary medieval rite of churching, the female ritual of purification of the womb after childbirth. Mills and Duffy do not comment at all upon the curious fact that the corporate procession of believers in Candlemas ritual theater was also the liturgical type of a female gynecological rite reenacted in the private calendar ritual of each new mother's childbirth, a women's ritual that coexisted uneasily at best with the corporate symbolism of Candlemas.

The lighted candle of the feast signaled not only the purity of Mary's body but also the ritual purification of the individual female body. The lighted, blessed candle was a familiar prop held in the hand of each medieval Christian mother as she sought ritual readmission to the parish community of believers in the womanly rite of churching. Why had the law in the Book of Leviticus specified a wait of forty days (in truth, thirty-three)[17] after the birth of a son and eighty days [*sic*] for the purification of mothers of female infants?, asked Jacobus de Voragine. Since the female body requires twice as much time to complete itself in the mother's womb, the soul is not infused into it on the fortieth day as with male infants, but only on the eightieth day. And "since Christ wished to be born as a man, He desired to honour man and to endow him with more grace; for this reason He allowed boys to grow more quickly and the mothers to be purified the sooner." Furthermore, explains the *Legenda Aurea*, since woman has "sinned more than man, [she] should therefore be unhappier; and as her suffering has been doubled on earth, so too should it be doubled in the womb."[18]

The official position of the church—tactfully stated as early as the famous 601 letter from Pope Gregory the Great to Saint Augustine of Canterbury, quoted by Bede,[19] and by the mid–sixteenth century polemically asserted by the Puritan reform movement—was that the churching of women was a ritual not of purification but of thanksgiving for safe delivery of a child. But as the rather ingenuous exegesis in the *Legenda Aurea* makes clear, in actual medieval practice and piety, the ceremonial churching of women was certainly about women's bodies and about women's problematic relationship to ecclesiastical blessing and control. For regardless of Jacobus de Voragine's concession that the purification of Mary marked the end of the Jewish purification and the beginning of the Christian purification, "which is the work of faith, and purifies the heart,"[20] it is woman's womb where indwells Eve's trouble, her suffering, and her curse.[21]

It is surely because the ritual of churching was so much a part of the ordinary fabric of women's lives that so few medieval written sources think to comment upon it—and so few medievalists have paused to notice it. Churching is no less than the purloined letter of women's experience, in such plain view it is invisible. Clarissa Atkinson's book, *The Oldest Vocation: Christian Motherhood in the Middle Ages* (Cornell University Press, 1991), for example, contains not a single sentence mentioning the ubiquitous ritual of churching after childbirth, the ceremony that was the ritual confirmation of—and in some ways the dramatic enactment of—the Christian motherhood that is her subject.

Even when the storm of controversy over churching among (male) Puritan apologists in the sixteenth and seventeenth centuries makes churching a celebrated subject, it is truly astonishing how little acknowledgment there is by early modern historians. As David Cressy has observed in an important and much-needed article on the post-Reformation churching of women, "What little discussion of churching one finds in the secondary sources" usually simply repeats Keith Thomas's brief remarks on churching as an obligatory purification rite that linked the Hebrew scriptural tradition with popular "magical elements."[22]

As for anthropologists, most have assumed taboo, misogyny, and reintegration to be full meaning and sufficient explanation of the rite.[23] William A. Christian Jr.'s testy remarks are not untypical:

> The churching of women after childbirth is another instance of the way that women are made to feel impure. Technically this is an act of thanksgiving ... [but] the ritual itself, and the name it is given by the Church are ... clear in their meaning.... The symbolism of the churching ceremony hardly betokens thanksgiving. The woman kneels at the end of the church holding a lighted candle; the priest sprinkles her with holy water and recites Ps. xxiii [sic], and then leads her to the altar rails.... The ritual has the woman being first purified with holy water, then escorted back into the most sacred part of the church by the priest. The Church may change what it says it means by the ritual, but the ritual itself speaks loud and clear its own meaning.[24]

But ritual, does not, of course, "speak loud and clear its own meaning" any more than other kinds of cultural performance do. Participants and spectators gloss and create meaning as much as they perform and witness; medieval devotional theater shaped expectation and belief but it also reflected and even created those things. Let us concede that at first glance—and in obvious tension to the communal parish procession of Candlemas—the late medieval churching ritual looks deeply misogynist: a new mother was isolated from the community during her lying-in time, then after the passing of about a month's interval—the precise number of days decreed by local custom and by class—the woman was brought veiled to the church porch to present the chrisom cloth of her baptized child (the white cloth signifying the purity of Baptism) and a lighted candle that when blessed by the priest symbolized the woman's own restored and purified body. She then processed into the church to be ritually readmitted by the priesthood to the Mass and to the community of the faithful; the climax of that ritual reincorporation was the priest's chanting of the awesome words of the 120th (121st) psalm, which solemnly assured the new mother that

> The sun shall not burn thee by day: nor the moon by night.
> The Lord keepeth thee from all evil: may the Lord keep thy soul.
> May the Lord keep thy coming in and thy going out; from hence-
> forth now and for ever. (Psalm 120:6–8; Douay-Rheims version)

The scoffing late-sixteenth-century dissenter Henry Barrow dismissed as idolatry the Church of England's adherence to the "popish feastes of Christmass, Al-Hallowes, Candlemass, etc. for your dividing and devising Christ's life into a stage-play" ... and the keeping of "an especial worship" to the Virgin Mary's "purification yeerly in your church."[25] But especially Barrow lambasts "the weoman's monethlie restraint and separation from your church, her comming after that just tyme wympeled, vealed, with her gosips and neighbours following her, her kneeling downe before and offring unto the priest, the prieste's churching, praying over her, blessing her from sonne and moone, delivering her in the end to her former vocation."[26]

In his "A Brief Discoverie of the False Church," written in Fleet Prison in the year 1589 or 1590, Barrow spelled out further his objections to the churching of women: "Is not all this abolutely Jewish? Though in deed the prieste's part savor more of poperie. Seeing therfore they will not have it a Jewish purification, let it be a mixt action of Judaisme and poperie. This trumperie is so grosse, as it deserveth no refutation, but a doung forke to cast it out."[27]

But Barrow's most vehement objection is both surprising and instructive. For it was not the misogyny of the medieval ceremony of the churching of women — which had been officially and euphemistically renamed in the 1552 prayer book "The Thankes Geuing of Women After Childe Birth, Commonly Called The Churchyng of Women"[28] — that Barrow objected to so much as its apparent privileging of the female body:

> To conclude, why should such solemne, yea, publike thankes ... be given openly in the church, more for the safe deliverance of these women, being ... yet a thing natural, ordinarie, and common, more than for sundrie other strange and marveilous deliverances from sicknes, manie dangers of death, and perilles both by sea and land, shewed by the mighty hand of God towardes men and women daily, if there lay not some high misterie and diepe point of divinitie in the matter? ... why should women have this prerogative?[29]

Why indeed? What Barrow sees clearly is that churching is "prerogative" and not subjugation. Even if local custom was a powerful compelling force, there is no proof that the churching of women in the fifteenth and sixteenth centuries was ever imposed from above by ecclesiastical authority or edict. Indeed, historical evidence suggests quite the opposite: "It would be easy to argue," William Coster has written, with some perplexity, "that the churching of women was not only religiously offensive, but personally insulting to these women. . . . But such a conclusion perhaps ignores the evidence that the majority of women continued to acquiesce in, many actively to support, the ceremony as a social necessity."[30]

Peter Rushton has even suggested that it was not the churching of women but rather its *rejection* by radical reformers that was the real attempt to exert social control over women's lives and bodies, since "what is evident throughout the period after the Reformation . . . is the general determination of women to be churched."[31] Even into the twentieth century, Rushton observes, it is clear that "churching is women's business and that it is only pressure from other women which ensures its survival."[32] What the historical facts seem to show is that medieval women sought out the ceremony and even after the Reformation continued to demand it; as Susan Doran and Christopher Durstone have observed, even though in the strictest days of the Puritan Interregnum in the 1640s the theaters were all closed and even the celebration of Christmas was forbidden, "in many parishes . . . mothers continued to be churched following childbirth."[33]

No single social meaning provides adequate explanation for the dogged survival of the churching ritual. Cressy has shown that in post-Reformation England, the "formal religious ceremony of thanksgiving [after childbirth] formed part of a larger social ritual with complex secular dimensions," that indeed, "like many other rituals, its outward form could mask a variety of meanings."[34] It is important to note that the most significant reason for the continuing ritual of churching must have been simple and urgent necessity; childbirth until the most recent time was as perilous as it was ordinary. It may indeed be true, as Barrow objects, that men were delivered from all manner of perils daily without benefit of private ritual prayers, psalms, and blessings, but a medieval wife had good reason to fear that her death could come in childbirth or of childbed fever;[35] she even knew (in some medieval parishes at least) that women who died in the throes of childbirth, tainted by the curse of Eve, were customarily refused burial in holy ground.[36] The terrifying spiritual as well as physical risk of motherhood in the Middle Ages was ever present in women's thoughts. Men as well as women died in fire or flood or perished of famine and plague and disease. Men died fighting wars. But, as the churching ritual existed to acknowledge, women passed through great pain and risk of death in bearing children. The Virgin Mary's intercession for wives who implored her protection in childbirth and whose pregnant bodies were blessed in her name in the Sarum Liturgy[37] was a crucial part, perhaps *the* crucial part, of medieval laywomen's understanding of both the public liturgy of Candlemas and the salvific private liturgy of churching.

If we look at late medieval Candlemas plays, then, as a medieval woman was likely to have viewed them, we may see that these plays of Mary's "churching" are about the powerful centrality of Mary's female body in a preordained plan for salvation—and also in the redemption of womankind. Mary's special election and grace are proclaimed by her miraculous virginity and by the intact purity of her womb, and by her relentless and empowering humility as well; the Mary of medieval Christendom subverted the authority of the Jewish law by submitting to it. In the fifteenth-century play of Mary's Purification from the East Anglian *N-Town Cycle*, for example, Mary insists she must go to the Temple "in Goddys syght / Puryfyed for to be / In clene sowle," despite Joseph's objection that "to be purefyed haue ʒe no nede ... For þu art ful clene, / Vndefowlyd in thought and dede."[38] As Mary processes into the Temple to stand before the altar, she is hailed by the aged Simeon as "Mary bryght ... lanterne of lyght!" but the first words of praise uttered by the old prophetess standing at his side are "All heyl, salver of seknes!... All heyl, þu modyr of mekenes!"[39] It is as healing mother that Anna Prophetissa recognizes and lauds Mary in a scene that proclaims the very paradox of triumphant Christian humility. Mary submits her body as meek mother only to be transformed into powerful healer and intercessor.

That women's bodies in their vulnerability could symbolize the humanity of Christ, the paradoxical empowerment of meek flesh, Caroline Walker Bynum and others have taught us to understand. But the late medieval churching of women is about the oxymoronic weakness and power of the female body that can no better be explained by Christlikeness than it can be explained by misogyny. What is in tension with the community ritual of Candlemas is nothing more nor less, I would argue, than a women's theater of considerable social and political importance, a theater that celebrated the female body in both the fleshly and the corporate senses of the word.

Royal churchings, the best recorded, were lavish spectacles. "The stately order," the "many priests bearing relics," and the "many scholars singing and carrying lights" who accompanied the sixty royal female attendants at Queen Elizabeth Woodville's churching in 1465 awed the Nuremberg statesman Gabriel Tetzel, who witnessed it during his visit to London.[40] When the infant princess grew up to bear in 1486 Henry VII's firstborn son—the ill-fated Prince Arthur—Elizabeth of York's churching, too, would have been an elaborately staged public drama that befitted its political importance.[41] The *Liber Regie Capelle* of about 1449 regulated the stately ceremonial of royal churchings: two duchesses were to lead the queen, dressed in the most elaborate and precious garments, in procession from her impressive state bed to church door and to altar. A duke escorted the queen and her female attendants, bearing in his hands a splendid golden candelabrum that burned with the symbolic light of the Queen's purified body.[42]

That the lesser nobility aped such lavish theatrical display can be inferred from the versified saint's life of Elizabeth of Hungary written in the 1440s for Elizabeth de Vere, the countess of Oxford, by the Suffolk poet and monk Osbern Bokenham. Pointedly extolling the humility of the saintly queen and mother Elizabeth of Hungary, Bokenham praises, as had the *Legenda Aurea*, the homiletic simplicity of Elizabeth, who wore no precious jewels or cloth of gold to her churchings, "as of ladyis of astate yt ys þe guyse," but who walked simply dressed and with her newborn child in her own arms to church, where she offered up a single candle.[43] And the French life of Saint Elizabeth of Hungary that Rutebeuf wrote for Isabelle, Queen of Navarre, between 1258 and 1270 tells us that even by the thirteenth century, townswomen were in turn emulating the churching attire of countesses:

> When the townswomen of the domain,
> Clothed in their mantles,
> Would go to attend the service of Purification Day,
> Each one would dress as a countess
> And pay much attention to her attire.
> But as for her [Saint Elizabeth], she would do otherwise
> And go in poor clothing,
> With bare feet.
> In the muddy road,
> She would dismount
> Without asking for a chair or a horse.
> She would enter the church, holding her child
> And carrying a lighted candle.
> She would put her load down on the altar
> Along with a lamb, thus imitating
> Our Lady at the temple,
> Who was her model.[44]

But it is not, I think, only the splendid visual spectacle of medieval queens and countesses and town wives processing to their churching in their finery and white veils that should concern us, but also its meaning to women themselves. The piety of *The Book of Margery Kempe* may differ in degree from that of ordinary fifteenth-century English wives and mothers, but surely not in kind. Thus it is instructive that Margery's account of being moved to ecstatic tears by her parish Candlemas procession so that "she could hardly bear up her candle to the priest as other folks did at the time of the offering" moves fluidly and inevitably in the very next sentence to her affective devotional response at viewing the ritual churching of the ordinary women of her parish:

> Sche had swech holy thowtys & meditacyons many tymes whan sche saw women ben purifyid of her childeryn. Sche thowt in hir sowle þat sche saw owr Lady ben purifijd & had hy contemplacyon in þe beheldyng of þe women wheche comyn to offeryn with þe women þat weryn purifijd. Hir mende was al drawyn fro þe erdly thowtys & erdly syghtys & sett al to-gedyr in gostly syghtys, whech wer so delectabyl & so deuowt þat sche myth not in þe tyme of fer-uowr wythstondyn hir wepyng.[45]

"The women that came to offer" and who gave Margery Kempe such "high contemplation" were the midwives and "gossips," "god-sibs" or appointed godmothers who assisted at the birth and presented the new-born child on behalf of the mother for baptism.[46] After the mother's month or so of confinement after childbirth, the midwives and gossips flanked by female relatives and neighbors also customarily accompanied the new mother to church, processing with her from church door to stand—or, by the sixteenth century, to sit in a special pew[47]—near the altar. If we try not only to see in our mind's eye the women in these rituals but to "stand with women as well," as Bynum has urged we must,[48] we may well conclude that the meaning of the purification ritual for the women who were churched must have been very different from the meaning projected by the celibate male elite who presided at the altar.[49] Churching was, after all, for women a theater of their own, the only liturgical ceremony in the medieval church provided by the clergy for women only. It is important to note, too, that the awesome Latin psalms and blessings, the holy water and burning candles, sanctified not only the body of the new mother, but the entire body of attending women. Even on those occasions when the father or other male attendants were present (as they tended to be, for example, in royal ceremonies), the men remained literally marginal, on the outskirts of the ceremony and its meaning. The symbolic and ritual center of this drama was a woman's body—and the privileged body of women who had served as childbed attendants in the exclusively female space of the childbirthing room. In the medieval lying-in chamber there was always a powerful taboo against the male presence; when, for example, the time for childbirth drew near in 1442 for Henry VI's queen, Margaret of Anjou, a royal degree excluded all men from the lying-in chamber and specified that a closed curtain be placed in her inner chamber that "shall never be ... drawn until she be purified.... After that traverse there may not openly no man officer or other come there nearer than the outer chamber.... Instead of men officers must be gentlewomen."[50]

And in this women's ceremony, it could even be argued, the most important female attendants had themselves a quasi-clerical status. Medieval midwives, because of the frequent urgent necessity to baptize dying infants, were by canon law required to be instructed in the "very words and form of baptism"[51] and were empowered by episcopal license to perform the baptismal sacrament. A mid-fifteenth-century manuscript of John Myrc's versified *Instructions for Parish Clerks* elaborately explains that parish priests must teach the words of baptism to midwives, must require midwives to have clean water ready to baptize the child if need arise, and must instruct them how the water and vessel should be decently disposed of. Myrc even reassures the parish priest that a midwife's bad Latin (Myrc's example is "patria et filia et spiritus santia," a baptism by female case endings!) doesn't matter so long as the intent and the "fyrste sylabul . . . ys gode wythouten fabul."[52] The midwife's power to administer the syllables and the sacrament of baptism was to be hotly contested by Puritan reformers, who saw clearly that it bestowed clerical privilege to those who, so they taught, were expressly forbidden it. Women, Calvin wrote in the *Institutes of the Christian Religion*, were not allowed to speak in church "and also not to teach, to baptize, or to offer."[53]

The late medieval churching of women, then, was much less an imposition of misogyny or of male, clerical power than a complexly encoded drama that assumed the female body's pollution, taboo, and danger—but that also acknowledged female corporate identity and power and, in the person of midwives, even gave the extraordinary privilege of the sacrament of Baptism, the power to save from eternal death. In Margery Kempe's *Book*, Margery's fervent identification with the community of women who preside at the churching ceremony is especially significant given what is surely the central healing (and sainthood-qualifying) miracle of Margery Kempe's *Book*, Margery's restoration of the woman hysterical from the trauma of childbirth to "hir witte & hir mende a-ȝen" so that she can be "browt to chirche & purifijd as other women be."[54] But even more interesting—and revealing—is the moment in *The Book of Margery Kempe* in which Margery tells how she opposed the efforts of a number of "ryche men, worshepful marchawntys, & haddyn gold a-now" who tried to wrest the sole privilege of christenings and purifications from her parish church of Saint Margaret for their own chapels-at-ease.[55] Margery, herself the namesake of that Saint Margaret who is patron saint of childbirth, prophesies that these rich men will not succeed—and so they do not. "And so, blyssed mot God ben, þe parysch cherch stod stylle in her worship & hyr degre as sche had don ij hundryd ȝer before & mor."[56] That for Margery Kempe the dignity of her parish church—and one infers from the insistent female pronouns the dignity of the holy Saint Margaret herself—resided more in monopolizing control over the churching of women than in administering the

Eucharist (which is never contested by Margery) offers startling evidence by a fifteenth-century lay witness of the perceived political power and devotional importance of this female ritual.

The churching of women, then, far from being woman's shameful obligation, was for Margery Kempe a solemn ceremony of blessing and empowerment, not only empowering the female body and the body of females who both submitted and presided in the ceremony but bestowing dignity and degree on the very church itself. The female body standing at the church door and then before the altar had by bearing forth a Christian child enfleshed matter and spirit, had by childbearing created and nourished and linked another human body to God and to God's teeming creation. That the womb labored under the painful curse of Eve's sin made it guilty, but medieval Christendom taught that the miraculously inviolate body of Mary had in triumphant humility bestowed its blessing and redemption upon women's bodies, even as the incarnate body of Christ who bled and who birthed new life had redeemed the vulnerabilty in all humankind.

Notes

1. *Meditations on the Life of Christ,* trans. Isa Ragusa and Rosalie B. Green (Princeton, N.J.: Princeton University Press, 1961), pp. 54–56. The *Meditationes,* long attributed to Saint Bonaventure, is now thought to have been written by Johannes de Caulibus, a Franciscan friar of San Gemignano in Tuscany. For a convenient summary of the problems of authorship and role of the text in Franciscan spirituality, see Nicholas Love, *Mirror of the Blessed Life of Jesus Christ,* ed. Michael G. Sargent, Garland Medieval Texts 18 (New York and London: Garland, 1992), pp. ix–xx.

2. "Vernacular Books in England in the Fourteenth and Fifteenth Centuries," *Modern Language Review* 15 (1920): 354.

3. Love, *Mirror,* p. 47.

4. Ibid., pp. 47–48.

5. Ibid., p. 48.

6. Jacobus de Voragine, *The Golden Legend,* trans. Granger Ryan and Helmut Ripperger (London: Longmans, Green, 1941; reprint, New York: Arno Press, 1969), p. 152.

7. Ibid.

8. *The Late Medieval Religious Plays of Bodleian MSS Digby 133 and E Museo 160,* ed. Donald C. Baker et al., Early English Text Society (EETS), o.s. 283 (Oxford: Oxford University Press, 1982), pp. 111, 115.

9. De Voragine, *Golden Legend,* p. 152.

10. David Mills, "Religious Drama and Civic Ceremonial," in *The Revels History of Drama in English: I, Medieval Drama* (London: Methuen, 1983), p. 159.

11. Eamon Duffy, *The Stripping of the Altars: Traditional Religion in England c. 1400–c. 1580* (New Haven, Conn., and London: Yale University Press, 1992), pp. 16–17.

12. See Alan H. Nelson, *The Medieval Stage* (Chicago: University of Chicago Press, 1974), p. 88.

13. Ibid., p. 192.

14. See Anna Jean Mill, *Medieval Plays in Scotland* (Edinburgh and London: Blackwood, 1927), p. 116.

15. Ibid., p. 116 n. 3.

16. See, for example, the 1476 altarpiece of the Virgin in the Burning Bush by Nicholas Froment in James Snyder, *Northern Renaissance Art* (Englewood Cliffs, N.J.: Prentice-Hall, and New York: Abrams, 1985), pp. 262–84 and fig. 259.

17. Leviticus 12:4–5 specifies that women shall be deemed unclean thirty-three days after the birth of a man child and sixty-six days after the birth of a maid child. The Gospel of Luke (2:21) simply says "after the days of [Mary's] purification, according to the law of Moses, were accomplished ... " (Douay-Rheims version).

18. Jacobus de Voragine, *Golden Legend*, p. 150.

19. See Bede, *Ecclesiastical History of the English People*, trans. Leo Sherley-Price and rev. R. E. Latham (Harmondsworth, England: Penguin Books, 1990), p. 83: "As to the interval that must elapse after childbirth before a woman may enter church, you are familiar with the Old Testament rule: that is, for a male child thirty-three days and for a female, sixty-six. But this is to be understood as an allegory, for were a woman to enter church and return thanks in the very hour of her delivery, she would do nothing wrong."

20. Jacobus de Voragine, *Golden Legend*, p. 150.

21. See Genesis 3:16: "To the woman also he said: I will multiply thy sorrows, and thy conceptions: in sorrow shalt thou bring forth children, and thou shalt be under thy husband's power, and he shall have dominion over thee" (Douay-Rheims).

22. David Cressy, "Purification, Thanksgiving and the Churching of Women in Post-Reformation England," *Past and Present* 141 (1993): 108. See William Coster, who observes that the churching of women, "though the only means by which, after childbirth, a woman could return to the community of the Church, and indeed to society in general ... is a subject that has received very scant scholarly attention" ("Purity, Profanity, and Puritanism: The Churching of Women, 1500–1700," in *Women in the Church*, ed. W. J. Sheils and Diana Wood, Studies in Church History 27 [Oxford: Blackwell, 1990], p. 377).

23. See Cressy, "Purification," p. 109: "The Polynesian word 'taboo' appears frequently in these discussions without much self-consciousness or criticism. Churching is presented as a classic *rite de passage* dealing with female pollution, as cultural response to the fear of women, and as a man-made instrument for their control."

24. William A. Christian, *Person and God in a Spanish Valley* (New York and London: Seminar Press, 1972), p. 154.

25. Henry Barrow, *The Writings of Henry Barrow, 1590–1591*, ed. Leland H. Carlson, Elizabethan Nonconformist Texts 5 (London: Allen and Unwin, 1966), p. 72.

26. Ibid.

27. Henry Barrow, *The Writings of Henry Barrow, 1587 to 1590*, ed. Leland Carlson, Elizabethan Nonconformist Texts 3 (London: Allen and Unwin, 1962), p. 463.

28. See *The First and Second Prayer Books of Edward VI*, ed. Douglas Harrison (New York: Dutton, 1968; London and Toronto: Dent, 1968), p. 428.

29. Barrow, *Writings, 1587–1590*, pp. 463–64.

30. Coster, "Purity," p. 386.

31. Peter Rushton, "Purification or Social Control? Ideologies of Reproduction and the Churching of Women after Childbirth," in *The Public and the Private*, ed. Eva Garnikow et al. (London: Heinemann, 1983), p. 124. (I am indebted to Susan Karant-Nunn for sharing with me, after I had presented an earlier draft of this paper at the Intersections conference, her forthcoming essay "Churching, A Women's Rite: Ritual Modification in Reformation Germany," in which I learned about Peter Rushton's study).

32. Rushton, "Purification," p. 125.

33. Susan Doran and Christopher Durston, *Princes, Pastors, and People: The Church and Religion in England, 1529–1689* (London and New York: Routledge, 1991), p. 91.

34. Cressy, "Purificaton," p. 111.

35. Christiane Klapisch-Zuber, who has studied fifteenth-century childbed mortality statistics, has concluded that even among wealthy, privileged Florentines, "one out of three Florentine women who died before their husbands did so bringing a child into the world or as an immediate consequence of childbirth" (see Christiane Klapisch-Zuber,

"Women and the Family," in *Medieval Callings*, ed. Jacques Le Goff and trans. Lydia G. Cochrane [Chicago: University of Chicago Press, 1991], p. 302).

36. Keith Thomas, *Religion and the Decline of Magic* (New York: Scribner, 1971), p. 39.

37. See *The Sarum Missal in English*, part 2, trans. Frederick E. Warren (London: De La More Press, 1911), p. 164: "so through the intercession of the most blessed mother of God thou wouldest deign to pour forth the light of thy grace upon their speedy delivery."

38. *The N-Town Play*, ed. Stephen Spector, EETS, supp. ser. 11 (Oxford: Oxford University Press, 1991), vol. 1, pp. 183–84, lines 97–110.

39. *N-Town Play*, I, p. 184, lines 123–26.

40. See *The Travels of Leo of Rozmital*, trans. and ed. Malcolm Letts, Hakluyt Society, 2nd ser. 108 (Cambridge: Cambridge University Press, 1957), pp. 45–48.

41. See Sydney Anglo, *Spectacle, Pageantry, and Early Tudor Policy* (Oxford: Clarendon Press, 1969), pp. 46–51. But as David Cressy observes ("Purification," p. 145), in all churchings the new mother was a conspicuously central "actor": "The ritual put her on display, as the centre of attention ... at her churching she came forward to the most prominent seat or pew by the altar, all eyes upon her."

42. Kay Staniland, "Royal Entry into the World," in *England in the Fifteenth Century: Proceedings of the 1986 Harlaxton Symposium*, ed. Daniel Williams (Woodbridge, Suffolk: Boydell Press, 1987), pp. 307–10.

43. Osbern Bokenham, *Legendys of Hooly Wummen*, ed. Mary S. Serjeantson, EETS, o.s. 206 (Oxford: Oxford University Press, 1938; reprint; New York: Kraus Reprints, 1971), p. 266, lines 9793–9800.

44. Rutebeuf, "Life of Saint Elizabeth of Hungary," in *The Lady as Saint: A Collection of French Hagiographic Romances of the Thirteenth Century*, trans. and ed. Brigitte Cazelles (Philadelphia: University of Pennsylvania Press, 1991), p. 159, lines 750–70.

45. Margery Kempe, *The Book of Margery Kempe*, ed. Sanford Brown Meech and Hope Emily Allen, EETS, o.s. 212 (London: Oxford University Press, 1940; reprint, 1961), p. 198.

46. A royal edict of 1486 even specified that at the confinement of Henry VII's queen, Elizabeth of York, "the Gossippes must be lodged nighe the Queenes Deliveraunce, that they ... may be ready to attend upon the Yonge Prince or Princesse to the Christeninge." See Phillis Cunnington and Catherine Lucas, *Costumes for Births, Marriages, and Deaths* (New York: Barnes and Noble, 1972), p. 23.

47. On midwives' pews and other women's pews and seats, see Margaret Aston, "Segregation in Church," in *Women in the Church*, ed. Sheils and Wood, pp. 237–94.

48. Caroline Walker Bynum has criticized the anthropologist Victor Turner for looking *at* women in religious life, while the "historian or anthropologist needs to stand *with* women as well." See Caroline Walker Bynum, "Women's Stories, Women's Symbols: A Critique of Victor Turner's Theory of Liminality," in *Anthropology and the Study of Religion*, ed. Robert L. Moore and Frank E. Reynolds (Chicago: Center for the Scientific Study of Religion, 1984), p. 109.

49. As David Cressy concludes in his study of churching in post-Reformation England, "The ceremony celebrated her survival, and offered the comforts of religion. It recognized her endurance of the pains and the perils of childbearing, and focused on the woman rather than her baby. It was, fundamentally, a thanksgiving. Was it a purification? Only if she thought herself unclean" (Cressy, "Purification," p. 145). Likewise, in an essay entitled "Churching, a Women's Rite: Ritual Modification in Early Modern Germany," Susan C. Karant-Nunn argues that churching was "multiply symbolic" in Reformation Germany, that the interpretation of the ritual varied from "women and men, magistrates and ordinary citizens, clergy and laity.... Each group had its own perceptions of churching" (in *History and Anthropology in Early Modern Europe: Papers from the Wolfenbüttel Conference 1991* (Wolfenbüttel, Germany: Herzog August Bibliothek, forthcoming). I am grateful to Professor Karant-Nunn for generously sharing this essay with me.

50. M. J. Tucker, "The Child as Beginning and End: Fifteenth and Sixteenth Century English Childhood," in *The History of Childhood*, ed. Lloyd deMause (New York: Harper

and Row, 1974), p. 238. Barbara Hanawalt has emphasized that the folklore sources that give evidence for peasant childbirth customs "illustrate the taboo on having a man present and the anxiety of both sexes at breaking it." See Barbara A. Hanawalt, *The Ties That Bound: Peasant Families in Medieval England* (New York and Oxford: Oxford University Press, 1986), p. 216.

51. Tucker, "The Child," p. 239.

52. John Myrc, *Instructions for Parish Priests,* ed. Edward Peacock, EETS, o.s. 31, 2nd ed. revised by F. J. Furnivall (London: Oxford University Press, 1902; reprint, Millwood, N.Y.: Kraus Reprint, 1981), pp. 3–5.

53. Joyce L. Irwin, *Womanhood in Radical Protestantism, 1525–1675* (New York and Toronto: Mellon Press, 1979), p. 159.

54. See Kempe, *Book,* p. 178, and Gail McMurray Gibson, *The Theater of Devotion* (Chicago and London: University of Chicago Press, 1989), pp. 64–65.

55. Kempe, *Book,* p. 59. Sara Beckwith includes an interesting political and economic discussion of the dispute between the parish church of Saint Margaret and the Saint Nicholas Chapel in *Christ's Body: Identity, Culture, and Society in Late Medieval Writings* (London and New York: Routledge, 1993), pp. 105–6. For a discussion of other English lay petitions to have churching rights transferred to chapels-at-ease, see Katherine L. French, "Women and the Medieval Parish," from her 1993 University of Minnesota dissertation "Community Identity and the Late Medieval Parish: The Example of Bath and Wells." (My thanks to Katherine French for sharing a draft of this chapter with me.)

56. Kempe, *Book,* p. 60.

CHAPTER 8

❖

"The Childe of Bristowe" and the Making of Middle-Class Adolescence

Barbara A. Hanawalt

The behavior of middle-class youth came to prominence in the literature, laws, court cases, guild regulations, and thinking of fifteenth-century English society in an obsessive way uncharacteristic of preceding centuries.[1] Books of advice for youth aspiring to make their way up the social ladder proliferated in manuscript form and spread even more with the invention of printing. Among the dominant metaphors were the relationship of the young to the old, the apprentice to the master, the uncultivated to the cultivated. The process of forming a concept of a societal ideal of middle-class adolescent behavior was, as Norbert Elias described, one in which meaning and form were picked up and polished in speech and writing and "tossed back and forth until they became efficient instruments for expressing what people had jointly experienced and wanted to communicate about."[2] In this chapter I will look at this process of polishing descriptions of adolescent behavior as they are circulated between literary and legal creations, on the one hand, and the actual experience of adolescence, on the other. The game of exchange between the literary and the historical leads to a fifteenth-century construction of adolescence. Although the ideal type may be seen in a number of written examples, the portrait appears most fully in a popular poem, "The Childe of Bristowe," and its variant, "The Merchant and His Son."[3] These didactic narratives are a fifteenth-century version of Horatio Alger stories, adventure tales in which an aspiring lad overcomes the obstacles set in his way to achieve good fame and fortune.

Historical conditions in the fifteenth century proved especially unsettling. In this century of disruption and transition, youth became a focus for anxieties about a better future. Disease and wars kept population low. The rise of new economic opportunities and the demise of serfdom changed the social hierarchy. Political realignments in Europe and England and a heightened lay piety accompanied by criticism of the church led to instability in the secular and ecclesiastical realms. It was a period of recognizable flux; one that inspired considerable comment from poets and moralists of the time. Among the concerns that occupied the middle ranks of English society, a rapidly expanding sector, were the values, virtues, and behavior that their class should maintain. Their anxieties centered on such questions as the most prestigious way of earning their wealth (law, trade, or landed estates), the appropriate education for their sons and marriages for their daughters, the type of clothing they should wear, the manners they should display, and their personal salvation. Fundamental to their unease was the shift in the old hierarchical order.

The predominant response of the middle class to the new social order of the fifteenth century was conservatism. In literature David Lawton has pointed to the general attribute of "dullness," not only as part of our modern reading of it, but as a desirable avocation on the part of its practitioners. Literature generally adopted a public rather than an individualistic voice. The message was an insistent one emphasizing morality, piety, and respect for hierarchy. In the writings of Lydgate, Hoccleve, and the other fifteenth-century poets, the moral lessons of books of advice were elevated to a grander scale of public poetry made for the monarch, among other powerful patrons. Literature for the education of princes is a grander version of the literature for the education of middle-class youth. The "dullness" of these poets was a virtue to them. While distorting the writing of their acknowledged master, Chaucer, to fit their own lessons in morality, they perceived themselves to be his dutiful apprentices, much as they saw master-apprentice relationships in general as the basis for a sound society.[4]

By looking at the various venues in which Chaucer's works appeared and were read, Seth Lerer has shown how Chaucerian tales were modified to fit with other "improving literature" and bound into books that were designed for the education of young readers of a household. Chaucer's texts became, in these versions, a vehicle for those compilers and authors who wrote "father Chaucer" as an instructor of youth. Although designed for children, the views expressed were not radically different from those found in fifteenth-century poets such as Hoccleve and Lydgate. As Lerer points out, the thrust of so much of the fifteenth-century literary messages indicates a new importance for childhood training.[5]

I would go beyond that generalization to suggest that the fifteenth-century literature, while it taught reading and conservative values to children, emphasized lessons needed in adolescence. The literature, along with and as part of historical experiences, produced the *Kultur* of which Elias speaks. The construction of middle-class behavior began to coalesce specifically around the adolescent years, and literature of all sorts, high and low, was directed toward an age group that was perceived to be most in need of instruction.

If authors aimed a major thrust of their moral messages at youth, so too did the regulations governing social life. Not knowing what the new social hierarchy would be, adults focused their attention on dictates of behavior that emphasized a public image, one that, as Elias points out, was self-conscious about the body and its uses. Guild regulations, even those of parish guilds, dictated the sober and pious behavior expected of their membership.[6] Sumptuary legislation attempted to enforce the social hierarchy of dress, the foods the population ate, and the places they sat at table.[7] Training for ritualized public behavior began with children and extended into adolescence in the form of manner books and moral tales for the literate and catchy rhymes for the illiterate.

The Paragon of Middle-Class Adolescence

To understand the process that produced a consensus on the making of middle-class adolescence, we can follow the "tossing to and fro" of the ideal attributes from the popular literature, particularly the two variants of "The Childe of Bristowe," to the regulatory measures for apprentices and youth. Since the plot of the poem is not well known, this first section includes a narrative along with a comparison of it to the prescriptive literature and regulations. The poems begin with Childe-William's background (the name is a shorthand that includes both poems, since he is baptized "William" in "The Merchant and His Son"). His birth and upbringing fit the ideal candidate for apprenticeship. His father, aside from his moral lapses into usury and neglect of charity and tithes, was "a squyer mykel of myght" with castles, towns, towers, forests, and fields. William's father in "The Merchant and His Son" was "a ryche franklyn of Ynglond" with many jewels, great treasure, horses, sheep, and land.[8] A fifteenth-century poem written for the mason's guild warns masters not to recruit from among serfs because the lord has the power to come and claim them. The demise of serfdom rendered the complaint out of date, but the lament rings true: "By olde tyme, wryten Y fynde / That prentes schulde be of gentyl kynde." Part of the reason for preferring gentry was that they increased the prestige of the master and the guild.[9] Gentlemen and yeomen's sons, like Childe-William, were more likely to enter prestigious guilds, such as the guild of long-distance merchants, than were sons of husbandmen.[10]

Not only was Childe-William well born, he also met the physical requirements of the merchant class, being "semely and feyre" with "lymes large and long."[11] By 1510 the Mercers' Guild in London had spelled out similar specifications for their apprentices. They had to be at least sixteen years old, free of birth, tall, lithe of limb, and not disfigured in body or members. But the wardens despaired of honest recruitment because "daily there be presented and also admitted divers apprentices which be very little in growing or stature." When reality fell short of the ideal, the wardens considered compelling the apprentices' friends to swear to their fitness, but decided against it.[12]

Childe-William met the educational and courtesy specifications as well. During the fifteenth century the guilds had begun to require higher standards of literacy from their apprentices. The goldsmiths, for instance, required apprentices to prove their skill by writing in "a book to be dormant in the treasury of the Hall." The book came to be known as the *Dormant*. The ironmongers had an *Apprentices' Book of Oaths*, which served a similar purpose. One goldsmith claimed that an apprentice he had taken from Banbury was so skilled in engraving letters that he naturally assumed that the young man could read and write when he could not.[13] No such mistake could be made about Childe-William.

> When the child was xij yere and more,
> His fader put hym unto lore
> to learne to be a clerke;
> so long he lernyd in clergie,
> til he was wise and wittye,
> and drad al dedis derke.

The alternative version, the more lively of the two, says that William "cowde hys gramer wonder wele: / hys felows cowde hym not amende."[14]

The literacy requirement coincided with the great popularity of advice and courtesy books, which, like the household reading books Lerer has described, were designed to instill moral virtues and provide instruction on polite behavior and proper public presentation for aspiring youth.[15] While the more famous of these books, such as John Russell's *Boke of Nurture*, were written for youth who planned to enter into noble households,[16] others, such as "The Young Children's Book," were specifically adapted to middle-class ideals. These stressed such injunctions as "you must eat what you get with your hands," since "a man's arms are for working as a bird's wings for flying."[17] The poems assure us that Childe-William had learned all of the needful lessons recommended: "he wax so curteise and bolde, / all marchauntz loved hym, yong and olde."[18]

The merchants' superior moral values, in contrast to the usurious, impious, and uncharitable behavior of Childe-William's gentry father,[19] also find their place in the advice books: "Use no swearing of falsehood in buying or selling, else shall you be shamed at the last. Get your money honestly, and keep out of debt and sin. Be eager to please and so live in peace and quiet."[20] Law, the other alternative for middle-class wealth, which his father advocates, meets with Childe-William's disapproval because the youth was afraid he would endanger his immortal soul.[21]

The youth aspires to become a merchant, even though his father shrewdly points out that he has "Seyn men bothe ryse and falle; hyt ys but caswelte" to be in "merchandyse."[22] The "Childe of Bristowe," however, claims an abiding desire to lead his life by "marchandise." As it turns out, Childe-William had made his own inquiries about a suitable master and tells his father that close by, at Bristol, there is a merchant who is a "just trew man" and that he wants to be apprenticed to him for seven years.[23]

The apprenticeship contracts presumed that the candidate was as well prepared and dedicated to middle-class values as was Childe-William.[24] While apprenticeship contracts contained economic elements involving fees, wages, and other payments, the emphasis was on the behavior expected from both parties. The apprentice swore not to marry and not to fornicate, including the wise precaution that he not have sexual relations with anyone of his master's household. He was not to engage in the temptations of the city, such as drinking, gaming, and going to the theater. He was not to gossip about his master's affairs, but remain loyal to his interest and not waste his money. He was expected to accept discipline without complaint and undertake not to leave the apprenticeship to serve another master or to run away. If he did run away, his sponsors could be fined and he could be barred from the craft.[25]

The master, likewise, accepted a series of obligations that regulated his behavior in this quasi-familial pact. He had to provide room, board, and clothing. He could not ask his apprentices to perform degrading tasks, such as carrying water, that were for menial servants.[26] He had to treat the youth as a younger member of his own status group. He had a duty, as did a father, to chastise his apprentice for wrongdoing, but he could not be abusive. Above all, he was to instruct the apprentice in his trade or craft without concealing trade secrets that would hinder the apprentice from becoming a master. Childe-William's father entered his son into such a contract: having traveled to Bristol, he "with the Marchaund cownant made." It was for seven years, and the youth was to live with his master. The merchant thereby agreed that if he were paid "gold gret plente, / the child hys prentys should be, / his science for to conne."[27]

By the late fourteenth and fifteenth centuries, entry into an apprenticeship was very expensive. The sponsor or the candidate himself would have to pay a varying amount to the master by way of an inducement to take the youth and to cover part of the expenses of lodging.[28] By the late fourteenth century the charge by the master was four to five marks.[29] In their charter of 1393, the goldsmiths tried to protect apprentices and their sponsors from unscrupulous demands by establishing a schedule of premiums to be paid to the master. If a ten-year contract was signed, then the minimum payment to the master was five pounds. If a shorter term was agreed to, then the premium was ten marks. Fines of five pounds could be levied on the masters for not abiding by these arrangements.[30] Premiums ranged from two to six pounds in other guilds.[31] In addition, candidates or their sponsors had to pay twenty to forty shillings for entrance into the Goldsmiths' Guild.[32] The mercers had similar entry fines for apprentices.[33]

The close, surrogate-familial relationship that developed between Childe-William and his master was not an unusual occurrence or simply a literary device, and it was certainly one that the middle class regarded as the most desirable outcome. The apprenticeship arrangement was a complex one. For the young person it meant leaving the natal home or school and moving into the house of a stranger. The master and his family would have a young, nonkinsperson in their household who became a part of the family. For both the apprentice and the master, the living arrangement was a potentially uncomfortable mix of familial and professional roles. The seven to ten years of working and living together could result in deep emotional conflict as well as attachment. The expenses of arranging the apprenticeship in a sense acted as a bond for the good behavior of the apprentice.[34] In Bristol, which was a much smaller commercial center, most masters would have one apprentice at a time. A master with only one apprentice in his lifetime could form a strong attachment to this surrogate son. Mortality of children in the cities of medieval Europe was very high, so their inhabitants might not have surviving sons of their own, as was true of Childe-William's master. Thus their emotional investment in their protégés became intensified.

As the narrative technique of medieval popular poetry dictates, however, it is time to "return to the story of the boy's father." Childe-William is happily placed with his master, loved by the community of merchants, learning his trade, and well on his way to becoming an honest merchant, but his father lies on his deathbed with considerable anxiety about his salvation. None of his fair weather friends will act as executor. This leaves his only son, who "drad al dedis derke." What is our hero to do? What do the insistent voices of advice manuals and poetry tell him?

One of the main goals of the guides was to inculcate in the young an understanding of and reverence for hierarchy and authority. With this injunction, we must again pick up the narrative of the poems as a guide to readers unfamiliar with this piece of popular poetry. Injunctions to filial piety, such as Childe-William exhibits, were typical of advice manuals:

And child, worship thy father and thy mother;
Look that thou grieve neither one nor other,
But ever, among them thou shalt kneel down,
And ask their blessing and benison.[35]

This same obedience was to extend to a master, who must also be treated with respect: "An thy master speak to thee, / take thy cap in hand."[36] It behooved a youth aspiring to either maintain his parents' social position or achieve a better one to learn the rules and take advantage of the opportunity a master could offer toward this goal.

Childe-William, of course, embodied these virtues. In spite of his father's sinful means of acquiring wealth, he agrees to act as his father's executor and save his soul at the cost of the inheritance he might expect. At the same time, he is completely loyal to his master and to his apprentice contract. Childe-William's master in return is continually described as loving his apprentice, even when he suspects him of gambling away his fortune.[37]

The two loyalties, to father and to master, dominate the poem, but the filial piety is expressed largely through the sacrifices that the young man must go through to save his father's soul. In this conventionally drawn center section of the poem, the apprentice tells his father that he must meet him in the death chamber in a fortnight after he dies so that he can see if his soul has been saved.[38] When he is dead, the young man sets about an elaborate expenditure on conventional funeral expenses: masses for his father's soul, alms to poor women and children to say prayers for his father, repair of roads and bridges in his father's name, and so on, until all his father's ready money has been spent. But when his father's burning soul appears in the chamber at the prescribed time, led by a devil with a chain and accompanied by a blast of lightning, the son promises to do more and asks him to return in another fortnight.[39]

Returning to his master, he explains that his father has died and that he must sell the whole of the inheritance he has gained, "croppe, rote and rynde." The merchant's response is anguished. Not only will his beloved apprentice be poorer, he will appear a fool to the merchant community:

> Thou schalt not selle they gode, Wyllyam,
>   be the counsel of me;
> Men wyll sey that here therof, that thou art nevyr lyke to the
>   [never like to thrive].
> All thys cuntre wyll speke therof, bothe woman,
>   chylde, and man,
> For to sele so sone awey all that thy fadur wan.[40]

The general anxiety about what others would think also was common to the advice literature. [41]

When arguments evoking public censure fail, the master suggests a loan to cover any short-term problems the apprentice may be having in trade. Loyal to his father's memory, the young man has not revealed what he is doing with the money, and the merchant assumes he has suffered a business setback. Apprentices at his stage of career did go to trade on their own if they had the capital, which Childe-William would have as executor of a wealthy father. The apprentice refuses the loan, arguing that if he must sell the land cheap, he would rather that his master own it than anyone else. The master pays him more than the asking price.[42]

In the surrogate-filial relationship of apprentice and master, such an arrangement would be the most honorable.

Taking the money back into the countryside, Childe-William has it proclaimed in churches and markets that he would repay any man or woman whom his father had ruined, providing that they would say prayers for his soul. Penniless once again following this distribution, he awaits the second visit of his father's ghost. This time it arrives all black but without flames. His father is not yet saved, but the ghost realizes that his son's approach to fair dealing in life has been better than his own.[43]

A suspicion of a business setback was one thing, but when the apprentice returned the second time and wanted to borrow money, the master became suspicious that he was behaving contrary to his contract, as a bad apprentice might do:

> [B]y my feith, y hold the mad;
> for thu has played atte dice,
> or at some other games nyce,
> and lost up, sone that thu had.

In the alternate version, the master suggests that he will end up on the gallows for whatever he is doing with so much money. Filial piety prevents him from confessing his drain of money, and the master says that he has heard that his "governaunce" was bad. When the apprentice suggests that he become his master's bondsman and servant in exchange for the loan, the master is forthcoming. Only in the alternative version does the author permit the master to make a sly comment to his wife that he is now assured of a reliable servant in his former apprentice.[44] That comment, in itself, is a hint about the problem of finding skilled labor in the fifteenth century. With a reduced supply of skilled artisans, masters tried to prolong apprentice contracts or force trained apprentices to continue working for low wages.

Returning once again to the country, Childe-William pays all the tithes that his father owed to various churches and continues to give alms in his father's name until he is again penniless. Returning to meet his father's ghost for the final time, he comes across a beggar who claims that his father owed him for a measure of grain. With nothing left to give, he takes his fine clothing off his back and gives it to the beggar. Reduced to his underwear, he enters the death chamber and is, at last, rewarded with a vision of his father's salvation.[45]

If the merchant was bothered about lending money to his apprentice, his appearance before him in his undergarments leads to a lecture about keeping up appearances. In a society in which clothes make the man, Childe-William was not making a good impression:

Wyllyam, he seyde, how ys hyt with the?
thow arte a rewful grome;
Hyt were almes, seyde the marchand, in preson the to caste:
For moche gode haste thou loste, and broght unto waste.
Y had thoght to have made the a man,
y pray Got to gyf the care,
Y wyll no more tryste to the, to go wyth my chaffare.[46]

His reaction was no different from that of the London mercers, who required their apprentices and servants, when going to the Mart, to wear capes, partellettes of silk, furred gowns, and double-turved cappys shoes, and slippers.[47]

The conclusion of the poem is, likewise, expressive of a middle-class ideal about how the master-apprentice relationship should resolve itself. The merchant has had his suspicions about the apprentice, but he has not been the financial loser in his arrangements with him. He also has never given up his quasi-paternal love. When the youth returns for the third time and explains his successful efforts to save his father's soul, all is forgiven. In the "Childe of Bristowe" he becomes the heir to his master, and in the "Merchant and His Son" he becomes his executor and marries his only daughter. In both conclusions he inherits all of his father's lands again, in addition to the wealth of his father-in-law. In the merchant's appointment of William as executor, the alternative version once again permits a sly laugh; the merchant realizes to what lengths the apprentice's filial piety has taken him on behalf of his father, and he presumes that he will do the same for a surrogate father. Both the merchant's present fortune and his afterlife are assured in the hands of this paragon of merchant virtues.[48]

Although the portrait may seem an overdrawn fiction, the master-apprentice relationship could result in such a comfortable conclusion in real life. Wills tell much about the familial bonds between the parties. Of the 3,330 men registering wills in the Husting Court, 3 percent left their apprentices bequests. Money (28 percent) and goods (33 percent) were the typical bequests. John Claydish, a pewterer in London, left one apprentice 13s. 4d. and a more junior apprentice 10s. A goldbeater, William Wylewan, left all his molds, including his best one, to his apprentice. His son would have the shop and other instruments. In other cases, the apprentice received the shop (7 percent) and tenements (8 percent). Some men remembered all of their apprentices, thus indicating a generally good relationship within the shop and household structure.[49] The relationship could become so close that the apprentice was made chief heir to the master.[50]

With the intimate familial environment, one might also expect that marriages could result from the relationship built upon trust and acquaintance. Thus Thomas Wood, who had two daughters, married one to a former apprentice, who went on to have a distinguished career in the Goldsmiths' Guild. Harry ap Richard claimed that he had been apprentice to William Griffith, late tailor of London, who had released him from his indenture of apprenticeship. He had agreed with William's widow to marry her and take over the business, but, he complained, she broke the contract and married someone else.[51]

The filial relationship might also be carried to the grave. Thomas Gauder, a pouchmaker, died young with a wife but no children. He left his brother and nephew his inheritance and also made a number of civic bequests. At the end of his life, his chief desire was to be buried in the same tomb as William Gauder, his late master. Richard Wycombe also valued the closeness of his relationship with his former master and his current apprentices; he provided for prayers for his master's soul and gave each of his current apprentices ten shillings.[52]

Negative Exempla: Ungoverned Youth

Although the poems about this paragon of mercantile virtue ring true with advice literature and historical prescriptions such as apprentice contracts and wills, one remains suspicious about the real and fictive fears all this assortment of evidence rails against. Elias observed that books of advice used the ploy of holding up examples of the "uncultured peasant" or the obverse of the cultured to show how improved were the manners of the civilized. The rustic and the rube were the negative examples that showed the positive virtues of culture to the consumers of social-climbing manuals. Negative examples were effective instructional tools. Likewise, guilds and cities made public examples of those youths who broke contracts or otherwise offended, so that their punishment would be a lesson to others who might be inclined to offend.

John Russell's *Boke of Nurture* provides one of the most interesting contrasts between "governed" and "ungoverned" youth. A manual for the duties of a butler and carver to the nobility, its introduction creates appositions that give an insight into the sort of benign, adolescent savage that can be turned into a paragon of virtue. The introduction juxtaposes wilderness to noble household, poacher to servitor, unruly to well governed, and naive youth to civilized man.

Russell meets his candidate for conversion in a fittingly wild environment, a forest in the "merry season of May." The young poacher, armed with bow and arrow, has the right physical appearance—he is slender and lean. But he is in despair because he cannot find service: "I serve myself and no other man." Russell immediately asks the obvious question for any aspiring, medieval youth: "Is thy governance good?" This child of nature confesses that he has tried to get a master, "but because I knew nothing good, and showed this wherever I went, every man denied me; day by day wanton and not overnice, reckless, lewd and chattering like a jay, every man refused me." Fortunately, he is educable and can come in from the wilderness.[53]

The contrast of wilderness to household provides an insight into the expectations that adults had when they viewed adolescents. The wilderness and the young savage's poaching stand for his disabilities in finding a position in civilized society. If he follows the advice of his adult mentor, he will no longer be an outcast, but can become a respected member of society.

The author of the fifteenth-century courtesy book *Lytyl John* uses a negative example whom he calls Ruskyn. He is not an untutored child of nature waiting to be rescued, but rather he has only partially learned his manners and turns out to be foppish. Lessons must be learned thoroughly, not by halves. The author compares him to Absolon in *The Miller's Tale*.[54]

One large body of literature, that of the "ages of man," defined adolescence as a life stage, in terms both of medical theory and of the type of behavior characteristic of each life period. Adolescence fell between the childish period of "wanton and wild," and the goal of adulthood to be "sad and wise." In the ancient physician's and philosopher's division of life stages into four (based on Pythagoras), adolescence was hot and dry as summer is and as fire is and its humor was red choler. In the division of the life cycle into seven, according to the planets (the Ptolemaic and Hippocratic periodization), youth's planet was Venus, which "implants an impulse toward the embrace of love."[55]

The morality play *Mundus et Infans* captures the difference between the pranks of the child and the "love-longing" of youth. Smart little Wanton, a child of seven to fourteen, is an engaging figure. Wanton tells of all his secret games with relish. He can spin a top, but he also uses his "scroug-stick" (whip for the top) to beat his playmates on the head. He manipulates his family by biting and kicking his brother or sister if they thwart him, but pouting and crying if his father or mother should interfere. He can "dance and also skip, . . . play at the cherry-pit, . . . and whistle you a fit." On the way to school he has learned to do all those things that moralists told him not to do. He stole fruit from gardens, went after birds' eggs, and ended up feeling the whip of his master.[56] Wanton is drawn along lines that can be seen in the behavior of real urban children from the ages of seven to fourteen.[57]

At fourteen, Wanton changes his name to Lust and Liking. Mundus tells him that the next seven years are to be all games and glee, all "love-longing in lewdness." He sets out in pursuit of women, revel, and riot.[58] But the playwright does not dwell on his carousing and conquests.

Other late medieval popular poetry, however, takes up the theme of male adolescent behavior. "The Mirror of the Periods of Man's Life," a lively moral lesson in verse, divides life into stages by years and qualities.

In the fourteenth year "knowliche of manhode he wynnes" (puberty), and through the early twenties the youth is a battleground for the struggle between the seven virtues and the seven sins. Reason dictates an education at Oxford or at the law, but lust has another institution in mind:

> Quod lust, "harp and giterne there may ye leere,
> And pickid staff and blucklere, there-with to plawe,
> At tauerne to make women myrie cheere,
> And wilde felaws to-gider draw.

Music, drink, mock fights, and wild companions vie with obedience, reason, and those other attributes that are to make one "sad and wise."[59]

Since urban centers attracted a large number of young men and women, the problems of "lust and love-longing" occupied urban courts. A few cases suffice to indicate that poets and moralists had real examples to draw upon. Richard, son of John le Mareschall of Smythfield, was charged with abducting Stephen of Hereford's wife. The neighbors were full of gossip about it. Richard had been seeing this woman for some time, but when Stephen was away at Winchester Fair, Richard was at his house all the time, and the neighbors and friends of Stephen determined to put a halt to it. Searching the house, they directed the adulterous wife to open a chest closed with iron and therein they found Richard. Richard left London and did not see her again. When she learned that her husband was returning, she left home with some of his goods. Finally, she got the ecclesiastical court to force Stephen into a reconciliation with her.[60]

Childe-William's master, curiously, was not worried about the sexual escapades of his apprentice, but suggested, instead, that he was unthrifty and had gambled away his money. Gambling, drinking in taverns, and wasting money on clothing was tempting. Three apprentices, Henry Pykard, Walter Waldeshef, and Roger Fynch, were charged in 1339 with being "addicted to playing knuckle-bones" at night and leading other apprentices into gambling. People in one ward found that Richard de Pelham was "a good man and true," but his son, Richard, was a "rorer."[61]

Apprentice contracts precluded gambling and unthrifty living, but the situation was hard to control when the older ones were abroad on their master's business. The mercers, in order "to avoid evil among the youth of the fellowship" when they were in Flanders, established six English houses there run by men of good reputation. The apprentices could eat only at these houses or face fines. They were to have only four groats worth of English beer (not the strong, continental beers) and no wine. They were not to play cards or other games for money and were not to dance, revel, or sit up past nine o'clock in the evening.[62]

The problems of apprentices went beyond their wild living; they could defraud their masters and even beat them. Again, a few examples suffice to show the type of problem that could arise. While masters were much more likely to abuse the relationship because they had the greater power, apprentices could also cause problems. Edward Bowden violently and suddenly beat his mistress, reviled her and tried to strangle her. The goldsmiths were outraged and called together "worshipful men" to decide what to do about Bowden. They concluded that he would only become worse if they sent him to prison. Instead, they had him stripped and beaten in the Goldsmiths' Hall kitchen until his blood flowed, so that his own body's pain and bleeding would instruct him about the damage he had done to his mistress. Twenty years earlier the goldsmiths had dealt with an attempted murder of a master by an apprentice.[63]

The story of Walter Prata indicates the sorts of ungovernable qualities in apprentices that scared masters. Stories like Walter's were reason enough to create literature and ordinances that emphasized honesty and obedience in apprentices. Walter was apprenticed in 1400 to John Lincoln, a liveried goldsmith. A precocious cheat, he engaged in false measures, shortchanging his master, and stealing from other apprentices. Finally, he became involved in an alchemy scheme with a Fleming. The account concludes that "in this wise he made much dis-ease among the men." The guild expelled him with no possibility of gaining readmission.[64]

The "sad and wise" were continually bothered by the misbehavior of adolescents, particularly apprentices. Thus the wardens of the Mercers' Company lamented to the membership that "they have lately known and herd that divers mennys apprentices have greatly mysordered theymself as well in spendyng grete Summes of mony of theyre Maisters goods in Riott as wel upon harlotes as at dyce, cardes and other unthryfty games as in their apparell," to the great hurt of all. They needed some ordinances to deal with the problem.[65] A few years later on May Day, 1517, a general riot among apprentices occurred, and the mercers and others heard from the king that they must do something about the "wild, undiscrete Parsones named to be menes apprentices and menes servauntes of this Citie."[66]

The concern over riot did not imply a decided culture of misrule among urban apprentices, and, indeed, the literature speaks of individual rather than group violations of propriety. London's fifteenth-century riots lacked the carnivalesque features that early modernists like to refer to as typical of a "youth culture." The most serious riots were attacks on foreigners and involved guildsmen, as well as apprentices and servants.[67]

Moralists could not accept that the planets alone made youth "ungovernable" and strove to educate them. Some writers argued that they turned out so badly because they were not adequately beaten. Others opined that their rebelliousness was the result of too much beating and that they became callous because of it. Still others felt that the home environment was so poisonous that young people lacked role models of how honorable people ought to behave.[68] How could they be expected to behave better than their elders? Medieval moralists, city fathers, and masters were perplexed about what to do with adolescents.

Fifteenth-Century Anxiety over Adolescence

Literary and historical examples of a new preoccupation with middle-class adolescence abound, and it is quite clear that the adults were honing an image of the ideal behavior expected of this group of youth. The literary examples reinforced the regulatory ones, with each contributing to a unified image. But the investigation of this particular intersection of history and literature leaves two major questions unanswered: a historical one about the sudden value placed on middle-class youth and a literary one about the audience for such poems as "The Childe of Bristowe."

A demographic explanation for the increased awareness of adolescence is initially attractive. If there were more adolescents in the population, then an older and smaller generation might feel threatened by their presence and feel that adult society could not properly assimilate or train them to be useful additions to the "sad and wise." Recalling the conflicts between youth and adults that our post World War II "baby boom" occasioned in the 1970s, this is an attractive hypothesis. But the fifteenth century was a period of low population growth. The concern about adolescence arose, not because of an overabundance of them, but because they were a scarce commodity. Scarcity produced a sense of concern for their proper nurturing and training.

The plague of 1349 and its subsequent visitations reduced the population of England by about one-third and in London by about one-half. The plague did not visit once, but kept returning. There is even some evidence that the young were particularly vulnerable to mortality from the plague. In addition, a number of other diseases made their first entry into Europe and England during the fifteenth century.[69] With a scarcity of children who survived into adulthood, parents in the country tried to keep their sons at home to compensate for the greatly reduced labor force.[70] The low rural population meant that opportunities to work for high wages or even to purchase or rent land made it easy for youth to marry and establish a family in the countryside.

From the point of view of the urban middle class, the scarcity of adolescents and the new opportunities in the countryside made it difficult to recruit apprentices. A husbandman's son would hesitate to accept the long-delayed adulthood that being an apprentice required. The steep costs of entry were also a hindrance. If a youth persisted in the goal, he might have to work longer as an agricultural servant to earn the money and meet the new requirements of literacy. The chief suppliers of apprentices, the husbandman ranks, therefore felt a pull to remain at home. Some crafts, such as the fursters (saddle makers), showed a reluctance to take apprentices at all. The city accused them of taking no apprentices in order to restrict the number of people practicing the trade and thereby raise prices. In their defense, they claimed that the pestilence had made it difficult to attract apprentices, and "they were feeble from a life of labor" and could not train them, in any case.[71]

Other guilds responded by lengthening the term of the apprenticeship contract to ten years. By making the apprentices serve longer, they were able to rely upon skilled labor at a very low cost to themselves in the last years of the apprenticeship. The goldsmiths by 1393 had already mandated that the term be ten years, but they agreed to reduce it for an extra fee or for sons of goldsmiths. By their own records, however, the average term was 10.6 years.[72] The trend toward longer terms was established by the first half of the fifteenth century, when only 41 percent were for eight years and 59 percent were for a longer period.[73] Scattered references to contract violations and guild ordinances indicate that the average length of a term was ten years in the fifteenth and sixteenth centuries.[74]

Because the young people were staying in the country longer before seeking apprenticeships, the age of entry into apprenticeship rose. In the early fourteenth century, fourteen was the usual age of entry into apprenticeship, and a city ordinance specified thirteen as the minimum age. But the age of entry crept up to fifteen or sixteen by the end of the fourteenth century.[75] During the course of the fifteenth century the age of entry into apprenticeship increased to at least sixteen, but eighteen was more common. Many of the elite London guilds, such as the mercers, goldsmiths, and ironmongers, began to require that their apprentices have an education before entering into their apprenticeships.[76] Thus they spent longer in grammar schools than apprentices of the previous century.

A change in the composition of the apprentices can also be noted as the fifteenth century wore on. More of the apprentices came from a husbandman background as opposed to gentry or merchant. By the middle of the sixteenth century 47 percent of the apprentices were sons of husbandmen, 23 percent were of yeoman origin, and another 23 percent were native Londoners, with only 7 percent being drawn from the gentry. By the sixteenth century, then, husbandmen formed the predominant group, whereas townsmen and yeomen dominated in the fifteenth century. Only the prestigious guilds, such as long-distance traders, could expect to recruit from the gentry and merchant class.[77]

We have, then, three factors that begin to explain the newfound concern with adolescence. The supply of adolescents appropriate for recruitment for apprenticeships was low until the end of the fifteenth century. Those who were recruited increasingly came from the husbandman class and, therefore, needed all the polish that the advice books could give to bring them up to guild standards. Guild standards were actually rising as the supply of qualified candidates was shrinking. Finally, the guilds and masters were trying to dominate and assimilate an older population of adolescents. A young man who entered apprenticeship at age fourteen was easier to train and control than a youth who entered apprenticeship at eighteen.

The lengthened terms of apprenticeship also created difficulties. In the fifteenth century apprentices did not finish their terms until they were twenty-eight, rather than twenty-one, as in the fourteenth century. Imposing the terms of apprenticeship contracts, which delayed sexual activity, marriage, dress, and independent living arrangements, was much more difficult for older apprentices. Guilds and masters were extending adolescent status to men who were essentially adult except for their dependent position.

A fear of these overgrown youths, combined with anxiety to do the best for them, led to literature and public policies reflective of generational and social status clashes. Teaching a subordinate position and respect for social hierarchy was essential for middle-class adolescents.

Reinforcing the efforts to construct an ethos for middle-class adolescents were the conservative values and "dullness" among fifteenth-century writers. As Lerer has pointed out, Lydgate in his *Testament* used the technique of juxtaposing the unruly qualities of youthful behavior, including pranks and thefts, to the desirable "commercial, social, and religious spheres of action" that the youths should adopt. Lydgate casts his piece as "autobiographical," as does Hoccleve in *La Male Regle*.[78] The use of this personal approach, in contrast to *Ratis Raving* or Russell's *Book of Nurture*, adds a weight of firsthand experience to traditional themes.

Hoccleve describes in his "autobiography" the attributes of a prolonged period of youthful indiscretions:

> But twenti wyntir past, continuelly,
> Excesse at borde hath leyd his knyf with me.

Following the "ages of man" literature he speaks of the pursuit "of Venus femel lusty children deere," particularly at "Poules Heed" tavern where he went "to talke of mirthe and to disport and pleye." He drank sweet wine, ate choice foods, and stumbled to bed to sleep it off.[79] It was Hoccleve's view that "for the more paart, youthe is rebel."

> O yowthe, allas, why wilt thow nat enclyne
> And unto reuled resoun bowe thee?
> Syn resoun is the verray, streighte lyne
> That ledith folk unto felicitee.

Even though friends and wise men tell youth that they will regret their excesses, they will not listen.[80]

In both Lydgate and Hoccleve are elements one finds in books of advice, in popular poetry, and in urban regulations and court cases. Lerer even finds that the cycle turns on itself and that the author of the popular "Poem to Apprentices" borrows directly from the organization of Lydgate's *Testament*.[81]

The vast expansion of literature for instruction of youth in the fifteenth century suggests an audience of increasingly literate children for whom parents bought books, and authors and scribes found a profit in writing them. While some of the pieces were adaptations and infantilizations of Chaucer, as Lerer has shown, the scribblers were also busy with experimentation to make moral lessons palatable and memorable to their audiences. Even Russell's *Book of Nurture* engages a young reader with a positive image before plunging into technical descriptions of carving and serving.

Much of the popular literature was designed to be memorized and even recited orally, rather than simply read. For instance, "Symon's Lesson of Wisdom for All Manner of Children" did not presume a literate audience:

All manner of children, ye lisen and hear
A lesson of wisdom that is written clear.
My child, I advise thee to be wise, take heed of this rhyme.

Other books organized the lessons in order such as "The ABC of Aristotle."[82]

The "Childe of Bristowe" and "The Merchant and His Son" are written in a way that would instill moral training through a good story.[83] The young hero is the ideal physical and social type—straight of limb, well educated, and gentle by birth—just the sort of youth an aspiring apprentice might identify with if given the poem early enough. His respect for father and master are tied into an adventure story with the requisite three episodes in saving his father's soul. The story carries the reader along with its adventure and rewards. The second version adds a touch of humor. Finally, Childe-William's patience and willingness to sacrifice any claim to his father's ill-gotten fortune is rewarded with the return of the property, a marriage, and full establishment as a merchant. In fifteenth-century fashion, the patience of the hero is likened to that of Job:

First was riche and sitthen bare,
And sitthen richer than ever he was.[84]

We cannot conclude that all of the fine lessons were picked up and put into practice, or even that their chief consumers were children and adolescents. While undoubtedly the ideal presented in these poems was what the "sad and wise" of the fifteenth century wished their sons and apprentices to imbibe, the fact that the two surviving examples appear in devotional rather than household books makes the reader wonder who was going to learn the lesson. Certainly, the historical sources speak of numerous apprentices who showed no signs of moving along the continuum of behavior from "wild and wanton" to "sad and wise," but the story of Childe-William does illustrate an agreement on an ideal type that can be found in both literature and history.

Notes

Seth Lerer was very helpful in reading a draft of this paper and sharing with me his own work on didactic literature of the fifteenth century. David Wallace, Ralph Hanna, and James Landman also offered considerable help in the final version.

1. I would agree with Mary Martin McLaughlin that the eleventh and twelfth centuries can be characterized by a new preoccupation with the experiences of childhood. Mary Martin McLaughlin, "Survivors and Surrogates: Children and Parents from the Ninth to the Thirteenth Centuries," in *The History of Childhood*, ed. Lloyd deMause (New York: Psychohistory Press, 1974), pp. 100–181.

2. Norbert Elias, *The Civilizing Process: The History of Manners*, trans. Edmund Jephcott (Oxford: Blackwell, 1979), p. 7. His own study relies heavily on sixteenth- to eighteenth-century books of advice. His chapter on medieval manners (pp. 60–70) puts the advice literature, including John Russell's *Book of Nurture*, in the category of courtly behavior. He does not see the shift of audience of advice literature to the middle class until the sixteenth century (p. 70). Jonathan Nicholls, *The Matter of Courtesy: Medieval Courtesy Books and the Gawain-Poet* (Woodbridge, Suffolk: Brewer, 1985) has pointed out that civility is an urban term and that courtesy came to include not only courtly ideals, but skills needed for a new age (pp. 13–14).

3. "The Childe of Bristowe" is preserved in the British Library Harleian MS 2382, fol. 118. The poems included within the manuscript are largely devotional literature, such as Lydgate's "Life of Our Lady," "The Testament of Dan John" in various parts, poems to the Virgin Mary, Chaucer's *Prioress's Tale*, and his life of Saint Cecilia. In other words, the poems are associated with devotional tracts and with Lydgate. No doubt the selections from Lydgate in this manuscript led Joseph Ritson, *Bibliographia Poetica* (London: Printed by C. Roworth for G. and W. Nicol, 1802) p. 71, to attribute the poem to Lydgate, as did Clarence Hopper, who edited it in 1859 for the Camden Society (*Camden Miscellany* 4). "The Childe of Bristowe" is the ninth entry following the *Long Charter of Christ*. "The Merchant and His Son" comes from Cambridge University Library MS no. Ff.2.38.59r. It, too, is bound with manuscripts of a moral and devotional nature, including part of William Lychfield's *Complaint of God*, proverbs of Solomon, meditations, mirrors of vices and virtues, several poems on the seven works of mercy, *The Charter of Christ*, and several poems about the Virgin, Saint Margaret, Saint Thomas, Mary Magdalen, and Saint Katherine. "The Merchant and His Son" appears in the latter part of the manuscript, which includes "How the Wyse Man Taght Hys Son," "The Story of the Adulterous Falmouth Squire," and a variety of romances. The two manuscript sources are both of the mid–fifteenth century and contain similar collections. Both poems appear in W. Carew Hazlitt, *Remains of the Early Popular Poetry of England*, 1 (London: John Russell Smith, 1864), pp. 110–52. W. F. Schirmer, *John Lydgate: A Study in the Culture of the Fifteenth Century*, trans. Anne E. Keep (Berkeley: University of California Press, 1961; originally published in German, 1952) lists the Ritson attribution in his appendix (pp. 275, 278), but does not consider the ascription as reliable. I am grateful to James Landman for looking up the two manuscripts in Cambridge and London.

4. David Lawton, "Dullness and the Fifteenth Century," *Journal of English Literary History* 54 (1987): 761–71.

5. Seth Lerer, *Chaucer and His Readers: Imagining the Author in Late Medieval England* (Princeton, N.J.: Princeton University Press, 1993); see chap. 3 in particular. His study of the household type of manuscript collection could be of major importance in putting in context the preservation of such manuscripts as "The Childe of Bristowe," as well as the variant versions of Chaucer's works. As these are currently bound and catalogued, however, the context seems to represent devotional literature rather than the sort of collections that Lerer has identified. The interchange brought about by the Intersections conference has proved how important these interdisciplinary workshops can be to the understanding of how fields work along parallel lines. It is possible, for instance, that there were different levels of books for advice for the young and that adults would find some of the stories for adolescents instructive.

6. Barbara A. Hanawalt, "Keepers of the Lights: Late Medieval English Parish Gilds," *Journal of Medieval and Renaissance History* 14 (1984): 137–48, speaks of the religious conservatism of the guilds. Barbara A. Hanawalt and Ben R. McRee, "The Guilds of *Homo Prudens* in Late Medieval England," *Continuity and Change* 7 (1992): 163–79, address the issues of social behavior in guild regulations. These are very close to the types of advice that appear in the general literature produced for the aspiring adolescent in that they address issues of behavior at table during guild feasts, moral relations with brother guildsmen, honor in business dealings, and so on. The guilds were, one may conclude, part of the general movement toward a definition of middle-class, conservative morality that characterized the fifteenth century.

7. See Frances Elizabeth Baldwin, *Sumptuary Legislation and Personal Regulation in England* (Baltimore, Md.: Johns Hopkins University Press, 1926), pp. 73–119, for discussion of the Lancastrian and Yorkist periods.

8. Hazlitt, *Early Popular Poetry*, "The Childe of Bristowe," p. 111, line 15; "The Merchant and His Son," p. 132, line 2.

9. H. S. Bennett, *England from Chaucer to Caxton* (London: Methuen, 1928), pp. 149–50.

10. Steve Rappaport, *Worlds within Worlds: Structures of Life in Sixteenth-Century London* (Cambridge: Cambridge University Press, 1989), pp. 304–5. Among the skinners and tailors, 32 percent of the apprentices had fathers who were merchants or craftsmen, 30 percent had yeomen fathers, 19 percent were husbandmen, 16 percent were gentry, and the other 3 percent had fathers from miscellaneous backgrounds (Sylvia L. Thrupp, *Merchant Class of Medieval London* [Chicago: University of Chicago Press, 1948], pp. 211–19).

11. Hazlitt, *Early Popular Poetry*, "The Childe of Bristowe," p. 112, lines 29–30.

12. Laetitia Lyell and Frank D. Watney, eds., *Acts of the Court of the Mercers' Company (London), 1453–1527* (Cambridge: Cambridge University Press, 1936), p. xi; Charles Welch, *History of the Cutlers' Company of London*, vol. 1 (London, printed privately, 1916), p. 114: cutlers required that the apprentices be "clean of limb and lith in their bodies without any deformity for the worship of the city."

13. Thomas Reddaway, *The Early History of the Goldsmiths' Company* (London: Edward Arnold, 1975), p. 147; Rappaport, *Worlds within Worlds*, p. 298; Walter Prideaux, ed., *Memorials of the Goldsmiths' Company, Being Gleanings from Their Records* (London: Eyre, 1896), p. 28.

14. Hazlitt, *Early Popular Poetry*, "The Childe of Bristowe," pp. 112–113, lines 37–42; "The Merchant and His Son," p. 134, lines 29–30.

15. Alice Green, *Town Life in the Fifteenth Century* (London: Macmillan, 1894), vol. 2, pp. 1–12, first made this observation about the role of courtesy books in the fifteenth century and their importance to the formation of urban manners.

16. See, for instance, Diane Bornstein, *Mirrors of Courtesy* (Hamden, Conn.: Archon Press, 1975), chap. 4.

17. Edith Rickert, ed., *The Babees' Book: Medieval Manners for the Young, Done into Modern English from Dr. Furnivall's Texts* (New York: Cooper Square, 1966), p. 22.

18. Hazlitt, *Early Popular Poetry,* "The Childe of Bristowe," p. 114, lines 82–83.

19. Ibid., p. 112, lines 10–16. The second version is more specific, explaining that when he lent 10s. he expected to get 11s. back, and he put the people under obligation and had them imprisoned when they did not make good on their debts. There is a whole catalog of his deceits, which are of great interest in themselves ("The Merchant and His Son," pp. 133–34, lines 11–24).

20. Rickert, *The Babees' Book,* "The Young Children's Book," p. 23.

21. Hazlitt, *Early Popular Poetry,* "The Childe of Bristowe," p. 113, lines 50–61: "they fare ful wel tha lerne no lawe." He goes on to say that he would never undertake a career that would "make God my foo." In "The Merchant and His Son" the boy makes less of a protest about the law but refuses to enter the profession (pp. 135–36, lines 40–48).

22. Ibid., "The Merchant and His Son," p. 135, lines 45–46.

23. Ibid., "The Childe of Bristowe," p. 113, lines 61–70.

24. A typical contract is that from the merchant tailors for 1451: "John Harrietsham contracts with Robert Lucy to serve the said Robert as well in the craft and in all his other works and doings such as he does and shall do, from Christmas day next ensuing for the term of 7 years. He is to receive 9s. 4d. at the end of the term, and he shall work one year after the seven at wages of 20s. Robert is to find his apprentice all necessaries, food, clothing, shoes, and bed and to teach him his craft in all its particulars without concealment. During the term the apprentice is to keep his master's secrets, to do him no injury and commit no excessive waste of his goods. He is not to frequent taverns, not to commit fornication in or out of his master's house, nor make any contract of matrimony nor affiance himself without his master's permission. He is not to play at dice, tables, or checkers or any other unlawful games but is to conduct himself soberly, justly, piously, well, and honorably, and to be a faithful and good servant according to the use and custom of London. For all his obligations Robert binds himself, his heir and his executors, his goods and chattels, present and future, wherever found (Charles M. Clode, *The Early History of the Guild of Merchant Tailors* [London: Harrison and Sons, 1888], p. 344). The process of drawing up the contract is described in another case. William Morton and Robert de Eye, a cutler, came to a verbal agreement, and Robert had a scrivener draw up an indenture of apprenticeship that contained clauses William had not agreed to. The contract said that he would pay the usual four marks for his first year, but Robert had added that he would have to pay a bond of forty pounds if he broke the contract. William refused and argued that his parents and friends would never have agreed to that. The mayor overturned the bond (*Calendar of Plea and Memoranda Rolls of the City of London,* ed. A. H. Thomas, vol. 3 [Cambridge: Cambridge University Press, 1929] p. 14 [1383]).

25. George Clune, *The Medieval Gild System* (Dublin: Browne and Nolan, 1943), pp. 91–94.

26. Reddaway, *Early History of the Goldsmiths,* p. 147.

27. Hazlitt, *Early Popular Poetry,* "The Childe of Bristowe," p. 114, lines 71–78.

28. Sylvia Thrupp, "The Grocers of London, A Study in Distributive Trade," in *Studies in English Trade in the Fifteenth Century,* ed. Eileen Power and M. M. Postan (London: Routledge, 1933), p. 255.

29. *Calendar of Plea and Memoranda Rolls,* vol. 3, pp. 14–15; Public Record Office C1/67/144; *Calendar of Letter Books of the City of London, Letter-Book G,* ed. Reginald R. Sharpe (London: John Edward Francis, 1905), p. 308 (1373): an eight-year apprenticeship cost 46s. 8d. Hereafter these will be referred to as *Letter Book,* with the corresponding letter of the alphabet.

30. Reddaway, *Early History of the Goldsmiths,* p. 73.

31. Thrupp, "Grocers of London," p. 256.

32. Prideaux, ed., *Memorials of the Goldsmiths' Company,* p. 15.

33. Lyell and Watney, eds., *Acts of Court of the Mercers' Company,* pp. 89, 193; Jean

M. Imray, "'*Les Bones Gentes de la Mercerye de Londres*': A Study of the Membership of the Medieval Mercers' Company," in *Studies in London History Presented to Philip Edmund Jones*, ed. A. E. J. Hollaender and William Kellaway (London: Hodder and Stoughton, 1969), pp. 157–58: in 1347, entry was a 2s. fee from master and likewise from the apprentice; in 1348 it was raised to 20s.; in 1357 to 3 li. 6s. 8d. About 12 percent were delinquent in paying fees, but most did eventually pay the fee along with a fine for delinquency. A. H. Johnson, *The History of the Worshipful Company of Drapers of London* (Oxford: Clarendon Press, 1914), p. 272: drapers set the fee at 13s. 4d. in the late fifteenth century but reduced it to 6s. 8d. in 1512.

34. One reason that the bonds could become close is that most business or craft establishments were small and a master might have only one apprentice during his lifetime. In London between 1349 to 1410, 457 master goldsmiths took in approximately 1,120 apprentices. During the course of their active years as masters, half had only one apprentice, 19 percent had two, 10 percent had three, 7 percent took four, and 14 percent took five or more (Reddaway, *Early History of the Goldsmiths*, p. 91). Reddaway warns that these figures must represent underreporting since not all apprentices were registered, regardless of the regulations.

35. Rickert, ed., *The Babees' Book*, "Symon's Lesson of Wisdom," p. 123.

36. Ibid., "Rhodes's Book of Nurture," p. 132.

37. Hazlitt, *Early Popular Poems*, "The Childe of Bristowe," p. 122, line 319, for an example, or p. 126, line 16: "The burger lovyd the child so wele." The youth always refers to his master as "dear master."

38. Ibid. The two poems deviate on the way the wealth is expended. In "The Childe of Bristowe" the youth expends all the cash on hand in the estate on prayers. He then sells his inheritance and finally his person (pp. 117–28). In "The Merchant and His Son" the action is compressed. He still meets the father's ghost three times, but the dispersal of cash on hand is omitted (pp. 138–49).

39. Ibid., "The Childe of Bristowe," pp. 115–21; "The Merchant and His Son," pp. 137–39. In the latter, the son makes more of a protest that his father should amend his ways before he dies, but the old man will not and leaves the child with his estate and his benediction.

40. Ibid., "The Merchant and His Son," p. 140, lines 110–14. In "The Childe of Bristowe," first version, the master simply says that he will be an unwise man if he sells his inheritance (p. 122, lines 298–300).

41. Rickert, ed., *The Babees' Book*, p. 46.

42. Hazlitt, *Early Popular Poetry*, "The Childe of Bristowe," pp. 121–22, lines 280–320; "The Merchant and His Son," pp. 140–41, lines 106–27.

43. Ibid., "The Childe of Bristowe," pp. 122–24; "The Merchant and His Son," pp. 145–47.

44. Ibid., "The Childe of Bristowe," pp. 125–26, lines 388–427; "The Merchant and His Son," pp. 144–45, lines 167–91.

45. Ibid., "The Childe of Bristowe," pp. 126–27, "The Merchant and His Son," pp. 146–49.

46. Ibid., "The Merchant and His Son," p. 150, lines 54–58.

47. Lydell and Watney, *Acts of the Mercers' Company*, p. 724.

48. Hazlitt, *Early Popular Poetry*, "The Childe of Bristowe," pp. 129–31, lines 496–552; "The Merchant and His Son," pp. 150–52, lines 250–90.

49. Guildhall, Commissary Court, 9051/1 18 (1393), 9171/5 225v. Richard Bradcock left an apprentice and two former apprentices his three best anvils and left his last two apprentices a clenching anvil each (Reddaway, *Early History of the Goldsmiths*, p. 285; see also, pp. 292, 294). See *Calendar of Wills Proved and Enrolled in the Court of Husting, London, A. D. 1258–1688*, ed. R. R. Sharpe (London: John C. Francis, 1890), vol. 2, for a goldsmith's bequest of tools to an apprentice (p. 144 [1371]). Hereafter this collection will be referred to as *Husting Wills*.

50. *Husting Wills*, 1:232 (1312); 2:233 (1383).

51. Public Record Office C1/64/313.

52. *Husting Wills*, 1:114 (1368), 19 (1361), 138 (1370) prayers for both master and mistress.

53. Rickert, ed., *The Babees' Book*, pp. 48–49.

54. Bornstein, *Mirrors of Courtesy*, pp. 82–83.

55. J. A. Burrow, *The Ages of Man: A Study in Medieval Writing and Thought* (Oxford: Oxford University Press, 1988), pp. 12–43.

56. G. A. Lester, ed., *Three Morality Plays: Mankind, Everyman, and Mundus et Infans*, (New York: Norton, 1981), pp. 115–16.

57. *Calendar of Plea and Memoranda Rolls of the City of London*, ed. A. H. Thomas, vol. 2 (Cambridge: Cambridge University Press, 1927), p. 36; *Memorials of London and London Life in the Thirteenth, Fourteenth, and Fifteenth Centuries*, ed. T. H. Riley (London: Longmans, Green, 1868), p. 268.

58. Lester, ed., *Three Morality Plays*, pp. 117–18.

59. Frederick J. Furnivall, ed., *Hymns to the Virgin and Christ, the Parliament of Devils, and Other Religious Poems*, Early English Text Society, o.s. 14 (London, 1868), p. 61.

60. R. B. Pugh, ed., *Calendar of London Trailbaston Trials under Commissions of 1305–06* (London: Her Majesty's Stationery Office, 1975), p. 84. For a more romantic love account, see Public Record Office C1/154/60.

61. *Calendar of Plea and Memoranda Rolls of the City of London*, ed. A. H. Thomas, vol. 1 (Cambridge: Cambridge University Press, 1926), p. 113; *Memorials of London Life in the Thirteenth, Fourteenth, and Fifteenth Centuries*, ed. Riley, p. 88 (1311).

62. Lyell and Watney, *Acts of the Mercers' Company*, p. 724 (1526).

63. *Letter Book C*, p. 123 (1303). Warin Fatting, an apprentice of Matilda Fatting, maimed an index finger of her right hand. He was pardoned, and he paid 35s. in recompense (Reddaway, *Early History of the Goldsmiths*, p. 147; Prideaux, ed., *Memorials of the Goldsmiths' Company*, pp. 18, 22).

64. Reddaway, *Early History of the Goldsmiths*, pp. 83–84, has reconstructed this young man's story from a lengthy record of his crimes, which appeared in the court book.

65. Lyell and Watney, eds., *Acts of the Mercers' Company*, pp. 418–19 (1513).

66. Ibid., pp. 444–45. City fathers had good reason to fear riots among the apprentices, as well as among other inhabitants of the city. The revolt in London in 1381 involved a number of servants. Trade fights led guild members to take to arms and attack one another. When adults began a fight, their servants and apprentices automatically joined in so that a crowd of five hundred or more could assemble quickly, and deaths often resulted. If the riots became serious, the king could threaten to take away the city's charter, and sometimes he did. It was not, therefore, mere moralizing that led the guilds and the city fathers to take a keen interest in suppressing youth riots along with others. See Charles Pendrill, *London Life in the Fourteenth Century* (Port Washington, N.Y.: Kennikat Press, 1971), pp. 133–69, for a discussion of trade fights and their consequences for the city. The most unruly group of apprentices were those of the bench, that is, those young men who were studying common law at the inns of court. These youth were in their late teens or early twenties and lived just outside the city gates in the Holbourn and Fleet area. Unlike the apprentices associated with merchant and craft guilds, they did not live in the master's house and so were not directly supervised. Instead, they lived in rooms, often with their own servants, and learned case law with jurists and through attending court. Their living arrangements permitted them to congregate with each other easily at taverns or in the streets. Together with their servants, they contributed substantially to violent crime and riot in the city (*Calendar of Plea and Memoranda Rolls*, 1:156–60, 213). The apprentices of the bench were as close as London came to having distinctive youth groups with a youth culture.

67. Apprentices as well as masters felt their wealth and grasp on London's markets and industries challenged by foreigners, particularly Lombards (Italians) and Germans (a lumping together of those from the low countries and German towns). In 1456 a major riot occurred between mercers' apprentices and Lombards. A young man had taken the

dagger of a Lombard and had broken it in two. He was immediately arraigned before the mayor at Guildhall and committed to the sheriff's custody. On his way home to dinner, the mayor was held up in the Cheap by a crowd of mercers' apprentices and other people who demanded that the youth be released. The mayor gave in, but this only encouraged the crowd and later in the day they attacked the Lombards in their homes and took goods. Some rioters were arrested and put into Newgate, but when the king's justices proposed to try them, the crowd threatened to ring the Common Bell, to signal for arming the city. Although some of the offenders were eventually hanged, the situation was so unstable that the king and queen left London for a time. In 1493 the mercers' apprentices rose against the German traders and collected a mob of servants, apprentices, and children. The merchants had prior warning and shut their gates in the Steelyard, which was the part of the city assigned to the Hanseatic merchants. The chronicler reporting the event was at pains to point out that no householders were involved in the attack, but only apprentices, servants, and journeymen (Pendrill, *London Life*, pp. 76–77). For an account of alien merchants in late fourteenth-century London, see Alice Beardwood, *Alien Merchants in England, 1350–1377: Their Legal and Economic Position* (Cambridge, Mass.: Harvard University Press, 1931).

68. G. R. Owst, *Literature and Pulpit in Medieval England* (Cambridge: Cambridge University Press, 1933), pp. 460–68.

69. See John Hatcher, *Plague, Population, and the English Economy, 1348–1530* (London: Macmillan, 1977), for a complete discussion of the effects of plague and the course it took in England.

70. Rappaport, *Worlds within Worlds*, p. 297.

71. *Calendar of Plea and Memoranda Rolls*, 1:235–39.

72. Reddaway, *Early History of the Goldsmiths*, pp. 73, 80.

73. *Calendar of Plea and Memoranda Rolls of the City of London*, ed. P. E. Jones, vol. 5 (Cambridge: Cambridge University Press, 1954); see index under "apprenticeship, length of term."

74. In sixty-five scattered cases of broken apprenticeship contracts that appear in the Mayor's Court, Chancery Petitions, and surviving company records for the fifteenth century, the average length of apprenticeship was for ten years. Sixteen years for a contract was not unknown; see Public Record Office C1/19/143. For the sixteenth century, see Rappaport, *Worlds within Worlds*, p. 109; George Unwin, *The Gilds and Companies of London* (London: Methuen, 1908), pp. 91–92; and Welch, *Cutlers' Company of London*, 1: 10–14. Cutlers required a seven-year term with extra service.

75. R. J. Mitchell and M. D. R. Leys, *A History of London Life* (London: Longmans, Green, 1958), pp. 46–47; Clune, *Medieval Gild System*, p. 88; *Letter Book E*, p. 272; *Letter Book F*; pp. 35; *Letter Book H*, pp. 165, 405.

76. Thrupp, *Merchant Class*, pp. 193; Clune, *Medieval Gild System*, pp. 87–88. By the sixteenth century the average age for entering an apprenticeship was eighteen to twenty-two, with some companies forbidding enrollment of apprentices under sixteen. The reason for late age of entry into apprenticeship was both the increased demand for literacy on the part of guilds and the need for adolescent labor at home (most apprentices were drawn from husbandmens' families) (Rappaport, *Worlds within Worlds*, pp. 295–98).

77. Rappaport, *Worlds within Worlds*, pp. 304–11. Thrupp, *Merchant Class*, pp. 218–19, makes a similar observation about the lesser companies in the fifteenth century.

78. Lerer, *Chaucer and His Readers*, pp. 108–10.

79. See Thomas Hoccleve, *Selected Poems*, ed. Bernard O'Donoghue (Manchester: Fyfield Books, Carcanet New Press, 1982), pp. 50–53, lines 111–209, for descriptions of his life.

80. Ibid., pp. 49–50, lines 57–96. David Wallace notes that Hoccleve was only about thirty-five and still unmarried when he wrote this poem in 1405. He seems to want to use this poem to distance himself from his own recent past and assert his adulthood.

81. Lerer, *Chaucer and His Readers*, pp. 109–10.

82. Rickert, *The Babees' Book*, pp. 22, 25, 122.

83. Lerer, *Chaucer and His Readers*, pp. 95–96, shows how the *Tale of Sir Thopas* and *Melibee* became adventure stories as well known to children as Robin Hood and other ballads.

84. *Early Popular Poetry*, "The Childe of Bristowe," p. 131; Lerer, *Chaucer and His Readers*, pp. 111–13.

❖

CHAPTER 9

Reciprocity and Exchange in the Late Medieval Household

Felicity Heal

The great household in late medieval England was the principal focus not only of elite consumption but also of social exchange. Noble households modeled themselves upon the greatest establishment of all, the royal court—that "new house of houses principal of England," as the *Black Book* of Edward IV called it. The royal household was identified as the heart of the realm, embodying its virtue and reputation: in 1485 Henry VII's parliament, passing the Act of Resumption, insisted, "Your Honorable Houshold ... must be kept and borne Worshipfully and Honorably, as it accordeth to the Honour of your Estate and your said Realme." Even heaven was conceived by the author of *Cleanness* as a household:

> He is so clene in his courte, the kyng that al weldez,
> And honeste in his housholde, and hagherlych served. (lines 17–18)

The late Middle Ages has, with much justification, been described as "the age of the household" and peculiarly of the noble household. Neither the court nor other competing focuses of power—the church, London, provincial centers, the legal system—had yet subverted the concentration of regional authority in the entourages of the nobility. Although the reintegration of royal authority under Edward IV and Henry VII began to change the map of political control, it is still possible for an early Tudor historian, with only slight exaggeration, to describe the society as a "federation of noble fiefdoms."[1]

It is not surprising, therefore, that the great household carried a heavy burden of social purposes and meanings for contemporaries. This complex of meanings is partially expressed in the two distinct Latin terms that were used to describe the household: *hospicium* and *familia.* The first normally referred to the practical domestic structure catering to the physical needs of the lord; the second to the grouping of the nuclear family, the retainers and personal henchmen. In the case of the royal household such a division was made explicit in the separation between two departments: that of the lord steward who regulated the "Household of Providence," and that of the lord chamberlain in charge of the "Household of Magnificence." Mere nobles managed with a less elaborated organization, but their domestic establishments were equally committed to a combination of practical provisioning and sociocultural display of power. In its upper echelons the aristocratic household existed to articulate and enhance the reputation of its head: senior servants personated and expressed his qualities.[2]

The purpose of this essay is to examine one set of the meanings attached to these complex domestic structures: those associated with the exchange of benefits and rewards. In this culture the maintenance of reputation demanded the display of good lordship and of largesse, the most material forms of that quality of magnanimity that the Aristotelian tradition placed at the heart of true aristocracy. Although there were several possible theaters for the representation of this aspect of magnanimity—the church and works of charity, the public environment of court and city, or even the battlefield—the individual household was its most natural locus. The household, because it intimately expressed the values of its head, could readily provide the environment for ritualized gestures of exchange, trading favors for adherence, deference for patronage, and hospitality for honor. These transactions largely fall within parameters defined by anthropologists as those of symbolic exchange—Bourdieu's "fake circulation of fake coin." The underlying benefits sought and given were real enough, but the form of the interchange was usually gestural, ritualized, and not obviously commercial. It is not always appropriate, however, to construct a sharp distinction between the symbolic and the commercial elements in these exchanges. The great household employed a full gamut of strategies in its interactions with "foreigners"—that is, all outsiders—and there were opportunities to enhance influence and promote social bonding in even the most mundane transactions. It is best to conceive of each interchange as possessing its own reality and its own ability to contribute to the affirmation of the lord and his establishment.[3]

A taxonomy of reciprocal exchanges in the late medieval household can appropriately begin from those transactions that involved the greatest social gulf between participating parties. The poor had, by definition, little or no material resource to offer in the exchange of benefits with the great. Langland complained that in consequence rich knights ignore the virtues of charity and "gyve wher no nede is." Indeed, the hierarchical nature of the great household tended to confine the poor to its margins, as the recipients of doles and the contents of the almsdish beyond the gates. On the rare occasions when they were allowed a more direct contact with the establishment, it was implicitly understood that their role was that of a foil for noble magnificence. For example, the herald of the earls of Northumberland (as late as the early sixteenth century) cried "larges" before the poor when they entered the hall to receive alms at Twelfth Night and the Saint George Feast; humility in the face of generosity was their required posture. At the feast of Reason in *Piers Plowman,*

Reson stod and stihlede • as for stywarde of halle.
Pacience and ich weren • yput to be mettes,
And seten by ous selue • at a syd-table. (C 16.40–42)

This, of course, Patience, as a humble and poor man, properly accepts.[4]
But a reciprocal element survived in these relationships. Any gesture by
the poor was, as Hugh Rhodes's *Boke of Nurture* reminds us, of great value:

A kynde pore mans harty rewarde
is worth the other three.

Above all, the prayers of the needy were an indispensable aid to salvation. The ritually inverted maundy ceremony—in which clothing was
given to the poor and their feet were washed by the noble—was therefore undertaken in a number of great households, including those of the
duke of Exeter in the early fifteenth century and the earl of Northumberland a century later. Occasionally almsmen had a permanent place in the
establishment: in the fourteenth century Katherine de Norwich kept thirteen poor in her household, as did the "good" duke, Thomas Beaufort, in
the next. Lady Margaret Beaufort continued this tradition into the early
Tudor period. Nevertheless, the fact that more nobles chose to found separate almshouses, to display their works of charity at a distance, suggests
that it was often difficult to reconcile the theory of reciprocal prayer
from the poor with the distasteful fact of their daily presence.[5]
It was in the great funeral and commemorative rituals after the death
of a magnate that the reciprocal relationship between the lord or lady
and the poor was most fully revealed. There the use of the dole and the
deliberate calling-in of the poor to receive benefit provided a focal moment in which the full power of domestic reciprocity was revealed. Endless examples of the elaboration of investment could be cited. Humphrey
Stafford planned that one hundred poor men at his funeral should march
in white robes, with a cross on breast and back. Lord Bardolf left money
for twenty-four men and twenty-four women from his estates to be clad
in black to act as torchbearers. Lord Warenne decided that sixty men in
white was sufficient, while most, even among the nobility, seem to have
settled for rather fewer of the newly clad poor. In addition, the routine
of dole or food or both for all comers was obligatory if the image of
largesse was to be sustained: Elizabeth Montague expected that at least
one thousand poor would be given money dole on the day of her burial,
and at the funeral of Isabel, Lady Berkeley, the hearse traveling to the west
country was met by five thousand to six thousand people, most of whom
were fed or given dole.[6]
A more complex world of exchange existed between the noble and
his immediate inferiors. Since the basic function of the *hospicium* was
the proper provisioning of the lord and his entourage, exchange here

often involved explicitly commercial transactions. The great household was, by the fifteenth century, preponderantly part of a rentier economy and dependent on market purchase for most of the bulk goods it consumed. There are exceptions to this generalization: some home farming continued — many lesser gentry households still produced for their own needs — and fishing rights, some pasture, and deer parks were often kept in hand and served as significant sources of provision. Nevertheless, most surviving accounts for the nobility point strongly toward the market, and cash transactions, as the main form of supply. Even the directly commercial transactions characteristic of the *hospicium,* however, were not automatically shorn of elements of social bonding or symbolic reciprocity. The recurrence of a small group of names in many of the household accounts suggests that transactional bonds were forged with those who could offer adequate surplus. Grain and sheep were two commodities particularly likely to be purchased in bulk from individuals. In the process the lines between tenants, suppliers, and caterers often appear blurred. Thomas Howard, first duke of Norfolk, for example, received part of his livestock from a Mr. Seyntlow, who also occasionally produced gifts, but who subsequently moved directly into the duke's service. Where guest lists survive among the household accounts, they often include the names of regular suppliers, as when Dame Alice de Bryene routinely welcomed John White, who provisioned for her, to her table.[7]

One consequence of these changes for the general story of reciprocity and exchange is that the decline of direct demesne exploitation enabled nobles, if they so wished, to lead a less peripatetic existence. For example, the household of Humphrey Stafford, first duke of Buckingham, purchased the vast majority of its needs from local markets in the mid–fifteenth century. In 1452–53 the duke used only two rural residences, although he also visited London and his power base of Stafford for brief periods. His example was followed by other members of the Stafford dynasty: the favored manors changed over time, but only the second duke was intensely mobile, and that is to be explained largely by external political pressures. Half a century earlier the much smaller household of Margaret de Brotherton was also relatively static as a result of the rentier status of its head: Margaret spent much of the year at Framlingham in Suffolk, and her officials depended on the markets of Framlingham, Diss, and Newmarket for most of their supplies. No doubt the gradual fixing of places of residence had mixed results for social relationships. When a noble entourage moved around far-flung estates, it offered obvious opportunities for the integration of dependents: Elizabeth, Lady Berkeley, traveling through her Warwickshire lands in 1420, routinely received local men at her table. Yet steady residence afforded a clearer focus for the wider *familia,* and perhaps a more systematic opportunity to cultivate magnificence.[8]

At the same period that the great household became more static, it also showed a tendency to grow in size and organizational complexity. The growth of retaining provides one explanation for this physical expansion: the riding household, which roughly corresponded to the military servants of a nobleman, might only account for about a third of the whole servant body, but it had a multiplier effect on the establishment as a whole. Although it is important not to exaggerate the size of entourages on the basis of some of the wilder estimates of contemporaries, it was not uncommon for men of the upper nobility to have 100 to 150 individuals within their *hospicium*. The enlarged household offered a variety of opportunities for elaborate hospitality and displays of largesse, and indeed for that "aggressive generosity" that was one of the cultural inheritances of earlier knightly society.[9]

The cash nexus provided the primary bond between the household and its suppliers. But older forms of exchange still appeared intermittently. Some are tenurial agreements to service the household with specified commodities in lieu of money rent. When these arrangements were strictly those of rent in kind they might create associations little different from those of commercial suppliers. In the household of the earls of Northumberland, for example, the tenants of Heigham supplied freshwater fish by contract. Such rents in kind are often, however, difficult to distinguish from tenant gifts: items such as hens, rabbits, and game birds were often produced by tenants by customary agreement. The rather modest household of Robert Waterton, esquire, of Methley, Yorkshire, received 140 capons and 90 hens principally in the form of "gifts" in 1416–17. These commodities were usually associated with the festival cycle of the household—presented as New Year or Easter "gifts"—and then they were explicitly linked with an obligation by the lord to reciprocate. The *"gestum,"* or tenant feast, was the occasion for hospitality given by the lord in return both for service done and rent-gifts produced. Fifteenth-century accounts record this duty being performed to tenants at New Year: Dame Alice de Bryene, for example, entertained three hundred tenants and others to dinner on January 1, 1413, a remarkable contrast with the twenty or so persons who usually dined with her. Songs and carols record the sense of these entertainments as rightfully due to the tenantry, the expressive reward in a relationship essentially economic and transactional. A north country carol of the early sixteenth century, for example, calls for

> Some ayle or beare gentill butlere
> some lycour thou has showe
> such as you mashe our throtts to wishe
> the best were that you brewe.[10]

Good relationships with tenants and suppliers, aimed at sustaining the household economy, merge into a wider range of transactional arrangements that were important for the lord and his *familia*. Gift giving is of particular interest here, since gestures of largesse served to modify the calculative elements of household behavior. A basic pattern of giving to and from the *hospicium* can be identified in many accounts. The values attributed to the donations were rarely large: the first duke of Buckingham received goods worth between eleven pounds and fourteen pounds per annum. This compares with nine hundred pounds in total domestic receipts in 1439. Thomas de Berkeley dispensed sixty-five pounds, or five percent of his income, in gifts and pensions in 1345. But value is of less interest here than what is represented by the gift. The majority of those included in the accounts were items of consumption, especially wild fowl, fish, and game. Many came from men whose status is not defined in the formal accounts, presumably therefore men who were not automatically part of the "community of honor," seeking to maintain identity, favor, or the like. We seem to encounter in these records strategies for the articulation of interpersonal relationships by the multiplication of small gestures. Indeed, the very modesty of the signs may be an essential element in their success: they did not threaten the fundamentally hierarchical relationships between donor and recipient, did nothing to subvert the magnificence of the lord.[11]

We should not underestimate the significance of these small gifts in sustaining the asymmetrical relationships between lord and dependent. It is the ability to use gifts as tokens of the circulation of goodwill that is crucial. Thus the thirteen gifts given by the third duke of Buckingham in 1516–17 are significant mainly because of their recipients and the fidelity to service that they betokened. Two beneficiaries were members of the duke's council, four were his annuitants, one was a legal adviser, and the rest were local Gloucestershire gentlemen or were from other areas where the duke held property. The most prestigious of consumption goods — venison — was regularly used to afforce local identities. For example, the keeper of Framlingham Park in Suffolk dispensed between one hundred and two hundred of the second duke of Norfolk's deer annually, largely to dependent neighbors, tenants, and servants. Such gifts interconnected with the giving of "rewards" to annuitants and the like who were bound to do the lord service; indeed, the language of rewards suggests the difficulty of establishing clear differences between types of transaction. Men were bound to others by material tokens, and the conceptual distance between the "free benevolence" and the fee was very narrow. This is shown particularly clearly in the case of the granting of livery. Livery in some measure combined the contrasting elements of wage and gift: it had the qualities of the former in that it rewarded service rendered and bound to further action; the latter in that it manifested the lord's largesse and secured embodiments of his magnificence. This is particularly obvious in the form that livery worn by knightly and senior retainers often took from the end of the fourteenth century: the wearing of chains, often of gold, badged with the lord's insignia. John of Gaunt introduced this practice into England, partly it would seem to provide clear social differentiation among the retinue—badges and plain cloth to lesser servants, chains and fur tippets to those with status. But it also expressed munifience—or, thinking in late-twentieth-century terms, one is tempted to say a powerful example of gift advertising—whose cultural impact may be judged by the number of examples of funeral effigies in which knights wear the lord's collar.[12]

"Gifts" of livery bound their recipients to a response. Few can have had the unconstrained quality suggested by Richard II, of all people, when he described his wearing of John of Gaunt's collar as a "signe de bon amour d'entier coer entre eux." The appearance of some freedom of action might be preserved between parties, but when a nobleman or woman called on the affinity, they were entitled to the direct reciprocation of their largesse. In the context of the household, those benefits were the provision of a proper "supporting cast" from the affinity whenever necessary. Francis Bacon has a delightful story of Henry VII's encounter with the earl of Oxford's retainers at Castle Hedingham. Men in the de Vere livery lined his route: Henry admired them, pretending to believe that they were purely domestic servants. The earl is supposed foolishly to have acknowledged that they were there "to do me service" and was promptly fined for retaining. The East Anglian gentry accepted this duty to appear in due time before the Mowbrays, de Veres, or Howards, in order to show the proper deference of the affinity. Margaret Paston expected to go to the lying-in of the last Mowbray duchess of Norfolk in 1476; a few years earlier her son John had been present when the duchess "took her chamber" for an earlier confinement. In the early sixteenth century Sir Thomas Le Strange was one of many Norfolk gentlemen who regularly felt obliged to visit the Howards at Kenninghall during the Christmas season. Similarly, the Gloucestershire gentry can be observed making their appearance at Thornbury Castle, the seat of the duke of Buckingham, in the twelve days of the Christmas season in 1507.[13]

Many of those bound in the relationship of liveried retainer with a lord were able to claim some near equality of status with him by virtue of their membership in the knightly classes and the "community of honor." Such men of honor among his followers had to be rewarded with high-status "gifts" and associated hospitality. But it was the stranger, in the sense of outsider, of honorable standing who demanded the most subtle response. Froissart's account of the household of that prince of chevaliers, Gaston de Foix, sketches one model of largesse in action. Froissart resided in de Foix's household for a time in the 1380s, and was deeply impressed by its integrity and order. The noble was "large and courtesse in gyftes. He could ryght well take where it parteyned to hym, and to delyver agayne where as he ought." No man of honor departed from his house without some gift, and yet, to Froissart's surprise, his treasure continued to multiply, partly because of his prudential estate management. It is important to note that de Foix did not expect to act purely as a cornucopia, spilling forth gifts to visiting knights; he played a part in a gift economy that sustained the reputation of all participants. The Black Prince was said by his biographer to have employed the same "tres noble largesse," having been committed to it from his youth onward.[14]

The household accounts occasionally reveal the giving of these large gifts: the Black Prince's wardrobe accounts record horses and jewels given to noble friends and close kin. Those of Edward Mortimer, earl of March, for 1413-14 show him receiving horses and hawks, as well as the predictable fish and wild fowl. Grand donations of venison are occasionally recorded by park-keepers. But it is in the transactions associated with hospitality that we can locate the best evidence of reciprocity in the late medieval household. Here the household ordinances are a valuable guide to expectations—articulated from the hegemonic perspective of the lord. Exquisite care was taken in these documents to ensure that the whole establishment directed itself toward upholding the honor of the lord and his reputation for generosity. When John Russell, steward to Humphrey, duke of Gloucester, sought to advise a marshal on the proper seating of guests, he emphasized that the "curtesie of court" must be learned in order that "the honoure and worshippe" of the lord be served. Two generations later, the author of ceremonial advice for the earl of Northumberland's household was insisting that gentlemen ushers should ensure that strangers were always generously served from cellar, buttery, or pantry, for "it is the lords honour."[15]

The household provided a theater in which exchanges of power between men of honor could be played out in ritual form. The nature of this theater can best be evoked by looking at one of the most detailed ordinances. It probably dates from the very early sixteenth century, and could possibly be part of the elaborate series of books of orders associated with the household of the fifth earl of Northumberland. The ordinances, "for the household of an earl," are much concerned with the drama of reciprocal relationships between the household and outsiders. Visitors were moved through a series of ceremonial moments. First the porter received them at the gate and immediately calculated their status. A man of knightly status or above was received with much formality: the head officers had to "repair to the gates" and convey him with due ceremony to the chamber. If the visitor was of particularly high birth, a baron or above, then the great gate might be opened, but only if he was of the same status as his host could he ride into the courtyard, "although after the old order of England [the visitor] most comonlie would not onles he were earnestlie required by the head officers who receyved him." When the lord had a visitor of higher standing than himself, then "the head officers of the said estate do delyver their staves to the head officers of the honorable personage," a situation that was most likely in the case of a royal visit.[16]

In *Sir Gawain and the Green Knight* we possess a powerful poetic vision of this hospitality in action, when Gawain comes at the Christmas season to the castle of Sir Bertilak. When the knight asks for harbor he is met by the porter, who swiftly brings men of the household to greet him. They "yolden hym the brode yate, yarked up wyde" (line 820), since they thought him worthy of the honor. When he reached the hall, Gawain was particularly distinguished, since the master of the house deliberately came from his chamber to greet him, saying "Ye ar welcum to wone as yow lykes. / That here is, al is yowre awen, to have at yowre wylle / and welde" (835–36).

The form of entertainment continues with all the ceremony that would be expected on both sides. For example, at the first meal he was given, Gawain

... calde hit a fest ful frely and ofte
Ful hendely, quen alle the hatheles rehayted hym at ones
as hende:
"This penaunce now ye take,
And eft hit schal amende." (894–98)

Gawain's manners as a guest prove impeccable, as might be anticipated in one reared in Arthur's court, and the language of the poet is full of exchanges of "courtesy" and "honour." These sentiments are most fully articulated at the moment on Saint John's Day when Gawain seeks to depart with the other Christmas guests. His host remarks:

"Iwysse, sir, quyl I leve, me worthes the better
That Gawayn has ben my gest at Goddes awen fest." (1035–36)

Gawain responds:

"Grant merci sir, ... in god fayth hit is yowres,
Al the honour is your awen — the heghe kyng yow yelde!
And I am, wyye, at your wylle, to worch youre hest
As I am halden therto, in hyghe and in lowe, bi right." (1037–40)

Knightly honor, and the need to maintain essential reputation, demanded that enemies as well as strangers experienced this largesse. At the beginning of a late-fourteenth-century version of *Morte Arthure,* the Roman ambassadors ordering Arthur to go to Rome are entertained lavishly at Carlisle, so that there might be "largesce on lofte."[17]

Lavish giving between men of honor was thus a powerful form of bonding; it was also a means of competing for status and reputation, a game at which no great lord could afford to lose. Since such grandiose forms of display were costly in money, time, and emotion, it was useful to be able to express "full largess" partially through the daily routines of the late medieval *hospicium* with a flow of tokens and gestures of the type already identified as characterizing exchange between nobles and their inferiors. In the 1519 household books of Sir Thomas Le Strange, the head of a well-established Norfolk gentry family, we see gifts of curlews, plovers, capons, and even swans being produced for the household by local clergy patronized by the knight. But his neighboring gentry and kin also contributed: a bottle of Rhenish wine from Henry Sherburn, nine plovers from Mr. Bedingfield, a cock pheasant and four woodcocks from Mr. Ashley. In his turn Le Strange tended to send fish to fellow gentlemen and to men of influence in the county. In 1521, for example, he paid five shillings for a porpoise, and divided it between Sir Thomas Bedingfield, Sir John Sheldon, Sir Roger Townshend, and the prior of Walsingham. He also gave half a conger eel to the bishop of Norwich, reserving the other half for himself like the prudent housekeeper he was.[18]

The most famous "text" of gift exchange of the early sixteenth century—the Lisle letters—shows similar preoccupation with the gestural element in exchange. The lord deputy of Calais and his wife procured endless fat quails, game birds, and other "trifles" for presentation to individuals in England. But here gifts carried meanings about identity and the circulation of interest that went beyond some simple affirmation of friendship. They were most commonly directed to the court, by the reign of Henry VIII the focus of the "community of honor," and they anticipated a return not of tokens to symbolize connections between individuals or households, but of patronage and political favor. The same is presumably true of the venison pasties distributed by the first earl of Cumberland a few years earlier. He sent them to court via his friend Henry Percy, heir to the Northumberland title, and the latter passed them to such worthies as the Lord Chamberlain and the papal ambassador, having decided that none were needed for Wolsey, who had been given earlier pasties, which he "dyd take ... veray thankfully, not withstanding my brother Daycar had not long be foyr presentyd ys Grace with vi pastes off astag."[19]

Thus a nobleman or woman interacted with a range of inferiors and equals through the medium of the household: they or their servants ensured that these exchanges were marked by the displays of generosity and largesse proper to the ranks of both parties. The strategies employed were presumably intended to contribute in a functional manner to the enhancement of reputation and the control of conflict and aggression for the participating individuals. This assumes, however, both a measure of structural constancy and a shared vocabulary of secure symbols and values among those participating in these exchanges. It is unwise to presume that such assured states existed for the late medieval great household. The comforts of good lordship and affinity have been much stressed in recent writing about the period, but we should not forget that element of "lethal competitiveness" in fifteenth-century culture that produced political crisis under Henry VI. The environment in which the great household had to operate was uncertain, discontinuous, and prone to sudden collapse. Its symbolic world was equally vulnerable: its capacity to enforce the specific conception of its head was uncertain, and the possibilities of subversion were ever present.[20]

The most obvious tension routinely experienced *within* the household was that of liberality versus prudential management. Good housekeeping was essential to noble honor, but magnanimity unchecked by fiscal caution could easily lead to disaster. If excess were permitted it would ultimately destroy those values that hospitality and generosity should maintain. Sir William Stonor was warned that his overlavish behavior "may breke your howshold with your honour and worschep." Grandeur had to be calculated and a fierce supervisory eye kept upon those servants whose duty it was to control the everyday finances of a great establishment. This was in practice what most households endeavored to do, but there were problems. Control meant extensive management and formalization of hierarchy, or it meant close personal supervision by a lord. And behind these practical difficulties, which occupy much time and attention in the records, it was no simple matter to establish the precise philosophy that should govern behavior. The fourteenth-century dialogue *Wynnere and Wastoure* provides the most vivid evidence of this problem. Waster is accused of pride, neglect of his property, abuse of his aristocratic position, and gluttony; Winner, of avarice, hoarding, failure of charity, and lack of bonhomie. The rhetoric seems conventional enough, yet the striking feature of the text is that no victor really emerges from the discourse. The monarch, who is adjudicating, dispatches Winner to Rome (to live in luxury with the pope), Waster to London (to encourage commerce and consumption). Each is needed: the two cannot readily exist in harmony. At the other end of our period, Skelton made failure to use measure in giving the central concern of his morality *Magnyfycence.*[21]

The problem of lavish consumption was important not only because of the need to secure the wealth of a noble house from one generation to another, but because its misuse was likely to lead to dishonor in the wider society. Gifts and hospitality were necessary parts of largesse; to be effective they needed to be congruent with the expectations of both donors and recipients. The gift may, in Hyde's words, "give increase" and so strengthen the bonds of community, but it also limits freedom of motion. Peter Idley, using as his source Albertanus of Brescia, advised his son of the dangers of love

... kept and conserved
Be riche presentis and giftis grete.

189

True alliance, he argues, can only be forged when the circulation of gifts is properly undertaken:

> For who with love woll make aliance,
> He must nedis yelde gyfte for gyfte,
> And thenne is frendship evenly shifte.

Beneficence required calculation in response: only by proper timing and expenditure could appropriate exchange be completed. William Worcester presented William Wayneflete, bishop of Winchester, with a copy of his translation of Cicero's *De senectute* in 1472, but "got no reward." His sense of insult was far greater than any disappointment at the loss of financial benefit: the gift had rebounded both to his own dishonor and to that of the recipient. An anticipated gift denied was an even more obvious form of insult: in 1468 the duke of Norfolk gave John Paston III no livery gown, "wherfor," the latter noted angrily, "I wayted not on hym."[22]

Among men of honor the misuse of the gift was corrosive and shaming. This notion provides the denouement for the prime literary example of gift exchange, that between Gawain and his host, Sir Bertilak. We have already seen that the normal transactions of honorable exchange between Gawain and his host were conducted on either side with the full resources of knightly courtesy. This was an expected social encounter; less predictable was the knight's offer to exchange "Quat-so-ever I wynne in the wod" for whatever advantages Gawain gained in the castle. Not that Gawain is seen as nonplussed by the agreement; he is evidently grateful for further guidance and for instruction on how to reach the Green Chapel and accedes with courtesy. Nevertheless the bargain is odd, as is suggested by its legal form and the fact that, before they retire to bed, the parties "recorded covenauntes ofte." And so the bargain proves. The exchanges of the first two days' winnings render both parties happy; those of the third are besmirched by guile and disillusion. Sir Bertilak purports to feel shamed by only having a fox skin to return for Gawain's kisses:

> "For I haf hunted al this day, and noght haf I geten
> Bot this foule fox felle — the fende haf the godes!"(lines 1943–44)

But both he and Gawain are aware that the loss of honor is actually that of the guest who has concealed the gift of the girdle. Although it is Gawain's fear and self-love that makes him vulnerable, he is wound into this snare by the intensifying pressures of gift exchange.[23]

In the real world of the fifteenth-century household it was probably the public shame of being bound by gifts as bribes that was most feared. The boundaries between acceptable and unacceptable behavior were always hard to define, especially when, as in the mid–fifteenth century, political authority was too weak to superimpose its own readings upon the "community of honor." The Pastons, whose ruthless pursuit of familial interest is famed, thought themselves thoroughly justified in using the gift as a means to an end. As part of their endless campaign to recover the manor of Caister from the Mowbrays, John Paston II proposed to give the duchess twenty pounds for the purchase of a horse and a saddle. He defended his action by reference to the proverbial wisdom that "men may nott lure none hawkys wyth empty handys." It was, perhaps, fear of allowing the gift to become a bribe that led Thomas Beaufort, duke of Exeter, to insist he would take "no gifts or rewards." Such austerity must have been unusual, but others may have also been cautious: the very detailed accounts of the first Howard, duke of Norfolk, contain few notes of rewards paid to those bringing gifts. An early entry acknowledging a servant who brought a greyhound from "my lord Lyle" obtrudes as quite exceptional. The magnificent man might give, but it behooved him not to be bound too closely by the donations of others.[24]

Hospitality, like other aspects of symbolic exchange, did not easily operate with mutually agreed systems of meaning. The genres of the courtesy text and the manuals of advice to servitors flourished partly because of the difficulty of establishing shared meanings in the competitive world of the fifteenth century. Disagreements about the placing of guests at the dinner table seem to have limited connection to the key values of aristocratic honor and magnanimity, but the texts are often obsessed with their importance. When John Russell, steward to Humphrey, duke of Gloucester, penned his advice to other servants, he showed intense preoccupation with the correct placing of popes, against emperors, against archbishops, and so on down the social order. In particularly casuistical mood he worries, for example, about the parents of a pope or cardinal, who might seek to claim equality of status with their son: "Therfore fader ne moder, they owe not to desire / to sytte or stond by theyre son, his state wille hit not require." Even the steward of the duke of Gloucester can rarely have been confronted in practice by such embarrassments. Rather his text should be read as an attempt to compel his readers to recognize the vulnerability of the household to the ambitions and assertiveness of strangers. Only by confronting the most arcane of possibilities could the good servant be ready to afforce his master's imposition of order within his establishment.[25]

Literary convention permitted poets to take this fear of dishonor through the offering of hospitality to extremes that were rarely experienced in daily life. Knightly challengers, who entered the household legitimately by virtue of their own status and of the open generosity of the host, could turn order into disorder by their rejection of the customary role of the guest. This the Green Knight does at the court of Arthur during the New Year feast. Even more threatening is Sir Degrevant, in the early-fifteenth-century romance, who appears in the castle of his neighbor earl after a tournament victory fully horsed:

Als thay were servede of the first mese
He rade up to the dese,
Mayden Mildore he chese
And chalanges that free. (lines 1217–20)

Sir Degrevant had legitimation for his action in that the earl had broken his word on the outcome of the tournament and was therefore already dishonored, but in riding into the hall he made this shame public in the most dramatic manner possible for a householder. Much the same gesture was made by the Scottish kings who attended King Arthur's coronation feast in Malory's *Morte Darthur*. They refused the gifts offered to them by the king "and said they had no joye to receyve no yeftes of a berdles boye that was come of lowe blood."[26]

Even the most assured forms of hospitality, based on relationships of friendship and near equality, could burden with obligations and uncertainties. In 1523 the fifth earl of Northumberland wrote to his northern neighbor Lord Clifford, expressing thanks for the "good cheire and costes I put you to att my last beinge with you, which if it lie in me I shall deserve." The language, although cordial, is replete with the sense of debts incurred. If this "burden of the spirit" was serious, rather than a mere rhetorical gesture, we would expect men to be cautious in acquiring indebtedness in this competitive society. One of the ways in which this is displayed is the apparent reluctance to trespass upon the hospitality of fellow peers. Several historians examining this period have noted the rather limited number of occasions, recorded in household accounts and correspondence, on which men and women of high status visited one another. There were, of course, grand ceremonial encounters at feasts marking rites of passage, episcopal enthronements, and the like. There were visits to kin and meetings of like-minded political associates. But when they traveled, the great households were far more likely to turn to the church, or their tenants and affinity, for accommodation. This is shown particularly well in the very full accounts of Richard Beauchamp, earl of Warwick, for 1431/32, and of his wife Elizabeth Berkeley a decade earlier: a number of journeys are documented in these texts, but in no case does hospitality seem to have been provided by a fellow peer. The rules for such social interchanges were well articulated, as we have seen, but their practice was no doubt cumbersome, costly, and fraught with possibilities of conflict or loss of face.[27]

It may be valuable to look again at the household ordinances with these issues in mind. These texts are not necessarily concerned with the management of outsiders, indeed the "orders for an earl's household" discussed above is unusual in the minute attention it gives to visitors. At the opposite extreme can be cited a document certainly associated with the household of the fifth earl of Northumberland: a volume of guidance for the officers on proper ceremonial at such times as high festivals, the christening or marriage of the earl's children, and the lying-in of the countess. The elaboration of ritual and gesture prescribed on these occasions would not have been out of place at Versailles: everything is governed by precise instructions about equipment, forms of processions, words, and music. Strangers, in the sense of outsiders, appear from time to time, but their roles are clearly coincidental when compared with the concern for proper "honorable" behavior within the household itself. If this is theater for the benefit of strangers, the latter were expected to sit quietly in the stalls for most of the performance. This was a document prepared for a household of more than two hundred persons, and its language of reciprocity and exchange is turned inward.[28]

This internal, introverted, unstable reading of the ordinances may offer a different perspective on the purposes of hierarchy and ceremonial. David Starkey, in his valuable article on the age of the household, described the noble virtue of magnanimity as having two aspects, generous condescension to inferiors and "cool self-sufficiency *vis-à-vis* equals." The second of these aspects is embodied in an ordinance like the Northumberland one. Dependent gentlemen and others could easily become the mere backdrop against which this ritual life was played out. When a meal was carried through the hall of one of these great houses, en route to the chamber, it was expected that all those who happened to be assembled in this major social room of the house should stand bareheaded, in an attitude of reverence, until the procession had moved on. There is also a clear impression that only the most pressing royal messenger, or the most powerful visitor, could be allowed to disrupt the full ritualism of the twice-daily meal, when the gates were shut and the establishment separated from external pressures. The response of the household servants, to whom the ordinances were directed, must have been more closely governed by the internal demands of formality and control than by the transactional pressures of the outer world.[29]

These "inward" rituals can perhaps be connected with changing perceptions of cultural behavior already touched upon earlier in this chapter. The noble, in ordering so large and elaborated a household, is displaying magnificence, a quality that transcends liberality and even largesse and that is the peculiar prerogative of the coterie of the great. As an Aristotelian virtue, there is nothing new in late medieval culture about the idea of magnificence, but its preoccupation with conspicuous consumption and grandeur is peculiarly fitted to the assumptions and needs of the great nobility of this period. Magnificence still required largesse, as Skelton's Redresse advised his master:

For of noblenesse the chefe poynt is to be lyberall,
So that your largesse be not to prodygall. (lines 2487–88)

And Cloked Colusyon's cynical advice that Magnificence need only give

Largesse in wordes — for rewardes are but small.
To make fayre promyse, what are ye the worse? (1760–61)

is condemned. But generosity was only part of a series of strategies, intended to display power through lavishness, and in the process it was shorn of some of its force as a form of interaction or social bonding. The magnificent man was, by definition, too elevated to need or expect any return for his giving. The relationships between individuals articulated in earlier feudal patterns of gift giving, and still strongly present in *Sir Gawain*, lost much of their reciprocal force when magnificence became the principal objective of the great nobility.[30]

The pursuit of magnificence cannot be confined exclusively to any one moment of the late Middle Ages, but it owed much to developments of the fifteenth century, especially to the Crown's need to display power in the aftermath of Henry VI's disastrous reign. The nobility experienced a similar desire for affirmation of status and stability. For all the relative economic security the great household provided for its head and members, and for all its capacity to integrate a region through its purchasing power, hospitality, and promotion of affinity, it remained a volatile and uncertain entity. Establishments that for a few years might display a monolithic authority were easily broken apart by death, political misadventure, or the simple choice of moving from one area of the country to another. Those earls of Northumberland, whose ordinances appear to be models of noble order and hierarchy, came from a family that had already suffered generations of violence and sudden death. Within a few years, the line was almost to succumb to the pressures of Tudor hostility. Loyalty from one's inferiors depended on an ability to command influence. The East Anglian gentry were in the habit of displaying allegiance to their dominant magnates, but moved with apparent lack of concern with the political winds to serve a Mowbray, a de Vere, or a Howard. Magnificence provided one means by which to defy the vagaries of fortune's wheel.[31]

At the beginning of the sixteenth century the ascendant figure upon fortune's wheel was the monarch. The Yorkist and early Tudor kings achieved a gradual mastery over the "community of honor." This did not automatically portend a sustained attack on noble power or the collapse of the household system, but it focused previously disaggregated activities upon the political center. Local patterns of reciprocity and exchange might be little affected, but those who sought honor from giving and largesse were now more likely to focus much of their energies on courtly calculation and display. Skelton's Magnificence is persuaded at one point in the text that he should bestow all his generosity on a few intimates:

> ... chose out ii, iii, of suche as you love best,
> And let all your fansyes upon them rest. (1769–70)

The fear was that actual monarchs would do the same. Therefore every art and gesture had to be employed to retain an individual and his family in the royal eye. This is the world of gift giving in which the Lisles excelled. No donation was too small to be used as political capital. When Honor Lisle on one occasion wanted "a token" from Henry VIII in return for her gift of fine preserve, her daughter Anne, who served at court, wrote that she could not press for it "for fear lest how his Grace would a'takyt it." Monarchs probably nurtured these anxieties. Both More and Shakespeare employed the incident of Richard III's request for strawberries from Morton: an apparently trivial test of obedience at a moment of high political drama, the fall of Lord Hastings. Formal gifts certainly became a test of political standing. The pattern of New Year gifts offered to the king, and the returns he made, were eagerly studied in the Henrician period as indicators of influence. This political calculus seems worlds removed from the "frank courtesie" of Froissart's knights.[32]

The court therefore became once again the principal theater of political reciprocity and exchange, a position it had always occupied in periods of strong government. But the noble and gentry household continued to provide a fertile environment for more modest exchanges of power and influence. The "community of honor" was still bonded partly by those servants who wound their way across muddy winter lanes bearing gifts of wigeon and partridge between neighboring gentlemen. And while reputation continued to be determined by the gestural displays necessary in an honor-shame society, no great man could escape from the need to give hospitality and offer the appearance of largesse. When Thomas More and his fellow humanists began their assault on the "trains of idle servants" that followed a great lord, they challenged a form of power that was central to noble identity. Strategies of elite influence would demand, long into the sixteenth century, that "lyberalyte ... [is] most convenyent ... [for] a prynce to use with all his hole intent."[33]

Notes

1. A. R. Myers, ed., *The Household of Edward IV: The Black Book and the Ordinance of 1478* (Manchester: Manchester University Press, 1959), p. 86; *Rotuli Parliamentorum* 6, p. 336; A. C. Cawley and J. J. Anderson, eds., *Pearl, Cleanness, Patience, Sir Gawain and the Green Knight* (London: Dent Dutton, 1962), p. 51; G. W. Bernard, *The Power of the Early Tudor Nobility: A Study of the Fourth and Fifth Earls of Shrewsbury* (Brighton: Harvester Press, 1985), p. 180.

2. In practice the linguistic categories between *familia* and *hospicium* are often blurred, but contemporaries used the differentiation in this form when it was necessary to do so:

Felicity Heal

M. Harris and J. M. Thurgood, eds., "The Account of the Great Household of Humphrey, First Duke of Buckingham, for the year 1452–3," *Camden Miscellany 27*, Camden Society, 4th ser. 29 (London: Royal Historical Society, 1984), p. 3; David Starkey, "The Age of the Household," in *The Context of English Literature: The Later Middle Ages*, ed. Stephen Medcalf (London: Methuen, 1981), pp. 254–56.

3. Pierre Bourdieu, *Outline of a Theory of Practice* (Cambridge: Cambridge University Press, 1977), pp. 6, 171–83. Bourdieu's discussion of symbolic capital and its contribution to the maintenance of honor in a community is particularly valuable for an understanding of this aspect of exchange; for a critique of current anthropological readings of symbolic exchange, see John Davis, *Exchange* (Buckingham: Open University Press, 1992), pp. 75–85.

4. Thomas Percy, ed., *The Northumberland Household Book* (London, 1770), p. 344; William Langland, *The Vision of William Concerning Piers the Plowman*, ed. W. W. Skeat, 2 vols. (Oxford: Clarendon Press, 1886), 1: 389.

5. Felicity Heal, *Hospitality in Early Modern England* (Oxford: Clarendon Press, 1990), pp. 68–69; Rhodes quote from F. J. Furnivall, ed., *The Babees Book*, Early English Text Society (EETS), o.s. 1 (London, 1868), p. 102; *Northumberland Household Book*, p. 346; C. M. Woolgar, ed., *Household Accounts from Medieval England*, 2 vols., British Academy Records of Social and Economic History, n.s. 17 (Oxford: Clarendon Press, 1992–93), 1: 177ff.; John Harvey, ed., *The Itineraries of William Worcestre* (Oxford: Clarendon Press, 1969), p. 357; M. K. Jones and M. G. Underwood, *The King's Mother: Lady Margaret Beaufort* (Cambridge: Cambridge University Press, 1992), p. 155.

6. J. T. Rosenthal, *The Purchase of Paradise* (London: Routledge, 1972), pp. 106–7; Claire Gittings, *Death, Burial and the Individual in Early Modern England* (London: Croom Helm, 1984), pp. 27–29; John Smyth, *Lives of the Berkeleys*, ed. John Maclean, 3 vols. (Gloucester, 1883), 2: 175–76.

7. For valuable introductions to the pattern of household accounting, see Woolgar, *Household Accounts from Medieval England*, part 1; Harris and Thurgood, eds., "Account of Humphrey, First Duke of Buckingham," introduction. See also Christopher Dyer, *Standards of Living in the Later Middle Ages: Social Change in England, c.1200–1520* (Cambridge: Cambridge University Press, 1989); K. A. Mertes, *The English Noble Household, 1250–1600* (Oxford: Blackwell, 1988). On patterns of supply see Mertes, *The Noble Household*, pp. 104–19; J. C. Ward, *English Noblewomen in the Later Middle Ages* (Harlow: Longman, 1992), pp. 58–64; Society of Antiquaries MS 77, fols. 22vff; M. K. Dale and V. B. Redstone, eds., *The Household Book of Dame Alice de Bryene, 1412–13* (Ipswich: Suffolk Institute of Archaeology and Natural History, 1931).

8. Harris and Thurgood, eds., "Account of Humphrey, First Duke of Buckingham," p. 5; John M. Ridgard, ed., *Medieval Framlingham: Select Documents, 1270–1524* (Suffolk Records Society 27, 1985), pp. 86–128; Rowena Archer, "The Estates and Finances of Margaret of Brotherton, ca.1320–99," *Historical Research* 60 (1987): 274–75; Longleat MS, Misc. Bk. 9.

9. Mertes, *The Noble Household*, pp. 14–15; Dyer, *Standards of Living*, pp. 50–54; Mark Girouard, *Life in the English Country House* (New Haven, Conn.: Yale University Press, 1978), pp. 14–28.

10. Percy, ed., *Northumberland Household Book*, p. 108; Woolgar, *Household Accounts*, part 2, pp. 505–6; Dale and Redstone, ed., *Household Book of Alice de Bryene*, p. 28; Heal, *Hospitality in Early Modern England*, p. 76; R. T. Davies, ed., *Medieval English Lyrics* (London: Faber and Faber, 1963), p. 217; P. J. King, ed., *Tudor Songs and Ballads* (London, 1978), p. 110.

11. British Library, Eg. 2208; Dyer, *Standards of Living*, p. 70; Daniel Gurney, ed., "The Household and Privy Purse Accounts of the Lestranges of Hunstanton," *Archaeologia* 25 (1834): 421, 447; for similar records of gifts in the household of the third duke of Norfolk, see Cambridge University Library, Pembroke MS 300, fols. 64ff.

12. B. J. Harris, *Edward Stafford, Third Duke of Buckingham, 1478–1521* (Stanford, Calif.: Stanford University Press, 1986), pp. 140–41; R. B. Manning, *Hunters and Poachers:*

196

A Cultural and Social History of Unlawful Hunting in England, 1485–1640 (Oxford: Clarendon Press, 1993), p. 10; Starkey, "The Age of the Household," p. 265; Simon Walker, *The Lancastrian Affinity, 1361–99* (Oxford: Clarendon Press, 1990), p. 95. For example, in Warwickshire, Walter Cokesey, Thomas Erdington I, Humphrey Stafford, and John Ferrers II all wear the Lancastrian collar (Christine Carpenter, *Locality and Polity: A Study of Warwickshire Landed Society, 1401–1499* [Cambridge: Cambridge University Press, 1992], p. 227).

13. Walker, *Lancastrian Affinity*, p. 96; Francis Bacon, *Works*, ed. James Spedding, 7 vols. (London, 1857–9), 6: 219–20; Norman Davis, ed., *The Paston Letters*, 2 vols. (Oxford: Clarendon Press, 1971–76), 1: 452, 602; *Archaeologia* 25 (1834): 549; Staffordshire Record Office, D1721/1/5, 56–58.

14. Froissart's *Cronycles*, trans. Lord Berners, 2 vols., 6 parts (Stratford on Avon: Blackwell, 1927), vol. 2, part 1, p. 120; B. J. Harwood, "*Gawain* and the Gift," *PMLA* 106 (1991): 485.

15. G. F. Beltz, *Memorials of the Most Noble Order of the Garter, from Its Foundation to the Present Time* (London, 1841), pp. 383–85; Woolgar, *Household Accounts*, part 2, pp. 598–601; Furnivall, ed., *The Babees Book*, pp. 191–92; Bodleian MS Eng. hist. b. 208, fol. 76.

16. British Library, Harleian MS 6815, fol. 23ff.

17. J. R. R. Tolkien and E. V. Gordons, eds., *Sir Gawain and the Green Knight* (Oxford: Clarendon Press, 1925), pp. 24ff; Edmund Brock, ed., *Morte Arthure*, EETS, o.s. 8 (London, 1865), pp. 5–8.

18. Harwood, "*Gawain* and the Gift," pp. 483–85. The lesser gifts that maintain social bonds can be found in many cultures; the Kabyles of Algeria, for example, maintain a system of "little presents" to "keep friendship going." See Bourdieu, *Outline of a Theory of Practice*, pp. 7–8; *Archaeologia* 25 (1834): 421, 447.

19. Muriel St. Byrne, ed., *The Lisle Letters*, 6 vols. (Chicago: University of Chicago Press, 1981); Barbara Hanawalt, "Lady Honor Lisle's Networks of Influence," in *Women and Power in the Middle Ages*, ed. Mary Erler and Maryanne Kowaleski (Athens: University of Georgia Press, 1988), pp. 194–96; Stafford Household Accounts, Staffordshire Record Office, D1721/1/5; A. G. Dickens, ed., *Clifford Letters of the Sixteenth Century*, Surtees Society 172 (London, 1962), p. 106.

20. Myers makes the point about the competitiveness of households in *The Black Book*, p. 2.

21. Dyer, *Standards of Living*, pp. 86ff; C. L. Kingsford, ed., *The Stonor Letters and Papers, 1290–1483*, 3 vols., Camden Society, 3rd ser. 29, 30, 34 (1919–24), 2: 98; Stephanie Trigg, ed., *Wynnere and Wastoure*, EETS, o.s. 297 (London, 1990); John Skelton, *The Complete English Poems*, ed. John Scattergood (London: Penguin, 1983), pp. 140–214.

22. Lewis Hyde, *The Gift: Imagination and the Erotic Life of Property* (New York: Random House, 1979), pp. 62, 71–73, 274; Charlotte D'Evelyn, ed., *Peter Idley's Instructions to His Son* (London: Oxford University Press, 1935), p. 100; Harvey, ed., *The Itineraries of William Worcestre*, p. 253; Davis, ed., *The Paston Letters*, 1:545.

23. Harwood, "*Gawain* and the Gift," pp. 485–89; for an interesting discussion of the legal and contractual elements in the text of *Gawain*, see R. J. Blanch and J. N. Wasserman, "Medieval Contracts and Covenants: The Legal Colouring of *Sir Gawain and the Green Knight*," *Neophilologus* 68 (1984): 598–610.

24. Davis, ed., *The Paston Letters*, 1:453; Harvey, ed., *The Itineraries of William Worcestre*, p. 357; Society of Antiquaries MS 77, fol. 1v.

25. Furnivall, ed., *The Babees Book*, pp. 185ff.

26. L. F. Casson, ed., *The Romance of Sir Degrevant*, EETS, o.s. 221 (London, 1949), p. 72; Eugène Vinaver, ed., *The Works of Sir Thomas Malory*, 3rd ed., 3 vols. (Oxford: Clarendon Press, 1990), 1: 17.

27. R. W. Hoyle, ed., "Letters of the Cliffords, Lords Clifford and Earls of Cumberland, c.1500–c.1565," *Camden Miscellany 31*, Camden Society, 4th ser. 44 (London: Royal Historical

Society, 1992), p. 90; Charles Ross, "The Household Accounts of Elizabeth Berkeley, Countess of Warwick, 1420–21," *Transactions of the Bristol and Gloucestershire Archaeological Society* 70 (1951): 81–105; H. A. Crome and R. H. Hilton, eds., "The Beauchamp Household Book," *University of Birmingham Journal* 2 (1949/50): 208–18; A. R. Myers, *Crown, Household and Parliament in Fifteenth-Century England* (London: Hambledon Press, 1985), p. 110.

28. Bodleian MS Eng. hist. b. 208.

29. Starkey, "The Age of the Household," pp. 254–55.

30. Thus Aristotle in the *Nicomachean Ethics* talks of the munificent man who will spend "for the sake of what is noble" (Aristotle, *The Nicomachean Ethics*, ed. John Warrington, [London: Dent Dutton, 1963], p. 75); Skelton, *English Poems*, pp. 189, 211.

31. Mervyn James, *Society, Politics and Culture in Early Modern England* (Cambridge: Cambridge University Press, 1986), pp. 48–90; Diarmaid MacCulloch, *Suffolk under the Tudors* (Oxford: Clarendon Press, 1986), pp. 54–66.

32. On the changing nature of the honor culture, see Mervyn James, "English Politics and the Concept of Honour," in his *Society, Politics and Culture*, pp. 308–415; Skelton, *English Poems*, p. 190; Byrne, ed., *Lisle Letters*, nos. 1620, 1653; Thomas More, *The History of King Richard III*, ed. R. S. Sylvester (New Haven, Conn.: Yale University Press, 1976), p. 47. This reading assumes that Morton had told More of the incident of the Holborn strawberries. Despite Alison Hanham's vigorous attack on the idea that Morton could have been an important source for More, this incident does not appear in the other sources and makes little sense unless we assume that it had been narrated by the cardinal or one of his immediate entourage (Alison Hanham, *Richard III and His Early Historians, 1483–1535* [Oxford: Clarendon Press, 1975], p. 168).

33. See Thomas More, *Utopia*, ed. Edward Surtz and J. H. Hexter (New Haven, Conn.: Yale University Press, 1965), p. 63; Thomas Starkey, *A Dialogue between Pole and Lupset*, ed. T. F. Mayer, Camden Society, 4th ser. 37 (London: Royal Historical Society, 1989), p. 87.

❖

CHAPTER 10

William Thorpe and His Lollard Community
Intellectual Labor and the Representation of Dissent
Rita Copeland

This chapter explores how a politically persuasive model of dissenting identity is produced through an intersection of historical and literary representations. It considers the role of professional intellectuals as articulate participants in social resistance, and how, as intellectuals, they can occupy the problematic space that official legal structures make for self-representation among dissenters. For the history of Lollardy these are especially difficult questions, because we must not only discover adequate historical grounds for recognizing medieval discourses of dissent, but also examine in a historically sensitive way the complex and often contradictory positions from which dissenters speak. Contemporary work in postcolonial theory and in discourses of resistance, much of which, of course, attends to the positioning of intellectuals, can help us to locate our historical inquiry in a vital, ongoing debate about dissent and its representations.

My focus is a text that has long been known but has not been much read in full, the so-called "Examination" or "Testament" of William Thorpe, which purports to be an account by the Lollard priest William Thorpe of his interrogation at the hands of Archbishop Thomas Arundel on August 7, 1407, while he was being held prisoner in the castle of Salt-wood in Kent.[1] According to the account, Thorpe had been arrested in April of that year in Shrewsbury for openly preaching Lollard doctrines in Saint Chad's Church.

The Middle English text of Thorpe's "Examination" has recently been edited by Anne Hudson. It has been known to modern readers in a semi-modernized form in A. W. Pollard's anthology, *Fifteenth-Century Prose and Verse*.[2] It is quite a long text: in Bodleian MS Rawlinson C. 208 of the early fifteenth century, the only extant manuscript of the English text, it runs to ninety-one folios. The account dramatically reenacts dialogue, usually Arundel's doctrinal questions and Thorpe's lengthy answers, but also elaborates the scene with other touches, such as the busy ministrations of Arundel's clerks, who frequently break into the dialogue, or descriptions of nonverbal actions such as people entering and leaving the room or Arundel withdrawing to a corner to confer privately with his clerks. It is also a very emotionally pressured scene. Thorpe often describes his state of mind when posed with a question or a new accusation (for example, "And I heerynge these wordis, thouȝte in myn herte that this was an vnleeful askynge" [p. 35: 365–66], or "And with this axynge [asking] I was astonyed, and anoon thanne I knew that I was sotilly bitraied, of a man that cam to me in to prisoun on the Fryday bifore" [p. 80: 1830–32]).[3] Similarly he describes how his interlocutors often lose their tempers and threaten him. Thorpe's prologue claims that he undertook the writing of this account, among other reasons, because his friends, hearing that he was to be removed from Shrewsbury to Canterbury and thinking that he would likely be examined by Arundel himself, bade him to write his "apposing" and "answering." Presumably he would have written this account when he was led back to prison following his refusal to submit to Arundel and make a recantation on August 7.

I begin with a scene that occurs toward the end of the "Examination," a scene that could be said to form the climax of this very moving, but not exactly suspenseful, text. After what seems an endless day of interrogation and cross-interrogation between Arundel and Thorpe, Arundel breaks into violent exasperation with Thorpe's passive-aggressive resistance and dogmatic refusals to submit to ecclesiastical authority:

And the Archebischop seide to me, "Submitte thee than now here wilfulli and mekeli to the ordenaunce of holi chirche whiche I shal schewe to thee."

And I seide "Sere [Sir], acordingli as I haue rehersid to ȝou I wole be now redy to obeie ful gladli to Crist the heed of al holi chirche, and to the lore and to the heestis [biddings] and to the counseilis of euery plesyng membre of him."

And than the Archebischop, smytyng with his fist fersli [fiercely] vpon a copbord [cupboard], spake to me with a grete spirit, seiynge, "Bi Iesu, but if thou leeue suche addiciouns, obeiynge thee now here withouten ony accepcioun to myn ordinaunce, or that I go out of this place I schal make thee as sikir [secure] as ony theef that is in Kent. And avise thee now what thou wolt do."

And than as if he hadde been angrid, the Archebischop wente from the copbord where he stood to a wyndowe. And than Maluerne and another clerk camen nerhond to me and thei spaken to me manye wordis ful plesyngeli, and also other wise, manassynge [menacing] me and counseilynge me ful bisili to submytte me, either ellis, thei seiden, I schulde not ascape ponyschinge ouer mesure. For I schulde, thei seiden, be degratid [degraded], cursid and brent and so thanne dampned. (pp.87–88: 2063–82)

This scene, with its gestural drama of the courtroom, the angry Arundel pounding the cupboard with his fist and striding to a window to emphasize his impatience by staring out, presumably at nothing, while his lackey clerks take over to play "good cop–bad cop" with the intransigent prisoner, by turns cajoling him and threatening him, highlights the task of representation that this text as a whole must perform: to stand in, as fully realized literary representation, for our historical knowledge of William Thorpe.[4] As a life, Thorpe barely exists beyond the page. Thorpe's historical identity, his (auto)biographical subjectivity, comes into being only through such a textual representation of an adversarial and indeed violent encounter. Thorpe's "Examination" exemplifies, in medieval and purportedly historical terms, what Nancy Armstrong and Leonard Tennenhouse have described, in terms of the psychological subject in the nineteenth-century novel, as "the violence of representation." The discursive strategies for producing psychological or, in Thorpe's case, historical depth of the individual are necessarily "acts of suppression" that essentialize the subject.[5] As we see in the textual drama of Thorpe's encounter with Arundel, the process of creating a self is one of opposition, positioning others "in a negative relationship to that self."[6] There is a kind of hegemonic power in writing as the victim: in his own narrative, Thorpe cannot come into being as a subject acting in history, in a culture of dissent, in his own (putative) autobiography, without enacting his own violence of representation, suppressing the difference of other modes of narrative identity in order to be an authentic spokesman for his own actions and a representative of his community.[7] In the most obvious sense of this, Thorpe must position himself—and his readers—in such a way against the events described as to see them as violent.

But a more basic mechanism of narrative suppression in this text is the denegation of its own literary character in favor of its claims to historicity. Outside this text, Thorpe's is a shadowy life. He has been tentatively identified with a priest named William Thorpe instituted to the vicarage of Marske, Cleveland (York diocese), in March of 1395, which would locate him in the north of England and thus confirm Arundel's statement at the opening of the "Examination": " 'William, I knowe wel that thou hast this twenti wyntir and more traueilid aboute bisili in the north lond and in othir diuerse contrees of Ynglond, sowynge aboute fals doctryne'" (p. 29: 180–83).[8] But for the interview with Arundel in August 1407 reported in this text, there is no external evidence.[9] The text states that the trial followed on his arrest in Shrewsbury in April 1407, but beyond the text there is no record of this arrest or of the outcome of the interview or even of what became of Thorpe.[10]

Here we may usefully compare Thorpe's autobiographical account of his interrogation with an interesting parallel in Lollard writing, the letter of Richard Wyche reporting his trial before Walter Skirlawe, bishop of Durham, which probably took place about 1402.[11] Wyche's letter, written from prison to an unnamed associate, strongly resembles Thorpe's "Examination" in the detail with which it reproduces the dialogue between Wyche and his examiners. But the historical cause and effect of Wyche's self-representation here extend beyond the internal framework of his letter: his defense and recantation (circa 1405) are recorded in the *Fasciculi Zizaniorum*, and continuous evidence of his activity (including letters to Hus in 1410, a summons to appear for questioning after the Oldcastle revolt, and another imprisonment in 1419–20) can be found up to his execution in London as a relapsed heretic in June 1440. A number of London chroniclers record that Wyche's execution produced popular unrest and that the authorities had to forbid people assembling at the sites where he was burned and buried.[12]

By contrast, the historical identity of Thorpe as a dissenter is almost entirely a creation of his very powerful self-narration. The only report in the "Examination" of an event in Thorpe's life for which there is possible external corroboration refers to an episode ten years earlier, in 1397. During the reported interview Arundel mentions his exile in 1397, and suggests that his departure must have been a turn of good fortune for Thorpe; Thorpe adds that on Arundel's banishment, he was released from the prison of Bishop Braybrooke of London where he was being held, saying that Braybrooke no longer found cause to hold him once Arundel was out of the country (p. 91: 2169–80).[13] There is some independent historical record of Braybrooke taking legal action against Thorpe. In the memorandum book of John Lydford, a diocesan official of Exeter, there are three entries concerning one William Thorpe: articles drawn up for Robert Braybrooke accusing Thorpe of heretical preaching in London; Thorpe's reply to Braybrooke's accusations, justifying his preaching on scriptural grounds; and the beginning of a mandate of excommunication against Thorpe.[14] There is no record that the mandate for excommunication was carried out. However, according to Hudson, the events recorded in these entries cannot be dated later than 1386.[15] In the "Examination," Thorpe states that Braybrooke freed him from prison when Arundel left the country (in 1397): since historical record suggests a previous pattern of Braybrooke's actions against Thorpe (although not necessarily including imprisonment at the time of the articles drawn up against Thorpe), it is possible that Thorpe's account refers to an arrest closer to 1397, perhaps predicated on earlier attempts to prosecute him. In both these episodes, Thorpe's case would seem to have remained incomplete, for he is never treated in the "Examination" as a relapsed heretic.

While this reference in the text is linked (however ambiguously) to earlier historical records of Thorpe, the actual proceedings reported here, the interview with Arundel, have no similar corroboration in external record. Yet, of course, the "Examination" asks to be read as historical record, as direct translation of a life, an event, occluding its own literary textuality. Thorpe's autobiographical account of his youth, which he gives early in the text, describes how he came to espouse Lollard doctrine through his education for the priesthood, his passage from orthodox to heterodox circles (pp. 37–42: 437–595). He situates the beginnings of his own nonconformity at the historical origins of the movement, with Wyclif's own Oxford circle, mentioning as teachers and colleagues Wyclif himself, John Aston, Philip Repingdon, Nicholas Hereford, and John Purvey, among others (pp. 40–41: 557–87). Here the life on the page reaches back thirty years into history, vivifying itself through identification with an earlier and indeed originary epoch.[16] Thorpe's dissenting subjectivity is seen to evolve not just from the narrative logic of his own life as recounted, but from the historical logic of earlier events, from a crucial, founding moment in the evolution of English nonconformity. The text reaches forward into later history, as well, its reception in the later fifteenth century and the Reformation establishing for it a kind of canonical solidity. Two manuscripts preserved in Vienna and Prague, containing Latin versions of the "Examination" and written in fifteenth-century Bohemian hands, indicate that it circulated in Hussite Bohemia. A modernized English text paired with a version of the examination of Oldcastle was printed in 1530, probably in Antwerp.[17] In 1543 John Bale translated it into Latin and inserted it into the manuscript of *Fasciculi Zizaniorum*.[18] And it was known to many generations through John Foxe's inclusion of it in the *Acts and Monuments*, a text that Foxe says he printed from a transcription by William Tyndale.[19]

The very ghostliness of this text as testimony to an event in history accounts for its fascination: in its fragmentary and allusive character it seems to float just beyond the historicity that it wants to seize. To express this in its simplest outlines, there is the Thorpe who exists almost fleetingly in historical document and whose fortunes are not known, and the Thorpe who emerges fully formed from this autobiographical text that claims historical veracity. Since so little else is recorded of him we must assume that the Thorpe who was known at least to later generations in England is the figure who emerges from this quasi-fictive, quasi-documentary account.[20] What is the role that such a text might play in the fashioning of a historical consciousness of dissent? We might almost ask whether, if Thorpe had not existed, he would have to have been invented: the text offers his historicized identity as a paradigm for constructing a dissenting subject.

Most important is the form that dissent takes in this text: dissent is defined here in terms of intellectual labor, represented through scenes of violent confrontation between the official voice of accusatory interrogation and Thorpe's own violently reactive hermeneutics. I use the term "intellectual labor" here in a way that recognizes, but is not always continuous with, the value it has acquired in contemporary Marxist revaluations of intellectual autonomy. Gramsci's influential essay on the "organic intellectual" has provided the point of departure for much critical debate about the possibility of intellectual agency within political structures, especially as such models of agency would challenge traditional categories of intellectual work as necessarily self-marginalizing.[21] For the Middle Ages the notion of "intellectual labor" represents a more tightly regulated (and more consciously self-marginalizing) sphere of professional activity than its standard application to postindustrial Europe typically implies. The question of autonomy as understood in contemporary contexts is certainly resonant with the ideological and institutional terms of intellectual professionalism in the Middle Ages. But the Lollard ideology instantiated in Thorpe's text has redefined intellectual labor as a form of struggle, identical with the political struggle that links Thorpe's persona with a historical community. It is through this nexus of representation, political opposition as intellectual labor, that Thorpe the dissenter is projected onto history as a knowable subject.

This text makes intellectual labor visible — representable — by dramatizing it as a violent clash of hermeneutical ideologies. Indeed in this courtoom drama it is less Thorpe who is on trial than Lollard hermeneutics itself. Underwriting the textual aims of Thorpe's documentary enterprise is the Lollard interpretive linchpin of the literal sense. In his prologue Thorpe states that his friends bade him, in writing his account,

> that I bisie me with alle my wittis to go as ny3 the sentence and the wordis as I can, both that weren there spoken to me and that I spake, enaunter this my writynge come ony tyme bifore the Erchebischop. And of this counseile I am ri3t glad, for in my conscience I was moued to bisie me hereaboute, and to axe herto the special help of God. (p. 25: 36–41)

By itself, of course, such a principle is not very telling, since Lollard thought hardly owns the commonplace of fidelity to "words and sentence." But this is one of the principles of classical and patristic translation theory that the Prologue to the Wycliffite Bible conspicuously borrows and alters to accord with the particular inflections of the Lollard hermeneutic of the "open" text:

> to translate aftir the sentence and not oneli aftir the wordis, so that the sentence be as opin either openere in English as in Latyn, and go not fer fro the lettre; and if the lettre mai not be suid in the translating, let the sentence euere be hool and open, for the wordis owen to serue to the entent and sentence, and ellis the wordis ben superflu either false.[22]

The notion of the open Scriptural text whose words affirm the truth of its sentence is fundamental to Wycliffite and Lollard doctrines of the literal sense. On Wyclif's view, elaborated in *De veritate sacrae scripturae,* Scripture is true in every word, its language always "proper" or literal, its very words identical with its mystical senses and thus with God's intention as the author of Scripture.[23] One implication for Lollard translation theory is that the meaning of Scripture is always accessible or "open" because the truth of God resides beyond the power of any particular human language to distort it: one language is as good as another to arrive at God's proper meaning because the truth of Scriptural language does not succumb to the empty distortions of common language.[24] The literal sense is the truth of God, not the words on the page of the physical codex; rhetorical distortion of meaning is the work of false and selfish readers, not of God's divine eloquence, which is beyond the power of any human language to constrain. Thus it is possible to translate Scripture into English accurately and truly.[25]

In 1407, the same year in which his interview with Thorpe supposedly took place, Thomas Arundel had drafted the orthodox opposition to vernacular Scriptures, arguing that language is idiomatic and that the vernacular cannot be trusted to render the meaning of Scripture faithfully. Arundel's Oxford *Constitutions* (formally issued in 1409) enforced as statutory law official opposition to vernacular Scripture:[26] on this view, Scriptural meaning is not open to all languages, and the literal sense is not adequate as an indicator of divine truths. Questions about the value of interpretation grounded in the literal sense had been, of course, material for comparatively open (if also at times vitriolic) public debate as recently as the turn of the century, as witnessed in the determinations on Bible translation of 1401 associated with Oxford, notably that of the Franciscan William Butler and the more even-handed explorations of the Oxford master Richard Ullerston.[27] But by 1407, Arundel's legal proscriptions had foreclosed the possibility of debate over the legitimacy of Lollard translations and their attendant hermeneutical assumptions about Scriptural language. It seems, then, especially appropriate that the year in which Arundel first encoded the orthodox hermeneutical view as law should also be the historical moment of the drama of interrogation between Arundel and Thorpe. Both historically and textually, 1407 becomes a kind of watershed year for the prosecution of Lollard hermeneutics, and Thorpe's "personal" account itself functions as historical "event."

Thorpe's narrative stages the conflict between official doctrine on Scripture and dissenting Lollard hermeneutics both as a broad political struggle between repression and resistance and as a violent clash of individual wills. Unlike other Lollard tracts, such as the *Lantern of Light* (circa 1410), which offer polemical responses to official accusations and restrictions and which must reconstruct, by extratextual reference, the coercive force of law, Thorpe's account places the official voice of law in the text, in the historical person of Arundel, who enacts ecclesiastical authority in his accusatory interrogations.[28] Thorpe's construction of himself in relation to Arundel here is crucial to the dramatic and ideological purposes of his text. Arundel must insinuatingly frame Thorpe as rhetorical, as a sophistic equivocator, so that Thorpe can extricate himself and show himself to be unrhetorical, to be a plain and basic reader of Scripture. It is useful for Thorpe to stage accusations of himself as a mystifier, temporarily allowing his opponents to voice what is actually a standard Lollard characterization of mendicant preaching:

> And the clerke seide to me, "this is ful derk mater and unsauery that thou schewist heere to vs."
> And I seide, "Sere, if ʒe that been maistris knowen not this sentence pleynli, ʒe mowen soore dreden lest the rewme of heuene be take awei fro ʒou as it was from the prynces of prestis and from the eldir men of the Jewis." (p. 79: 1804–9)

When Arundel examines Thorpe on disendowment of the clergy, the exchange must take the form of disputed readings of the same Scriptural text, Paul's Epistle to the Hebrews, chapter 7, on tithing. Thorpe's patient elaboration of his views on temporal goods is punctuated with Arundel's exasperated interjections:

> And I seide, "Sere, Seint Poul seith that tithis weren ʒouen [given] in the olde lawe to Leuytis and to prestis that camen of the lynage of Leu. But oure prestis, he seith, camen not of the lynage of Leu, but of the lynage of Iuda, to which Iuda no tithis weren bihoten for to ʒeue. And therfore, Poul seith, sith the presthode is chaungid fro the generacioun of Leu to the generacioun of Iuda, it is necessarie that chaunginge be maad of the lawe, so that prestis lyuen now withouten tithis and other dewtees that thei now cleymen, suynge Crist and hise apostlis in wilful pouert, as thei haue ʒouun [sic] to hem ensaumple...."
> And the Archebischop seide to me with a grete spirit, "Goddis curse haue thou and [thine] for this techinge! For thou woldist herebi make the olde lawe more free and parfyt than the newe lawe. For thou seist that it was leeful to Leuytis and to prestis to take tithis in the olde lawe and so to ioien [enjoy] her priuylege, but to vs prestis now in the newe lawe thou seist it is not leeful to take tithis. And thus thou ʒeuest to Leuytis of the olde lawe more fredam than to prestis of the newe lawe."
> And I seide, "Ser, I merueile that ʒe undirstonde this pleyne tixt [text] of Poul thus." (pp. 70–71: 1520–47)

Here Thorpe voices the Lollard hermeneutic of literalism, which is seen to be a better, truer, "plainer" way of reading than Arundel's twisted, self-interested mystification of the "plain text"; but even more, Thorpe's literalist exposition performs the dramatic action of patient endurance that can be seen to emerge triumphant from a violent, agonistic struggle. This is, of course, the mode of the hagiographer, and Thorpe as the subject of his own quasi-hagiographical narrative constructs and projects his martyr's identity through the scholastic discourse of hermeneutics.

This kind of struggle is replayed with variations throughout the text. One prominent example of hermeneutics on trial translates the scene of courtroom interrogation into the terms of schoolroom interrogation. In the last section of the text, Arundel interrogates Thorpe on the charges of having preached against the lawfulness of swearing. Thorpe invokes Chrysostom as an authority on the sinfulness of swearing, but his explanation meets with scornful exasperation from Arundel and his clerks. Thorpe's response is to retreat further into the originary authority of Chrysostom, framing Lollard opinion as purist conservatism: "And I seide, 'Sere, this is not myn opynyoun, but it is the opynyoun of Crist oure sauyore, and of Seynt Iame, and of Crissostom and of othir dyuerse seyntis and doctouris'" (p. 76: 1694–96). This proves to have been an unwise move, for on this the Archbishop decides to quiz Thorpe on his knowledge of the Church Fathers, and just happens to have a text of Chrysostom on hand for discussion:

> And thanne the Archebischop badde a clerke rede this omelie of Crissostom, whiche omelie this clerk helde in his honde writen in a rolle, whiche rolle the Archebischop made to be taken fro my felowe at Cauntirbirie. And so thanne this clerk redde this omelie til that he came to a clause where Crisostom seith that it is synne to swere wele. And than a clerke, Maluerne as I gesse, seide to the Archebischop, "Ser, I preie ȝou, witith of him how that he vndirstondith Crisostom here seiynge it to be synne to swere wele."
>
> And so the Archebischop askide me, how I vndirstod here Crisostom. And certis I was sum deele agast to answere herto, for I hadde not bisyed me to stodie aboute the witt ther of. But, liftynge vp my mynde to God, I preied him of grace. (p. 76: 1694–1708)

The fear of the prisoner under interrogation is transformed here into the nightmare of the unprepared student: I didn't know that there was going to be a question about Chrysostom, he says, and I didn't study for it. But it is precisely through this kind of hermeneutical testing that the intellectual struggle of the schoolroom becomes the site for the fashioning of a dissenting identity.

The recent work of Barbara Harlow on the literature of modern political detention demonstrates powerfully how interrogation blurs the practices of prison and school, a paradigm that emerges sharply from William Thorpe's fifteenth-century prison narrative.[29] In the "scholastic" examination just quoted, we see how what Harlow calls an "academically sanctioned question" (here Arundel asking Thorpe how he understands this passage of Chrysostom), when posed in the violently pressured context of political detention, "exposes the coercive machinery of political containment that is complicitously prescribed by certain established literary-critical practices."[30] As represented in this scene, the exegetical methods of the orthodox schools do not serve to produce knowledge, but rather to contain or suppress the possibility of doctrinal difference. In the largest (and unexpressed) sense, what is at stake for Thorpe in this scholastic interrogation is his freedom or even his life, an implication that extends the logic of university examination practices to its most brutal dimension. On the other hand, detainees can also exploit the discipline of the prison as a space for "schooling" in counterhegemonic critical practices. In other words, where prison can be transformed into a school, the scene of learning is also the scene of resistance.[31] Thorpe's discipline here is to recall, through God's grace, the scriptural map that governs exposition of any set text, and to produce a coherent reading of Chrysostom that does not compromise his own doctrinal integrity. Thus in the heresy trial as scholastic examination, Thorpe can emerge as the triumphant intellectual martyr-hero, subduing Arundel, his hostile examiner, who is reduced to assenting that "Crissostom myȝte be thus vndirstonde" (p. 77: 1731).

The examination on Chrysostom continues at this point in the text with Thorpe and his interrogators briefly exchanging roles: Thorpe, having proven his intellectual mastery in exposition of patristic authority, now subjects Arundel and his clerk to interrogation about the difference between the Gospel as physical codex and the Gospel as the Word of God, leading them through a brief course on Wyclif's distinctions among the five grades of Scripture and the identification of its spiritual truth with its literal sense.[32] The dialogue form of the text, which replicates both prison interrogation and classroom examination, underscores the common terms of these two discursive spheres and allows a subtle transformation of one into the other: Arundel the political master, probing the prisoner for weakness in his resolve, gives way to Thorpe the intellectual master examining Arundel like a teacher revealing the weaknesses of a student. The spheres of the political and academic converge: having risen to the scholastic challenge, Thorpe emerges here as the political master, converting the discipline of his own interrogation into the disciplined "schooling" of his wayward opponents.[33]

In terms of the Lollard critical genre of dissenting hermeneutics and the staging of that genre through the dramatic dialogue (echoing the related genres of polemic and school text), Thorpe can readily achieve the legitimacy of authentic representation. The text, however, also asks us to transfer this structure of representation to the terms of the experience of an individual life, to recognize in this text a particular political struggle at a given moment in history. Thorpe's analysis of what it would mean for him to recant, of the bad example it would set to many people if he were to make an abjuration, locates him in relation to a knowable community at a specific historical moment:

> "If ... I schulde now forsake thus sodeynli, schortli and vnwarned, *al the lore* that I haue bisied me fore this thritti ʒeer and more, my conscience schulde euer be herwith ouer mesure vnquyetid. And also, ser, I knowe wel that manye men and wymmen schulden ben herthoruʒ greetli troublid and sclaundrid; and, as I seide, ser, to ʒou bifore, for myn vntruthe and false cowardise many oon schulde be putt into ful greet repreef. ʒhe, ser, I dreede that many oon, as thei myʒten thanne iustli, wolden curse me ful bittirli.... For, if aftir ʒoure counseile I lefte vttirli *al my loore,* I schulde herthoruʒ ... ʒeue occasioun to many men and wymmen of ful sore hurtynge; ʒhe, ser, as it is ful lickli to me, if I consentide thus to ʒoure wille, I schulde herynne bi myn yuel ensaumple in that that in me were sle so manye folkis goostli that I schulde neuere deserue to haue grace of God to edefien his chirche, neithir mysilf ne ony other lyf. And thanne I were moost wrecchidli ouercomen and vndon both bifore God and man." (pp. 38–39: 470–98; emphasis added)

In this moving speech, Thorpe equates his intellectual labor over the years—"al my loore"— with the very substance of his political struggle: to abandon these would be not only to disavow the means by which he *represents* himself, makes himself knowable to the community of "many men and wymmen," but also to forsake the work of *representing* his community, speaking on behalf of the many. The other members of Wyclif's circle, Hereford, Purvey, and Philip Repingdon, who have publically recanted and in fact joined the upper echelons of the clergy, are for Thorpe examples of those who have cut themselves off from any legitimate claim to represent themselves or their communities authentically.[34] As Thorpe says of them:

> "[F]or to the poynt of truth that these men schewiden out sumtyme, these wolden not now strecche forth her lyues, but bi ensaumple eche of hem of other, as her wordis and her werkis schewen, thei bisien hem thoruʒ her feynyng for to sclaundre and to pursue Crist in his membris rather than thei wolde be pursued." (p. 39: 512–16)

Because they will not now "stretch forth their lives," they have violated the terms of communal and historical self-representation. As Anne Middleton has noted of this passage, the recanters "have become radically and irreversibly unknowable, not only to either side but even to themselves."[35]

What are the conditions of a dissenter's "stretching forth a life"? Thorpe stretches forth a life as a legible text: in his work, the "confecting" of a dissenting identity is a coherent literary gesture.[36] This is "representation" in the sense of *Darstellung*, "re-presentation" in the mode of art or philosophy. Thorpe's life is invented and represented through the image of intellectual labor. But the purpose of this text is also "representation" in the political sense of *Vertretung*, speaking on behalf of others.[37] As an intellectual, Thorpe refuses to abstract himself from the community for which he speaks. Intellectual labor therefore is not only what defines Thorpe narratively, but also, as I have suggested, what promises to link this ghostly narrative to a historical community of Lollards for whom he is both example and spokesman. From what cultural position can Thorpe speak, how do we understand his privilege to speak for himself and his community, what historical role does this text play in a heretical movement? In other words, what are the politics of Thorpe's interview with Arundel?

We can begin by considering Thorpe's relationship, both cultural and symbolic, to the community of dissenters for whom he speaks, those "many men and women" for whom his example of "stretching forth a life" is so powerful. The key issues around which that relationship is organized are the competition between the powers of an old academic elite and new counter-hierarchical textual communities, and the clerical-intellectual affiliations of later Lollard society. Within the text Thorpe is a site of these cultural markers. He is interrogated as a heterodox reader of Scripture: as an academically trained preacher he promulgates dissenting hermeneutics, but he also represents the participation of his heretical community in textual culture.

Lollard society, in ways that are perhaps more pronounced than among its antecedents in continental heretical movements, organizes itself through textuality, with reading communities and textual transmission among all social levels of its adherents, whether those members are literate or not.[38] Thorpe, however, occupies a transitional historical position with regard to his Lollard constituency. He represents the academic inner core of the oppositional movement. Thorpe can be seen as one of the last links with the founding academic circle of Wycliffite heterodoxy at Oxford. He may well have been a younger contemporary of Hereford, Purvey, and Aston; he indicates that they were already fully engaged in their revisionist work by the time that he entered their circle:

> "Maister Ion Aston tauȝte and wroot acordingli and ful bisili.... Also Filip of Repintoun whilis he was a chanoun of Leycetre, Nycol Herforde, ... and Ioon Purueye, and manye other whiche weren holden riȝtwise men and prudent, tauȝten and wroten bisili this forseide lore of Wiclef, and conformeden hem therto. And with alle these men I was ofte homli and I comownede [conversed] with

hem long tyme and fele [many], and so bifore alle othir men I chees wilfulli to be enformed bi hem and of hem, and speciali of Wiclef himsilf, as of the moost vertuous and goodlich wise man that I herde of owhere either knew. And herfore of Wicleef speciali and of these men I toke the lore whiche I haue tauȝte and purpose to lyue aftir, if God wole, to my lyues ende." (p. 41: 570–83)

Had the movement taken a different course, had its first-generation Oxford core not been so effectively eliminated through persecutions and recantations, someone like Thorpe would have been a likely candidate to be part of a second-generation link between the founding circle and an ever-widening popular reformist community. Instead, he is one of the few remaining representatives of that first "inner core," and he speaks for a movement that is taking on a nonacademic life of its own, its leadership increasingly in the hands of unbeneficed lower clergy and self-taught laymen, with few direct ties to its original academic center.[39] Here the historical irony of 1407 is especially acute. Even if, as the most recent research suggests, Lollardy's ties with Oxford were not eradicated by the end of the fourteenth century and the new century saw a resurgence of Wycliffism among a new generation of schoolmen, the very kinds of academic practices that could foster this interest were the target of Arundel's *Constitutions* in 1407, which put into place the legal apparatus for surveillance of the universities in order to purge them completely of heterodox activity.[40] The position from which Thorpe speaks, asserting the continuing links between the academic center and the broader social movement, is at that very moment becoming obsolete.

But it is also Thorpe's role as a member of that academic circle that authorizes him to speak here, and to speak, after all, at such length of himself. The basic rhetorical assumption that makes the text operate so persuasively is that Thorpe is important enough to Arundel to take up so much of the archbishop's time (the text continuously underscores this: Arundel's obsequious clerks are fond of reminding the archbishop at crucial moments that he is a busy man, that it has been a long day, and that he should have done with the intransigent Thorpe who has wasted enough of his time). To borrow the terms of James C. Scott's analysis of the relations of power and representation between dominant and subordinate groups, Thorpe is a "renegade member of a dominant elite."[41] While Thorpe speaks on behalf of an extended constituency of men and women who presumably range from a few Latinate clergy like himself (and fewer Latinate laypeople) to a greater number of semiliterate and nonliterate members of Lollard vernacular textual communities, he has, in fact, most in common with Arundel. One of the unstated premises of the text is that Arundel and Thorpe comfortably speak the same language of intellectual institutions, operating and interacting in the dominant professional terms of academic discourse.[42] Thus while the drama of the text clearly marks the boundary between subordination and power, the imprisoned heretic confronting his ecclesiastical prosecutor, the discourse of the text blurs that boundary, as Arundel the archbishop and Thorpe the former Oxford scholar engage as intellectual equals in an intense debate over the finer points of doctrine, what Thorpe even calls at one point (although contemptuously) "scole mater" (p. 55: 1030), a shorthand (and thus insider) term for subjects of debate in the university schools. The discursive relationship between Thorpe and Arundel constitutes what Scott would call the "hidden transcript" of dominant classes: the text presents the way that the powerful, academic elite speak among themselves. Arundel treats Thorpe, not with condescension, such as he might show to a social inferior (here we may recall Arundel's indulgent paternalism with Margery Kempe, whose interview with him is similarly long, lasting "tyl sterrys apperyed in the fyrmament"),[43] but with muscular attention, as if trying to reclaim someone who has broken ranks with his own class. On Scott's analysis, "renegade members of the dominant elite who ignore the standard script" are especially dangerous to official powers because they break the "naturalization of power made possible by a united front."[44] Here the renegade scholar-priest has devoted his life to dismantling the authorizing power of clerical exegesis, and the text of the "Examination" performs, as public transcript, the hidden transcript of the dominant class negotiating the limits and contradictions of exegetical power.

But how does Thorpe, as a defector from the sanctioned norms of the academic elite, propose to speak on behalf of the politically subordinate—indeed, in this context, "subaltern"—members of a heretical community? I recognize the problem of using terms such as "subordinate" or "subaltern" to describe the lower echelons of Lollard society, because these terms commonly suggest a kind of economic as well as political disenfranchisement that is not consistent with what we know of the composition of Lollard social groups, which consist far more of lower middle and artisan classes than economically marginal laborers.[45] But I use such terms to characterize a lack of access to a legible political self-articulation of the sort that the academic Thorpe can achieve. The very discursive tools of professional intellectual work that empower him to engage Arundel with such authority also effectively separate him from the rank and file of those dissenters on behalf of whom he would "stretch forth" his life in words. With the rare exception of such a *laicus litteratus* as Walter Brut, whose trial for heresy in the court of Bishop Trefnant of Hereford in 1393 attracted unusual interest from the authorities because he produced lengthy and learned expositions of his beliefs, lay dissenters—especially nonliterates from the artisan and lower classes—receive fairly perfunctory attention from the authorities as *individual political subjects*.[46] How can Thorpe's narrative, startling in its autobiographical assurance and political individuation, really serve to "stretch forth" an exemplary life for all those who do not command such authority to speak for themselves?

The contradictions of this text, its dramatization of an exemplary scene of resistance through the historicized voice of one who is neither marginal nor subordinate, are also its fundamental driving forces. In the real social terms of Lollard dissenters in the fifteenth century, Thorpe's marginality is his education and professional rank. Lollard communities certainly have their own pedagogical structures, but these constitute a subversive order that operates against professionally sanctioned norms of intellectual work. Similarly, Lollards have a collective oppositional voice, but not the voice of individuated intellectual agency modeled in this text. It is as an intellectual that Thorpe emerges as historically knowable, his subjectivity defined in representational terms by the plausibility of his institutional importance to Arundel, while so many other members of his movement—surely with their own stories—were efficiently processed through the examination system and now remain merely names and occupations affixed to formulaic abjurations in diocesan records.[47]

The crucial ideological operation of this text is to suppress such contradictions, to assimilate them into the smooth hegemony of "writing as the victim." The text thus projects a dissenting self that is on the one hand historically particularized but on the other hand designed for general consumption, to be a common example for all dissenters. This common identity is confected through writing in what Anne McClintock has described as the "voice of the disempowered [which] becomes, in part, a way of lessening the marginalization of privilege."[48] This is not to suggest that Thorpe does not speak, in a very real way, as a prisoner on trial before an aggressive and powerful adversary: there is no pretense in his legal disempowerment. But his voice also commands the power of an individual, autobiographical subjectivity. The text's use of the first-person singular immediately establishes Thorpe as the "centered, univocal speaking 'I' of canonized male autobiography,"[49] a tangible signature of self that the legal conventions of narrative representation deny to most of those dissenters, men and women, for whom he proposes to "stretch forth" a life. Court transcripts of Lollard trials in the fifteenth century typically grant the dissenter the first-person singular only through the format of his or her abjuration, that is, only at the moment at which the dissenting subjectivity is erased through submission to ecclesiastical authority.[50]

The effect of the text is thus to elide Thorpe's legal disempowerment with the discursive barriers to self-representation of ordinary dissenters. This is, of course, a problem that needs to be approached with some sensitivity, for the critique that I make of this text and its application to a historical community is not to be confused with a critique of the "historical" Thorpe himself. Insofar as we can imagine that the interview with Arundel took place in the way reported here, we must recognize Thorpe as someone whose life or freedom was at stake, and who spoke with authenticity and courage as a dissenter who happened to be an articulate and politically visible intellectual. The existential effects of a life "stretched forth" in thirty years of heterodox preaching, that life narrated in Thorpe's text as personal history, are not erased under pressure of the institutional discourses that supply the common currency of the dialogue between Thorpe and Arundel. But as a literary construction the text holds out as exemplary a model of self-representation that, however persuasive, cannot be available to the larger community for which it speaks.

I have borrowed from Gayatri Chakravorty Spivak the framework of the double sense of "representation." In her critique of Western intellectual "representation" of the colonial subaltern "Other," Spivak considers the collapsing of *Darstellung*, artistic re-presentation or "staging of the world," with *Vertretung*, political representation of oppressed groups, as a form of "epistemic violence." She argues that "representing [subalterns], the intellectuals represent themselves as transparent," assuming that subalterns, whom Western intellectuals have constructed through their own language as "Other," as the shadow subject of the Subject of Europe, can speak for themselves:

> It is impossible for contemporary French intellectuals to imagine the kind of Power and Desire that would inhabit the unnamed subject of the Other of Europe.... In the constitutions of that Other of Europe, great care was taken to obliterate the textual ingredients with which such a subject could cathect [in terms of its own power and desire], could occupy (invest?) its itinerary—not only by ideological and scientific production, but also by the institutions of the law.[51]

In order for Western intellectuals to represent themselves as transparent "relayers" of theoretical practice who let the oppressed speak for themselves, it is necessary for them to deny the unrepresentability of subaltern subjects on the terms that intellectual discourse appropriates them. The space that Western intellectual paradigms benevolently create for the self-voicing of subalterns is not one that can make the subaltern subject's itinerary, her complex investment of motive and power, visible to representation. The true project for European intellectuals in confronting the real (as opposed to the imagined, homogeneous) "difference" of Third World subaltern groups "is not to represent (*vertreten*) them [i.e., subalterns] but to learn to represent (*darstellen*) ourselves [i.e., intellectuals]."[52]

I suggest that something of the same process of denial and suppression of difference is at work in Thorpe's "Examination." In order to "represent" his community, Thorpe must represent himself, must realize himself historically as a life. But in the process the text must deny the "unrepresentability" of the lives that it seeks to represent. The text works as "stretching forth a life" only if it succeeds in suppressing the real political and institutional differences between professional intellectuals, who can invest their own power and desire as concrete and authoritative experience, and the ordinary dissenters, whose potential for historicizing self-narration (beyond the admission of heretical beliefs and activities) is, more often than not, of little interest to the prosecuting agencies. The counterhierarchism of Lollard social thought about lay and clerical intellectual powers, the insistence on the democratizing force of vernacular Scripture (which would level off the power differential between lay and clergy), is certainly complicit in this "act of suppression," because it promises an undoing of hierarchies that are never undone in the practices of legal representation. In its English-language form, Thorpe's own text participates in the promise of democratization, as if in expectation of its own wide circulation and consumption by which it can subversively bequeath a didactic apparatus to present and future communities. But in a larger sense the text actually operates within the very power relations whose validity it denies. Certainly the orthodox ecclesiastical structures cannot accord official recognition to the idea of democratization. For Arundel's court and any other episcopal court, the difference between clerical academics and their semieducated lay followers is acutely important and necessary to preserve. The very leisure with which Thorpe's text allows him to expound his readings of Scripture is a sign of the structures of privilege with which this narrative model of dissent is complicit, even as it palpably denies them. To borrow Lora Romero's formulation of this issue with respect to the position of contemporary minority intellectuals and the work of (self-)representation, a text like this "fortifies the institutional practices that deny participants in popular movements the right to represent themselves."[53] In the narrative of Thorpe, the representation of dissent as intellectual labor becomes a textual violence of its own. The persuasive appeal of Thorpe's account is predicated on a violent suppression of difference between possible modes of narrative self-representation, and ultimately of the difference between artistic representation and *Vertretung*. These two distinct and perhaps even incompatible projects are elided together under the promise of stretching forth a life. On the real logic of this text, then, it is intellectual labor that confers individuated political subjectivity in history.

The text of Thorpe's interrogation exposes a set of contradictions that we can begin to understand as a kind of violence to the project of impossible representation: it gives us a quasi-fictional text that stands in for history, and a quasi-representative voice that must stand in for those voices that it cannot fully represent. In this narrative, the dissenting subject is invented through the scene of intellectual labor that is asked to constitute a model of political struggle. Through this scene of violent engagement Thorpe offers himself as example to his community. But the text offers us few clues about how to imagine the trajectory from his story to those many voices, with their own itineraries of motive and power, that did not or could not narrate themselves and so have fallen silent.

Notes

For their comments and suggestions on this essay at various stages of its preparation I would like to thank David Aers, Maria Damon, Kathy Eden, Andrew Elfenbein, Barbara Hanawalt, Ralph Hanna, Barbara Harlow, Bruce Holsinger, Steven Kruger, James Landman, William Marvin, Miri Rubin, Larry Scanlon, Ruth Shklar, Paul Strohm, and David Wallace.

1. The critical literature on Thorpe's "autobiographical" narrative is not extensive: Anne Hudson, *The Premature Reformation: Wycliffite Texts and Lollard History* (Oxford: Clarendon, 1988), esp. pp. 220–23; Ritchie D. Kendall, *The Drama of Dissent: The Radical Poetics of Nonconformity, 1380–1590* (Chapel Hill: University of North Carolina Press, 1986), pp. 58–67; Stephen Greenblatt, *Renaissance Self-Fashioning: From More to Shakespeare* (Chicago: University of Chicago Press, 1980), pp. 77–78; Anne Middleton, "William Langland's 'Kynde Name': Authorial Signature and Social Identity in Late Fourteenth-Century England," in *Literary Practice and Social Change in Britain, 1380–1530*, ed. Lee Patterson (Berkeley and Los Angeles: University of California Press, 1990), pp. 15–82 (on Thorpe, see p. 74). An article by John Fines, "William Thorpe: An Early Lollard," *History Today* 18 (1968): 495–503, offers a lively historical introduction to the "Examination."

2. Anne Hudson, *Two Wycliffite Texts*, Early English Text Society (EETS), o. s. 301 (Oxford: Oxford University Press, 1993); Alfred W. Pollard, *Fifteenth-Century Prose and Verse* (London: Constable, 1903), pp. 101–67. Hudson's edition appeared after I had completed the preliminary draft of this study, for which I used the text in MS Rawlinson C. 208. I have brought my textual citations and notes into accordance with Hudson's new authoritative edition. A portion of the text was earlier printed by Anne Hudson in her anthology, *Selections from English Wycliffite Writings* (Cambridge: Cambridge University Press, 1978), pp. 29–33. The title of the work presents some problems, as the Rawlinson MS of the English text gives no title to the work. In her new edition Hudson supplies the title "Testimony of William Thorpe." But since the sixteenth century the text has been known by the title "Examination of William Thorpe," as given in the Antwerp print (circa 1530) of the English text. This is the title used in Pollard's edition, by which many modern readers have come to know Thorpe's text. In this essay I have kept the older title.

3. Here and throughout, the text is cited by page number of Hudson's EETS edition, followed after the colon by the line numbers in Hudson's text. The character thorn has been replaced throughout with the letters *th*. I have occasionally provided glosses of individual words in brackets. In using Hudson's text I have not reproduced her indications of textual emendations.

4. On the quasi-dramatic genre of Thorpe's and other Lollard texts, see Kendall, *The Drama of Dissent*, pp. 50–89; on the performative and often technically dramatic character of medieval judicial discourse, see Jody Enders, *Rhetoric and the Origins of Medieval*

Drama (Ithaca, N.Y.: Cornell University Press, 1992), esp. chap. 2, "From Legal Ritual to Dramatic Representation in Classical Antiquity and the Middle Ages," and chap. 3, "The Theater of the Basoche and the Medieval Dramatic Continuum."

5. Nancy Armstrong and Leonard Tennenhouse, "Introduction: Representing Violence, or 'How the West Was Won,'" in *The Violence of Representation: Literature and the History of Violence*, ed. Armstrong and Tennenhouse (London and New York: Routledge, 1989), pp. 6–7. Armstrong and Tennenhouse situate their discussion in relation to the early modern and explicitly fictional terms of Brontë's novel *Jane Eyre*. In adapting their argument to a medieval text and its historical moment I am, by implication, locating the category "subjectivity" at a premodern historical juncture. On the debate about the "emergence of the subject," see the excellent article by David Aers, "A Whisper in the Ear of Early Modernists; or, Reflections on Literary Critics Writing the 'History of the Subject,'" in *Culture and History, 1350–1600*, ed. David Aers (Detroit, Mich.: Wayne State University Press, 1992), pp. 177–202.

6. Armstrong and Tennenhouse, "Representing Violence," p. 8.

7. Compare Armstrong and Tennenhouse, "Representing Violence," pp. 8–9.

8. Margaret Aston, *Thomas Arundel: A Study of Church Life in the Reign of Richard II* (Oxford: Clarendon, 1967), p. 326 and n. 2. On the possible problems of accepting this identification, see Hudson, *Two Wycliffite Texts*, p. xlvii.

9. On the absence of any record of this examination in Arundel's Canterbury and Lambeth registers, see Hudson, *Two Wycliffite Texts*, pp. xlv–xlvi, and *The Premature Reformation*, p. 14 and n. 43.

10. Hudson's speculations about Thorpe's fortunes are interesting and worth quoting here: "A list of beliefs, drawn largely from Wyclif's *De Eucharistia*, ascribed to 'Wylhelmi Torp, cuius librum ego habeo' appears in Prague Metropolitan Chapter Library MS D. 49, ff. 179v–181v.... Taken together with the two copies of Thorpe's Examination preserved in Bohemia, it is tempting to speculate that Thorpe, like [Peter] Payne, fled from persecution in England to Prague" (*Selections from English Wycliffite Writings*, p. 156). These conjectures are reprised, with some qualifications, in the introduction to *Two Wycliffite Texts*, pp. lii–liii.

11. The letter, preserved only in one Bohemian manuscript, is printed by F. D. Matthew, *English Historical Review* 5 (1890): 530–44. See Hudson, *Premature Reformation*, pp. 221–22, and on similarities between the letter of Wyche and Thorpe's account, see *Two Wycliffite Texts*, pp. xlvii, lvii–lix.

12. M. G. Snape, "Some Evidence of Lollard Activity in the Diocese of Durham in the Early Fifteenth Century," *Archaeologia Aeliana*, 4th ser., 39 (1961): 355–61; *Fasciculi Zizaniorum*, ed. W. W. Shirley, Rolls Series (London: Longman, 1858), pp. 370–82, 501–5; John A. F. Thomson, *The Later Lollards* (Oxford: Oxford University Press, 1965), pp. 15, 148–50; Hudson, *Premature Reformation*, pp. 160, 172, 381, 449.

13. On Thomas Arundel's exile from 1397–99, see Aston, *Thomas Arundel*, pp. 362–73.

14. *John Lydford's Book*, ed. Dorothy M. Owen, Devon and Cornwall Record Society 19 and Historical Manuscripts Commission Joint Publications Series 22 (London, 1974), pp. 108–12 (items 206 and 209).

15. See Hudson, *Two Wycliffite Texts*, pp. xlviii–l, on the evidence for dating the records in the Lydford memorandum book, the difficulties of reconciling the Lydford records with the events narrated in the "Examination," and possible explanations for the reported arrest by Braybrooke that led to Thorpe's release in 1397.

16. It is interesting to note that at this point the very manuscript page (fol. 22r and fols. 24v–25r) reinforces the historicity of Thorpe's narrative: marginal notations list the names of the Oxford circle that Thorpe mentions, as if to index the history lesson in the original figures of the Lollard movement that the narrative produces.

17. On the Latin versions and the 1530 print in English, see Hudson, *Two Wycliffite Texts*, pp. xxviii–xxxi, and *Premature Reformation*, p. 14 n. 42. The hands of the Vienna

Rita Copeland

manuscript (Vienna Österreichische Nationalbibliothek MS 3936) can be dated circa 1420; those of the Prague manuscript (Prague Metropolitan Chapter Library MS O. 29), circa. 1430. Pollard bases his modernized version of the text on the 1530 Antwerp print, and also provides a text of the Oldcastle examination from the same print (*Fifteenth-Century Prose and Verse*, pp. 175–89).

18. Only five folios of Bale's Latin translation survive in the manuscript, Bodleian e Mus. 86 (fols. 98v to 103v): see *Fasciculi Zizaniorum*, p. lxxii. Hudson (*Premature Reformation*, p. 490 and n. 276) notes that Bale was also responsible for a tractate entitled *A boke called Thorpe and Oldecastell*, printed in Zurich in 1543.

19. *The Acts and Monuments of John Foxe*, ed. S. R. Cattley, vol. 3 (London, 1837), pp. 239–85. On Foxe's ascription of the text to Tyndale, see Hudson, *Two Wycliffite Texts*, pp. xxxiii–xxxvi.

20. Thorpe offers something of an inverse analogy to the shadowy author of *Piers Plowman*, who, as Anne Middleton has recently argued, disperses himself into the strong textual lives that he creates—textual lives that take on a historical authenticity of their own, as in the afterlife of the Plowman himself as virtual narrator-author of the text and as authenticator of dissenting social movements (Middleton, "Getting a Life: Langland, Chaucer, and Authorship in the Nineties," Gayley Lecture, University of California at Berkeley, March 11, 1993). Where the historical Langland seems almost to submerge himself in order to represent other (fictive) lives as historically possible, the life of the quasi-historical Thorpe of the "Examination" is foregrounded as historically necessary so that his narrative can represent the reality of other dissident voices.

21. Antonio Gramsci, "The Formation of the Intellectuals," in *Selections from the Prison Notebooks of Antonio Gramsci*, ed. and trans. Quintin Hoare and Geoffrey Nowell Smith (New York: International Publishers, 1971; reprint, 1989), pp. 5–14. Among recent treatments, see especially Nancy Armstrong and Leonard Tennenhouse, *The Imaginary Puritan: Literature, Intellectual Labor, and the Origins of Personal Life* (Berkeley and Los Angeles: University of California Press, 1992), pp. 114–39, and R. Radhakrishnan, "Toward an Effective Intellectual: Foucault or Gramsci?" in *Intellectuals: Aesthetics, Politics, Academics*, ed. Bruce Robbins (Minneapolis: University of Minnesota Press, 1990), pp. 57–100.

22. Text quoted from Hudson, *Selections from English Wycliffite Writings*, p. 68. The entire prologue is printed in Josiah Forshall and Frederic Madden, eds., *The Holy Bible ... made from the Latin Vulgate by John Wycliffe and his Followers*, vol. 1 (Oxford: Oxford University Press, 1850), pp. 1–60 (this passage, from chap. 15, p. 57).

23. Wyclif, *De veritate sacrae scripturae*, ed. Rudolf Buddensieg, vol. 1 (London: Wyclif Society, Trübner, 1906; reprint, New York: Johnson Reprint; Frankfurt: Minerva, 1966), p. 5, lines 1–11; p. 43, lines 17 ff.

24. Compare Wyclif's remarks in *De contrarietate duorum dominorum*: "Lingwa enim, sive hebrea, sive greca, sive latina, sive anglica, est quasi habitus legis domini. Et per quemcunque talem habitum eius sentencia magis vere cognoscitur a fideli, ipse est codex plus racionabiliter acceptandus" (*John Wyclif's Polemical Works*, ed. Rudolf Buddensieg, vol. 2 [London: Wyclif Society, Trübner, 1883], p. 700, lines 29–33). On this passage and its elaboration in other Lollard (and anti-Lollard) polemic, see Anne Hudson, "Lollardy: The English Heresy?" in Hudson, *Lollards and Their Books* (London: Hambledon Press, 1985), pp. 152–53 (originally published in *Studies in Church History* 18 [1982]: 261–83).

25. These questions are treated at greater length in Rita Copeland, "Rhetoric and the Politics of the Literal Sense in Medieval Literary Theory: Aquinas, Wyclif, and the Lollards," in *Interpretations: Medieval and Modern*, ed. Piero Boitani and Anna Torti, J. A. W. Bennett Memorial Lectures, Perugia, 1992 (Cambridge: Brewer, 1993), pp. 1–23.

26. The text of the *Constitutions* is printed in D. Wilkins, ed., *Concilia Magnae Britanniae et Hiberniae*, vol. 3 (London, 1737), pp. 314–19. An English translation is given in Foxe, *Acts and Monuments*, 3:242–48.

27. Butler's determination is printed in Margaret Deanesly, *The Lollard Bible* (Cambridge: Cambridge University Press, 1920), pp. 399–418; on Ullerston's text, preserved in Vienna Hofbibliothek MS 4133, see Anne Hudson, "The Debate on Bible Translation, Oxford, 1401," in Hudson, *Lollards and Their Books*, pp. 67–84 (originally published in *English Historical Review* 90 [1975]), which clarifies the relationship between Ullerston's Latin text and an English version of it printed by Deanesly (*The Lollard Bible*, pp. 437–45, incorrectly attributed by Deanesly to John Purvey).

28. *The Lantern of Light*, ed. Lilian M. Swinburn, EETS, o.s. 151 (London: Kegan Paul, 1917). The *Lantern* repeatedly invokes the restrictions of the *Constitutions*, even naming them as one of the false laws by which the Antichrist assaults God's servants: "& principali thise newe constituciouns" (p. 17); see also pp. 14, 17–18. For references to *De heretico comburendo* (1401), see p. 43 and especially p. 100, which notes the penalties of imprisonment and even death for those found in possession of "Godes lawe in englische." There are, of course, many polemical Lollard texts that employ the conventional literary device of debate, staging a dialogue between an opponent and an adherent of Lollard belief, but they do not claim the historicity of Thorpe's account; see Anne Hudson, "A Lollard Quaternion," in Hudson, *Lollards and Their Books*, pp. 193–200 (originally published in *Review of English Studies*, n.s. 22 [1971]). See also Hudson, *Premature Reformation*, pp. 222–23, on overt and submerged dialogue in other Lollard texts.

29. Barbara Harlow, *Barred: Women, Writing, and Political Detention* (Hanover and London: Wesleyan University Press, 1992), p. 10.

30. Harlow, *Barred*, p. 8.

31. Harlow, *Barred*, pp. 10, 12; compare pp. 27–28.

32. See *De veritate sacrae scripturae*, pp. 107–9, 111. These difficult elements of Wyclif's thought on Scripture are explained with great clarity by Alastair Minnis, "'Authorial Intention' and 'Literal Sense' in the Exegetical Theories of Richard FitzRalph and John Wyclif: An Essay in the Medieval History of Biblical Hermeneutics," *Proceedings of the Royal Irish Academy* 75 (1975): 1–31 (see especially 13–14).

33. Toward the end of the text (pp. 86–87), Thorpe again reverses the interrogation, battering Arundel with a series of questions about faith to which the Archbishop can only respond "yea." This leads to the scene in which Arundel strikes the cupboard with his fist and gives up in exasperation. I am indebted here to Miri Rubin's comments on the dialogue form of the text and its imaging of classroom practice (as in didactic texts), which allows for a reversal of the roles of examiner and student.

34. In addition to Hereford, Purvey, and Repingdon, Thorpe mentions Robert Bowland as a recanter (p. 39). In Arundel's register for 1401 a clerk of this name is accused of immorality with a nun, but Bowland's connections with heretical activities are unclear. See Hudson, *Two Wycliffite Texts*, p. 111.

35. Middleton, "William Langland's 'Kynde Name,'" p. 74.

36. See Middleton, "William Langland's 'Kynde Name,'" pp. 67–70, on the "confected names and improvised identities" (p. 70) of the rebels in the literature of the 1381 Revolt, and her remarks (pp. 73–76) on identity and community as "the enacted reclamation of founding texts," exemplified in Thorpe, Kempe, and Langland's own self-naming (p. 74).

37. This formulation of *Darstellung* and *Vertretung* as a "double session of representations" is from Gayatri Chakravorty Spivak, "Can the Subaltern Speak?" in *Marxism and the Interpretation of Culture*, ed. Cary Nelson and Lawrence Grossberg (Urbana and Chicago: University of Illinois Press, 1988), pp. 271–313; on this formulation, see pp. 275–79.

38. On the dynamics of literacy among earlier continental reformist movements, see Brian Stock, *The Implications of Literacy: Written Language and Models of Interpretation in the Eleventh and Twelfth Centuries* (Princeton, N.J.: Princeton University Press, 1983), pp. 90–91. As Stock notes, heretical and reformist discourse does not originate with nonliterate popular constituencies: rather, heretics represent the "cutting edge of literacy." The leaders are educated, and the structure of a dissident community consists of a "small

inner core of literates," and then semiliterates and nonliterates, all grouped around a program of textual interpretation elaborated through the preaching of the literate leaders. See also the collection *Heresy and Literacy, 1000–1530,* ed. Peter Biller and Anne Hudson (Cambridge: Cambridge University Press, 1994), which appeared in print after the present essay was completed and at press.

39. A convenient account of this trend can be found in M. D. Lambert, *Medieval Heresy: Popular Movements from Bogomil to Hus* (London: Edward Arnold, 1977), pp. 256–59.

40. See Anne Hudson,"Wycliffism in Oxford, 1381–1411," in *Wyclif in His Times,* ed. Anthony Kenny (Oxford: Clarendon, 1986), pp. 67–84; for more detail, see Hudson, *Premature Reformation,* pp. 60–119, esp. pp. 82, 84, 99, 117.

41. James C. Scott, *Domination and the Arts of Resistance: Hidden Transcripts* (New Haven, Conn.: Yale University Press, 1990).

42. On the class identification of schoolmen and the traditional hostility of the class to *illiterati,* see Alexander Murray, *Reason and Society in the Middle Ages* (Oxford: Clarendon, 1978; reprint 1985), pp. 234–57. R. I. Moore argues that in the High Middle Ages the antagonism of professional intellectuals against *illiterati* was transferred onto the prosecution of heresy: see Moore, *The Formation of a Persecuting Society: Power and Deviance in Western Europe, 950–1250* (Oxford: Blackwell, 1987), pp. 138–40.

43. *The Book of Margery Kempe,* ed. Sanford Brown Meech and Hope Emily Allen, EETS 212 (London and Oxford: Milford, 1940), p. 37.

44. Scott, *Domination and the Arts of Resistance,* p. 67.

45. On the artisan and middle-class composition of Lollard society, see, for example, Derek Plumb, "The Social and Economic Spread of Rural Lollardy: A Reappraisal," *Studies in Church History* 23 (1986): 111–29; J. F. Davis, "Lollard Survival and the Textile Industry in the Southeast of England," *Studies in Church History* 3 (1966): 191–201; and, more generally, Hudson, *Premature Reformation,* pp. 128–34.

46. The proceedings against Walter Brut, including his own written answers to the charges brought against him, are printed in the *Registrum Johannis Trefnant, episcopi Herefordensis,* ed. William W. Capes, Canterbury and York Series 20 (London: Canterbury and York Society, 1916), pp. 278–365.

47. An excellent example of standardized questions and abjurations is in Anne Hudson, "The Examination of Lollards," in Hudson, *Lollards and Their Books,* pp. 125–40 (originally published in *Bulletin of the Institute of Historical Research* 46 [1973]). Thomson's remarks on the standardization of examinations are illuminating (even if also dismissive and probably too generalizing about literacy among the Lollards): "This might suggest that the court officers [of the Coventry persecutions in 1511–12] were following some formulary, as the charges are arranged in the same order [as in other records], but were allowed to modify the wording as long as the substance remained unaltered. This method of questioning the accused on a series of beliefs was probably general — as many of the Lollards were ignorant and illiterate it would *a priori* seem the only effective way of eliciting their views — and even in persecutions where no list of articles has been preserved the form of the abjurations would suggest that this was done" (Thomson, *The Later Lollards,* p. 226).

48. Anne McClintock, " 'The Very House of Difference': Race, Gender, and the Politics of South African Women's Narrative in *Poppie Nongena,*" in *The Bounds of Race: Perspectives on Hegemony and Resistance,* ed. Dominick LaCapra (Ithaca, N.Y.: Cornell University Press, 1991), p. 203. McClintock's study concerns a black South African woman, known as "Poppie Nongena," who was displaced, along with her family, during the Soweto uprisings of 1976, and who dictated her autobiography to a popular Afrikaans author, Elsa Joubert, under whose name the book appeared. The book was enormously successful, in large part because its public reception could assimilate the subaltern voice into the norms of the dominant white literary establishment.

49. McClintock, " 'The Very House of Difference,' " p. 209.

50. On the problem of self-representation in judicial documents, compare Paul Strohm's account of Thomas Usk's "textual self-assertion" in his "Appeal" and the effacement of Usk's textual agency and subjectivity in the official judicial documents drawn up for his arraignment. See "The Textual Vicissitudes of Usk's 'Appeal,'" in Strohm, *Hochon's Arrow: The Social Imagination of Fourteenth-Century Texts* (Princeton, N.J.: Princeton University Press, 1992), pp. 145–60.

51. Spivak, "Can the Subaltern Speak?" pp. 275, 280.

52. Ibid., pp. 285, 288–89.

53. Lora Romero, " 'When Something Goes Queer': Familiarity, Formalism, and Minority Intellectuals in the 1980's," *Yale Journal of Criticism* 6 (1993): 128.

Afterword

❖

What Happens at Intersections?

Paul Strohm

Going Downtown

Ralph Hanna is right about our common contemporary experience when he describes intersections as places of collision and danger. An alternative understanding—congenial to the centuries covered by this volume even if only latently available today—would treat the intersection as a *carrefour*: a crossroad or market square, a place where roads converge and persons with different origins and destinations tarry for purposes of acquaintance and exchange. This notion of the crossroad opens a possibility not of fast transit but of potential commingling, in which persons at least temporarily occupy and enjoy the same space. As a crossroad, marked by crowded and stimulating disarray, the intersection may serve as a figure for an interdisciplinary aspiration.

However untidy and noisy and inefficient, the crossroad is a place of considerable stimulus; a place of risk and profit; a place of exchange, where one gives something away to get something back. What we must be prepared to give away in the interdisciplinary case is a measure of security, as expressed through the established procedures of our primary disciplines and as reinforced by referees and panels and personnel committees. But must this rather considerable resignation be made?

One might argue, on behalf of our disciplines, that they are considerably less ruly places than they were a decade ago, and a good deal of work that might be considered interdisciplinary goes on within them. Nevertheless, much of what might be called "disciplinarily based interdisciplinarity" possesses the appearance of risk rather than its reality. It curtails risk by never quite going all the way "downtown," remaining always in sight of the security of its disciplinary home. We have all experienced crude renderings of such adventures-in-the-sight-of-home. The historian does it when pillaging literary texts for "illuminating details" or "reflections of life," while ignoring the text as a total representational system or the uses to which it was put or the complexity (and likely conventionality) of its referential relation to the world outside its bounds. The literary person does it when ignoring the enunciatory circumstances and social affiliations of a text, or by relaxing into the comfortable skepticism of the view that a text accounts only for what Ralph Hanna calls a

"Mimetic Real," without an identifiable connection to the social circumstances of its production.

Appropriately nuanced accounts of the representational relations of texts to social and political circumstances—accounts, that is, that avoid the historian's frequent simplification of the issues attending textuality and the litterateur's despair about the problems of historical reference—remain rare and are sometimes insufficiently appreciated when they occur. An earlier volume in this series, *Chaucer's England: Literature in Historical Context*, reflected an interdisciplinarity that was more disciplinarily based.[1] Reception of that volume, as indicated by reviews published thus far, suggests that historians and literary people tend to be rather well satisfied with the efforts of their disciplinary companions, and less so with those of the unfamiliar discipline. Extreme in this regard is the review of one historian who finds that his colleagues "share a distinctive tone and methodology: pragmatic, empirical, arguing closely from texts and documents, concerned to augment as well as to reinterpret knowledge," whereas the literary essays "are generally associative and freewheeling, sometimes more reliant on supposition than on deduction, and occasionally written in a language which is opaque to the point of unintelligibility."[2] The criteria of the review are suggested by the author's enthusiasm for the way his fellow historians wield "evidence," set over against the litterateurs' inability to resist "the baleful influence of literary theory." His suggestion would appear to be that the problems of using literary "evidence" in historical analysis remain sufficiently tractable that the literary practitioners have no excuse for going the long way round and routing their conclusions through unnecessary and extraneous theory. Yet surely—and I here address historians as well as my fellow literary scholars—if we are to find some ground for common discussion independent of the self-reinforcing and frequently limiting assumptions revealed in what I consider this reviewer's "field jingoism," then theory (understood as the attempt to grasp the assumptions of our endeavor from outside rather than from within its self-defined terms) must play a role in that endeavor.[3]

The crucial question—posed one last time in the spatial metaphor latent in the idea of "intersection"—would seem to be how to "leave home," disobeying our disciplinary elders by getting out in the traffic. But, if leaving home is not simply to be a lark or a solitary adventure, it definitely does involve an act of decisive relocation, the claiming of a new perspective on disciplinary space. Entailed by this relocation are several emancipatory moves. As described by Michel de Certeau, the first of these moves is one of self-emancipation from disciplinarily regulated space. But he is not content to stop with the resultant "soft" interdisciplinarity "that today insinuates itself into the interstices between the fields defined by different sciences, that merely takes advantage of their play as if from a vacant, uncertain, and unavowed space between them, or that allows each science the ease of assigning to others what exceeds the limits of its own explanation." Remaining for him is a necessary step beyond disciplinary free fall, in which "interdisciplinarity ... would attempt to apprehend epistemological constellations as they reciprocally provide themselves with the new delimitation of their objects and a new status for their procedures."[4]

Certeau's demand is that interdisciplinarity claim a proper place for itself, not just floating freely among and between existing disciplines but grounding its endeavor in distinctive objects of attention and disciplinarily emancipated procedures for studying them — or, revising his formulation to more nearly encompass the order in which insights are actually produced, distinctive objects *together with* the new procedures that illuminate them. Much is required of these new "procedures." Obviously, they must establish their worth competitively, both by producing new insights about existing objects and study and by directing fresh attention to previously neglected objects. At the same time, they must exonerate themselves of the suspicion under which they will automatically be placed: that of merely serving as stalking horse, lightly disguised but on stakeout to serve the interests of a previously existing disciplinary configuration.[5]

Several emergent configurations present themselves as possible embodiments of "new procedure." A provisional and very incomplete list might include the Freudian/Lacanian analysis of the text's (and textual subject's) necessary self-estrangement from its own desire; the feminist and postcolonialist analysis of steps necessary to hear the voice of the suppressed "other"; gender as analytical category and the emergence of gender hybridity and "queering" as sites of destabilizing analysis; the analytical power of structuration theory and its insight that texts, gestures, and actions are conceived and achieve intelligibility only within structure. Although amply present within existing departmental units, none of these tendencies can yet be said to have *quite* concluded its deal, by consolidating a "proper" disciplinary home. Rather, and probably appropriately, they exist as provocations, as sources of challenge to disciplinary certainties. (If disciplinary boundaries result from phobic incapacity for disorder, each of these tendencies retains, as observed by Diane Elam of feminist deconstruction, its capacity to precipitate a disciplinary anxiety attack!)[6] This very unrootedness with regard to traditional configurations certainly satisfies the first and goes a long way toward satisfying the second of Certeau's criteria.

Although medievalists are not accustomed to finding themselves in a methodological vanguard, I argue that this volume, developed from the Minnesota Intersections conference, occasions the collective disclosure of yet another powerful procedure, potentially "interdisciplinary" in all of Certeau's senses. This procedure is most conveniently summarized as the analysis of practices — with the word *practice* embracing both writing and behavior, symbol and matter. As an academic endeavor, the study of practices draws textuality, its occasions, its uses, and the events it describes into a socially performative totality.

As a point of theoretical attachment for the study of practices I would cite the work of Pierre Bourdieu, especially in his fusion of the economic and the noneconomic, the material and the symbolic, treating "all practices, including those purporting to be disinterested or gratuitous, and hence non-economic, as economic . . . as directed towards the maximizing of material or symbolic profit." Crucial to Bourdieu's theory, and of special interest to students of the written record, is his theory of symbolic capital, which as "a transformed and thereby *disguised* form of physical 'economic' capital, produces its proper effect inasmuch . . . as it conceals the fact that it originates in 'material' forms of capital which are also, in the last analysis, the source of its effects."[7] But, if Bourdieu possesses a heightened awareness of the material affiliations of the symbolic, so does he regard the "economic," and the whole conception of "profit," symbolically, with a concomitantly flexible sense of the varied forms in which "profit" can arise. Bourdieu's analytical flexibility has a payoff of its own, in that it permits him to recognize the varied motives from which participants engage in a practice, the differential rewards they seek from it, the multiple meanings a practice can produce.[8]

The Productivity of Practices

One of the advantages of "practice" as a grounding for study of texts and events is the subtlety with which it can register different kinds of social productivities and uses. In the hands of a skillful analyst, a practice may be viewed not just as a static consequence of someone's resolve, but as a site and occasion of varied social symbolisms in its own right. A case in point would be Gail Gibson's multiply valenced account of the ceremonial churching of women. She views this practice as indeterminate in effect, sometimes urging meanings on spectators and sometimes receptive of its spectators' varied construals and uses. It both generates and receives significations, registering misogynistic meanings (in its implication of the childbearing woman's *need* for purification) and affirmative female meanings (as a celebration of the centrality of the female body in salvation history). Moreover, these meanings might not be simply alternative, but simultaneous, depending on the differing perspectives of the participants involved. Thus, as she incisively suggests, "the meaning of the purification ritual for the women who were churched was very different from the meaning projected by the celibate male elite who presided at the altar."

Central to the churching ritual is, for Gibson, the female body, as alternately (or simultaneously) vulnerable and empowered, and thus as endlessly productive of meanings. Her analysis might be connected, in turn, with Miri Rubin's observations about the paradoxical productivity of the suffering child-body, issuing in disturbing images of child torture and abuse and also in private devotions and even in foundational and aggrandizing accounts of institutional destinies. First originating on the margins of authorized discourse, these accounts of children's suffering and potentially meaningless pain were transmuted into virtue via devotional and textual practice. Practice may, in this sense, be regarded as a system for channeling potentially inchoate and semantically overloaded symbolisms into devotional and/or social use, as when blood may be variously treated as a determinant of character (in medical theory), as an emblem of personal sacrifice (in flagellant observance), as a tangible representation of God (at the altar), as a concomitant of inquiry and truth (in judicial torture).

Felicity Heal's observations on "Reciprocity and Exchange in the Late Medieval Household" offer rich insight into a cluster of exchange practices occurring in the households of the nobility, among and between different kinds of clients. These practices cut across the realms of the symbolic and the commercial, involving exchange of "favors for adherence, deference for patronage, and hospitality for honor." Exchange, so described, is always "for" something, issuing in enhanced influence and in different forms of social bonding. Funereal gifts to impoverished mourners produce honor, courteous reciprocations between lords and tenants support otherwise asymmetrical relations, liveried retention creates a "community of honor." On the negative side, the inconsistent maintenance of shared meanings through symbolic exchange has the potential to fray sensibilities, giving way in the later fifteenth century to the anti-interactive and more static and less productive aspects of the emergent ideal of "magnificence."

A complex rendering of the assumption that social practice can (among other things) produce texts informs Ruth Karras's discussion of social mores, in the sense that social behaviors are registered in — and can be retrieved from — prescriptive texts. Cutting across traditionally literary and historical texts, she considers church court records and didactic literature as official "answers," from which may be inferred the unspoken challenges or "questions" posed by excluded or proscribed social practices. A case in point involves the analysis of male sexual transgression in ecclesiastical models (the ecclesiastical courts treat male adultery as less significant than female adultery) and in literature (*Dives and Pauper* finds adultery a greater sin for a man than a woman) — suggesting a split between church theory and what might be called an "unwritten discourse of practice." She thus posits unwritten practice as productive of theory, although not in a direct or simple or merely reflective way; rather, the challenging practice may be affirmed or negated, acknowledged or even explicitly denied in the different judgmentally or ideologically informed records and writings that it provokes.

Merging the Domains: Material and Symbolic

Karras's research model would seem to effect a distinction between behavior and belief; between, that is, the material and symbolic domains of practice. She partially overcomes this apparent conceptual obstacle by an implied theory of mixed "discourses of practice." Other, sometimes more thoroughgoing, solutions to the same dilemma recur within this volume. One of the most resolute is Heal's refusal to segregate the commercial and symbolic aspects of hospitable exchange. In her analysis, written texts, material exchanges, and gestural theatrics all blend into a single, and internally diverse, meaning-making system. A similar insistence is implicit in Miri Rubin's treatment of the material body as a screen for fantasy and point of departure for performances. In accord with this position is her refusal to treat the body as a "text," even though it might frequently be marked and written upon. Her fruitful compromise is to consider the body as an interpretative site, a place of "messy secrets," and an engine of meanings. Blood, as premier bodily fluid, cannot be confined either to the literal or the symbolic, but enjoys constant fluidity of existence.

Particularly relevant here is Sarah Beckwith's discussion of the complications introduced into ritual symbolization via instantiation and practice. In her analysis, the resistant and very real material body of the city enters into a complicated dialogue with the symbolic body of the Corpus Christi plays in a way that leaves neither untransformed. Bourdieu's "ritual practice" is reworked and fruitfully complicated as the superimposition of ritual (with its aspirations to timeless unity) on civic space (with its historical differentiation and implication in ties of ownership and use). This superimposition not only assigns meaning to civic space but exacerbates and reveals contradictions of public and private, obligation and exemption, in civic custom and ownership. Similarly, occurrence of the plays in real space before an actual audience highlights issues of understanding and cognition, and throws the focus back on the polysemousness at their symbolic center. The oppositions at the center of the symbol, from which the symbol is constructed and which it holds in uneasy balance, are thus articulated and rendered visible only via practice in space and time. Their difference not quite obliterated, the respective domains of the symbolic and the material are thus seen as completely interdependent—and their dialogue as endlessly productive of meaning.

At its most successful—and I here I might cite Beckwith's analysis as a proximate example of considerable conceptual success—a theory of "practice" can assist in overcoming some of the fruitless dichotomies and procedural impasses that block historical and literary research and that prevent members of the two groups from sharing their findings with each other. One undoubted impasse involves the tendency of historians to stabilize certain of their texts as reliable "evidence" of material practice, and that of literary scholars—precisely by calling them "texts"—to treat all written categories as interpretations of reality in their own right and as inevitably value-laden. Marjorie McIntosh's "Finding Language for Misconduct" would seem to risk the reinscription of this dichotomy, especially in its working distinction between "textual environment" and "material context." Yet her article abounds in constructive operational suggestions for overcoming precisely such categorizations, as in her analysis of what might be considered the "rhetoric" of legal documents (exemplified by a memorable analysis of the word *fovere*, with its implication of misplaced hospitality or nurture) and also her sense of the degree to which texts not only reflect practice but seek reciprocally to influence it (as when jury presentments move blame from prostitution to "the people who make bawdry possible"). An additional conceptual refinement of this essay is the care taken to register and explain the relative autonomy of different discursive practices; rather than simply explain differing local languages as the effect of different degrees of responsiveness to "reality," McIntosh explains linguistic variation among and between categories of texts in terms of differing conditions of enunciation, purpose, and historical context—as in her discussion of ecclesiastical secular jurisdictions or the appearance and subsequent disappearance of concern over "hedgebreaking."

Another essay that wrestles with an apparent dichotomy is Barbara Hanawalt's analysis of the "game of exchange" between the literary and the historical—"between literary and legal creations, on the one hand, and the actual experience of adolescence, on the other"—in the construction of fifteenth-century adolescence. Hanawalt's urbane progress through an enormous variety of texts—including literary, legal, advisory, and customary—puts her light-years beyond the mere reflection theories proscribed by Hanna. Nonetheless, the suggestion that representations might be "tossed back and forth" between the realms of text and experience would seem to define a pretextual category of "actual experience" to which appeal might be made. My own view (shared, I believe, with Hanna) is that experience is itself produced only within structure, and that structure is linguistically, if not textually, expressed.[9] A possible resolution of this dilemma may be discovered within Hanawalt's own investigative practice. Returning to the action of "tossing back and forth" different conceptions of behavior, I would suggest that the reciprocal action here described is not just between experiences and textualizations, but between and among different structurations; structurations that are formatively active across and between established categories of behavior and speech and writing. Seen in this way, the key categories of "wild and wanton" and "sad and wise" behavior might be seen as equally and indifferently available to writers, moralists, apprentices, and masters, and to all sorts of other social theorists and actors as well.

An ultimate horizon in the merger of material and symbolic, event and textualization, and practice and performance, is approached in Seth Lerer's reflections on the relation between the spectatorial response to the *Croxton Play of the Sacrament* and the punishment for cutpurses in the Lydd decree. The enterprise of his study is everywhere to "blur constructively the line between viewer and actor, practice and performance, history and fiction." Eroding the line by constantly crossing and recrossing it, Lerer argues for the spectatorial aesthetics of the Lydd punishments as a fiction of power and the eventfulness of the Croxton play as an experience of social reincorporation. As flexibly as he deals with the question of the "line," however, Lerer's interpretation risks its perpetuation, in a refined and subtle form. Alternatively, *what if there were no line?* What if, rather than injecting elements of the aesthetic into social ritual and the reverse, we were simply to adopt the assumption that ALL spectacles — theatrical and civic — are inextricably implicated in history and do social work via their processes of semiosis? The process of restoring history to a performance or a text would be greatly simplified if, in effect, we started with the assumption that history was present all along. Lerer effectively suggests at several points in his argument that all social texts and all written texts are simultaneously "historical and imaginative," and this simple fusion would seem to sweep many of our methodological difficulties aside.

The Text's Entry into Time

To one degree or another, the contributors to this volume concern themselves with (and capitalize on) the position of the analyst: a position that, according to Bourdieu, is immensely bolstered by the fact that "for the analyst, time no longer counts" — that, no longer in any uncertainty as to what may happen, the analyst is free to overcome the effects of time through totalization. Yet, as he adds, "the detemporalizing effect ... that science produces when it forgets the transformation it imposes on practices inscribed in the current of time ... is never more pernicious than when exerted on practices defined by the fact that their temporal structure, direction, and rhythm are *constitutive* of their meaning."[10] Seen as static, as possible structurations of behavior, the practices under consideration here would run the risk of detemporalization; the contemporary literary analyst faces a particular temptation to treat the text as an inscription of its own reading scene, an allegory of its own reception, an account of its own processes. For the most part, our contributors have resisted this temptation, and have carefully historicized their texts' inscription, in terms of the pressures that bear upon them and are realized within them. But the task of returning temporality to a text is itself fraught with conceptual dangers — one of which is, paradoxically, that of taking the text's self-historicization at face value!

I pause, in this regard, over Rita Copeland's analysis of William Thorpe's self-representation within an implied history of Lollard dissent. Her suggestion is that the account of Thorpe's examination before Archbishop Arundel may be read in terms of his attempt to project a particular historicized identity (realized, in this case, in terms of intellectual labor) as a paradigm for a knowable subject. In his spirited opposition to Arundel, Thorpe is seen as example and spokesperson of contrary tendencies in the Lollard movement, embracing the verbal mastery of an "old academic elite" and the dissenting force of "new counter-hierarchical textual communities." Yet, in Copeland's analysis, "Thorpe ... occupies a transitional historical position with regard to his Lollard constituency. He represents the academic inner core of the oppositional movement." As such, Thorpe's self-representation of his own oppositional centrality actually stands somewhere to the side of the conditions of contemporary struggle in the first decade of the fifteenth century.

Copeland tells us, in other words, that the text is not to be returned to its own time via an uncritical acceptance of its own projection of a relation to history through its strategic creation of an exemplary self. Refusing to allow the text to elide the circumstances of its own composition, she effects its reinsertion into time through a more arduous reconstruction of the "examination scene" in terms of its historical play of interests, institutional compulsions, and power, and (especially) its exclusion of unrepresented voices. Some of the most interesting things to be learned from texts in their relations to history, she suggests, are the very things that texts lack the interest or ability to tell us about themselves.

Untying the (Historical) Text

At the conference that produced this collection of essays, Barbara Hanawalt paused during her enumeration of William, "Childe of Bristow's," cumulative filial virtues to observe, "The little prig has something to tell us!" I would seize on her mixture of impatience, enjoyment, and historical faith as an emblem for this volume. Emblematized is the search for a place between existing disciplines from which texts can be read in order to grasp what they might "tell us"—sometimes willingly and sometimes grudgingly—about themselves and about history. At a recent literary symposium I heard mockery of the idea that one might hear "voices" in an archive, and this idea must be indeed criticized if it is taken to suggest that these voices speak unbidden or that they are wholly transparent or that the researcher has only to transcribe what they mean to say. But each text does "speak" to historical practice, if we can refine the procedures and conceptual tools by which we coax or otherwise elicit its voice. These procedures and tools may—in fact must—involve theory, and in these remarks I have sought to delineate a "theory of practice" that seems to be variously and richly adumbrated in the present contributions.

231

Notes

1. Barbara Hanawalt, ed., *Chaucer's England: Literature in Historical Context* (Minneapolis: University of Minnesota Press, 1992).

2. J. R. Maddicott, review of *Chaucer's England, Medium Aevum* 62 (1993): 331–32.

3. Each field might begin by admitting freely that the other possesses something it needs. Again following Ralph Hanna, I would cite the historian's archival/diplomatic skills, with the access they open to new materials and the subtlety they encourage in the interpretation of the circumstances and implications of texts in the details of their preservation and presentation (pp. 8–9), and the litterateur's familiarity with issues of textuality, grounded in firsthand encounters with "medieval discursive habits" (p. 24). Suppose, that is, that we take each other at our best, rather than, as is still usually true, at our worst (as when the literary person still uncritically treats an overgeneralized or discredited historical metanarrative *as* history, or when the historical person uncritically assumes a relationship of commensurability between "literary history" and other historical registers).

4. Michel de Certeau, *The Writing of History* (New York: Columbia University Press, 1988), p. 291.

5. I am thinking, for example, of the uneasy suspicions of the historian informed by the litterateur that his or her "documents" are really just "texts," or the equivalent response of the litterateur told by the historian that insight into past configurations is "properly historical" only if diachronic and oriented to perception of "change over time" — or that he or she can demonstrate historical sincerity only by doing archival work. In each case, the presence of a veiled disciplinary polemic undermines the advice giver's suasive force.

6. Diane Elam, "Ms. en Abyme: Deconstruction and Feminism," *Social Epistemology* 4 (1990): 293–308.

7. Pierre Bourdieu, *Outline of a Theory of Practice* (Cambridge: Cambridge University Press, 1977), p. 183.

8. On the productivity of "practice" within the realm of the symbolic, and also on practice as mediatory between representation and interpretation, see Roger Chartier, *Cultural History: Between Practices and Representations* (London: Polity Press, 1988), esp. pp. 1–17.

9. In addition to Bourdieu, see Anthony Giddens, *Central Problems in Social Theory: Action, Structure, and Contradiction in Social Analysis* (Berkeley: University of California Press, 1979), and David Carr, *Time, Narrative and History* (Bloomington: University of Indiana Press, 1986).

10. Bourdieu, *Outline of a Theory of Practice*, p. 9.

Contributors

❖

Sarah Beckwith teaches English and cultural studies at the University of Pittsburgh. She is the author of *Christ's Body: Identity, Culture, and Society in Medieval Writing* (1993). She is currently working on a book on medieval theater, *Signifying God: Social Act and Symbolic Relation in York's Play of Corpus Christi.*

Rita Copeland teaches English at the University of Minnesota. She is the author of *Rhetoric, Hermeneutics and Translation in the Middle Ages* (1991) and the editor of *Criticism and Dissent in the Middle Ages* (forthcoming).

Gail McMurray Gibson is Kenan Professor of English and Humanities at Davidson College. She is the author of *The Theater of Devotion: East Anglican Drama and Society in the Late Middle Ages* (1994) and numerous articles on medieval literature, drama, iconography, and spirituality.

Barbara A. Hanawalt is professor of history and director of the Center for Medieval Studies at the University of Minnesota. Among her publications are *Crime in East Anglia in the Fourteenth Century: Norfolk Gaol Delivery Rolls, 1307–1316* (1976); *Crime and Conflict in English Communities, 1300–1348* (1979); *The Ties That Bound: Peasant Families in Medieval England* (1986); and *Growing Up in Medieval London: The Experience of Childhood in History* (1993). She has also edited and contributed to several collections of essays, including three for the center. Her current research is on dispute management in medieval London and London women in the Middle Ages.

Ralph Hanna III teaches English at the University of California, Riverside. He is particularly interested in non-Chaucerian materials, especially alliterative poetry (including *Piers Plowman*) and prose translation.

Felicity Heal is fellow and tutor in modern history at Jesus College, Oxford. She is the author of *Hospitality in Early Modern England* (1990) and, with Clive Holmes, of *The Gentry in England and Wales, 1500–1700* (1994). She has also written extensively on the English Reformation and

233

is preparing a new volume on the Reformation in Britain for Oxford University Press.

Ruth Mazo Karras teaches history at Temple University. She is the author of *Slavery and Society in Medieval Scandinavia* (1988). Her current research interests are in the areas of gender and sexualities, and her book *Common Women: Prostitution and Sexuality in Medieval England* is forthcoming in 1996 from Oxford University Press.

Seth Lerer is professor of English at Stanford University and the author of *Boethius and Dialogue: Literary Method in "The Consolation of Philosophy"* (1985), *Literacy and Power in Anglo-Saxon Literature* (1991), and *Chaucer and His Readers* (1993).

Marjorie K. McIntosh is professor of medieval and early modern English history at the University of Colorado at Boulder. She has written about a range of topics dealing with social, economic, and religious history of the period between 1200 and 1640, including two studies of the royal manor and Liberty of Havering, *Autonomy and Community* (1986) and *A Community Transformed* (1991). Her essay in this collection stems from her current research on how local communities in England regulated social behavior and how they responded to the problems of poverty between 1350 and 1600.

Miri Rubin teaches medieval history at Oxford University. She is interested in social and cultural history, with particular inclinations toward the use of anthropological and literary critical approaches in the study of late medieval culture. Among her current research interests are narratives about Jews, the body, and the workings of gender.

Paul Strohm teaches English and medieval studies at Indiana University. He has written *Social Chaucer* (1989) and *Hochon's Arrow* (1992) and is currently investigating textuality and Lancastrian kingship.

David Wallace is Paul W. Frenzel Chair in Medieval Studies and professor of English at the University of Minnesota. He is currently editing *The Cambridge History of Medieval English Literature*; his new book, *Chaucerian Polity: Absolutist Lineages and Associational Forms in England and Italy*, is forthcoming from Stanford University Press.

Index